Microsoft® Office 365™
PUBLISHER 2016

INTRODUCTORY

JOY STARKS
Indiana University
Purdue University
Indianapolis

SHELLY CASHMAN SERIES®

Australia • Brazil • Japan • Korea • Mexico • Singapore • Spain • United Kingdom • United States

CENGAGE
Learning®

Shelly Cashman Microsoft Office 365 & Publisher 2016: Introductory
Joy L. Starks

SVP, GM Skills & Global Product Management: Dawn Gerrain

Product Director: Kathleen McMahon

Senior Product Team Manager: Lauren Murphy

Product Team Manager: Andrea Topping

Associate Product Manager: Melissa Stehler

Senior Director, Development: Marah Bellegarde

Product Development Manager: Leigh Hefferon

Senior Content Developer: Alyssa Pratt

Developmental Editor: Lyn Markowicz

Product Assistant: Erica Chapman

Manuscript Quality Assurance Project Leader: Jeffrey Schwartz

Senior Production Director: Wendy Troeger

Production Director: Patty Stephan

Content Project Manager: Arul Joseph Raj, Lumina Datamatics

Manufacturing Planner: Julio Esperas

Designer: Diana Graham

Text Design: Joel Sadagursky

Cover Template Designer: Diana Graham

Cover Images: karawan/Shutterstock.com; Click Bestsellers/Shutterstock.com

Compositor: Lumina Datamatics

Vice President, Marketing: Brian Joyner

Marketing Director: Michele McTighe

Marketing Manager: Stephanie Albracht

Microsoft and the Office logo are either registered trademarks or trademarks of Microsoft Corporation in the United States and/or other countries. Cengage Learning is an independent entity from the Microsoft Corporation, and not affiliated with Microsoft in any manner.

Mac users: If you are working through this product using a Mac, some of the steps may vary. Additional information for Mac users is included with the Data Files for this product.

For product information and technology assistance, contact us at
Cengage Learning Customer & Sales Support, 1-800-354-9706.

For permission to use material from this text or product, submit all requests online at **www.cengage.com/permissions.** Further permissions questions can be emailed to **permissionrequest@cengage.com.**

Library of Congress Control Number: 2015957836

ISBN: 978-1-305-87119-9

Cengage Learning
20 Channel Center Street
Boston, MA 02210
USA

Cengage Learning is a leading provider of customized learning solutions with employees residing in nearly 40 different countries and sales in more than 125 countries around the world. Find your local representative at **www.cengage.com.**

Cengage Learning products are represented in Canada by Nelson Education, Ltd.

To learn more about Cengage Learning, visit **www.cengage.com.**
Purchase any of our products at your local college store or at our preferred online store **www.cengagebrain.com.**

Printed in the United States of America
Print Number: 01 Print Year: 2016

Microsoft® Office 365™
PUBLISHER 2016

INTRODUCTORY

Microsoft Office 365™
PUBLISHER 2016

INTRODUCTORY

Contents

Microsoft **Office 365 & Publisher 2016**

MODULE ONE
Creating a Flyer

MODULE TWO
Publishing a Trifold Brochure

Productivity Apps for School and Work

Corinne Hoisington

Lochlan keeps track of his class notes, football plays, and internship meetings with OneNote.

Zoe is using the annotation features of Microsoft Edge to take and save web notes for her research paper.

Nori is creating a Sway site to highlight this year's activities for the Student Government Association.

Hunter is adding interactive videos and screen recordings to his PowerPoint resume.

© Rawpixel/Shutterstock.com

Being computer literate no longer means mastery of only Word, Excel, PowerPoint, Outlook, and Access. To become technology power users, Hunter, Nori, Zoe, and Lochlan are exploring Microsoft OneNote, Sway, Mix, and Edge in Office 2016 and Windows 10.

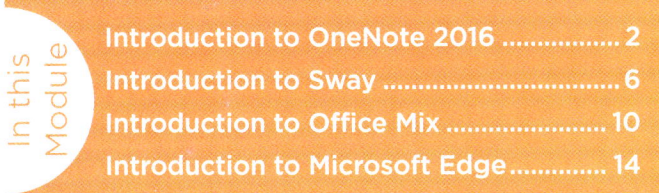

Learn to use productivity apps!
Links to companion **Sways**, featuring **videos** with hands-on instructions, are located on www.cengagebrain.com.

Introduction to OneNote 2016

notebook | section tab | To Do tag | screen clipping | note | template | Microsoft OneNote Mobile app | sync | drawing canvas | inked handwriting | Ink to Text

As you glance around any classroom, you invariably see paper notebooks and notepads on each desk. Because deciphering and sharing handwritten notes can be a challenge, Microsoft OneNote 2016 replaces physical notebooks, binders, and paper notes with a searchable, digital notebook. OneNote captures your ideas and schoolwork on any device so you can stay organized, share notes, and work with others on projects. Whether you are a student taking class notes as shown in **Figure 1** or an employee taking notes in company meetings, OneNote is the one place to keep notes for all of your projects.

Figure 1: OneNote 2016 notebook

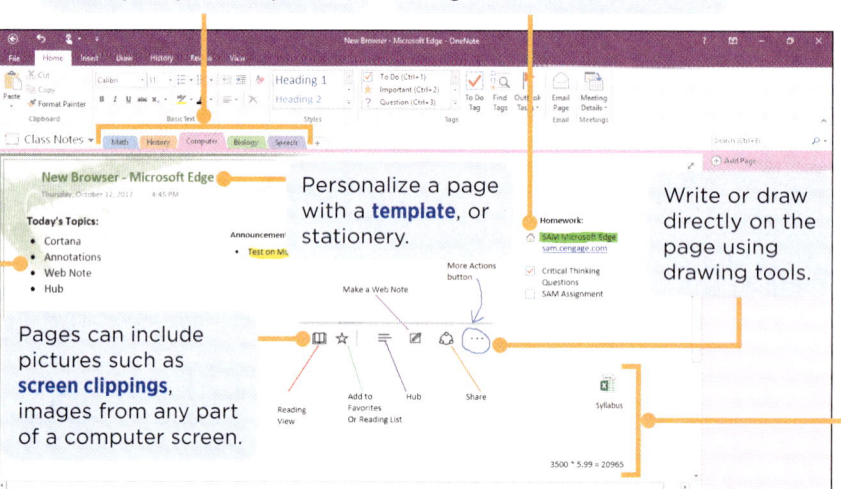

Each **notebook** is divided into sections, also called **section tabs**, by subject or topic.

Use **To Do tags**, icons that help you keep track of your assignments and other tasks.

Type on a page to add a **note**, a small window that contains text or other types of information.

Personalize a page with a **template**, or stationery.

Write or draw directly on the page using drawing tools.

Pages can include pictures such as **screen clippings**, images from any part of a computer screen.

Attach files and enter equations so you have everything you need in one place.

Creating a OneNote Notebook

OneNote is divided into sections similar to those in a spiral-bound notebook. Each OneNote notebook contains sections, pages, and other notebooks. You can use One-Note for school, business, and personal projects. Store information for each type of project in different notebooks to keep your tasks separate, or use any other organization that suits you. OneNote is flexible enough to adapt to the way you want to work.

When you create a notebook, it contains a blank page with a plain white background by default, though you can use templates, or stationery, to apply designs in categories such as Academic, Business, Decorative, and Planners. Start typing or use the buttons on the Insert tab to insert notes, which are small resizable windows that can contain text, equations, tables, on-screen writing, images, audio and video recordings, to-do lists, file attachments, and file printouts. Add as many notes as you need to each page.

Syncing a Notebook to the Cloud

OneNote saves your notes every time you make a change in a notebook. To make sure you can access your notebooks with a laptop, tablet, or smartphone wherever you are, OneNote uses cloud-based storage, such as OneDrive or SharePoint. **Microsoft OneNote Mobile app**, a lightweight version of OneNote 2016 shown in **Figure 2**, is available for free in the Windows Store, Google Play for Android devices, and the AppStore for iOS devices.

If you have a Microsoft account, OneNote saves your notes on OneDrive automatically for all your mobile devices and computers, which is called **syncing**. For example, you can use OneNote to take notes on your laptop during class, and then open OneNote on your phone to study later. To use a notebook stored on your computer with your OneNote Mobile app, move the notebook to OneDrive. You can quickly share notebook content with other people using OneDrive.

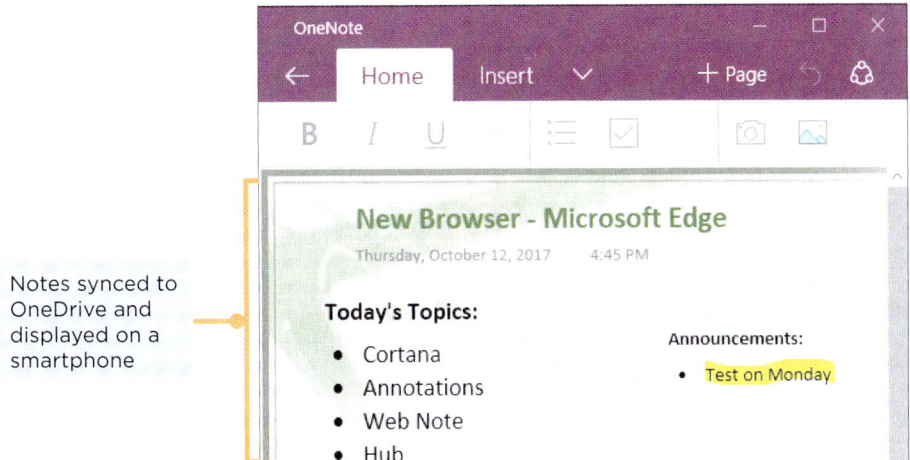

Figure 2: Microsoft OneNote Mobile app

Notes synced to OneDrive and displayed on a smartphone

Taking Notes

Use OneNote pages to organize your notes by class and topic or lecture. Beyond simple typed notes, OneNote stores drawings, converts handwriting to searchable text and mathematical sketches to equations, and records audio and video.

OneNote includes drawing tools that let you sketch freehand drawings such as biological cell diagrams and financial supply-and-demand charts. As shown in **Figure 3**, the Draw tab on the ribbon provides these drawing tools along with shapes so you can insert diagrams and other illustrations to represent your ideas. When you draw on a page, OneNote creates a **drawing canvas**, which is a container for shapes and lines.

On the Job Now

OneNote is ideal for taking notes during meetings, whether you are recording minutes, documenting a discussion, sketching product diagrams, or listing follow-up items. Use a meeting template to add pages with content appropriate for meetings.

Figure 3: Tools on the Draw tab

Draw tab

Pens and highlighters are in the Tools group.

Insert rectangles and lines from the Shapes group.

Lines and shapes are in the Shapes group.

Make drawings using pens in the Tools group.

Insert text using the Type button in the Tools group.

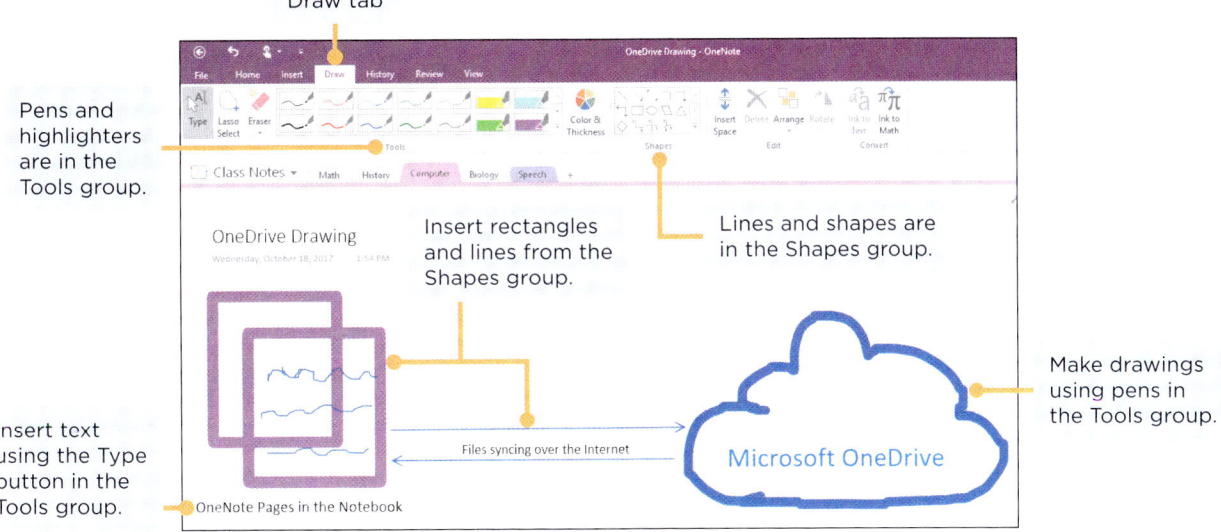

Converting Handwriting to Text

When you use a pen tool to write on a notebook page, the text you enter is called **inked handwriting**. OneNote can convert inked handwriting to typed text when you use the **Ink to Text** button in the Convert group on the Draw tab, as shown in **Figure 4**. After OneNote converts the handwriting to text, you can use the Search box to find terms in the converted text or any other note in your notebooks.

Figure 4: Converting handwriting to text

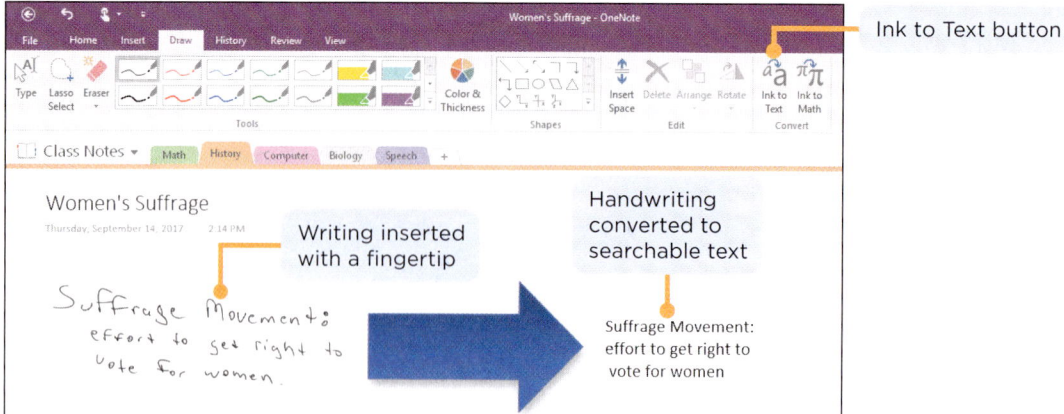

Ink to Text button

Women's Suffrage

Thursday, September 14, 2017   2:14 PM

Writing inserted with a fingertip

Handwriting converted to searchable text

Suffrage Movement: effort to get right to vote for women

On the Job Now

Use OneNote as a place to brainstorm ongoing work projects. If a notebook contains sensitive material, you can password-protect some or all of the notebook so that only certain people can open it.

Recording a Lecture

If your computer or mobile device has a microphone or camera, OneNote can record the audio or video from a lecture or business meeting as shown in **Figure 5**. When you record a lecture (with your instructor's permission), you can follow along, take regular notes at your own pace, and review the video recording later. You can control the start, pause, and stop motions of the recording when you play back the recording of your notes.

Figure 5: Video inserted in a notebook

Record Video button

Audio & Video Recording tab

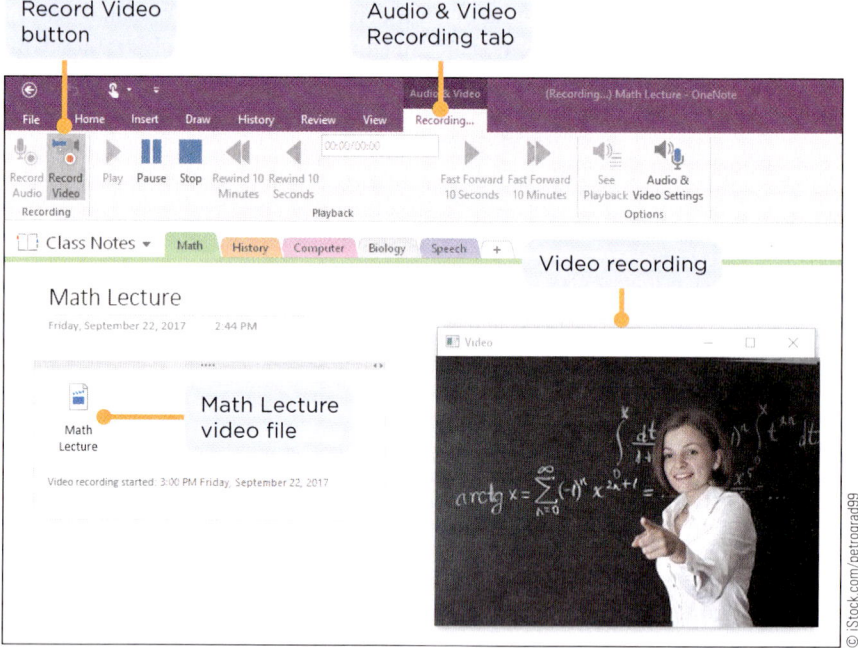

Video recording

Math Lecture video file

© iStock.com/petrograd99

Try This Now

1: Taking Notes for a Week

Learn to use OneNote!
Links to companion **Sways**, featuring **videos** with hands-on instructions, are located on www.cengagebrain.com.

As a student, you can get organized by using OneNote to take detailed notes in your classes. Perform the following tasks:

  a. Create a new OneNote notebook on your Microsoft OneDrive account (the default location for new notebooks). Name the notebook with your first name followed by "Notes," as in **Caleb Notes**.
  b. Create four section tabs, each with a different class name.
  c. Take detailed notes in those classes for one week. Be sure to include notes, drawings, and other types of content.
  d. Sync your notes with your OneDrive. Submit your assignment in the format specified by your instructor.

2: Using OneNote to Organize a Research Paper

You have a research paper due on the topic of three habits of successful students. Use OneNote to organize your research. Perform the following tasks:

  a. Create a new OneNote notebook on your Microsoft OneDrive account. Name the notebook **Success Research**.
  b. Create three section tabs with the following names:

  - **Take Detailed Notes**
  - **Be Respectful in Class**
  - **Come to Class Prepared**

  c. On the web, research the topics and find three sources for each section. Copy a sentence from each source and paste the sentence into the appropriate section. When you paste the sentence, OneNote inserts it in a note with a link to the source.
  d. Sync your notes with your OneDrive. Submit your assignment in the format specified by your instructor.

3: Planning Your Career

Note: This activity requires a webcam or built-in video camera on any type of device.

Consider an occupation that interests you. Using OneNote, examine the responsibilities, education requirements, potential salary, and employment outlook of a specific career. Perform the following tasks:

  a. Create a new OneNote notebook on your Microsoft OneDrive account. Name the notebook with your first name followed by a career title, such as **Kara - App Developer**.
  b. Create four section tabs with the names **Responsibilities, Education Requirements, Median Salary**, and **Employment Outlook**.
  c. Research the responsibilities of your career path. Using OneNote, record a short video (approximately 30 seconds) of yourself explaining the responsibilities of your career path. Place the video in the Responsibilities section.
  d. On the web, research the educational requirements for your career path and find two appropriate sources. Copy a paragraph from each source and paste them into the appropriate section. When you paste a paragraph, OneNote inserts it in a note with a link to the source.
  e. Research the median salary for a single year for this career. Create a mathematical equation in the Median Salary section that multiplies the amount of the median salary times 20 years to calculate how much you will possibly earn.
  f. For the Employment Outlook section, research the outlook for your career path. Take at least four notes about what you find when researching the topic.
  g. Sync your notes with your OneDrive. Submit your assignment in the format specified by your instructor.

Introduction to Sway

Sway site | responsive design | Storyline | card | Creative Commons license | animation emphasis effects | Docs.com

Expressing your ideas in a presentation typically means creating PowerPoint slides or a Word document. Microsoft Sway gives you another way to engage an audience. Sway is a free Microsoft tool available at Sway.com or as an app in Office 365. Using Sway, you can combine text, images, videos, and social media in a website called a **Sway site** that you can share and display on any device. To get started, you create a digital story on a web-based canvas without borders, slides, cells, or page breaks. A Sway site organizes the text, images, and video into a **responsive design**, which means your content adapts perfectly to any screen size as shown in **Figure 6**. You store a Sway site in the cloud on OneDrive using a free Microsoft account.

Figure 6: Sway site with responsive design

You can display a Sway presentation in a web browser.

Sway uses responsive design to make sure pages fit perfectly on any device.

© iStock.com/marinello, © iStock.com/marekuliasz

Creating a Sway Presentation

You can use Sway to build a digital flyer, a club newsletter, a vacation blog, an informational site, a digital art portfolio, or a new product rollout. After you select your topic and sign into Sway with your Microsoft account, a **Storyline** opens, providing tools and a work area for composing your digital story. See **Figure 7**. Each story can include text, images, and videos. You create a Sway by adding text and media content into a Storyline section, or **card**. To add pictures, videos, or documents, select a card in the left pane and then select the Insert Content button. The first card in a Sway presentation contains a title and background image.

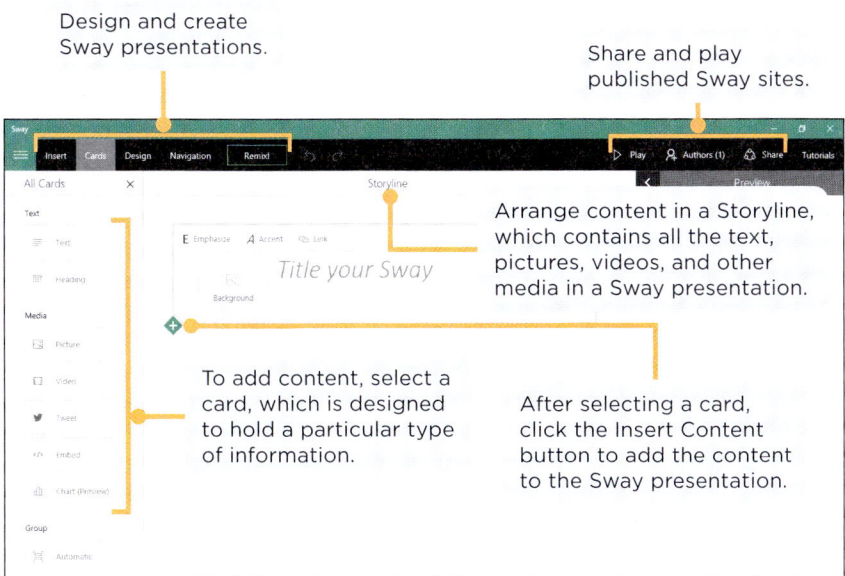

Design and create Sway presentations.

Share and play published Sway sites.

Arrange content in a Storyline, which contains all the text, pictures, videos, and other media in a Sway presentation.

To add content, select a card, which is designed to hold a particular type of information.

After selecting a card, click the Insert Content button to add the content to the Sway presentation.

Adding Content to Build a Story

As you work, Sway searches the Internet to help you find relevant images, videos, tweets, and other content from online sources such as Bing, YouTube, Twitter, and Facebook. You can drag content from the search results right into the Storyline. In addition, you can upload your own images and videos directly in the presentation. For example, if you are creating a Sway presentation about the market for commercial drones, Sway suggests content to incorporate into the presentation by displaying it in the left pane as search results. The search results include drone images tagged with a **Creative Commons license** at online sources as shown in **Figure 8**. A Creative Commons license is a public copyright license that allows the free distribution of an otherwise copyrighted work. In addition, you can specify the source of the media. For example, you can add your own Facebook or OneNote pictures and videos in Sway without leaving the app.

On the Job Now

If you have a Microsoft Word document containing an outline of your business content, drag the outline into Sway to create a card for each topic.

Figure 8: Images in Sway search results

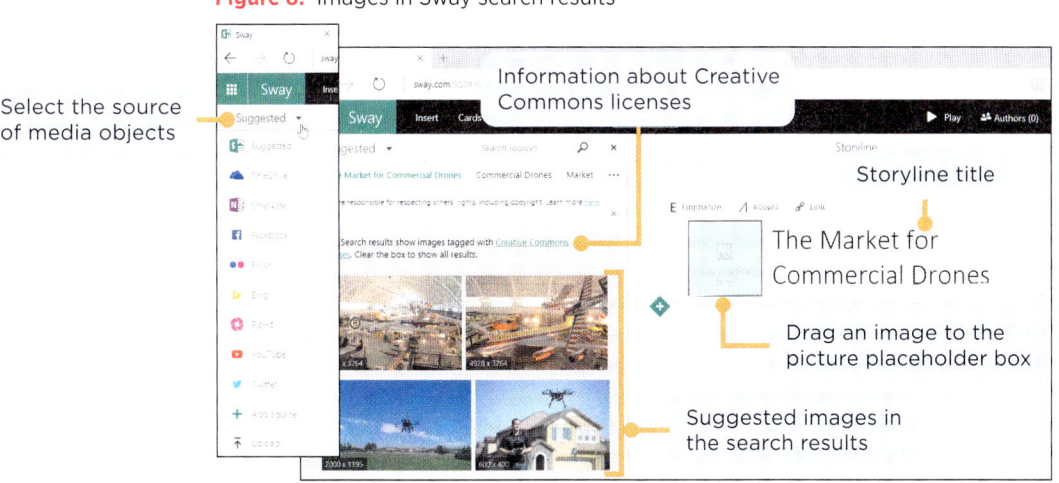

Select the source of media objects

Information about Creative Commons licenses

Storyline title

The Market for Commercial Drones

Drag an image to the picture placeholder box

Suggested images in the search results

Designing a Sway

Sway professionally designs your Storyline content by resizing background images and fonts to fit your display, and by floating text, animating media, embedding video, and removing images as a page scrolls out of view. Sway also evaluates the images in your Storyline and suggests a color palette based on colors that appear in your photos. Use the Design button to display tools including color palettes, font choices, **animation emphasis effects**, and style templates to provide a personality for a Sway presentation. Instead of creating your own design, you can click the Remix button, which randomly selects unique designs for your Sway site.

Publishing a Sway

Use the Play button to display your finished Sway presentation as a website. The Address bar includes a unique web address where others can view your Sway site. As the author, you can edit a published Sway site by clicking the Edit button (pencil icon) on the Sway toolbar.

Sharing a Sway

When you are ready to share your Sway website, you have several options as shown in **Figure 9**. Use the Share slider button to share the Sway site publically or keep it private. If you add the Sway site to the Microsoft **Docs.com** public gallery, anyone worldwide can use Bing, Google, or other search engines to find, view, and share your Sway site. You can also share your Sway site using Facebook, Twitter, Google+, Yammer, and other social media sites. Link your presentation to any webpage or email the link to your audience. Sway can also generate a code for embedding the link within another webpage.

Figure 9: Sharing a Sway site

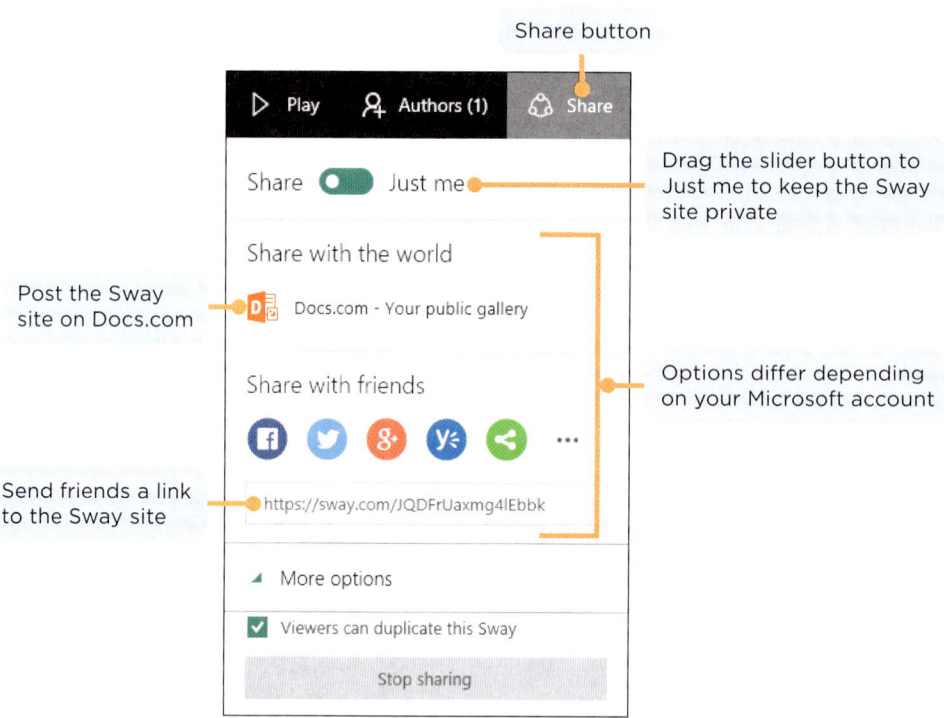

Try This Now

1: Creating a Sway Resume

Sway is a digital storytelling app. Create a Sway resume to share the skills, job experiences, and achievements you have that match the requirements of a future job interest. Perform the following tasks:

a. Create a new presentation in Sway to use as a digital resume. Title the Sway Storyline with your full name and then select a background image.
b. Create three separate sections titled **Academic Background, Work Experience**, and **Skills**, and insert text, a picture, and a paragraph or bulleted points in each section. Be sure to include your own picture.
c. Add a fourth section that includes a video about your school that you find online.
d. Customize the design of your presentation.
e. Submit your assignment link in the format specified by your instructor.

2: Creating an Online Sway Newsletter

Newsletters are designed to capture the attention of their target audience. Using Sway, create a newsletter for a club, organization, or your favorite music group. Perform the following tasks:

a. Create a new presentation in Sway to use as a digital newsletter for a club, organization, or your favorite music group. Provide a title for the Sway Storyline and select an appropriate background image.
b. Select three separate sections with appropriate titles, such as Upcoming Events. In each section, insert text, a picture, and a paragraph or bulleted points.
c. Add a fourth section that includes a video about your selected topic.
d. Customize the design of your presentation.
e. Submit your assignment link in the format specified by your instructor.

3: Creating and Sharing a Technology Presentation

To place a Sway presentation in the hands of your entire audience, you can share a link to the Sway presentation. Create a Sway presentation on a new technology and share it with your class. Perform the following tasks:

a. Create a new presentation in Sway about a cutting-edge technology topic. Provide a title for the Sway Storyline and select a background image.
b. Create four separate sections about your topic, and include text, a picture, and a paragraph in each section.
c. Add a fifth section that includes a video about your topic.
d. Customize the design of your presentation.
e. Share the link to your Sway with your classmates and submit your assignment link in the format specified by your instructor.

Introduction to Office Mix

add-in | clip | slide recording | Slide Notes | screen recording | free-response quiz

Bottom Line

- Office Mix is a free PowerPoint add-in from Microsoft that adds features to PowerPoint.
- The Mix tab on the PowerPoint ribbon provides tools for creating screen recordings, videos, interactive quizzes, and live webpages.

To enliven business meetings and lectures, Microsoft adds a new dimension to presentations with a powerful toolset called Office Mix, a free add-in for PowerPoint. (An **add-in** is software that works with an installed app to extend its features.) Using Office Mix, you can record yourself on video, capture still and moving images on your desktop, and insert interactive elements such as quizzes and live webpages directly into PowerPoint slides. When you post the finished presentation to OneDrive, Office Mix provides a link you can share with friends and colleagues. Anyone with an Internet connection and a web browser can watch a published Office Mix presentation, such as the one in **Figure 10**, on a computer or mobile device.

Figure 10: Office Mix presentation

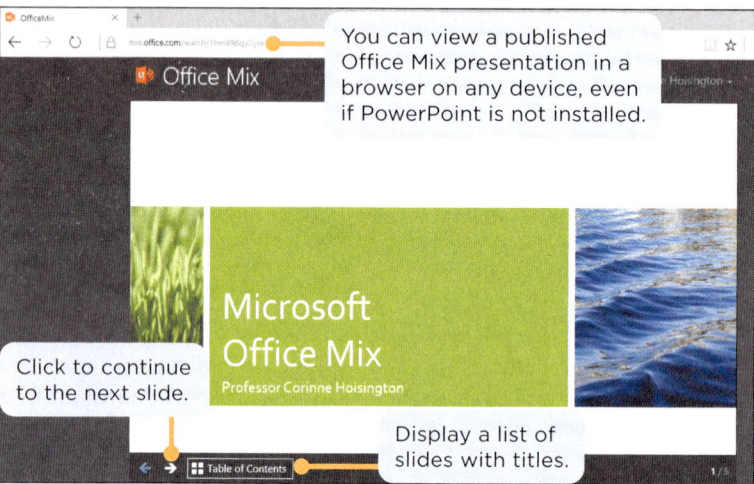

Adding Office Mix to PowerPoint

To get started, you create an Office Mix account at the website mix.office.com using an email address or a Facebook or Google account. Next, you download and install the Office Mix add-in (see **Figure 11**). Office Mix appears as a new tab named Mix on the PowerPoint ribbon in versions of Office 2013 and Office 2016 running on personal computers (PCs).

Learn to use Office Mix!

Links to companion **Sways**, featuring **videos** with hands-on instructions, are located on www.cengagebrain.com.

Figure 11: Getting started with Office Mix

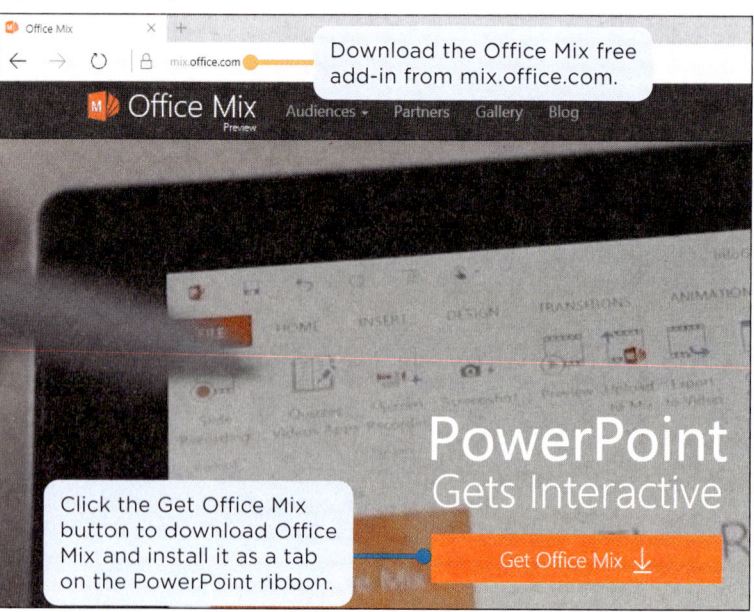

Capturing Video Clips

A **clip** is a short segment of audio, such as music, or video. After finishing the content on a PowerPoint slide, you can use Office Mix to add a video clip to animate or illustrate the content. Office Mix creates video clips in two ways: by recording live action on a webcam and by capturing screen images and movements. If your computer has a webcam, you can record yourself and annotate the slide to create a **slide recording** as shown in **Figure 12**.

Figure 12: Making a slide recording

Record your voice; also record video if your computer has a camera.

Use the Slide Notes button to display notes for your narration.

For best results, look directly at your webcam while recording video.

Use inking tools to write and draw on the slide as you record.

Choose a video and audio device to record images and sound.

When you are making a slide recording, you can record your spoken narration at the same time. The **Slide Notes** feature works like a teleprompter to help you focus on your presentation content instead of memorizing your narration. Use the Inking tools to make annotations or add highlighting using different pen types and colors. After finishing a recording, edit the video in PowerPoint to trim the length or set playback options.

The second way to create a video is to capture on-screen images and actions with or without a voiceover. This method is ideal if you want to show how to use your favorite website or demonstrate an app such as OneNote. To share your screen with an audience, select the part of the screen you want to show in the video. Office Mix captures everything that happens in that area to create a **screen recording**, as shown in **Figure 13**. Office Mix inserts the screen recording as a video in the slide.

Figure 13: Making a screen recording

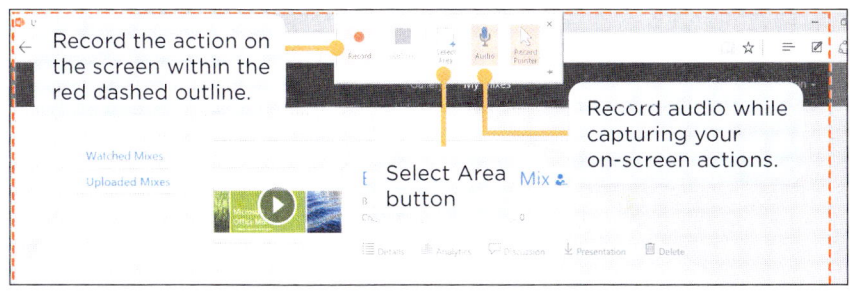

Record the action on the screen within the red dashed outline.

Record audio while capturing your on-screen actions.

Select Area button

Inserting Quizzes, Live Webpages, and Apps

To enhance and assess audience understanding, make your slides interactive by adding quizzes, live webpages, and apps. Quizzes give immediate feedback to the user as shown in **Figure 14**. Office Mix supports several quiz formats, including a **free-response quiz** similar to a short answer quiz, and true/false, multiple-choice, and multiple-response formats.

Figure 14: Creating an interactive quiz

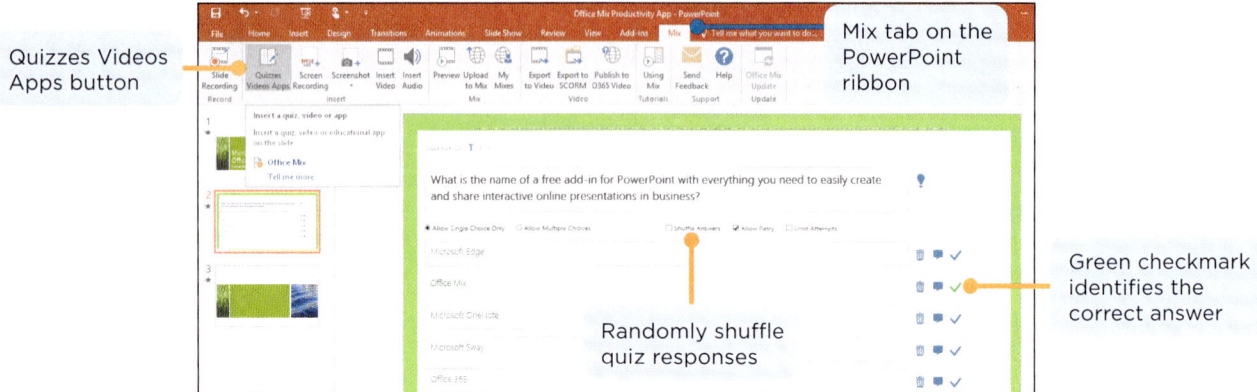

Sharing an Office Mix Presentation

When you complete your work with Office Mix, upload the presentation to your personal Office Mix dashboard as shown in **Figure 15**. Users of PCs, Macs, iOS devices, and Android devices can access and play Office Mix presentations. The Office Mix dashboard displays built-in analytics that include the quiz results and how much time viewers spent on each slide. You can play completed Office Mix presentations online or download them as movies.

Figure 15: Sharing an Office Mix presentation

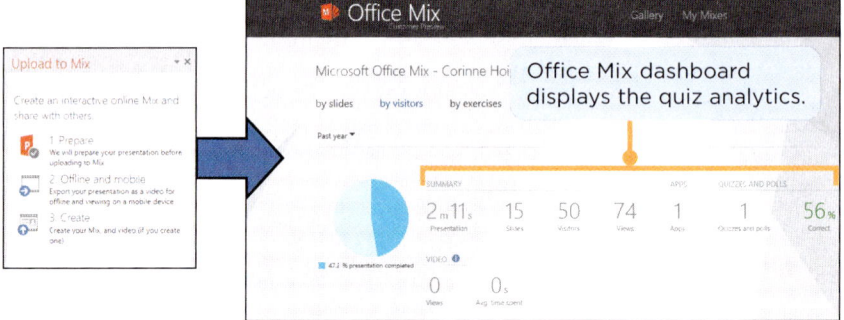

Try This Now

Learn to use Office Mix!
Links to companion **Sways**, featuring **videos** with hands-on instructions, are located on www.cengagebrain.com.

1: Creating an Office Mix Tutorial for OneNote

Note: This activity requires a microphone on your computer.

Office Mix makes it easy to record screens and their contents. Create PowerPoint slides with an Office Mix screen recording to show OneNote 2016 features. Perform the following tasks:

a. Create a PowerPoint presentation with the Ion Boardroom template. Create an opening slide with the title **My Favorite OneNote Features** and enter your name in the subtitle.
b. Create three additional slides, each titled with a new feature of OneNote. Open OneNote and use the Mix tab in PowerPoint to capture three separate screen recordings that teach your favorite features.
c. Add a fifth slide that quizzes the user with a multiple-choice question about OneNote and includes four responses. Be sure to insert a checkmark indicating the correct response.
d. Upload the completed presentation to your Office Mix dashboard and share the link with your instructor.
e. Submit your assignment link in the format specified by your instructor.

2: Teaching Augmented Reality with Office Mix

Note: This activity requires a webcam or built-in video camera on your computer.

A local elementary school has asked you to teach augmented reality to its students using Office Mix. Perform the following tasks:

a. Research augmented reality using your favorite online search tools.
b. Create a PowerPoint presentation with the Frame template. Create an opening slide with the title **Augmented Reality** and enter your name in the subtitle.
c. Create a slide with four bullets summarizing your research of augmented reality. Create a 20-second slide recording of yourself providing a quick overview of augmented reality.
d. Create another slide with a 30-second screen recording of a video about augmented reality from a site such as YouTube or another video-sharing site.
e. Add a final slide that quizzes the user with a true/false question about augmented reality. Be sure to insert a checkmark indicating the correct response.
f. Upload the completed presentation to your Office Mix dashboard and share the link with your instructor.
g. Submit your assignment link in the format specified by your instructor.

3: Marketing a Travel Destination with Office Mix

Note: This activity requires a webcam or built-in video camera on your computer.

To convince your audience to travel to a particular city, create a slide presentation marketing any city in the world using a slide recording, screen recording, and a quiz. Perform the following tasks:

a. Create a PowerPoint presentation with any template. Create an opening slide with the title of the city you are marketing as a travel destination and your name in the subtitle.
b. Create a slide with four bullets about the featured city. Create a 30-second slide recording of yourself explaining why this city is the perfect vacation destination.
c. Create another slide with a 20-second screen recording of a travel video about the city from a site such as YouTube or another video-sharing site.
d. Add a final slide that quizzes the user with a multiple-choice question about the featured city with five responses. Be sure to include a checkmark indicating the correct response.
e. Upload the completed presentation to your Office Mix dashboard and share your link with your instructor.
f. Submit your assignment link in the format specified by your instructor.

Introduction to Microsoft Edge

Reading view | Hub | Cortana | Web Note | Inking | sandbox

Microsoft Edge is the default web browser developed for the Windows 10 operating system as a replacement for Internet Explorer. Unlike its predecessor, Edge lets you write on webpages, read webpages without advertisements and other distractions, and search for information using a virtual personal assistant. The Edge interface is clean and basic, as shown in **Figure 16**, meaning you can pay more attention to the webpage content.

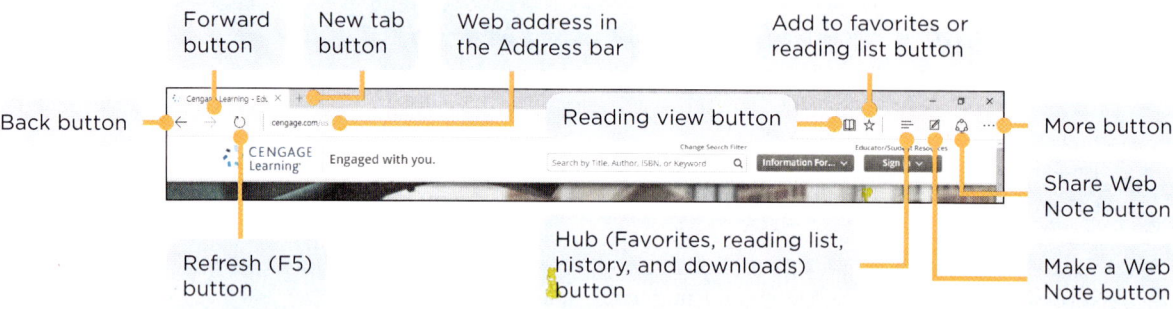

Figure 16: Microsoft Edge tools

Browsing the Web with Microsoft Edge

One of the fastest browsers available, Edge allows you to type search text directly in the Address bar. As you view the resulting webpage, you can switch to **Reading view**, which is available for most news and research sites, to eliminate distracting advertisements. For example, if you are catching up on technology news online, the webpage might be difficult to read due to a busy layout cluttered with ads. Switch to Reading view to refresh the page and remove the original page formatting, ads, and menu sidebars to read the article distraction-free.

Consider the **Hub** in Microsoft Edge as providing one-stop access to all the things you collect on the web, such as your favorite websites, reading list, surfing history, and downloaded files.

Locating Information with Cortana

Cortana, the Windows 10 virtual assistant, plays an important role in Microsoft Edge. After you turn on Cortana, it appears as an animated circle in the Address bar when you might need assistance, as shown in the restaurant website in **Figure 17**. When you click the Cortana icon, a pane slides in from the right of the browser window to display detailed information about the restaurant, including maps and reviews. Cortana can also assist you in defining words, finding the weather, suggesting coupons for shopping, updating stock market information, and calculating math.

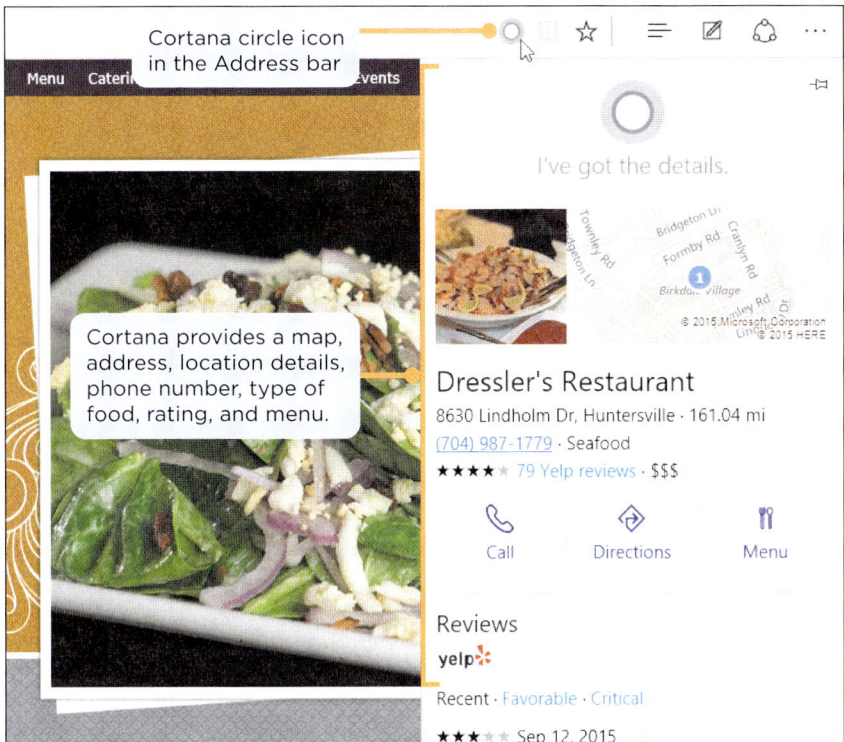

Cortana circle icon in the Address bar

Cortana provides a map, address, location details, phone number, type of food, rating, and menu.

I've got the details.

Dressler's Restaurant
8630 Lindholm Dr, Huntersville · 161.04 mi
(704) 987-1779 · Seafood
★★★★★ 79 Yelp reviews · $$$

Call   Directions   Menu

Reviews
yelp

Recent · Favorable · Critical
★★★☆☆ Sep 12, 2015

Annotating Webpages

One of the most impressive Microsoft Edge features are the **Web Note** tools, which you use to write on a webpage or to highlight text. When you click the Make a Web Note button, an **Inking** toolbar appears, as shown in **Figure 18**, that provides writing and drawing tools. These tools include an eraser, a pen, and a highlighter with different colors. You can also insert a typed note and copy a screen image (called a screen clipping). You can draw with a pointing device, fingertip, or stylus using different pen colors. Whether you add notes to a recipe, annotate sources for a research paper, or select a product while shopping online, the Web Note tools can enhance your productivity. After you complete your notes, click the Save button to save the annotations to OneNote, your Favorites list, or your Reading list. You can share the inked page with others using the Share Web Note button.

On the Job Now

To enhance security, Microsoft Edge runs in a partial sandbox, an arrangement that prevents attackers from gaining control of your computer. Browsing within the **sandbox** protects computer resources and information from hackers.

Figure 18: Web Note tools in Microsoft Edge

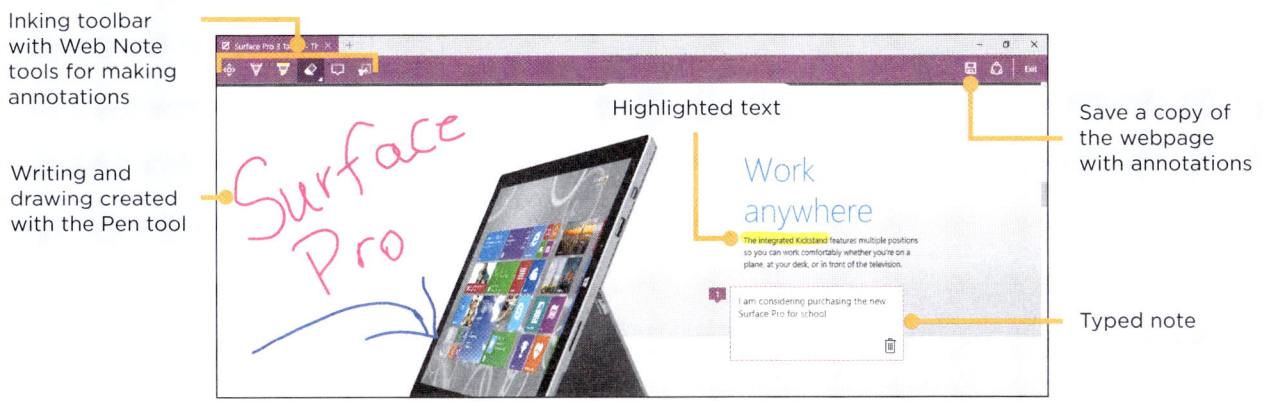

Inking toolbar with Web Note tools for making annotations

Writing and drawing created with the Pen tool

Highlighted text

Work anywhere

The integrated Kickstand features multiple positions so you can work comfortably whether you're on a plane, at your desk, or in front of the television.

I am considering purchasing the new Surface Pro for school.

Save a copy of the webpage with annotations

Typed note

Try This Now

1: Using Cortana in Microsoft Edge

Note: This activity requires using Microsoft Edge on a Windows 10 computer.

Cortana can assist you in finding information on a webpage in Microsoft Edge. Perform the following tasks:

a. Create a Word document using the Word Screen Clipping tool to capture the following screenshots.

- Screenshot A—Using Microsoft Edge, open a webpage with a technology news article. Right-click a term in the article and ask Cortana to define it.
- Screenshot B—Using Microsoft Edge, open the website of a fancy restaurant in a city near you. Make sure the Cortana circle icon is displayed in the Address bar. (If it's not displayed, find a different restaurant website.) Click the Cortana circle icon to display a pane with information about the restaurant.
- Screenshot C—Using Microsoft Edge, type **10 USD to Euros** in the Address bar without pressing the Enter key. Cortana converts the U.S. dollars to Euros.
- Screenshot D—Using Microsoft Edge, type **Apple stock** in the Address bar without pressing the Enter key. Cortana displays the current stock quote.

b. Submit your assignment in the format specified by your instructor.

2: Viewing Online News with Reading View

Note: This activity requires using Microsoft Edge on a Windows 10 computer.

Reading view in Microsoft Edge can make a webpage less cluttered with ads and other distractions. Perform the following tasks:

a. Create a Word document using the Word Screen Clipping tool to capture the following screenshots.

- Screenshot A—Using Microsoft Edge, open the website **mashable.com**. Open a technology article. Click the Reading view button to display an ad-free page that uses only basic text formatting.
- Screenshot B—Using Microsoft Edge, open the website **bbc.com**. Open any news article. Click the Reading view button to display an ad-free page that uses only basic text formatting.
- Screenshot C—Make three types of annotations (Pen, Highlighter, and Add a typed note) on the BBC article page displayed in Reading view.

b. Submit your assignment in the format specified by your instructor.

3: Inking with Microsoft Edge

Note: This activity requires using Microsoft Edge on a Windows 10 computer.

Microsoft Edge provides many annotation options to record your ideas. Perform the following tasks:

a. Open the website **wolframalpha.com** in the Microsoft Edge browser. Wolfram Alpha is a well-respected academic search engine. Type **US$100 1965 dollars in 2015** in the Wolfram Alpha search text box and press the Enter key.

b. Click the Make a Web Note button to display the Web Note tools. Using the Pen tool, draw a circle around the result on the webpage. Save the page to OneNote.

c. In the Wolfram Alpha search text box, type the name of the city closest to where you live and press the Enter key. Using the Highlighter tool, highlight at least three interesting results. Add a note and then type a sentence about what you learned about this city. Save the page to OneNote. Share your OneNote notebook with your instructor.

d. Submit your assignment link in the format specified by your instructor.

Office 2016 and Windows 10: Essential Concepts and Skills

Objectives

You will have mastered the material in this module when you can:

- Use a touch screen
- Perform basic mouse operations
- Start Windows and sign in to an account
- Identify the objects on the Windows 10 desktop
- Identify the versions and apps of Microsoft Office 2016
- Run an app
- Identify the components of the Microsoft Office ribbon

- Create folders
- Save files
- Change screen resolution
- Perform basic tasks in Microsoft Office apps
- Manage files
- Use Microsoft Office Help and Windows Help

This introductory module uses Publisher 2016 to cover features and functions common to Office 2016 apps, as well as the basics of Windows 10.

Roadmap

In this module, you will learn how to perform basic tasks in Windows and Publisher. The following roadmap identifies general activities you will perform as you progress through this module:

1. SIGN IN to an account.
2. USE WINDOWS.
3. USE features in Publisher that are common across Office APPS.
4. FILE and folder MANAGEMENT.
5. SWITCH between APPS.
6. SAVE and manage FILES.
7. CHANGE SCREEN RESOLUTION.

8. **EXIT APPS**.

9. **USE ADDITIONAL** Office **APP FEATURES**.

10. **USE** Office and Windows **HELP**.

At the beginning of the step instructions throughout each module, you will see an abbreviated form of this roadmap. The abbreviated roadmap uses colors to indicate module progress: gray means the module is beyond that activity, blue means the task being shown is covered in that activity, and black means that activity is yet to be covered. For example, the following abbreviated roadmap indicates the module would be showing a task in the USE APPS activity.

1 SIGN IN | 2 USE WINDOWS | **3 USE APPS** | **4 FILE MANAGEMENT** | **5 SWITCH APPS** | **6 SAVE FILES**
7 CHANGE SCREEN RESOLUTION | **8 EXIT APPS** | **9 USE ADDITIONAL APP FEATURES** | **10 USE HELP**

Use the abbreviated roadmap as a progress guide while you read or step through the instructions in this module.

Introduction to the Windows 10 Operating System

Windows 10 is the newest version of Microsoft Windows, which is a popular and widely used operating system (Figure 1). An **operating system (OS)** is a set of programs that coordinate all the activities among computer or mobile device hardware.

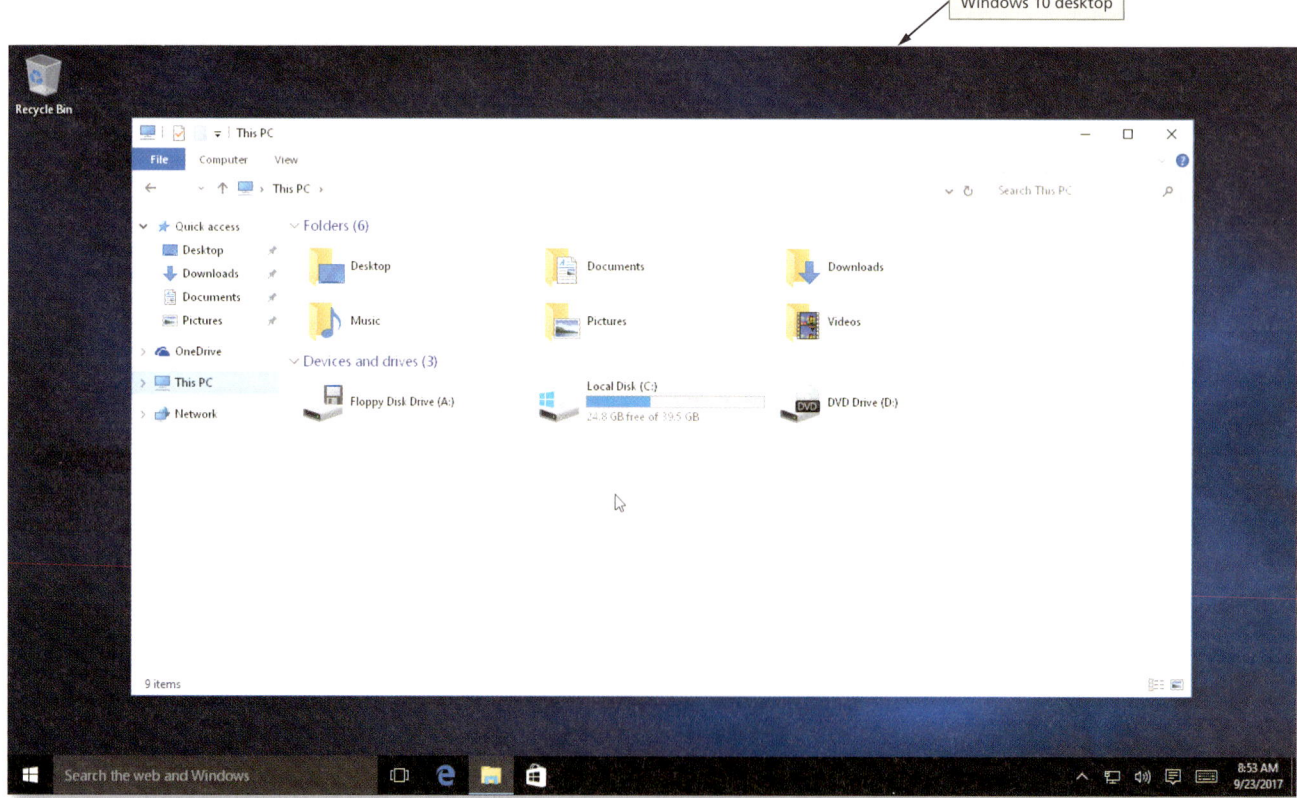

Figure 1

The Windows operating system simplifies the process of working with publications and apps by organizing the manner in which you interact with the computer. Windows is used to run apps. An application, or **app**, consists of programs designed to make users more productive and/or assist them with personal tasks, such as desktop publishing or browsing the web.

Using a Touch Screen and a Mouse

Windows users who have computers or devices with touch screen capability can interact with the screen using gestures. A **gesture** is a motion you make on a touch screen with the tip of one or more fingers or your hand. Touch screens are convenient because they do not require a separate device for input. Table 1 presents common ways to interact with a touch screen.

If you are using your finger on a touch screen and are having difficulty completing the steps in this module, consider using a stylus. Many people find it easier to be precise with a stylus than with a finger. In addition, with a stylus you see the pointer. If you still are having trouble completing the steps with a stylus, try using a mouse.

Table 1 Touch Screen Gestures

Motion	Description	Common Uses	Equivalent Mouse Operation
Tap	Quickly touch and release one finger one time.	Activate a link (built-in connection). Press a button. Run a program or an app.	Click
Double-tap	Quickly touch and release one finger two times.	Run a program or an app. Zoom in (show a smaller area on the screen, so that contents appear larger) at the location of the double-tap.	Double-click
Press and hold	Press and hold one finger to cause an action to occur, or until an action occurs.	Display a shortcut menu (immediate access to allowable actions). Activate a mode enabling you to move an item with one finger to a new location.	Right-click
Drag, or slide	Press and hold one finger on an object and then move the finger to the new location.	Move an item around the screen. Scroll.	Drag
Swipe	Press and hold one finger and then move the finger horizontally or vertically on the screen.	Select an object. Swipe from edge to display a bar such as the Action Center, Apps bar, and Navigation bar (all discussed later).	Drag
Stretch	Move two fingers apart.	Zoom in (show a smaller area on the screen, so that contents appear larger).	None
Pinch	Move two fingers together.	Zoom out (show a larger area on the screen, so that contents appear smaller).	None

Will the screen look different if you are using a touch screen?
The Windows and Microsoft Office interface varies slightly if you are using a touch screen. For this reason, you might notice that your Windows or Publisher screens looks slightly different from the screens in this book.

CONSIDER THIS

BTW

Pointer
If you are using a touch
screen, the pointer may not
appear on the screen as you
perform touch gestures. The
pointer will reappear when
you begin using the mouse.

Windows users who do not have touch screen capabilities typically work with a mouse that has at least two buttons. For a right-handed user, the left button usually is the primary mouse button, and the right mouse button is the secondary mouse button. Left-handed people, however, can reverse the function of these buttons.

Table 2 explains how to perform a variety of mouse operations. Some apps also use keys in combination with the mouse to perform certain actions. For example, when you hold down the CTRL key while rolling the mouse wheel, text on the screen may become larger or smaller based on the direction you roll the wheel. The function of the mouse buttons and the wheel varies depending on the app.

Table 2 Mouse Operations

Operation	Mouse Action	Example*	Equivalent Touch Gesture
Point	Move the mouse until the pointer on the desktop is positioned on the item of choice.	Position the pointer on the screen.	None
Click	Press and release the primary mouse button, which usually is the left mouse button.	Select or deselect items on the screen or run an app or app feature.	Tap
Right-click	Press and release the secondary mouse button, which usually is the right mouse button.	Display a shortcut menu.	Press and hold
Double-click	Quickly press and release the primary mouse button twice without moving the mouse.	Run an app or app feature.	Double-tap
Triple-click	Quickly press and release the primary mouse button three times without moving the mouse.	Select a paragraph.	Triple-tap
Drag	Point to an item, hold down the primary mouse button, move the item to the desired location on the screen, and then release the mouse button.	Move an object from one location to another or draw pictures.	Drag or slide
Right-drag	Point to an item, hold down the right mouse button, move the item to the desired location on the screen, and then release the right mouse button.	Display a shortcut menu after moving an object from one location to another.	Press and hold, then drag
Rotate wheel	Roll the wheel forward or backward.	Scroll vertically (up and down).	Swipe
Free-spin wheel	Whirl the wheel forward or backward so that it spins freely on its own.	Scroll through many pages in seconds.	Swipe
Press wheel	Press the wheel button while moving the mouse.	Scroll continuously.	None
Tilt wheel	Press the wheel toward the right or left.	Scroll horizontally (left and right).	None
Press thumb button	Press the button on the side of the mouse with your thumb.	Move forward or backward through webpages and/or control media, games, etc.	None

*Note: The examples presented in this column are discussed as they are demonstrated in this module.

Scrolling

A **scroll bar** is a horizontal or vertical bar that appears when the contents of an area may not be visible completely on the screen (Figure 2). A scroll bar contains **scroll arrows** and a **scroll box** that enable you to view areas that currently cannot be seen on the screen. Clicking the up and down scroll arrows moves the screen content up or down one line. You also can click above or below the scroll box to move up or down a section, or drag the scroll box up or down to move to a specific location.

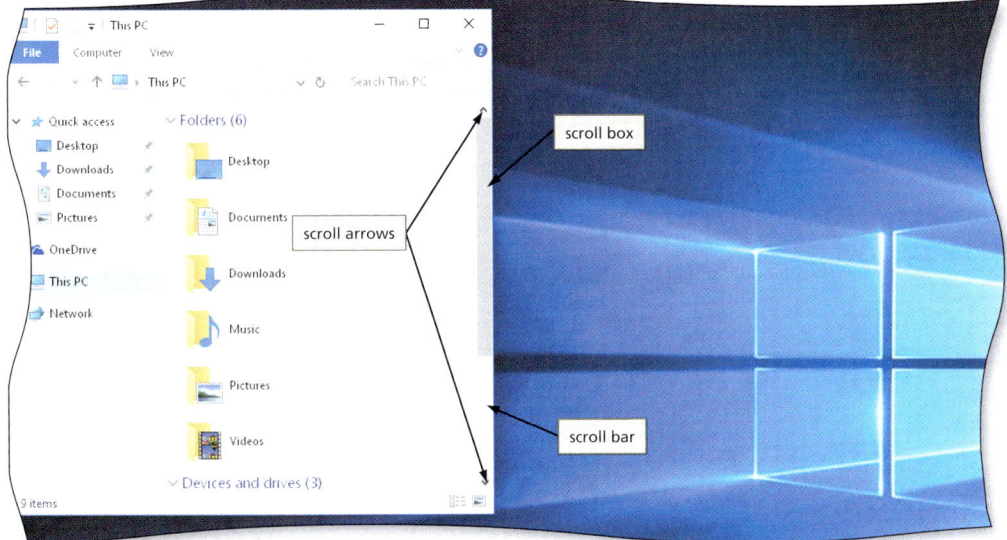

Figure 2

Keyboard Shortcuts

In many cases, you can use the keyboard instead of the mouse to accomplish a task. To perform tasks using the keyboard, you press one or more keyboard keys, sometimes identified as a **keyboard shortcut**. Some keyboard shortcuts consist of a single key, such as the F1 key. For example, to obtain help in many apps, you can press the F1 key. Other keyboard shortcuts consist of multiple keys, in which case a plus sign separates the key names, such as CTRL+ESC. This notation means to press and hold down the first key listed, press one or more additional keys, and then release all keys. For example, to display the Start menu, press CTRL+ESC, that is, hold down the CTRL key, press the ESC key, and then release both keys.

Starting Windows

It is not unusual for multiple people to use the same computer in a work, educational, recreational, or home setting. Windows enables each user to establish a **user account**, which identifies to Windows the resources, such as apps and storage locations, a user can access when working with the computer.

Each user account has a user name and may have a password and an icon, as well. A **user name** is a unique combination of letters or numbers that identifies a specific user to Windows. A **password** is a private combination of letters, numbers, and special characters associated with the user name that allows access to a user's account resources. An icon is a small image that represents an object; thus, a **user icon** is a picture associated with a user name.

When you turn on a computer, Windows starts and displays a **lock screen** consisting of the time and date (Figure 3). To unlock the screen, click the lock screen. Depending on your computer's settings, Windows may or may not display a sign-in screen that shows the user names and user icons for users who have accounts on the computer. This **sign-in screen** enables you to sign in to your user account and makes the computer available for use (shown in Figure 4). Clicking the user icon begins the process of signing in, also called logging on, to your user account.

BTW

Minimize Wrist Injury
Computer users frequently switch between the keyboard and the mouse while using Publisher; such switching strains the wrist. To help prevent wrist injury, minimize switching. For instance, if your fingers already are on the keyboard, use keyboard keys to scroll. If your hand already is on the mouse, use the mouse to scroll. If your hand is on the touch screen, use touch gestures to scroll.

Figure 3

At the bottom of the sign-in screen (shown in Figure 4) is the 'Connect to Internet' button, 'Ease of access' button, and a Shut down button. Clicking the 'Connect to Internet' button displays a list of each network connection and its status. You also can connect to or disconnect from a network. Clicking the 'Ease of access' button displays the Ease of access menu, which provides tools to optimize a computer to accommodate the needs of the mobility, hearing, and vision impaired users. Clicking the Shut down button displays a menu containing commands related to putting the computer or mobile device in a low-power state, shutting it down, and restarting the computer or mobile device. The commands available on your computer or mobile device may differ.

- The Sleep command saves your work, turns off the computer fans and hard drive, and places the computer in a lower-power state. To wake the computer from sleep mode, press the power button or lift a laptop's cover, and sign in to your account.
- The Shut down command exits running apps, shuts down Windows, and then turns off the computer.
- The Restart command exits running apps, shuts down Windows, and then restarts Windows.

To Sign In to an Account

1 SIGN IN | 2 USE WINDOWS | 3 USE APPS | 4 FILE MANAGEMENT | 5 SWITCH APPS | 6 SAVE FILES
7 CHANGE SCREEN RESOLUTION | 8 EXIT APPS | 9 USE ADDITIONAL APP FEATURES | 10 USE HELP

The following steps, which use SCSeries as the user name, sign in to an account based on a typical Windows installation. ***Why?*** *After starting Windows, you might be required to sign in to an account to access the computer or mobile device's resources.* You may need to ask your instructor how to sign in to your account.

- Click the lock screen (shown in Figure 3) to display a sign-in screen.

- Click the user icon (for SCSeries, in this case) on the sign-in screen, which depending on settings, either will display a second sign-in screen that contains a Password text box (Figure 4) or will display the Windows desktop (shown in Figure 5).

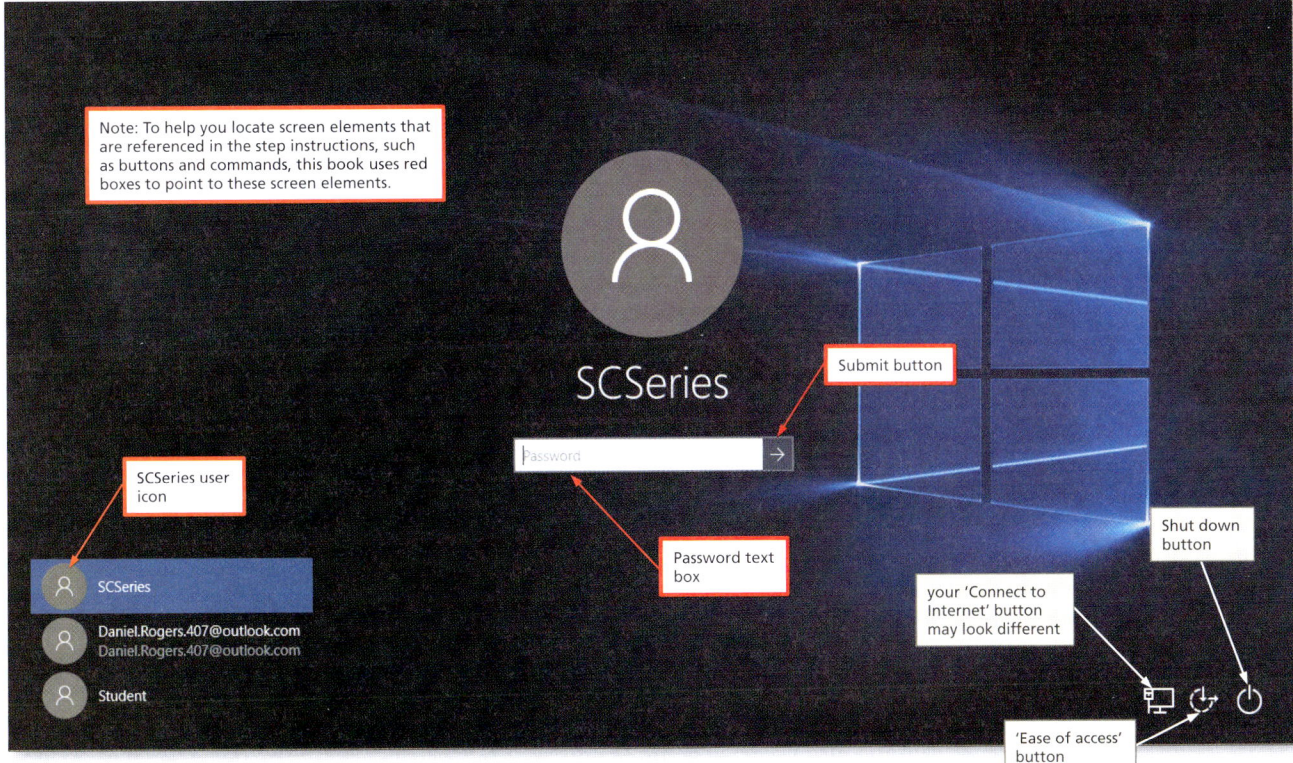

Figure 4

Q&A

Why do I not see a user icon?
Your computer may require you to type a user name instead of clicking an icon.

What is a text box?
A text box is a rectangular box in which you type text.

Why does my screen not show a Password text box?
Your account does not require a password.

- If Windows displays a sign-in screen with a Password text box, type your password in the text box.

- Click the Submit button (shown in Figure 4) to sign in to your account and display the Windows desktop (Figure 5).

Q&A

Why does my desktop look different from the one in Figure 5?
The Windows desktop is customizable, and your school or employer may have modified the desktop to meet its needs. Also, your screen resolution, which affects the size of the elements on the screen, may differ from the screen resolution used in this book. Later in this module, you learn how to change screen resolution.

How do I type if my tablet has no keyboard?
You can use your fingers to press keys on a keyboard that appears on the screen, called an on-screen keyboard, or you can purchase a separate physical keyboard that attaches to or wirelessly communicates with the tablet.

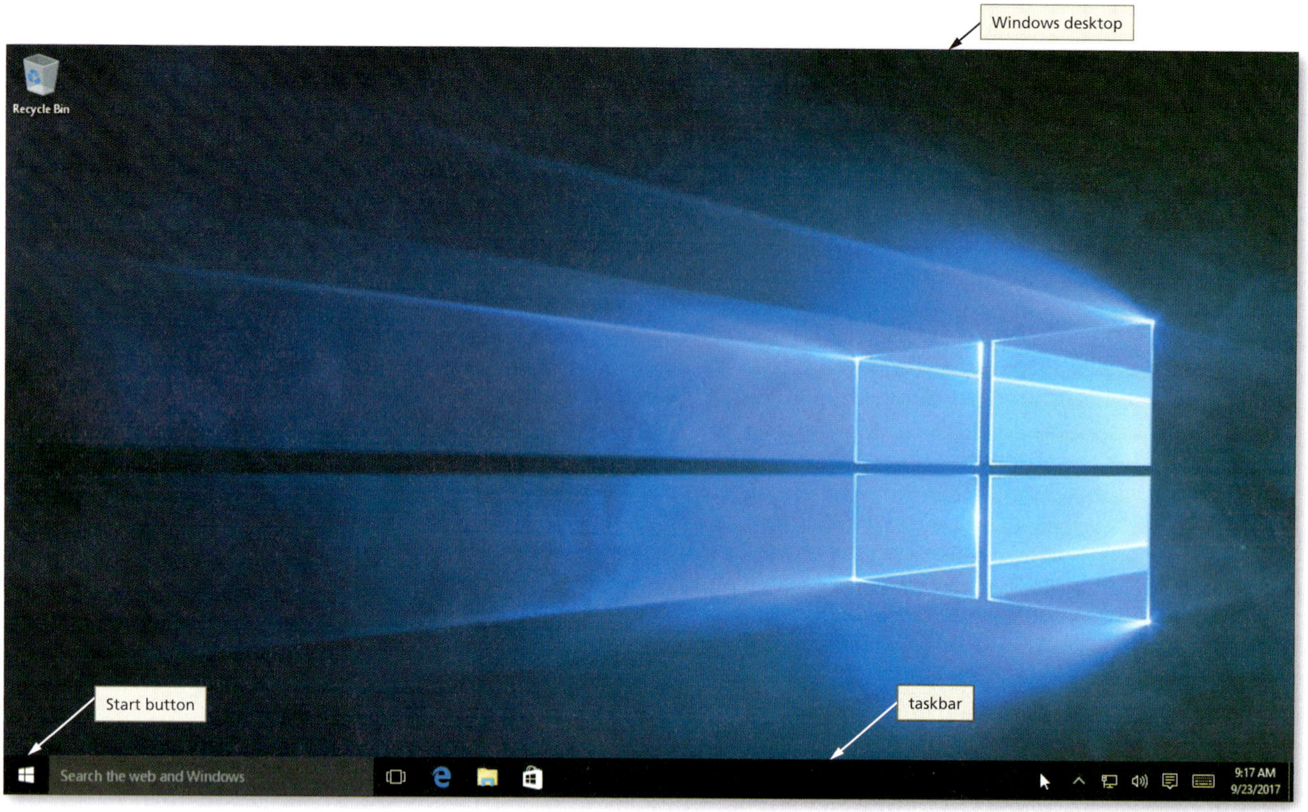

Figure 5

The Windows Desktop

The Windows 10 desktop (Figure 5) and the objects on the desktop emulate a work area in an office. Think of the Windows desktop as an electronic version of the top of your desk. You can perform tasks such as placing objects on the desktop, moving the objects around the desktop, and removing items from the desktop.

When you run an app in Windows 10, it appears on the desktop. Some icons also may be displayed on the desktop. For instance, the icon for the **Recycle Bin**, the location of files that have been deleted, appears on the desktop by default. A **file** is a named unit of storage. Files can contain text, images, audio, and/or video. You can customize your desktop so that icons representing programs and files you use often appear on your desktop.

Introduction to Microsoft Office 2016

Microsoft Office 2016 is the newest version of Microsoft Office, offering features that provide users with better functionality and easier ways to work with the various files they create. This version of Office also is designed to work more optimally on mobile devices and online.

Microsoft Office 2016 Apps

Microsoft Office 2016 includes a wide variety of apps, such as Word, PowerPoint, Excel, Access, Outlook, Publisher, and OneNote:

- **Microsoft Word 2016**, or Word, is a full-featured word processing app that allows you to create professional-looking documents and revise them easily.

- **Microsoft PowerPoint 2016**, or PowerPoint, is a complete presentation app that enables you to produce professional-looking presentations and then deliver them to an audience.

- **Microsoft Excel 2016**, or Excel, is a powerful spreadsheet app that allows you to organize data, complete calculations, make decisions, graph data, develop professional-looking reports, publish organized data to the web, and access real-time data from websites.

- **Microsoft Access 2016**, or Access, is a database management system that enables you to create a database; add, change, and delete data in the database; ask questions concerning the data in the database; and create forms and reports using the data in the database.

- **Microsoft Outlook 2016**, or Outlook, is a communications and scheduling app that allows you to manage email accounts, calendars, contacts, and access to other Internet content.

- **Microsoft Publisher 2016**, or Publisher, is a desktop publishing app that helps you create professional-quality publications and marketing materials that can be shared easily.

- **Microsoft OneNote 2016**, or OneNote, is a note-taking app that allows you to store and share information in notebooks with other people.

Microsoft Office 2016 Suites

A **suite** is a collection of individual apps available together as a unit. Microsoft offers a variety of Office suites, including a stand-alone desktop app, Microsoft Office 365, and Microsoft Office Online. **Microsoft Office 365**, or Office 365, provides plans that allow organizations to use Office in a mobile setting while also being able to communicate and share files, depending upon the type of plan selected by the organization. **Microsoft Office Online** includes apps that allow you to edit and share files on the web using the familiar Office interface.

During the Office 365 installation, you select a plan, and depending on your plan, you receive different apps and services. Office Online apps do not require a local installation and can be accessed through OneDrive and your browser. **OneDrive** is a cloud storage service that provides storage and other services, such as Office Online, to computer and mobile device users.

How do you sign up for a OneDrive account?

- Use your browser to navigate to onedrive.live.com.

- Create a Microsoft account by clicking the Sign up button and then entering your information to create the account.

- Sign in to OneDrive using your new account or use it in Publisher to save your files on OneDrive.

CONSIDER THIS

Apps in a suite, such as Microsoft Office, typically use a similar interface and share features. Once you are comfortable working with the elements and the interface, and performing tasks in one app, the similarity can help you apply the knowledge and skills you have learned to another app(s) in the suite. For example, the process for saving a file in Publisher is the same in Word, PowerPoint, Excel, and some of the other Office apps. While briefly showing how to use Publisher, this module illustrates some of the common functions across the Office apps and identifies the characteristics unique to Publisher.

Running and Using An App

To use an app, you must instruct the operating system to run the app. Windows provides many different ways to run an app, one of which is presented in this section (other ways to run an app are presented throughout this module). After an app is running, you can use it to perform a variety of tasks. The following pages use Publisher to discuss some elements of the Office interface and to perform tasks that are common to other Office apps.

Publisher

Publisher is a full-featured desktop publishing app that allows you to create many types of personal and business publications, including flyers, brochures, advertisements, catalogs, mailing labels, and newsletters. Publisher also provides tools that enable you to create webpages and save these webpages directly on a web server. Publisher has many features designed to simplify the production of publications and add visual appeal. Using Publisher, you easily can change the shape, size, and color of text. You also can include borders, shading, tables, images, pictures, charts, and web addresses in publications.

To Run an App Using the Start Menu and Create a Blank Publication

1 SIGN IN | **2 USE WINDOWS** | 3 USE APPS | 4 FILE MANAGEMENT | 5 SWITCH APPS | 6 SAVE FILES
7 CHANGE SCREEN RESOLUTION | 8 EXIT APPS | 9 USE ADDITIONAL APP FEATURES | 10 USE HELP

Across the bottom of the Windows 10 desktop is the taskbar. The taskbar contains the **Start button**, which you use to access apps, files, folders, and settings. A **folder** is a named location on a storage medium that usually contains related publications.

Clicking the Start button displays the Start menu. The **Start menu** allows you to access programs, folders, and files on the computer or mobile device and contains commands that allow you to run programs, store and search for publications, customize the computer or mobile device, and sign out of a user account or shut down the computer or mobile device. A **menu** is a list of related items, including folders, programs, and commands. Each **command** on a menu performs a specific action, such as saving a file or obtaining help. *Why?* When you *install an app, for example, the app's name will be added to the All apps list on the Start menu.*

The following steps, which assume Windows is running, use the Start menu to run Publisher and create a blank publication based on a typical installation. You may need to ask your instructor how to run Publisher on your computer. Although the steps illustrate running the Publisher app, the steps to run any Office app are similar.

- Click the Start button on the Windows 10 taskbar to display the Start menu (Figure 6).

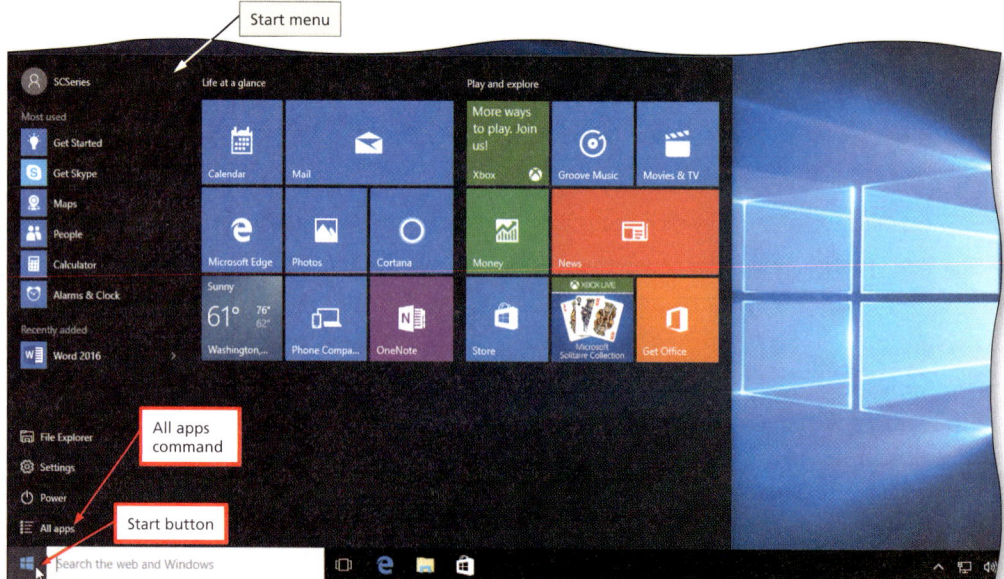

Figure 6

- Click All apps at the bottom of the left pane of the Start menu to display a list of apps installed on the computer or mobile device. If necessary, scroll to display the app you wish to run, Publisher 2016, in this case (Figure 7).

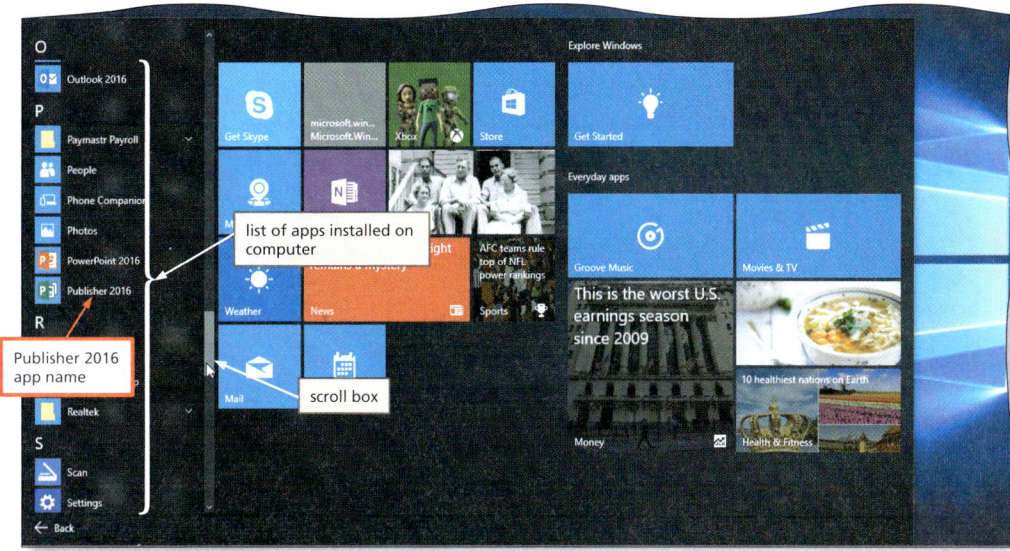

Figure 7

- If the app you wish to run is located in a folder, click or scroll to and then click the folder in the All apps list to display a list of the folder's contents.

- Click, or scroll to and then click the app name (Publisher 2016, in this case) in the list to run the selected app (Figure 8).

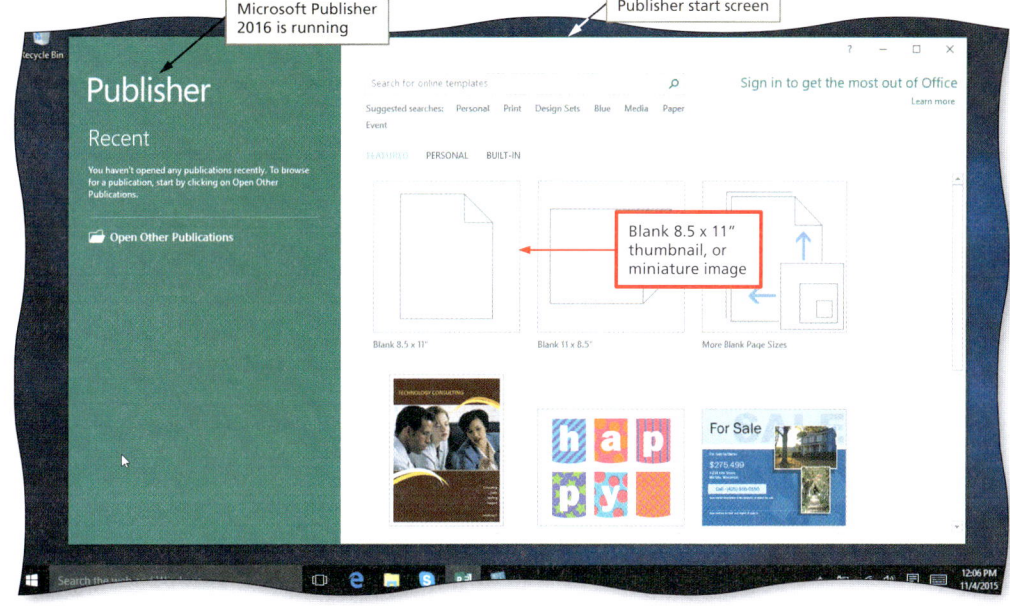

Figure 8

- Click the Blank 8.5 x 11" thumbnail on the Publisher start screen to create a blank publication in the Publisher window (Figure 9).

Q&A

Publisher opened with a blank publication. Did I do something wrong?

No. Someone may have turned off the New template gallery. To turn it back on, click File on the ribbon, click the Options tab (Backstage view), and then click the 'Show the New template gallery when starting Publisher' check box (Publisher Options dialog box).

What happens when you run an app?

Some apps provide a means for you to create a blank publication, as shown in Figure 8; others immediately display a blank publication in an app window, such as the Publisher window shown in Figure 9. A **window** is a rectangular area that displays data and information. The top of a window has a **title bar**, which is a horizontal space that contains the window's name.

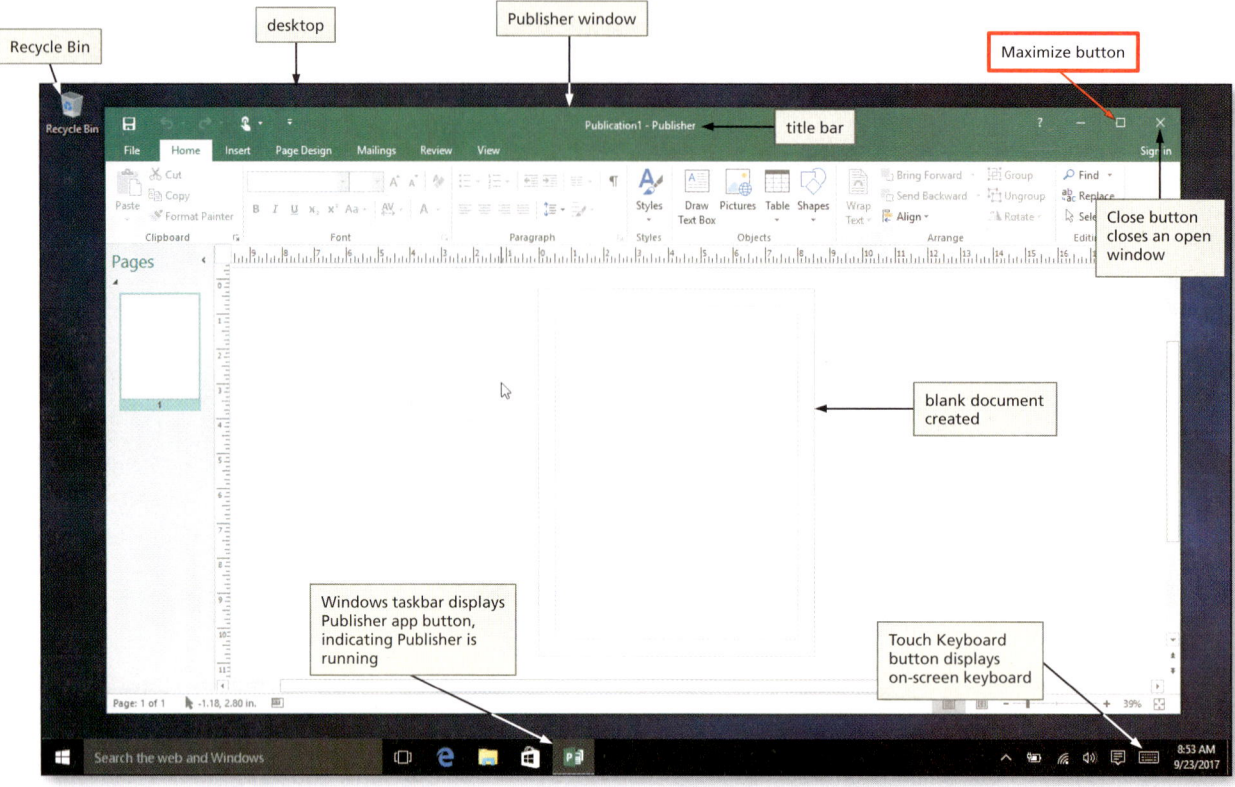

Figure 9

Other Ways

1. Type app name in search box, click app name in results list

2. Double-click file created in app you want to run

To Maximize a Window

1 SIGN IN | 2 USE WINDOWS | 3 USE APPS | 4 FILE MANAGEMENT | 5 SWITCH APPS | 6 SAVE FILES

7 CHANGE SCREEN RESOLUTION | 8 EXIT APPS | 9 USE ADDITIONAL APP FEATURES | 10 USE HELP

Sometimes content is not visible completely in a window. One method of displaying the entire contents of a window is to **maximize** it, or enlarge the window so that it fills the entire screen. The following step maximizes the Publisher window; however, any Office app's window can be maximized using this step. *Why? A maximized window provides the most space available for using the app.*

- If the Publisher window is not maximized already, click the Maximize button (shown in Figure 9) next to the Close button on the Publisher window's title bar to maximize the window (Figure 10).

Q&A

What happened to the Maximize button?

It changed to a Restore Down button, which you can use to return a window to its size and location before you maximized it.

How do I know whether a window is maximized?

A window is maximized if it fills the entire display area and the Restore Down button is displayed on the title bar.

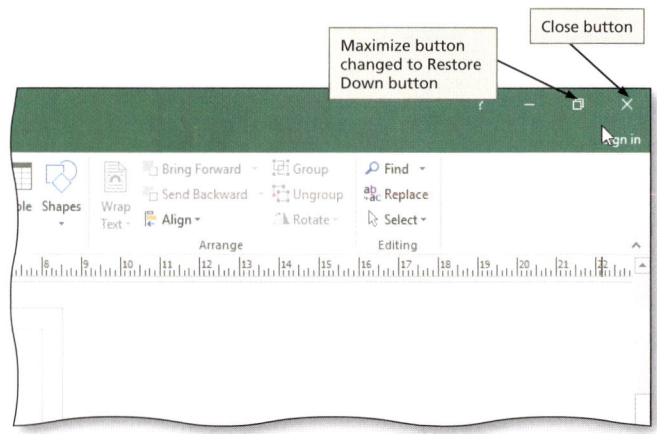

Figure 10

Other Ways

1. Double-click title bar

2. Drag title bar to top of screen

Publisher Window, Ribbon, and Elements Common to Office Apps

The Publisher window consists of a variety of components to make your work more efficient and publications more professional. These include the ribbon, mini toolbar, shortcut menus, workspace, Quick Access Toolbar, and Microsoft Account area. Most of these components are common to other Microsoft Office apps; others are unique to Publisher.

When you run Publisher, the default (preset) view is Single Page view, which shows the publication on a mock sheet of paper in the workspace (Figure 11).

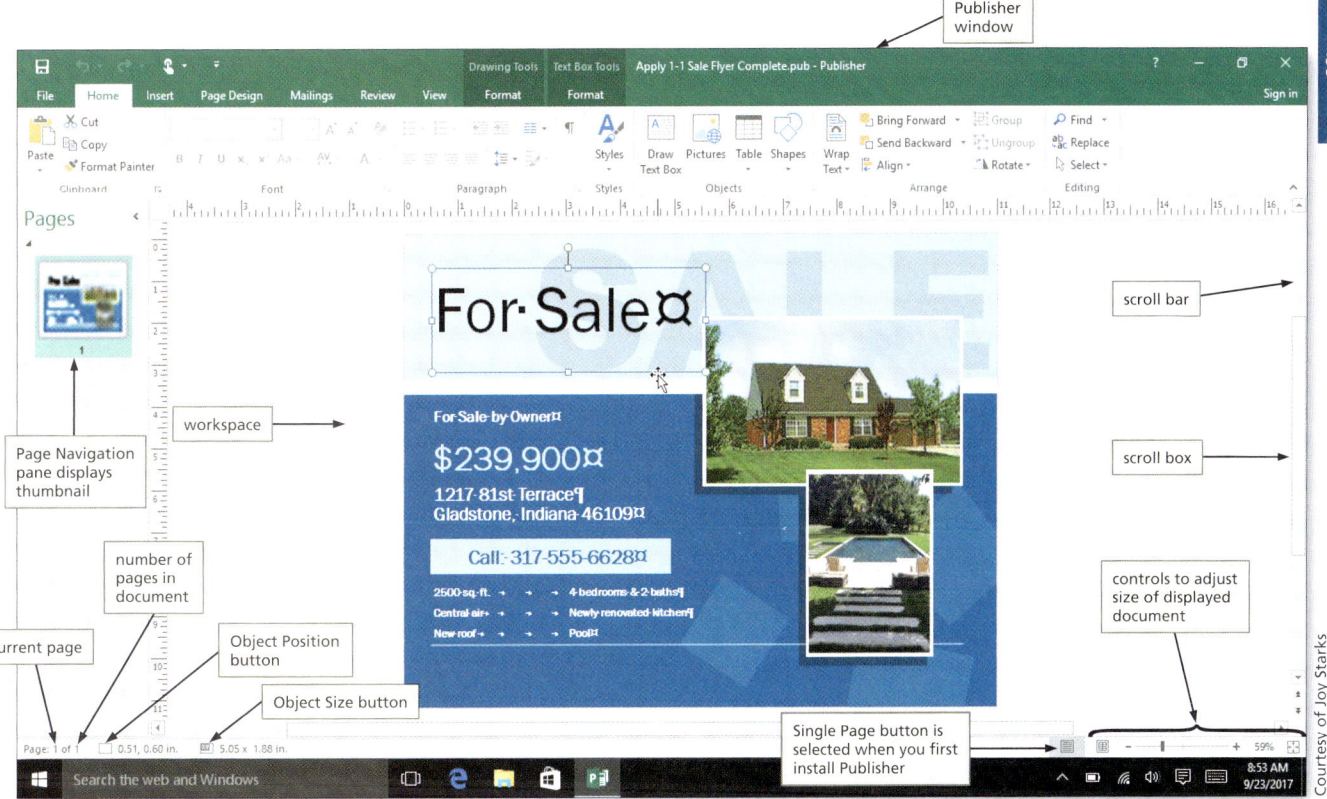

Figure 11

Scroll Bars You use a scroll bar to display different portions of a publication in the workspace. At the right edge of the workspace is a vertical scroll bar. If a publication is too wide to fit in the workspace, a horizontal scroll bar also appears at the bottom of the workspace. On a scroll bar, the position of the scroll box reflects the location of the portion of the publication that is displayed in the workspace.

Status Bar The status bar, located at the bottom of the Publisher window above the Windows taskbar, presents information about the publication, the dimensions and location of selected objects, and the status of certain commands and keys; it also provides controls for viewing the publication. As you type text or perform certain tasks, various indicators and buttons may appear on the status bar.

The left side of the status bar in Figure 11 shows the current page followed by the total number of pages in the publication, the Object Position button, and the Object Size button. The right side of the status bar includes buttons and controls you can use to change the view of a publication and adjust the size of the displayed publication.

Ribbon   The ribbon, located near the top of the window below the title bar, is the control center in Publisher and other Office apps (Figure 12). The ribbon provides easy, central access to the tasks you perform while creating a publication. The ribbon consists of tabs, groups, and commands. Each **tab** contains a collection of groups, and each **group** contains related commands. When you run an Office app, such as Publisher, it initially displays several main tabs, also called default or top-level tabs. All Office apps have a Home tab, which contains the more frequently used commands.

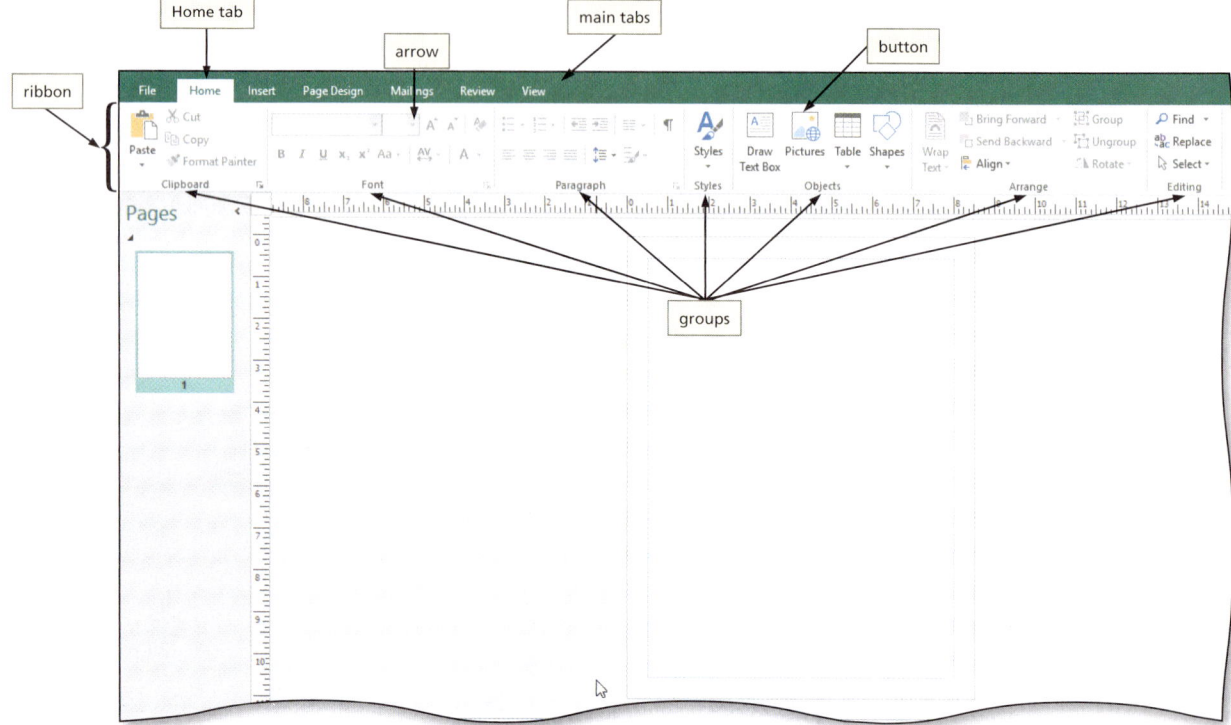

Figure 12

In addition to the main tabs, the Office apps display **tool tabs**, also called contextual tabs (Figure 13), when you perform certain tasks or work with objects such as pictures or tables. If you insert a picture in a Publisher publication, for example, the Picture Tools tab and its related subordinate Format tab appear, collectively referred to as the Picture Tools Format tab. When you are finished working with the picture, the Picture Tools Format tab disappears from the ribbon. Publisher and other Office apps determine when tool tabs should appear and disappear based on tasks you perform. Some tool tabs, such as the Table Tools tab, have more than one related subordinate tab.

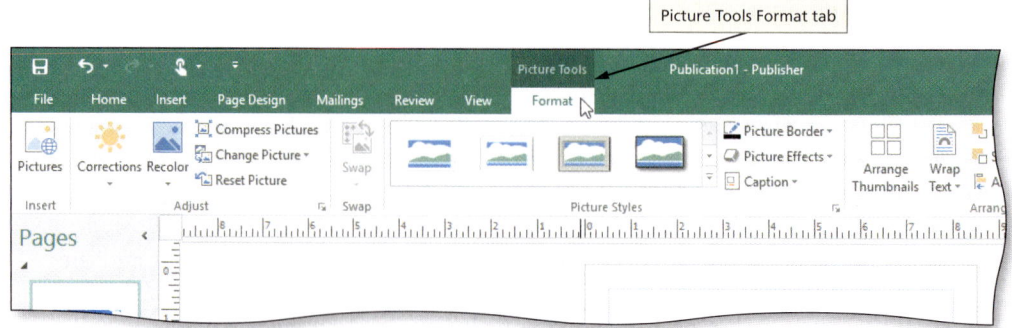

Figure 13

Items on the ribbon include buttons, boxes, and galleries (shown in Figure 13). A **gallery** is a set of choices, often graphical, arranged in a grid or in a list. You can scroll through choices in an in-ribbon gallery by clicking the gallery's scroll arrows. Or, you can click a gallery's More button to view more gallery options on the screen at a time.

Some buttons and boxes have arrows that, when clicked, also display a gallery; others always cause a gallery to be displayed when clicked. Most galleries support **live preview**, which is a feature that allows you to point to a gallery choice and see its effect in the publication — without actually selecting the choice (Figure 14). Live preview works only if you are using a mouse; if you are using a touch screen, you will not be able to view live previews.

BTW

Tell Me Box

Some apps display a **Tell Me box** that appears to the right of the tabs on the ribbon, which functions as a type of search box that helps you to perform specific tasks in an Office app. As you type in the Tell Me box, the word-wheeling feature displays search results that are refined as you type. The Tell Me box also lists the last five commands accessed from the box.

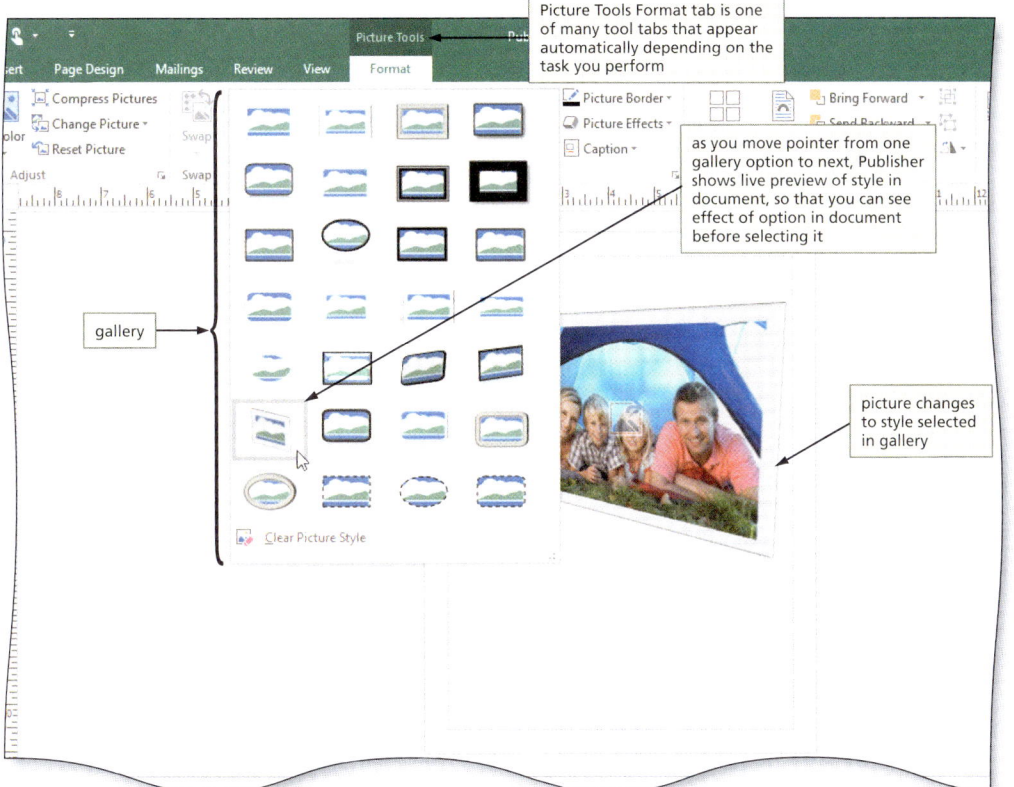

Picture Tools Format tab is one of many tool tabs that appear automatically depending on the task you perform

as you move pointer from one gallery option to next, Publisher shows live preview of style in document, so that you can see effect of option in document before selecting it

gallery

picture changes to style selected in gallery

©iStock.com/monkeybusinessimages

Figure 14

Some commands on the ribbon display an image to help you remember their function. When you point to a command on the ribbon, all or part of the command becomes highlighted in a shade of gray, and a ScreenTip appears on the screen. A **ScreenTip** is an on-screen note that provides the name of the command, available keyboard shortcut(s), a description of the command, and sometimes instructions for how to obtain help about the command (Figure 15).

BTW

ScreenTips

You can turn ScreenTips on and off in the Publisher Options dialog box (Backstage View | Options tab).

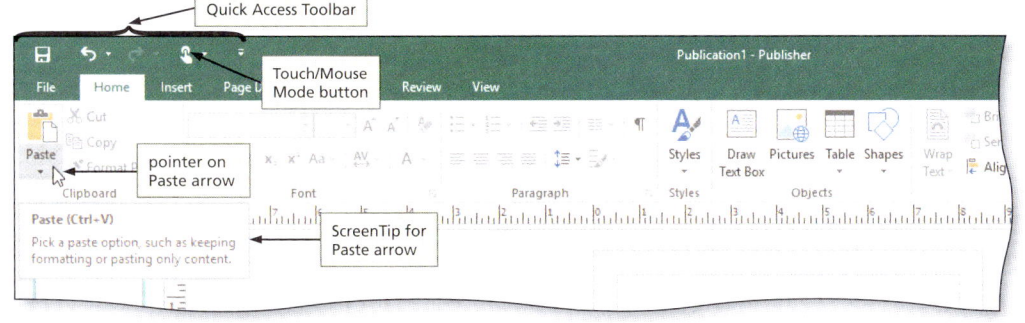

Quick Access Toolbar

Touch/Mouse Mode button

pointer on Paste arrow

ScreenTip for Paste arrow

Figure 15

BTW
Touch Mode
The Office and Windows interfaces may vary if you are using Touch mode. For this reason, you might notice that the function or appearance of your touch screen in Publisher differs slightly from this module's presentation.

Some groups on the ribbon have a small arrow in the lower-right corner, called a **Dialog Box Launcher**, that when clicked, displays a dialog box or a task pane with additional options for the group (Figure 16). When presented with a dialog box, you make selections and must close the dialog box before returning to the publication. A **task pane**, in contrast to a dialog box, is a window that can remain open and visible while you work in the publication.

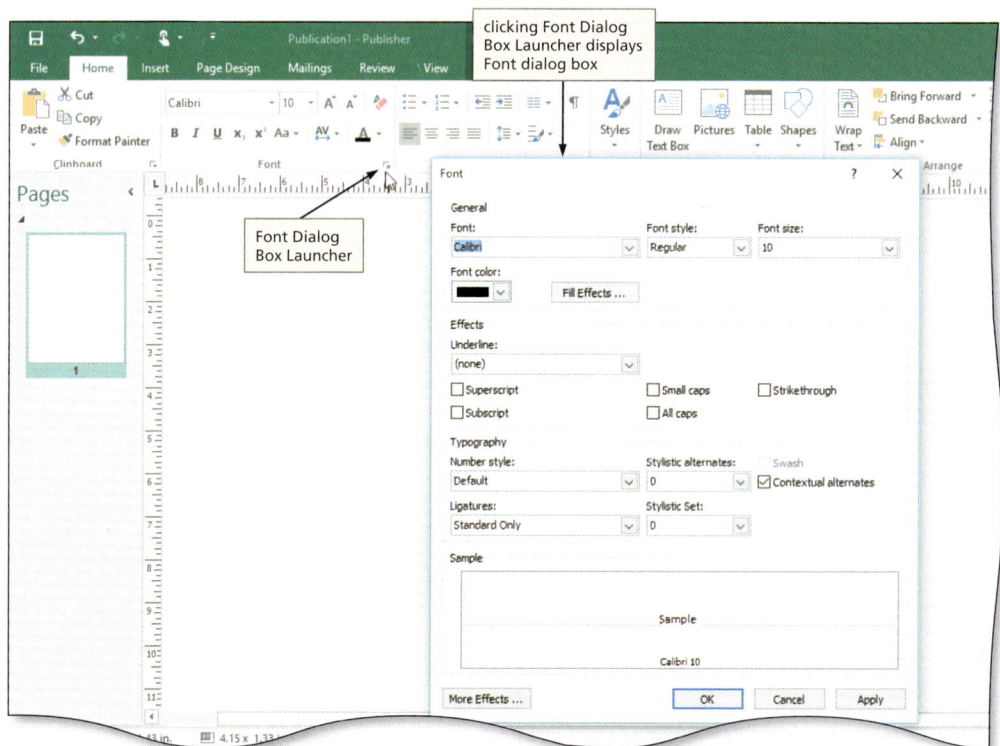

Figure 16

BTW
Turning Off the Mini Toolbar
If you do not want the mini toolbar to appear, click File on the ribbon to open the Backstage view, click the Options tab in the Backstage view, if necessary, click General (Options dialog box), remove the check mark from the 'Show Mini Toolbar on selection' check box, and then click the OK button.

Mini Toolbar   The **mini toolbar**, which appears automatically based on tasks you perform, contains commands related to changing the appearance of text in a publication (Figure 17). If you do not use the mini toolbar, it disappears from the screen. The buttons, arrows, and boxes on the mini toolbar vary, depending on whether you are using Touch mode versus Mouse mode. If you right-click an object in the publication, Publisher displays both the mini toolbar and a shortcut menu, which is discussed in a later section in this module.

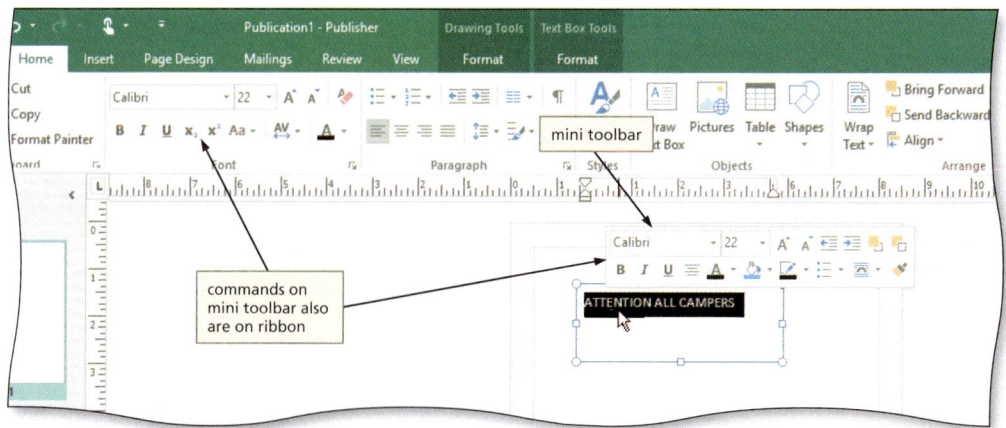

Figure 17

All commands on the mini toolbar also exist on the ribbon. The purpose of the mini toolbar is to minimize hand or mouse movement.

Quick Access Toolbar The **Quick Access Toolbar**, located initially (by default) above the ribbon at the left edge of the title bar, provides convenient, one-click access to frequently used commands (shown in Figure 15). The commands on the Quick Access Toolbar always are available, regardless of the task you are performing. The Touch/Mouse Mode button on the Quick Access Toolbar allows you to switch between Touch mode and Mouse mode. If you primarily are using touch gestures, Touch mode will add more space between commands on menus and on the ribbon so that they are easier to tap. While touch gestures are convenient ways to interact with Office apps, not all features are supported when you are using Touch mode. If you are using a mouse, Mouse mode will not add the extra space between buttons and commands. The Quick Access Toolbar is discussed in more depth later in the module.

KeyTips If you prefer using the keyboard instead of the mouse, you can press the ALT key on the keyboard to display **KeyTips**, or keyboard code icons, for certain commands (Figure 18). To select a command using the keyboard, press the letter or number displayed in the KeyTip, which may cause additional KeyTips related to the selected command to appear. To remove KeyTips from the screen, press the ALT key or the ESC key until all KeyTips disappear, or click anywhere in the app window.

BTW

Full Screen Mode
Some apps have a **Full Screen mode**, which hides all the commands and just displays the current file or document.

BTW

More Ribbon Options
Some apps display a 'Ribbon Display Options' button on the title bar with additional ribbon commands, such as Auto-hide.

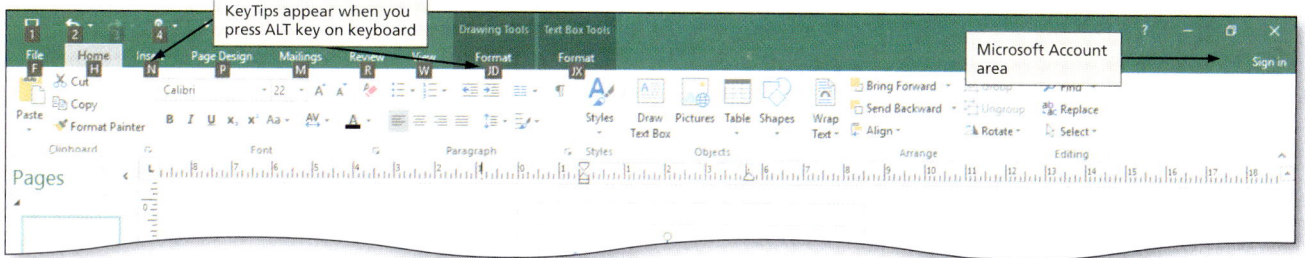

Figure 18

Microsoft Account Area In this area, you can use the Sign in link to sign in to your Microsoft account. Once signed in, you will see your account information. Some apps also display a picture if you have included one in your Microsoft account.

To Display a Different Tab on the Ribbon

1 SIGN IN | 2 USE WINDOWS | 3 USE APPS | 4 FILE MANAGEMENT | 5 SWITCH APPS | 6 SAVE FILES
7 CHANGE SCREEN RESOLUTION | 8 EXIT APPS | 9 USE ADDITIONAL APP FEATURES | 10 USE HELP

When you run Publisher, the ribbon displays seven main tabs: File, Home, Insert, Page Design, Mailings, Review, and View. The tab currently displayed is called the **active tab**.

The following step displays the Insert tab, that is, makes it the active tab. *Why? When working with an Office app, you may need to switch tabs to access other options for working with a publication.*

- Click Insert on the ribbon to display the Insert tab (Figure 19).

- Click the other tabs on the ribbon to view their contents. When you are finished, click Insert on the ribbon to redisplay the Insert tab.

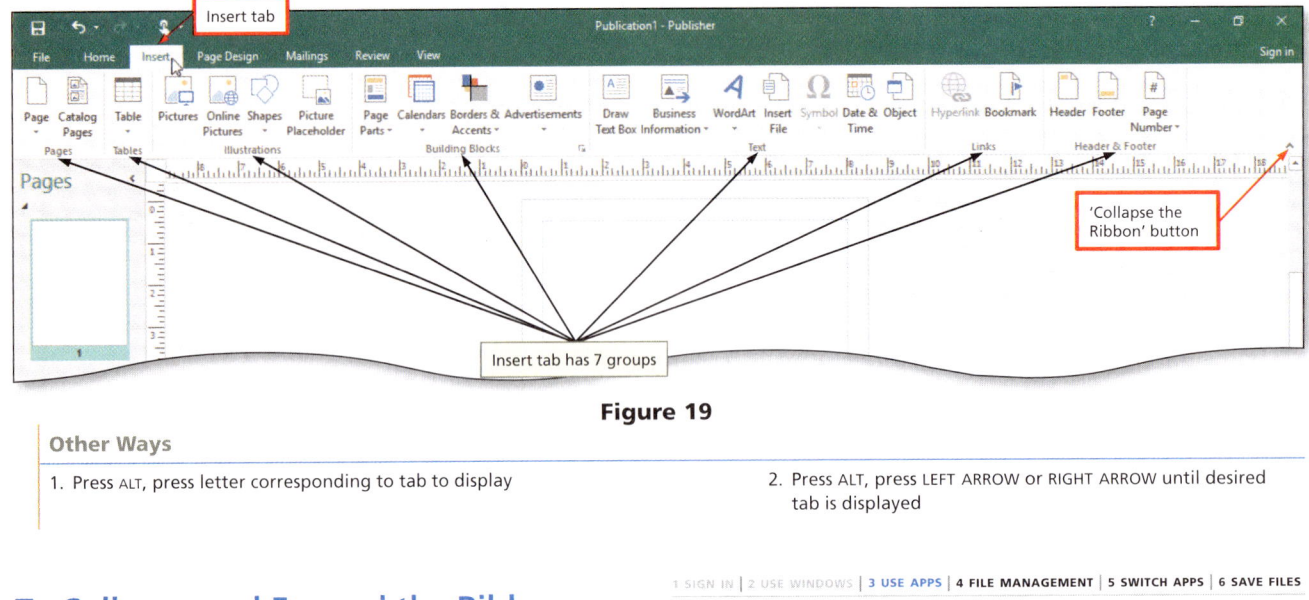

Figure 19

Other Ways

1. Press ALT, press letter corresponding to tab to display

2. Press ALT, press LEFT ARROW or RIGHT ARROW until desired tab is displayed

To Collapse and Expand the Ribbon

1 SIGN IN | 2 USE WINDOWS | 3 USE APPS | 4 FILE MANAGEMENT | 5 SWITCH APPS | 6 SAVE FILES
7 CHANGE SCREEN RESOLUTION | 8 EXIT APPS | 9 USE ADDITIONAL APP FEATURES | 10 USE HELP

To display more of a publication or other item in the window of an Office app, some users prefer to collapse the ribbon, which hides the groups on the ribbon and displays only the main tabs. Each time you run an Office app, such as Publisher, the ribbon appears the same way it did the last time you used that Office app. The modules in this book, however, begin with the ribbon appearing as it did at the initial installation of Office or Publisher.

The following steps collapse and expand the ribbon in Publisher. *Why? If you need more space on the screen to work with your publication, you may consider collapsing the ribbon to gain additional workspace.*

- Click the 'Collapse the Ribbon' button on the ribbon (shown in Figure 19) to collapse the ribbon (Figure 20).

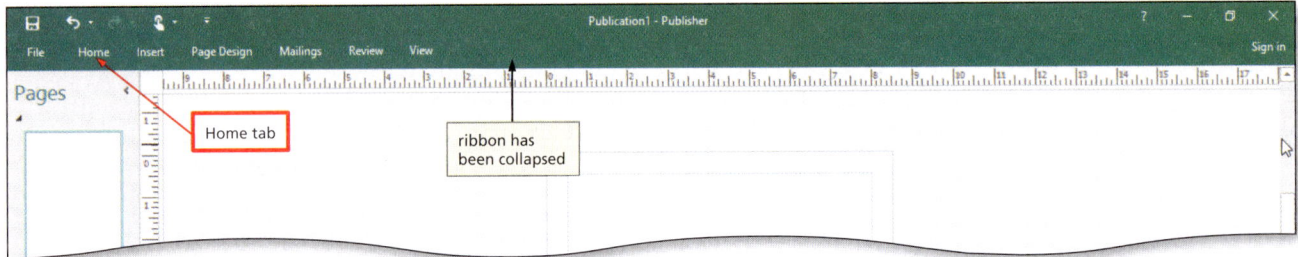

Figure 20

Q&A What happened to the 'Collapse the Ribbon' button?

The 'Pin the ribbon' button replaces the 'Collapse the Ribbon' button when the ribbon is collapsed. You will see the 'Pin the ribbon' button only when you expand a ribbon by clicking a tab.

- Click Home on the ribbon to expand the Home tab (Figure 21).

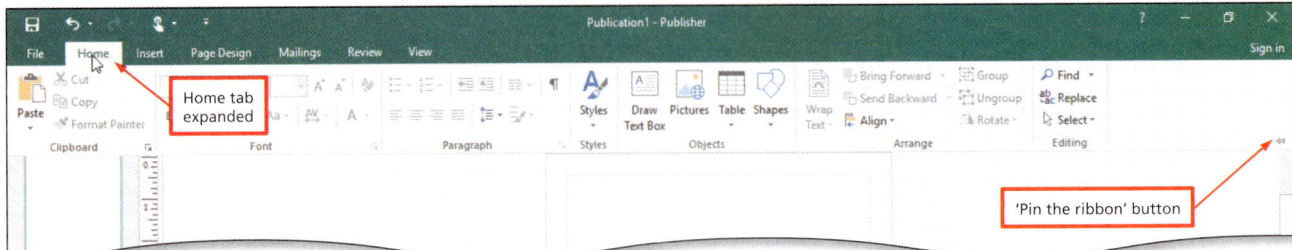

Figure 21

Q&A

Why would I click the Home tab?

If you want to use a command on a collapsed ribbon, click the main tab to display the groups for that tab. After you select a command on the ribbon and resume working in the publication, the groups will be collapsed once again. If you decide not to use a command on the ribbon, you can collapse the groups by clicking the same main tab or clicking in the app window.

Experiment

• Click Home on the ribbon to collapse the groups again. Click Home on the ribbon to expand the Home tab.

 3

• Click the 'Pin the ribbon' button on the expanded Home tab to restore the ribbon.

Other Ways

1. Double-click a main tab on the ribbon

2. Press CTRL+F1

To Use a Shortcut Menu to Relocate the Quick Access Toolbar

1 SIGN IN | 2 USE WINDOWS | 3 USE APPS | 4 FILE MANAGEMENT | 5 SWITCH APPS | 6 SAVE FILES
7 CHANGE SCREEN RESOLUTION | 8 EXIT APPS | 9 USE ADDITIONAL APP FEATURES | 10 USE HELP

When you right-click certain areas of the Publisher and other Office app windows, a shortcut menu will appear. A **shortcut menu** is a list of frequently used commands that relate to an object. *Why? You can use shortcut menus to access common commands quickly.* When you right-click the status bar, for example, a shortcut menu appears with commands related to the status bar. When you right-click the Quick Access Toolbar, a shortcut menu appears with commands related to the Quick Access Toolbar. The following steps use a shortcut menu to move the Quick Access Toolbar, which by default is located on the title bar.

1

• Right-click the Quick Access Toolbar to display a shortcut menu that presents a list of commands related to the Quick Access Toolbar (Figure 22).

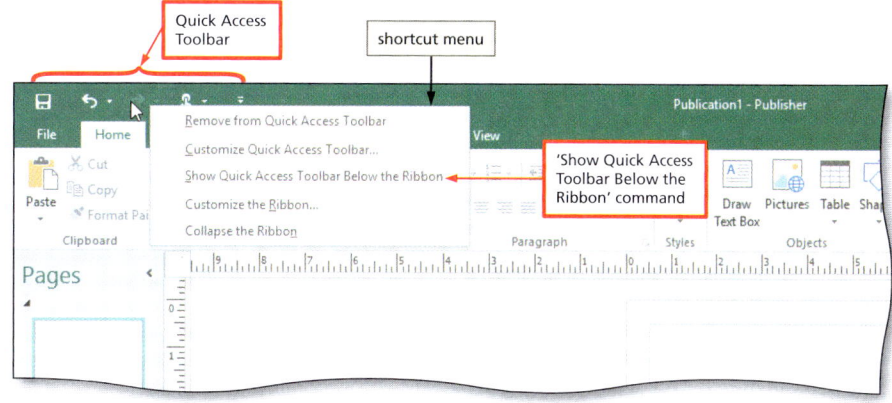

Figure 22

2

• Click 'Show Quick Access Toolbar Below the Ribbon' on the shortcut menu to display the Quick Access Toolbar below the ribbon (Figure 23).

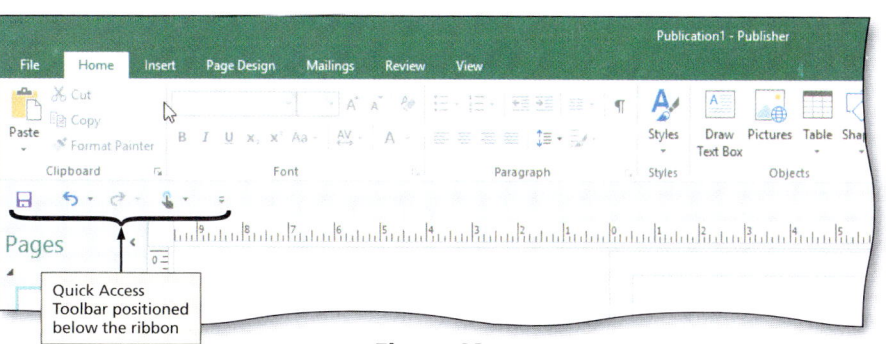

Figure 23

- Right-click the Quick Access Toolbar again to display the shortcut menu (Figure 24).

- Click 'Show Quick Access Toolbar Above the Ribbon' on the shortcut menu to return the Quick Access Toolbar to its original position.

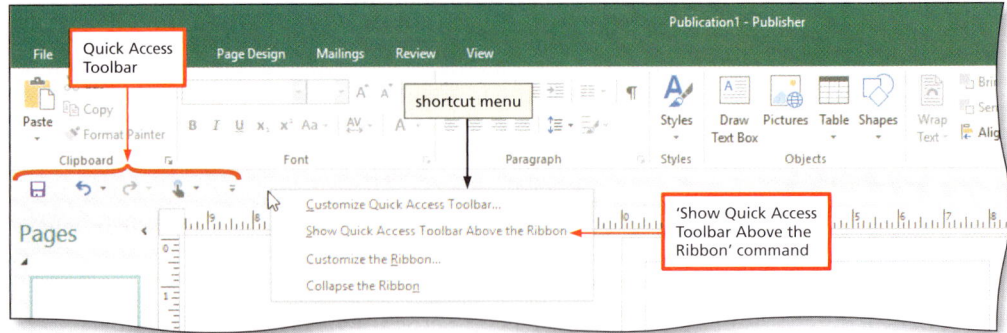

Figure 24

Other Ways

1. Click 'Customize Quick Access Toolbar' button on Quick Access Toolbar, click 'Show Below the Ribbon' or 'Show Above the Ribbon'

To Customize the Quick Access Toolbar

1 SIGN IN | 2 USE WINDOWS | 3 USE APPS | 4 FILE MANAGEMENT | 5 SWITCH APPS | 6 SAVE FILES
7 CHANGE SCREEN RESOLUTION | 8 EXIT APPS | 9 USE ADDITIONAL APP FEATURES | 10 USE HELP

The Quick Access Toolbar provides easy access to some of the more frequently used commands in the Office apps. By default, the Quick Access Toolbar contains buttons for the Save, Undo, and Redo commands. If your computer or mobile device has a touch screen, the Quick Access Toolbar also might display the Touch/Mouse Mode button. You can customize the Quick Access Toolbar by changing its location in the window, as shown in the previous steps, and by adding more buttons to reflect commands you would like to access easily. The following steps add the Quick Print button to the Quick Access Toolbar in the Publisher window. *Why? Adding the Quick Print button to the Quick Access Toolbar speeds up the process of printing.*

- Click the 'Customize Quick Access Toolbar' button to display the Customize Quick Access Toolbar menu (Figure 25).

Q&A

Which commands are listed on the Customize Quick Access Toolbar menu?
It lists commands that commonly are added to the Quick Access Toolbar.

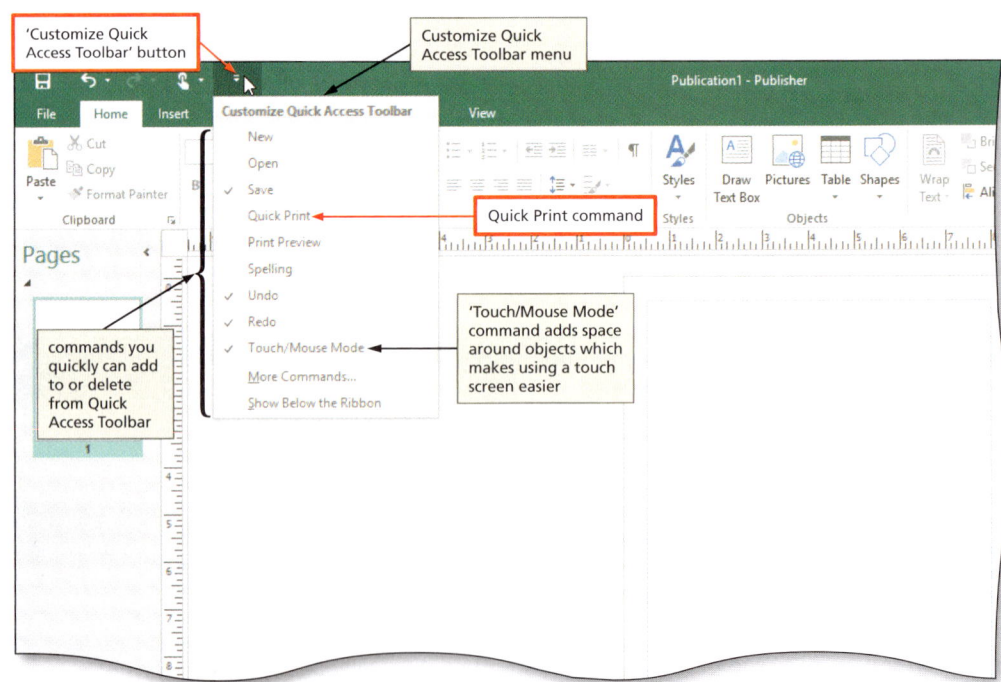

Figure 25

- Click Quick Print on the Customize Quick Access Toolbar menu to add the Quick Print button to the Quick Access Toolbar (Figure 26).

Q&A
How would I remove a button from the Quick Access Toolbar?
You would right-click the button you wish to remove and then click 'Remove from Quick Access Toolbar' on the shortcut menu or click the 'Customize Quick Access Toolbar' button on the Quick Access Toolbar and then click the button name in the Customize Quick Access Toolbar menu to remove the check mark.

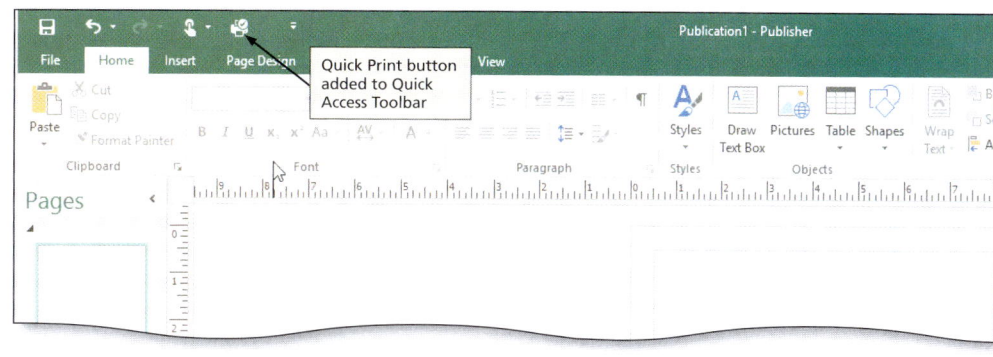

Figure 26

To Zoom Using a Function Key

1 SIGN IN | 2 USE WINDOWS | 3 USE APPS | 4 FILE MANAGEMENT | 5 SWITCH APPS | 6 SAVE FILES
7 CHANGE SCREEN RESOLUTION | 8 EXIT APPS | 9 USE ADDITIONAL APP FEATURES | 10 USE HELP

If text is too small to read easily, or if objects are too small to manipulate, you may want to zoom. When you zoom, Publisher changes the magnification of the text or other object on the page. Zooming does not change the font size of text; nor does it change the size of objects, such as pictures and shapes. The following step uses the F9 key to change the magnification to 100%. *Why? The function key is a quick way to zoom; you will learn many ways to zoom in future modules.*

- Press the F9 key on the keyboard. If your mobile device does not display function keys, click the Zoom In button on the task bar several times until your display is magnified to 100% (Figure 27).

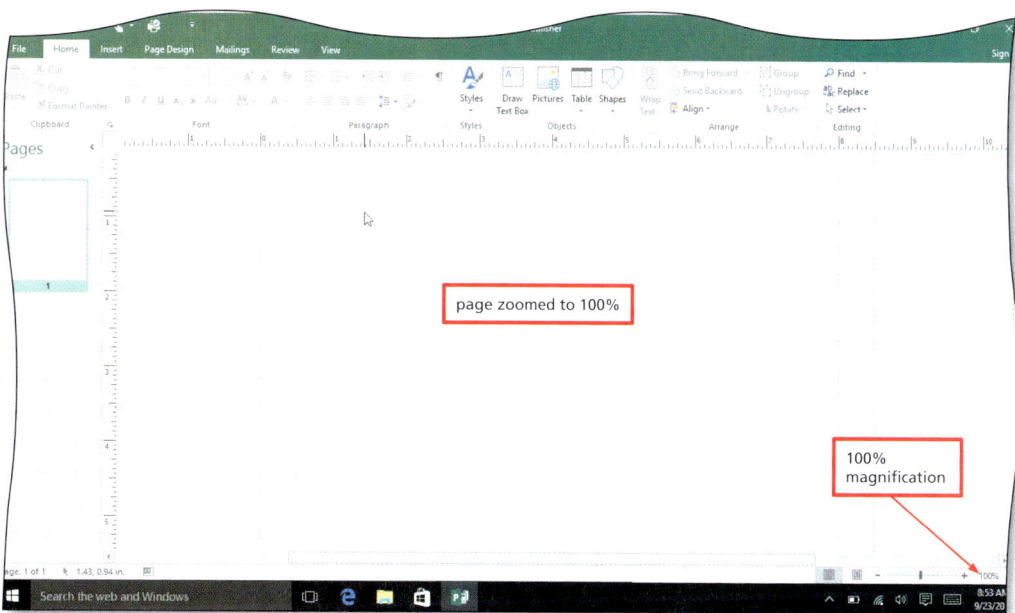

Figure 27

Other Ways

1. Click 100% button (View tab | Zoom group)
2. Type 100% in Zoom box (View tab | Zoom group)
3. Drag Zoom slider on taskbar

To Enter Text in a Publication

Many times, the first step in creating a publication is to enter text or replace text in a template by typing on the keyboard. Publisher uses text boxes to hold text. If the publication contains no text box, Publisher creates one for you when you begin to type.

The following steps type this first line of a flyer. *Why? To begin creating a flyer, for example, you type the headline in the publication.*

- Type **ATTENTION ALL CAMPERS** as the text (Figure 28).

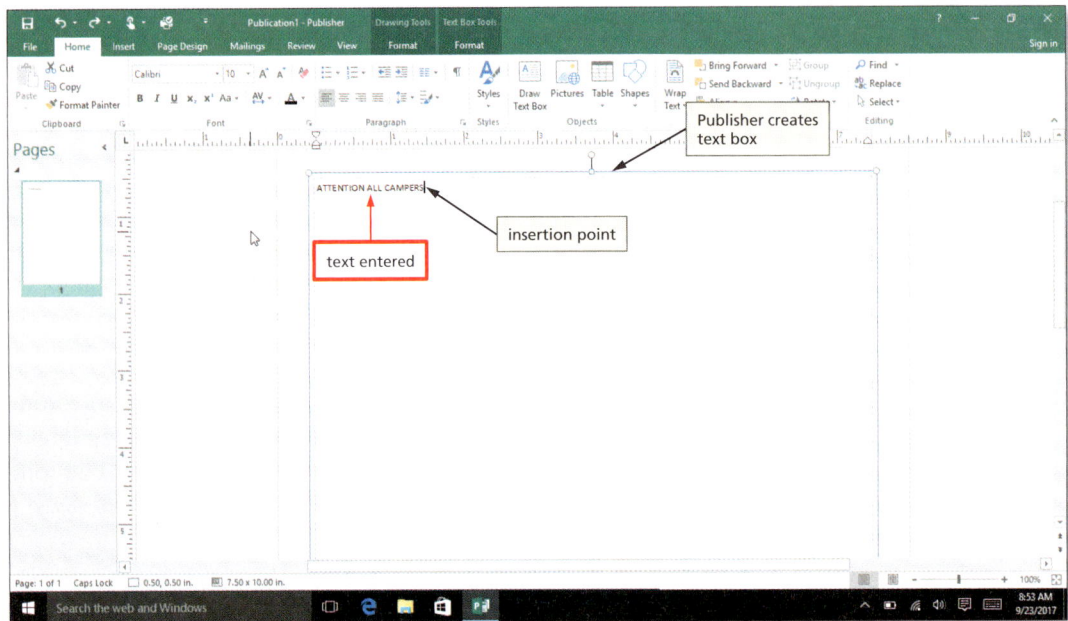

Figure 28

Q&A

What is the blinking vertical bar to the right of the text?
The blinking bar is the insertion point, which indicates where text, graphics, and other items will be inserted in the publication. As you type, the insertion point moves to the right, and when you reach the end of a line, it moves down to the beginning of the next line.

What if I make an error while typing?
You can press the BACKSPACE key until you have deleted the text in error and then retype the text correctly.

- Press the ENTER key to move the insertion point to the beginning of the next line (Figure 29).

Q&A

Why did blank space appear between the entered text and the insertion point?
Each time you press the ENTER key, Publisher creates a new paragraph and inserts blank space between the two paragraphs. Depending on your settings, Publisher may or may not insert a blank space between the two paragraphs.

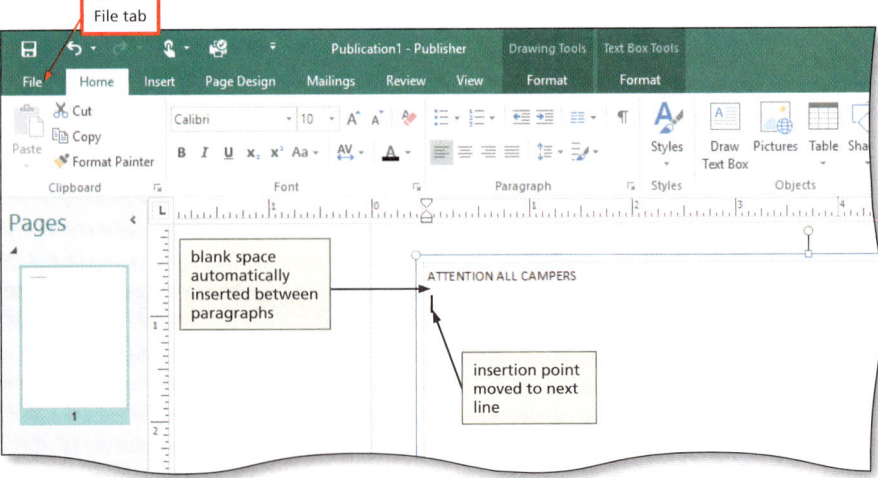

Figure 29

Publication Properties

You can organize and identify your files by using publication properties, which are the details about a file, such as the project author, title, and subject. For example, a class name or publication topic can describe the file's purpose or content.

CONSIDER THIS

Why would you want to assign publication properties to a publication?
Publication properties are valuable for a variety of reasons:

• Users can save time locating a particular file, because they can view a file's publication properties without opening the file.

• By creating consistent properties for files having similar content, users can better organize their files.

• Some organizations require users to add publication properties so that other employees can view details about these files.

To Change Publication Properties

You can change the publication properties while working with the file in an Office app. When you save the file, the Office app (Publisher, in this case) will save the publication properties with the file. The following steps change publication properties. *Why? Adding publication properties will help you identify characteristics of the file without opening it.*

• Click File on the ribbon (shown in Figure 29) to open the Backstage view and then, if necessary, click the Info tab in the Backstage view to display the Info gallery.

• Click the Publication Properties button (Backstage view | Info tab) to display the Publication Properties menu (Figure 30).

Q&A What is the purpose of the File tab on the ribbon and what is the Backstage view?
The File tab opens the Backstage view for each Office app, including Publisher. The **Backstage view** contains a set of commands that enable you to manage publications and provides data about the publications.

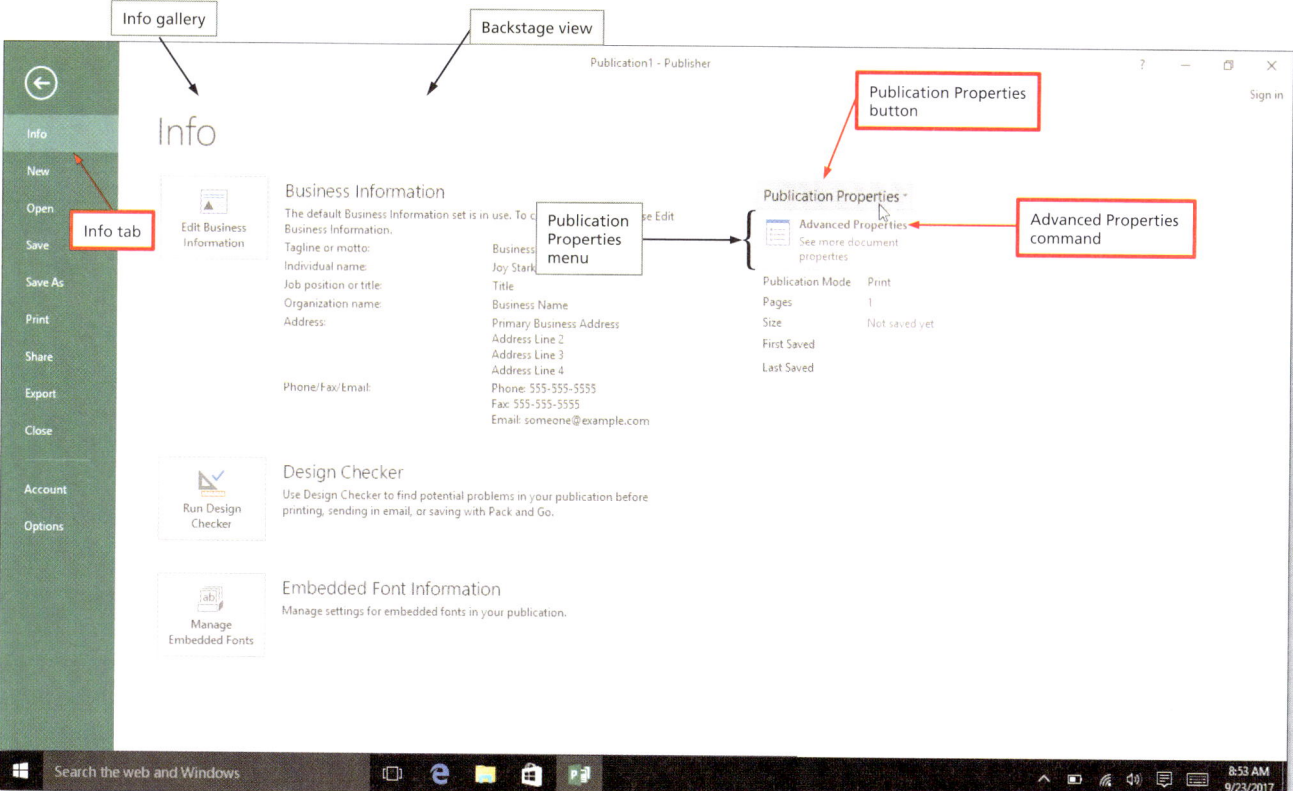

Figure 30

2

• Click Advanced Properties on the menu to display the Publication1 Properties dialog box.

• Click the Comments text box (Publication1 Properties dialog box) and then type CIS 101 Assignment in the text box (Figure 31).

Q&A

What is the purpose of the Info gallery in the Backstage view?
The Info tab, which is selected by default when you click File on the ribbon, displays the Info gallery, where you can protect a publication, inspect a publication, and manage versions of a publication, as well as view all the file properties, such as when the file was created.

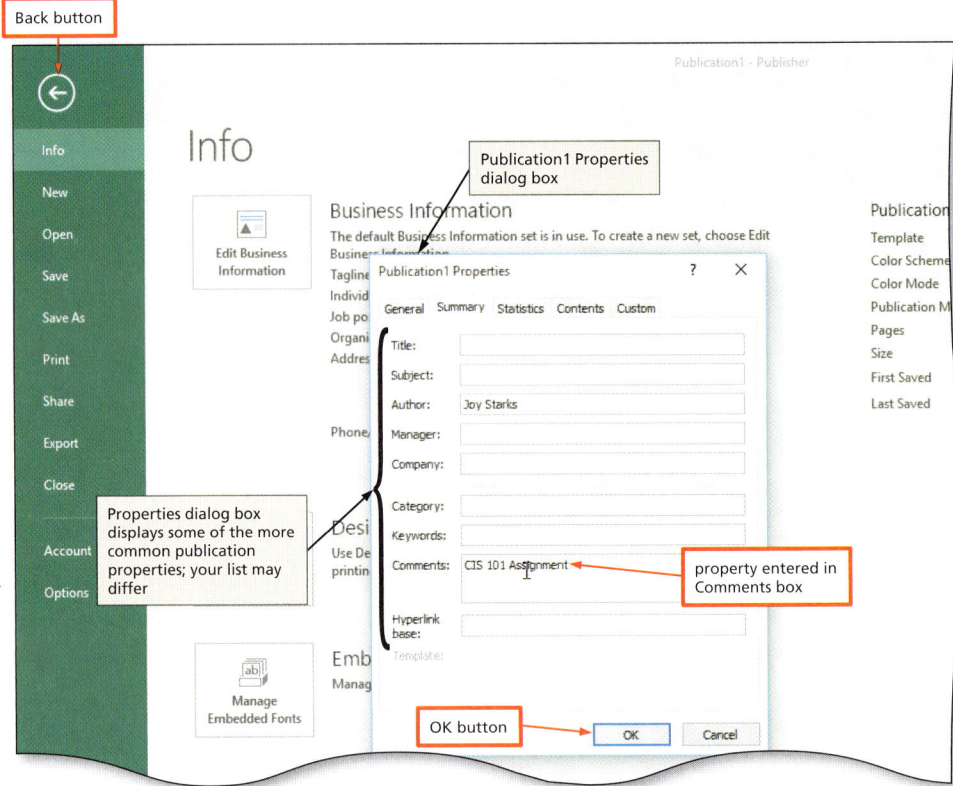

Figure 31

3

• Click the OK button (Publication1 Properties dialog box) to close the dialog box.

• Click the Back button in the upper-left corner of the Backstage view to return to the publication.

Other Ways

1. In File Explorer window, right-click file icon, click Properties on shortcut menu, click Comments text box (Properties dialog box), enter comment, click OK button

BTW

Document Properties
Some apps allow you to make property changes directly in Backstage view. In Microsoft Word, for example, you can click to the right of the property on the Info tab, to display a text box allowing you to enter or change that property.

Printing, Saving, and Organizing Files

While you are creating a publication, the computer or mobile device stores it in memory. When you save a publication, the computer or mobile device places it on a storage medium, such as a hard disk, solid state drive (SSD), USB flash drive, or optical disc. The storage medium can be permanent in your computer, may be portable where you remove it from your computer, or may be on a web server you access through a network or the Internet.

A saved publication is referred to as a file. A **file name** is the name assigned to a file when it is saved. When saving files, you should organize them so that you easily can find them later. Windows provides tools to help you organize files.

Printing a Publication

After creating a publication, you may want to print it. Printing a publication enables you to distribute it to others in a form that can be read or viewed but typically not edited.

What is the best method for distributing a publication?

The traditional method of distributing a publication uses a printer to produce a hard copy. A **hard copy** or **printout** is information that exists on a physical medium, such as paper. Hard copies can be useful for the following reasons:

- Some people prefer proofreading a hard copy of a publication rather than viewing it on the screen to check for errors and readability.

- Hard copies can serve as a backup reference if your storage medium is lost or becomes corrupted and you need to recreate the publication.

Instead of distributing a hard copy of a publication, users can distribute the publication as an electronic image that mirrors the original publication's appearance. The electronic image of the publication can be sent as an email attachment, posted on a website, or copied to a portable storage medium, such as a USB flash drive. Two popular electronic image formats, sometimes called fixed formats, are PDF by Adobe Systems and XPS by Microsoft. In Publisher, you can create electronic image files through the Save As dialog box and the Export, Share, and Print tabs in the Backstage view. Electronic images of publications, such as PDF and XPS, can be useful for the following reasons:

- Users can view electronic images of publications without the software that created the original publication (e.g., Publisher). For example, to view a PDF file you use a program called Adobe Reader, which can be downloaded free from Adobe's website.

- Sending electronic publications saves paper and printer supplies. Society encourages users to contribute to **green computing**, which involves reducing the electricity consumed and environmental waste generated when using computers, mobile devices, and related technologies.

To Print a Publication

1 SIGN IN | 2 USE WINDOWS | 3 USE APPS | 4 FILE MANAGEMENT | 5 SWITCH APPS | 6 SAVE FILES
7 CHANGE SCREEN RESOLUTION | 8 EXIT APPS | 9 USE ADDITIONAL APP FEATURES | 10 USE HELP

With the publication opened, you may want to print it. *Why? Because you want to see how the text will appear on paper; you want to print a hard copy on a printer.* The following steps print a hard copy of the contents of the publication.

1

- Click File on the ribbon to open the Backstage view.

- Click the Print tab in the Backstage view to display the Print gallery (Figure 32).

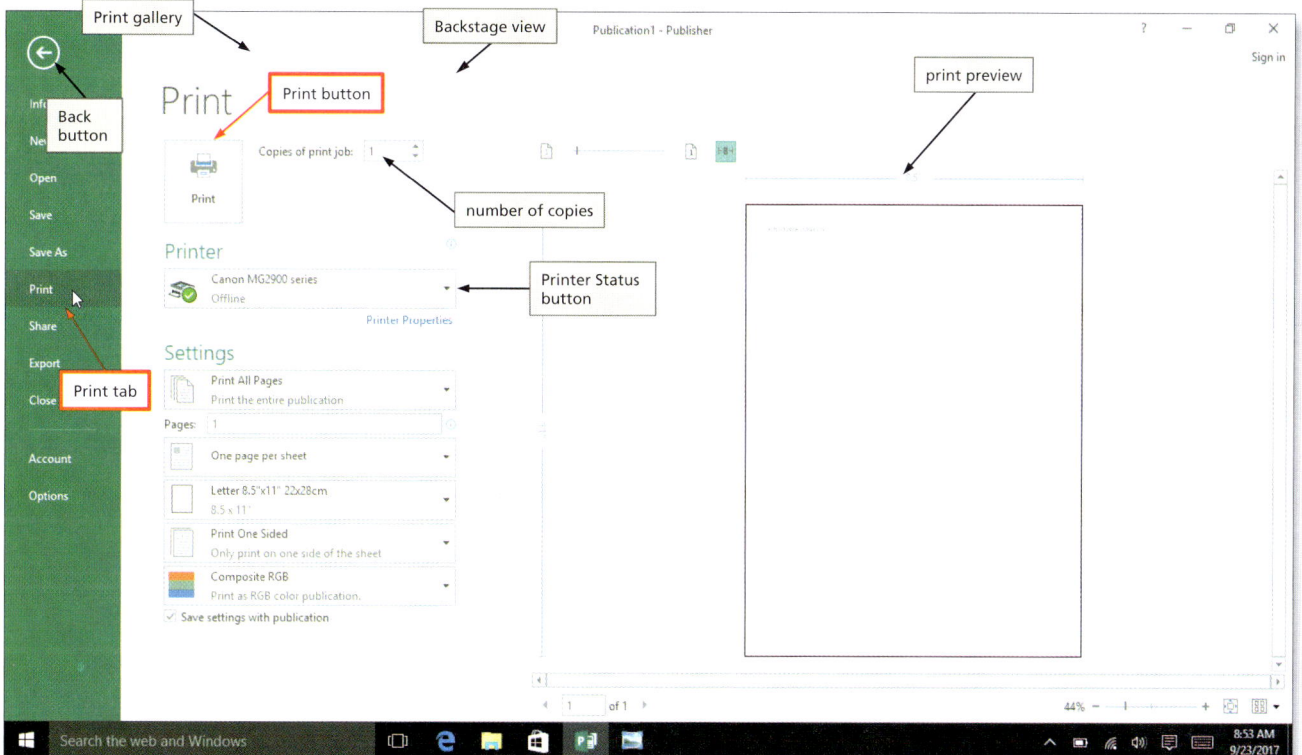

Figure 32

How can I print multiple copies of my publication?
Increase the number in the 'Copies of print job' box in the Print gallery.

What if I decide not to print the publication at this time?
Click the Back button in the upper-left corner of the Backstage view to return to the publication.

2

- Verify that the selected printer will print a hard copy of the publication. If necessary, click the Printer Status button to display a list of available printer options and then click the desired printer to change the currently selected printer.

3

- Click the Print button in the Print gallery to print the publication on the currently selected printer.

- When the printer stops, retrieve the hard copy (Figure 33).

What if I want to print an electronic image of a publication instead of a hard copy?
You would click the Printer Status button in the Print gallery and then select the desired electronic image option, such as Microsoft XPS Document Writer, which would create an XPS file.

ATTENTION ALL CAMPERS

Figure 33

Other Ways

1. Press CTRL+P

Organizing Files and Folders

A file contains data. This data can range from a research paper to an accounting spreadsheet to an electronic math quiz. You should organize and store files in folders to avoid misplacing a file and to help you find a file quickly.

If you are taking an introductory computer class (CIS 101, for example), you may want to design a series of folders for the different subjects covered in the class. To accomplish this, you can arrange the folders in a hierarchy for the class, as shown in Figure 34. The hierarchy contains three levels. The first level contains the storage medium, such as a hard drive. The second level contains the class folder (CIS 101, in this case), and the third level contains seven folders, one each for a different Office app that will be covered in the class (Word, PowerPoint, Excel, Access, Outlook, Publisher, and OneNote).

When the hierarchy in Figure 34 is created, the storage medium is said to contain the CIS 101 folder, and the CIS 101 folder is said to contain the separate Office folders (i.e., Publisher, Word, PowerPoint, Excel, etc.). In addition, this hierarchy easily can be expanded to include folders from other classes taken during additional semesters.

The vertical and horizontal lines in Figure 34 form a pathway that allows you to navigate to a drive or folder on a computer or network. A **path** consists of a drive letter

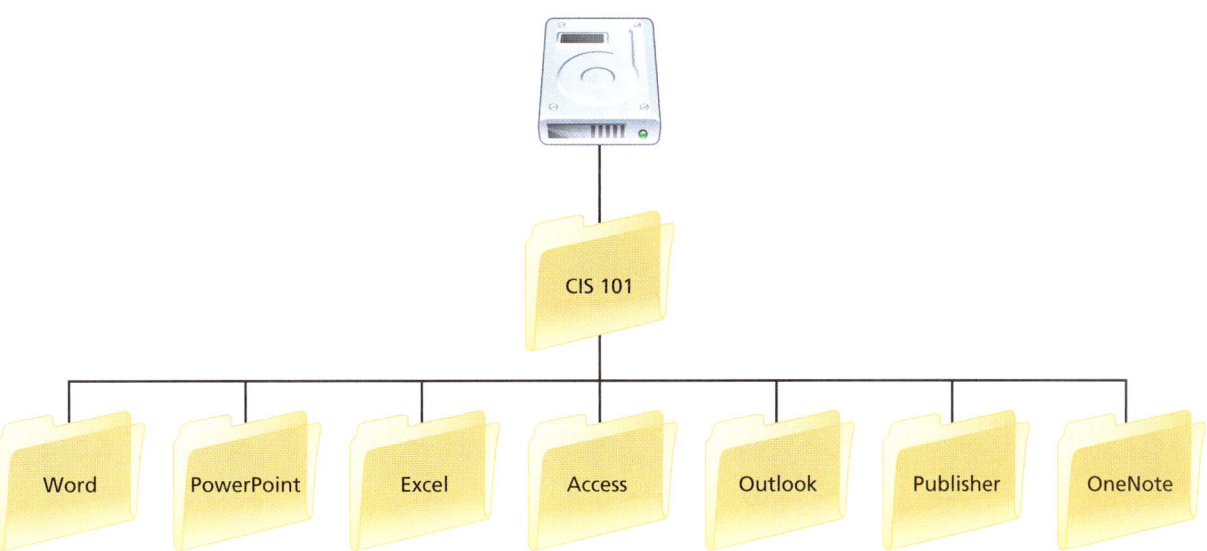

Figure 34

(preceded by a drive name when necessary) and colon, to identify the storage device, and one or more folder names. A hard drive typically has a drive letter of C. Each drive or folder in the hierarchy has a corresponding path.

By default, Windows saves publications in the Documents folder, music in the Music folder, photos in the Pictures folder, videos in the Videos folder, and downloads in the Downloads folder.

The following pages illustrate the steps to organize the folders for this class and save a file in a folder:

1. Create the folder identifying your class.
2. Create the Publisher folder in the folder identifying your class.
3. Save a file in the Publisher folder.
4. Verify the location of the saved file.

To Create a Folder

1 SIGN IN │ 2 USE WINDOWS │ 3 USE APPS │ **4 FILE MANAGEMENT** │ **5 SWITCH APPS** │ **6 SAVE FILES**
7 CHANGE SCREEN RESOLUTION │ **8 EXIT APPS** │ **9 USE ADDITIONAL APP FEATURES** │ **10 USE HELP**

When you create a folder, such as the CIS 101 folder shown in Figure 34, you must name the folder. A folder name should describe the folder and its contents. A folder name can contain spaces and any uppercase or lowercase characters, except a backslash (\), slash (/), colon (:), asterisk (*), question mark (?), quotation marks ("), less than symbol (<), greater than symbol (>), or vertical bar (|). Folder names cannot be CON, AUX, COM1, COM2, COM3, COM4, LPT1, LPT2, LPT3, PRN, or NUL. The same rules for naming folders also apply to naming files.

The following steps create a class folder (CIS 101, in this case) in the Documents folder. *Why? When storing files, you should organize the files so that it will be easier to find them later.*

- Click the File Explorer button on the taskbar to run File Explorer.
- If necessary, double-click This PC in the navigation pane to expand the contents of your computer.
- If necessary, click the 'Expand the Ribbon' button to expand the ribbon.
- Click the Documents folder in the navigation pane to display the contents of the Documents folder in the file list (Figure 35).

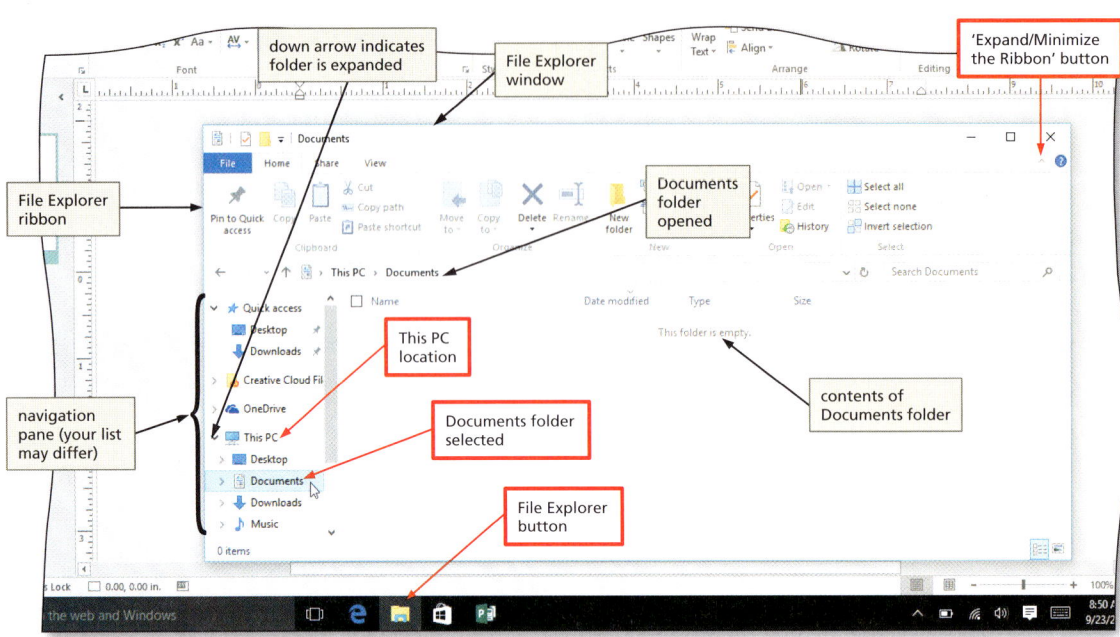

Figure 35

 2

- Click the New folder button on the Quick Access Toolbar to create a new folder with the name, New folder, selected in a text box (Figure 36).

Q&A Why is the folder icon displayed differently on my computer or mobile device?
Windows might be configured to display contents differently on your computer or mobile device.

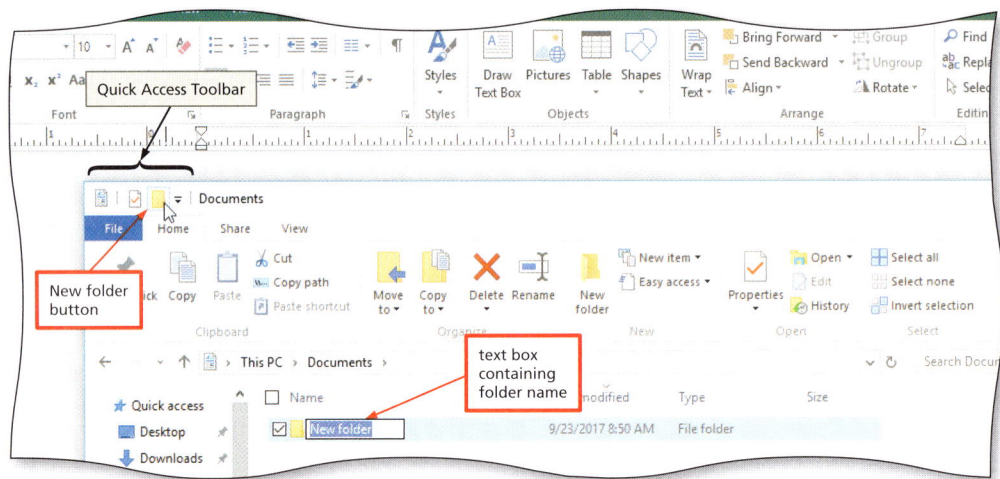

Figure 36

3

- Type CIS 101 (or your class code) in the text box as the new folder name.

    If requested by your instructor, add your last name to the end of the folder name.

- Press the ENTER key to change the folder name from New folder to a folder name identifying your class (Figure 37).

Q&A What happens when I press the ENTER key?
The class folder (CIS 101, in this case) is displayed in the file list, which contains the folder name, date modified, type, and size.

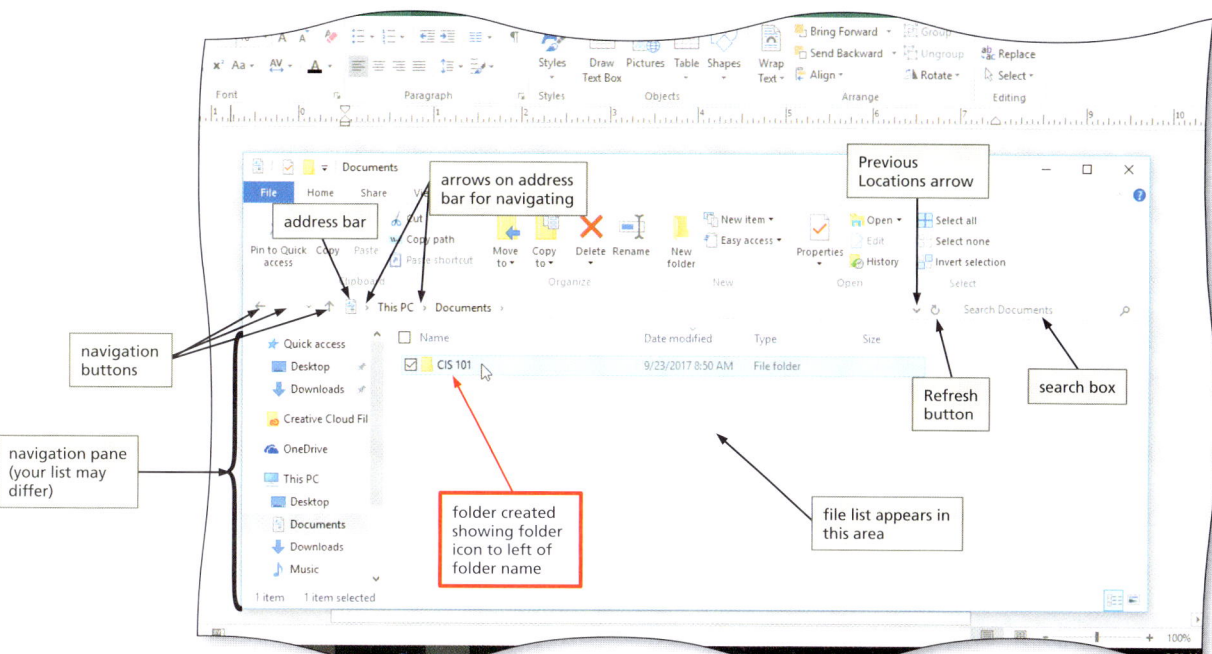

Figure 37

Other Ways

1. Press CTRL+SHIFT+N
2. Click New folder button (Home tab | New group)

Folder Windows

The File Explorer window is called a folder window. Recall that a folder is a specific named location on a storage medium that contains related files. Most users rely on **folder windows** for finding, viewing, and managing information on their computers. Folder windows have common design elements, including the following (shown in Figure 37).

- The **address bar** provides quick navigation options. The arrows on the address bar allow you to visit different locations on the computer or mobile device.

- The buttons to the left of the address bar allow you to navigate the contents of the navigation pane and view recent pages.

- The **Previous Locations arrow** displays the locations you have visited.

- The **Refresh button** on the right side of the address bar refreshes the contents of the folder list.

- The **Search box** contains the dimmed words, Search Documents. You can type a term in the search box for a list of files, folders, shortcuts, and elements containing that term within the location you are searching.

- The **ribbon** contains four tabs used to accomplish various tasks on the computer or mobile device related to organizing and managing the contents of the open window. This ribbon works similarly to the ribbon in the Office apps.

- The **navigation pane** on the left contains the Quick access area, the OneDrive area, the This PC area, and the Network area.

- The **Quick access area** shows locations you access frequently. By default, this list contains links only to your Desktop, Downloads, Documents, and Pictures.

To Create a Folder within a Folder

With the class folder created, you can create folders that will store the files you create using Publisher. The following step creates a Publisher folder in the CIS 101 folder (or the folder identifying your class). *Why? To be able to organize your files, you should create a folder structure.*

- Double-click the icon or folder name for the CIS 101 folder (or the folder identifying your class) in the file list to open the folder.

- Click the New folder button on the Quick Access Toolbar to create a new folder with the name, New folder, selected in a text box folder.

- Type `Publisher` in the text box as the new folder name.

- Press the ENTER key to rename the folder (Figure 38).

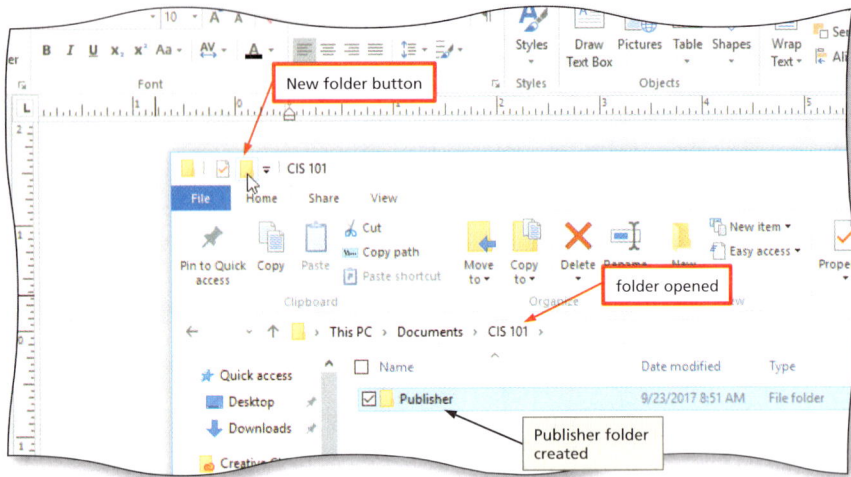

Figure 38

Other Ways

1. Press CTRL+SHIFT+N

2. Click New folder button (Home tab | New group)

To Expand a Folder, Scroll through Folder Contents, and Collapse a Folder

Folder windows display the hierarchy of items and the contents of drives and folders in the file list. You might want to expand a folder in the navigation pane to view its contents, scroll through its contents, and collapse it when you are finished viewing its contents. *Why? When a folder is expanded, you can see all the folders it contains. By contrast, a collapsed folder hides the folders it contains.* The following steps expand, scroll through, and then collapse the folder identifying your class (CIS 101, in this case).

- Double-click the Documents folder in the This PC area of the navigation pane, which expands the folder to display its contents and displays a down arrow to the left of the Documents folder icon (Figure 39).

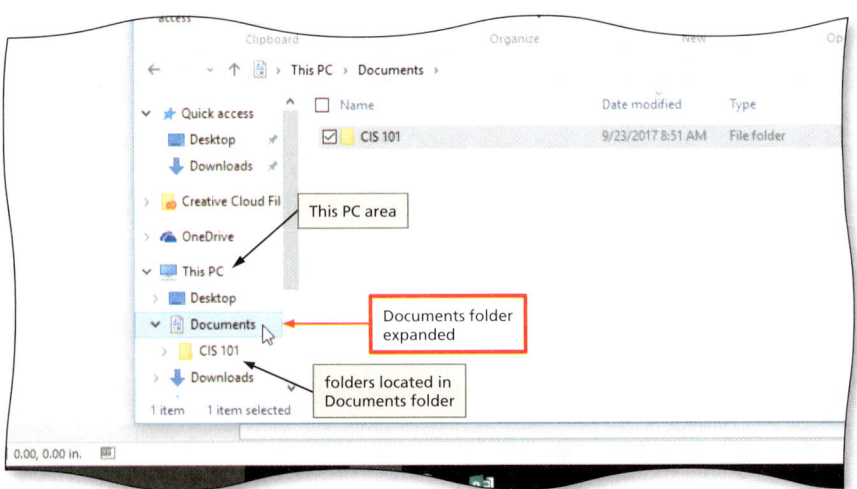

Figure 39

- Double-click the CIS 101 folder, which expands the folder to display its contents and displays a down arrow to the left of the folder icon (Figure 40).

Experiment

- Drag the scroll box down or click the down scroll arrow on the vertical scroll bar to display additional folders at the bottom of the navigation pane. Drag the scroll box up or click the scroll bar above the scroll box to move the scroll box to the top of the navigation pane. Drag the scroll box down the scroll bar until the scroll box is halfway down the scroll bar.

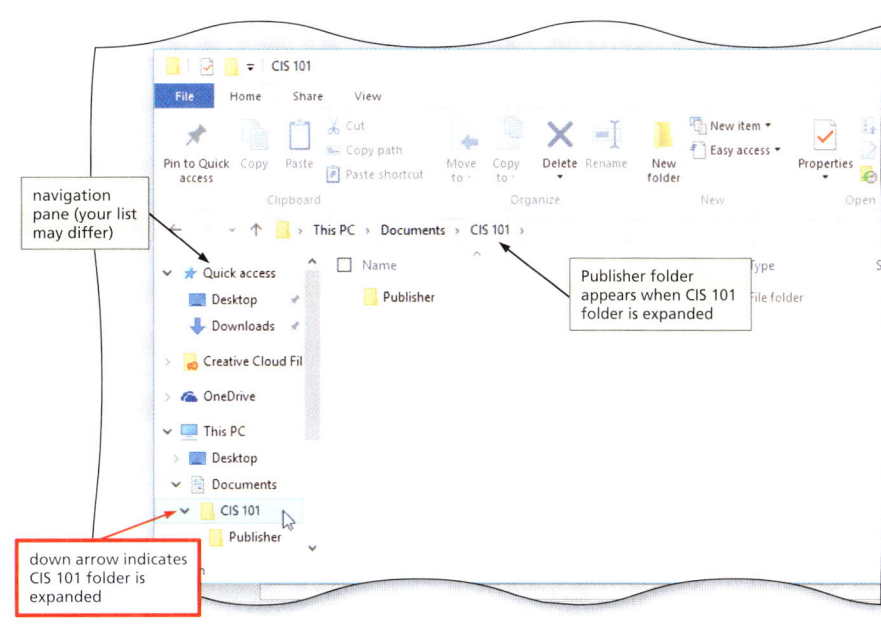

Figure 40

- Double-click the folder identifying your class (CIS 101, in this case) to collapse the folder (Figure 41).

Q&A Why are some folders indented below others?
A folder contains the indented folders below it.

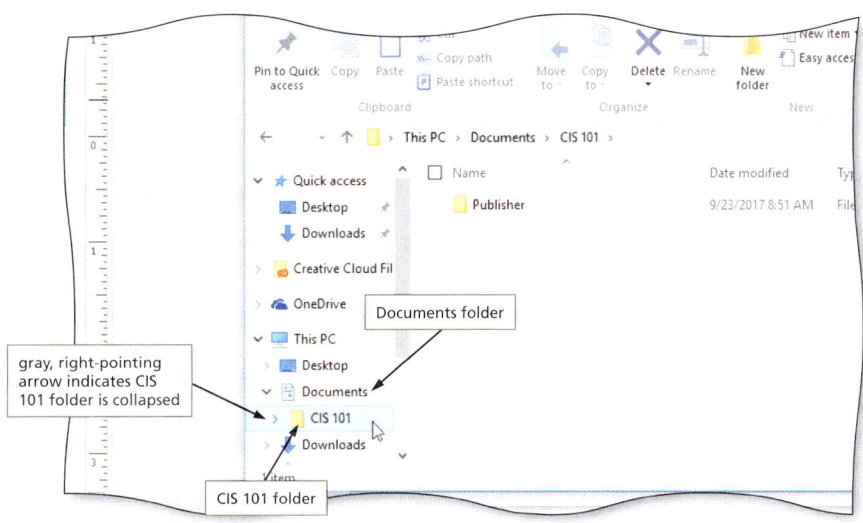

Figure 41

Other Ways

1. Point to display arrows in navigation pane, click arrow to expand or collapse
2. Select folder to expand or collapse using arrow keys, press RIGHT ARROW to expand; press LEFT ARROW to collapse

To Switch from One App to Another

1 SIGN IN | 2 USE WINDOWS | 3 USE APPS | 4 FILE MANAGEMENT | **5 SWITCH APPS** | **6 SAVE FILES**
7 CHANGE SCREEN RESOLUTION | 8 EXIT APPS | 9 USE ADDITIONAL APP FEATURES | 10 USE HELP

The next step is to save the Publisher file containing the headline you typed earlier. Publisher, however, currently is not the active window. You can use the button on the taskbar and live preview to switch to Publisher and then save the publication in the Publisher window.

Why? *By clicking the appropriate app button on the taskbar, you can switch to the running app you want to use.* The following steps switch to the Publisher window; however, the steps are the same for any active Office app currently displayed as a button on the taskbar.

- Point to the Publisher app button on the taskbar to see a live preview of the open publication(s) or the window title(s) of the open publication(s), depending on your computer's configuration (Figure 42).

Q&A

What if I am using a touch screen?
Live preview will not work if you are using a touch screen. If you are using a touch screen and do not have a mouse, proceed to Step 2.

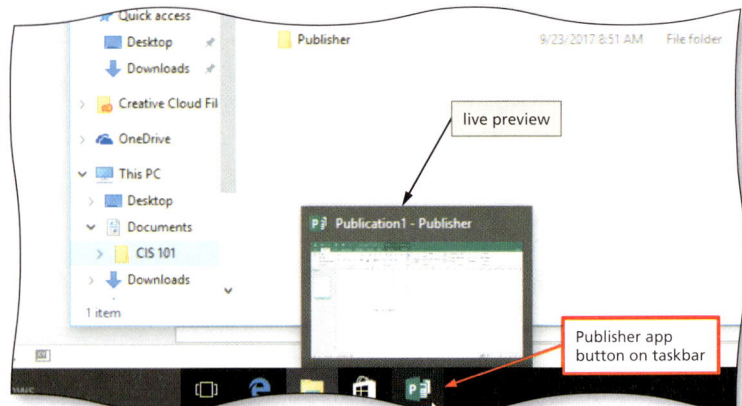

Figure 42

2

- Click the Publisher app button or the live preview to make the app associated with the app button the active window (Figure 43).

Q&A

What if multiple publications are open in an app?
Click the desired live preview to switch to the window you want to use.

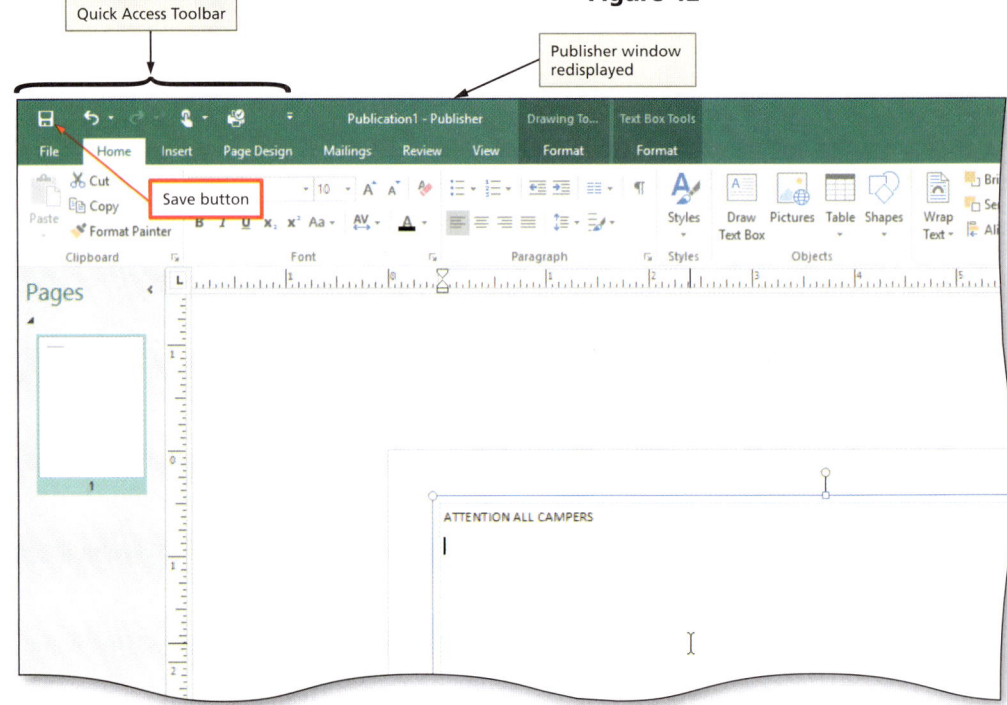

Figure 43

Other Ways

1. Press ALT+TAB until app you wish to display is selected

To Save a File in a Folder

1 SIGN IN | 2 USE WINDOWS | 3 USE APPS | 4 FILE MANAGEMENT | 5 SWITCH APPS | 6 SAVE FILES
7 CHANGE SCREEN RESOLUTION | 8 EXIT APPS | 9 USE ADDITIONAL APP FEATURES | 10 USE HELP

With the Publisher folder created, you can save the publication shown in the Publisher window in the Publisher folder. *Why? Without saving a file, you may lose all the work you have completed and will be unable to reuse or share it with others later.* The following steps save a file in the Publisher folder contained in your class folder (CIS 101, in this case) using the file name, Campers.

1

- Click the Save button (shown in Figure 43) on the Quick Access Toolbar, which depending on settings, will display either the Save As gallery in the Backstage view (Figure 44) or the Save As dialog box (Figure 45).

Q&A What if the Save As gallery is not displayed in the Backstage view?
Click the Save As tab to display the Save As gallery.

How do I close the Backstage view?
Click the Back button in the upper-left corner of the Backstage view to return to the Publisher window.

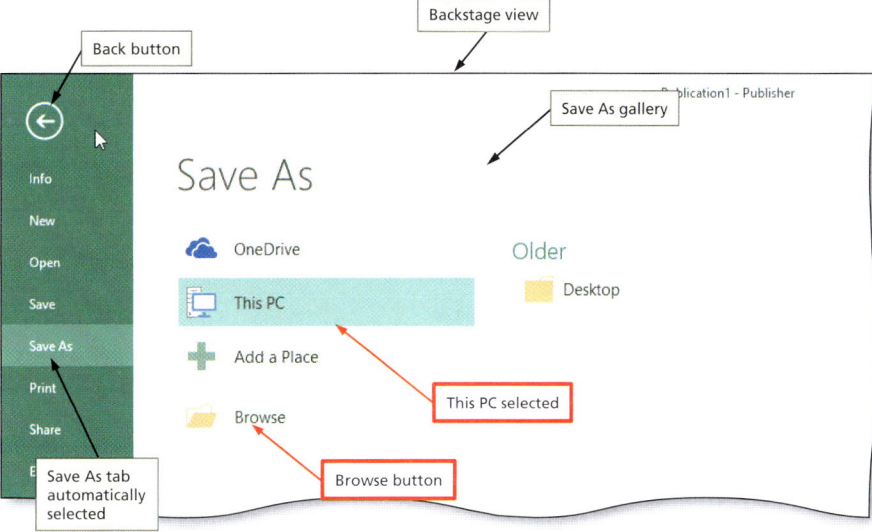

Figure 44

2

- If your screen displays the Backstage view, click This PC, if necessary, to display options related to saving on your computer or mobile device; if your screen already displays the Save As dialog box, proceed to Step 3.

Q&A What if I wanted to save on OneDrive instead?
You would click OneDrive. Saving on OneDrive is discussed in a later section in this module.

- Click the Browse button to display the Save As dialog box (Figure 45).

Q&A Why does a file name already appear in the File name box?
Publisher automatically suggests a file name the first time you save a publication. The file name normally consists of the first few words contained in the publication. Because the suggested file name is selected, you do not need to delete it; as soon as you begin typing, the new file name replaces the selected text.

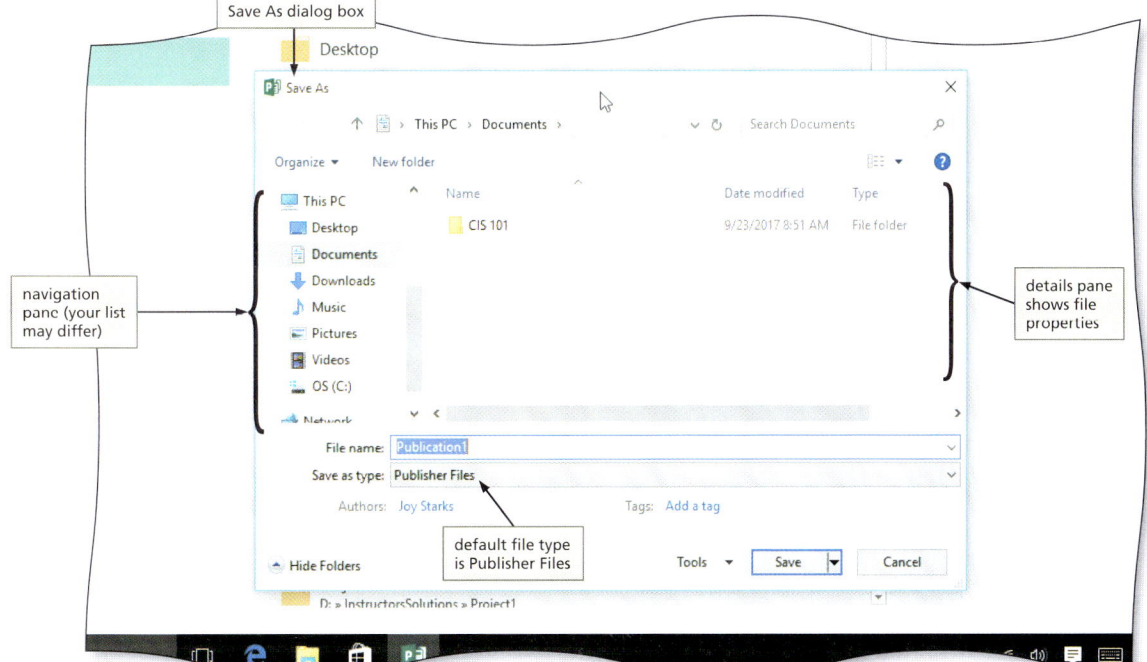

Figure 45

3

- Type `Campers` in the File name box (Save As dialog box) to change the file name. Do not press the ENTER key after typing the file name because you do not want to close the dialog box at this time (Figure 46).

Q&A What characters can I use in a file name?
The only invalid characters are the backslash (\), slash (/), colon (:), asterisk (*), question mark (?), quotation mark ("), less than symbol (<), greater than symbol (>), and vertical bar (|).

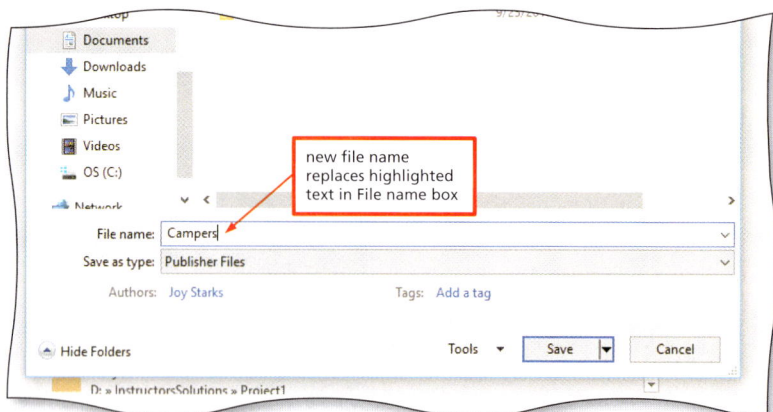

Figure 46

4

- Navigate to the desired save location (in this case, the Publisher folder in the CIS 101 folder [or your class folder] in the Documents folder) by performing the tasks in Steps 4a and 4b.

4a

- If the Documents folder is not displayed in the navigation pane, drag the scroll bar in the navigation pane until Documents appears.

- If the Documents folder is not expanded in the navigation pane, double-click Documents to display its folders in the navigation pane.

- If your class folder (CIS 101, in this case) is not expanded, double-click the CIS 101 folder to select the folder and display its contents in the navigation pane (Figure 47).

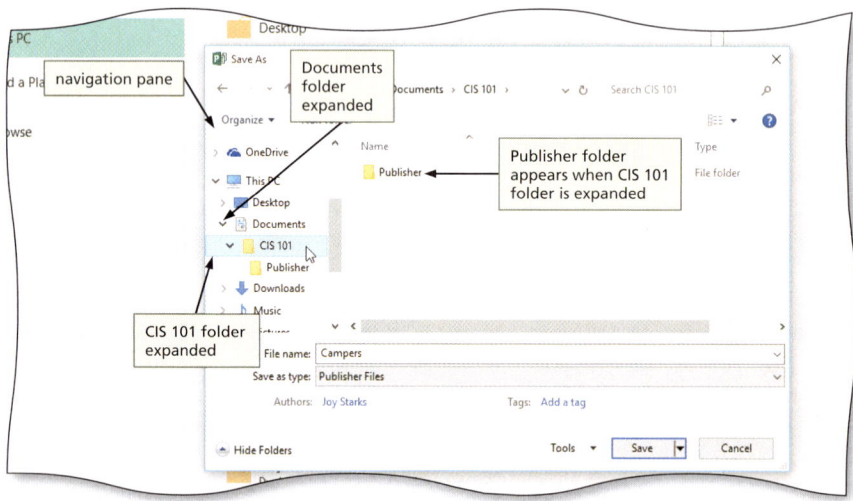

Figure 47

Q&A What if I do not want to save in a folder?
Although storing files in folders is an effective technique for organizing files, some users prefer not to store files in folders. If you prefer not to save this file in a folder, select the storage device on which you wish to save the file and then proceed to Step 5.

4b

- Click the Publisher folder in the navigation pane to select it as the new save location and display its contents in the file list (Figure 48).

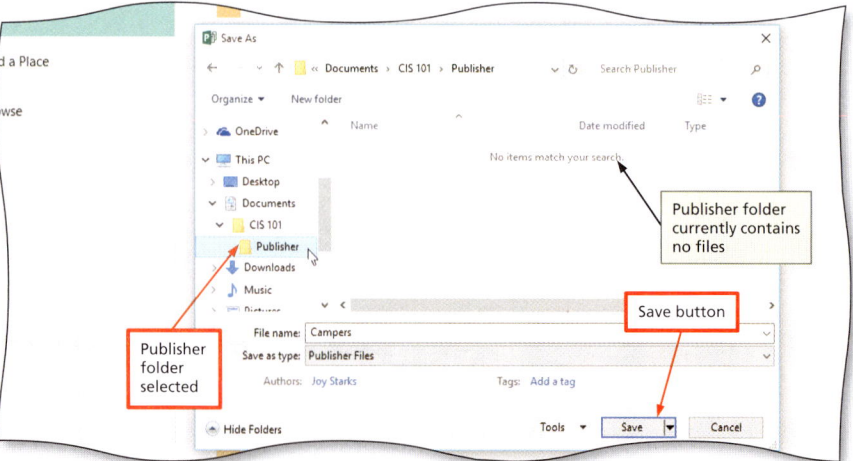

Figure 48

5

- Click the Save button (Save As dialog box) to save the publication in the selected folder in the selected location with the entered file name (Figure 49).

Q&A How do I know that the file is saved?
While an Office app, such as Publisher, is saving a file, it briefly displays a message on the status bar indicating the amount of the file saved. In addition, the file name appears on the title bar.

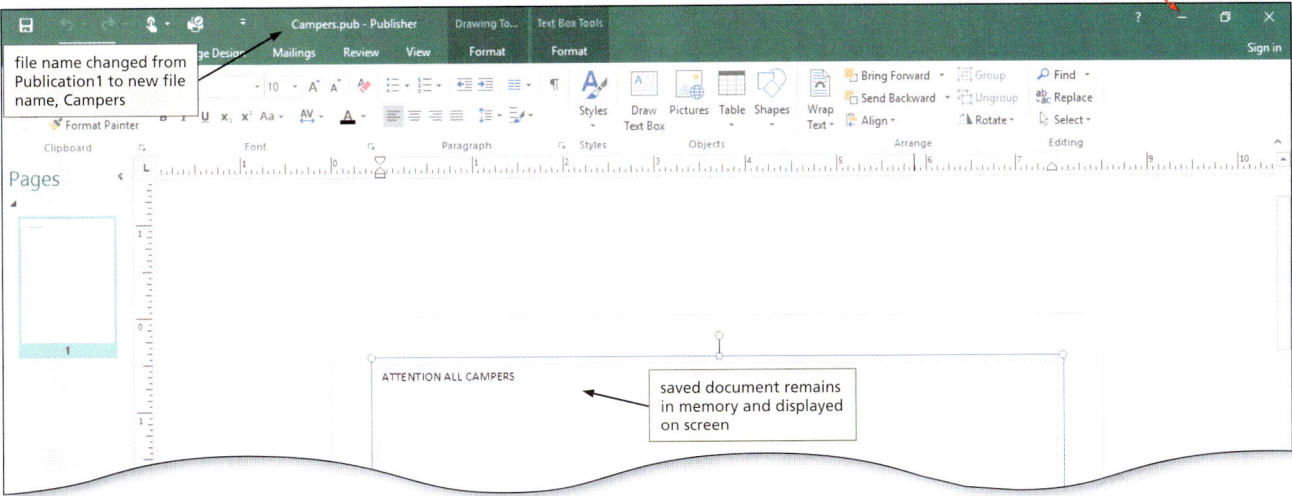

Figure 49

Other Ways

1. Click File on ribbon, click Save As tab in Backstage view, click This PC, click Browse button, type file name (Save As dialog box), navigate to desired save location, click Save button

2. Press F12, type file name (Save As dialog box), navigate to desired save location, click Save button

How often should you save a publication?

It is important to save a publication frequently for the following reasons:

- The publication in memory might be lost if the computer is turned off or you lose electrical power while an app is running.

- If you run out of time before completing a project, you may finish it at a future time without starting over.

CONSIDER THIS

Navigating in Dialog Boxes

Navigating is the process of finding a location on a storage device. While saving the Campers file, for example, Steps 4a and 4b navigated to the Publisher folder located in the CIS 101 folder in the Documents folder. When performing certain functions in Windows apps, such as saving a file, opening a file, or inserting a picture in an existing publication, you most likely will have to navigate to the location where you want to save the file or to the folder containing the file you want to open or insert. Most dialog boxes in Windows apps requiring navigation follow a similar procedure; that is, the way you navigate to a folder in one dialog box, such as the Save As dialog box, is similar to how you might navigate in another dialog box, such as the Open dialog box. If you chose to navigate to a specific location in a dialog box, you would follow the instructions in Steps 4a and 4b.

BTW

File Type

Depending on your Windows settings, the file type .pub may be displayed immediately to the right of the file name after you save the file. The file type .pub is a Publisher file.

Office 2016 and Windows 10 Module

To Minimize and Restore a Window

Before continuing, you can verify that the Publisher file was saved properly. To do this, you will minimize the Publisher window and then open the CIS 101 window so that you can verify the file is stored in the CIS 101 folder on the hard drive. A **minimized window** is an open window that is hidden from view but can be displayed quickly by clicking the window's button on the taskbar.

In the following example, Publisher is used to illustrate minimizing and restoring windows; however, you would follow the same steps regardless of the Office app you are using. *Why? Before closing an app, you should make sure your file saved correctly so that you can find it later.*

The following steps minimize the Publisher window, verify that the file is saved, and then restore the minimized window.

- Click the Minimize button on the Publisher window title bar (shown in Figure 49) to minimize the window (Figure 50).

Q&A Is the minimized window still available?
The minimized window, Publisher in this case, remains available but no longer is the active window. It is minimized as a button on the taskbar.

- If the File Explorer window is not open on the screen, click the File Explorer button on the taskbar to make the File Explorer window the active window.

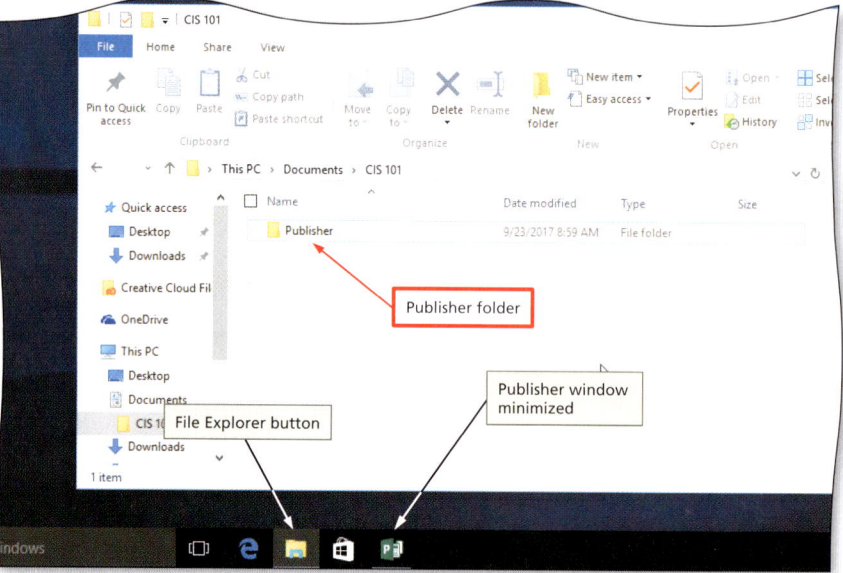

Figure 50

- Double-click the Publisher folder in the file list to select the folder and display its contents (Figure 51).

Q&A Why does the File Explorer button on the taskbar change?
A selected app button indicates that the app is active on the screen. When the button is not selected, the app is running but not active.

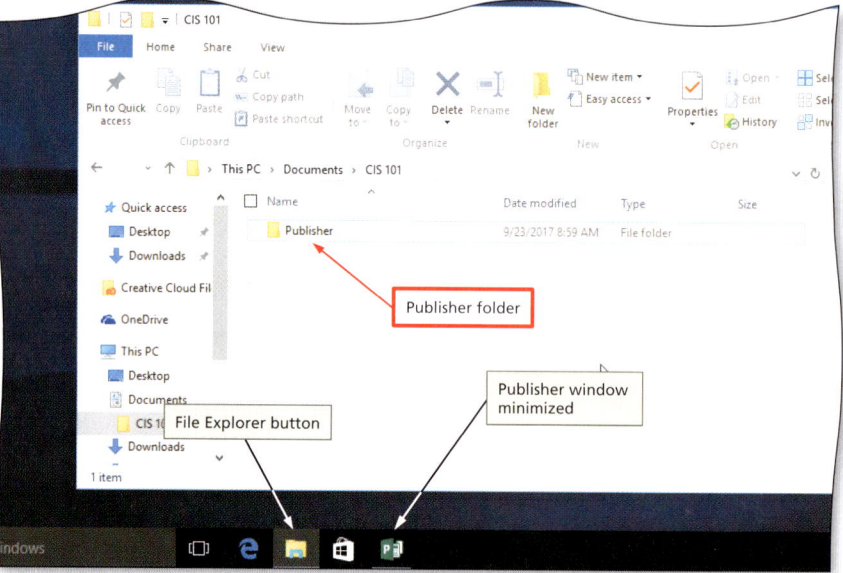

- After viewing the contents of the selected folder, click the Publisher button on the taskbar to restore the minimized window (as shown in Figure 49).

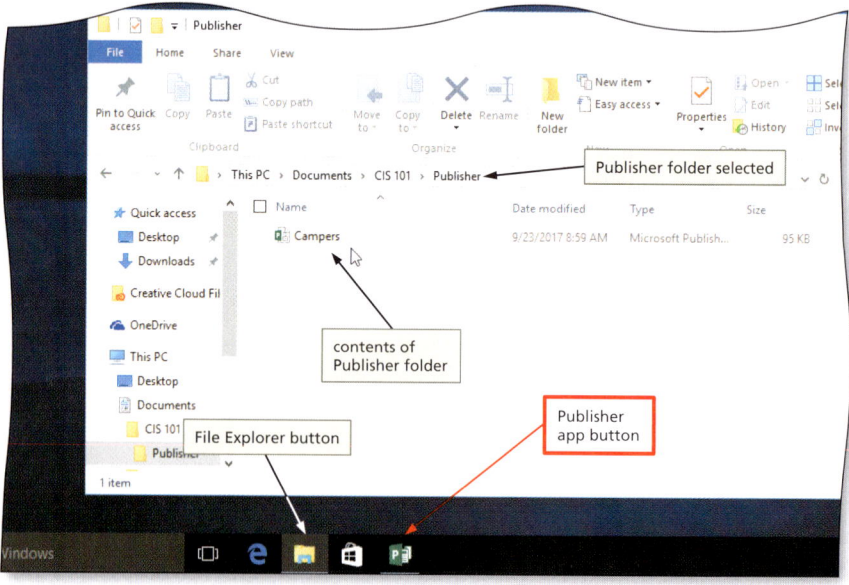

Figure 51

Other Ways

1. Right-click title bar, click Minimize on shortcut menu, click taskbar button in taskbar button area
2. Press WINDOWS+M, press WINDOWS+SHIFT+M
3. Click Publisher app button on taskbar to minimize window; click Publisher app button again to restore window

To Save a File on OneDrive

One of the features of Office is the capability to save files on OneDrive so that you can use the files on multiple computers or mobile devices without having to use an external storage device, such as a USB flash drive. Storing files on OneDrive also enables you to share files more efficiently with others, such as when using Office Online and Office 365.

In the following example, Publisher is used to save a file on OneDrive. *Why? Storing files on OneDrive provides more portability options than are available from storing files in the Documents folder.*

You can save files directly on OneDrive from within an Office app. The following steps save the current Publisher file on OneDrive. These steps require you have a Microsoft account and an Internet connection.

①

- Click File on the ribbon to open the Backstage view.

- Click the Save As tab in the Backstage view to display the Save As gallery.

- Click OneDrive in the left pane to display OneDrive saving options or a Sign In button, if you are not signed in to your Microsoft account already (Figure 52).

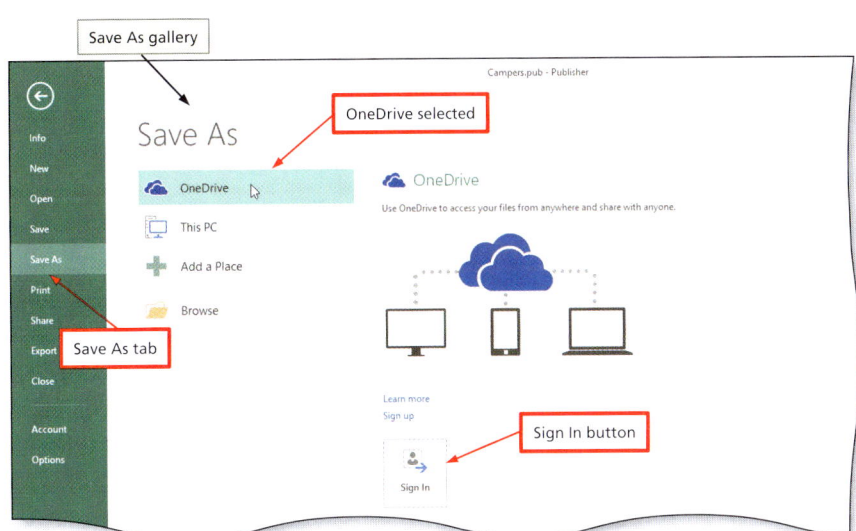

Figure 52

②

- If your screen displays a Sign In button (shown in Figure 52), click it to display the Sign in dialog box (Figure 53).

Q&A What if the Sign In button does not appear?

If you already are signed into your Microsoft account, the Sign In button will not be displayed. In this case, proceed to Step 3.

- Follow the instructions on the screen to sign in to your Microsoft account.

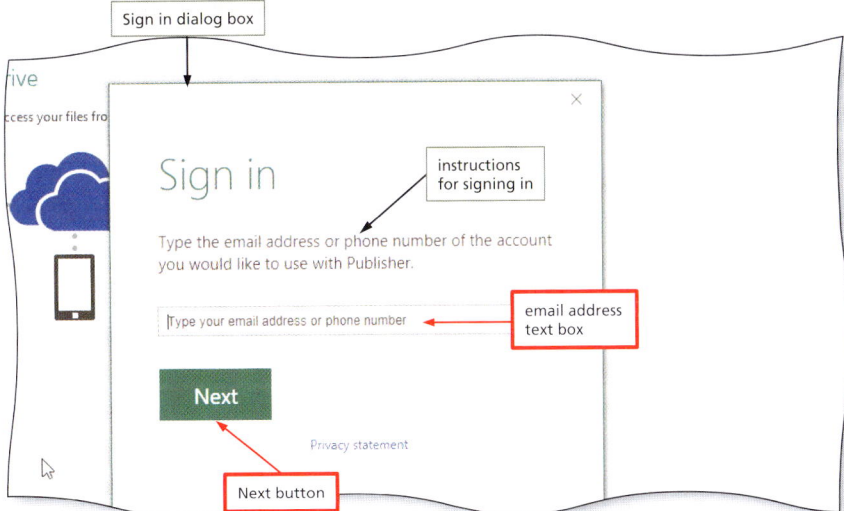

Figure 53

3

- Click the Documents folder in the right pane to display the Save As dialog box (Figure 54).

Why does the path in the OneDrive address bar in the Save As dialog box contain various letters and numbers? The letters and numbers in the address bar uniquely identify the location of your OneDrive files and folders.

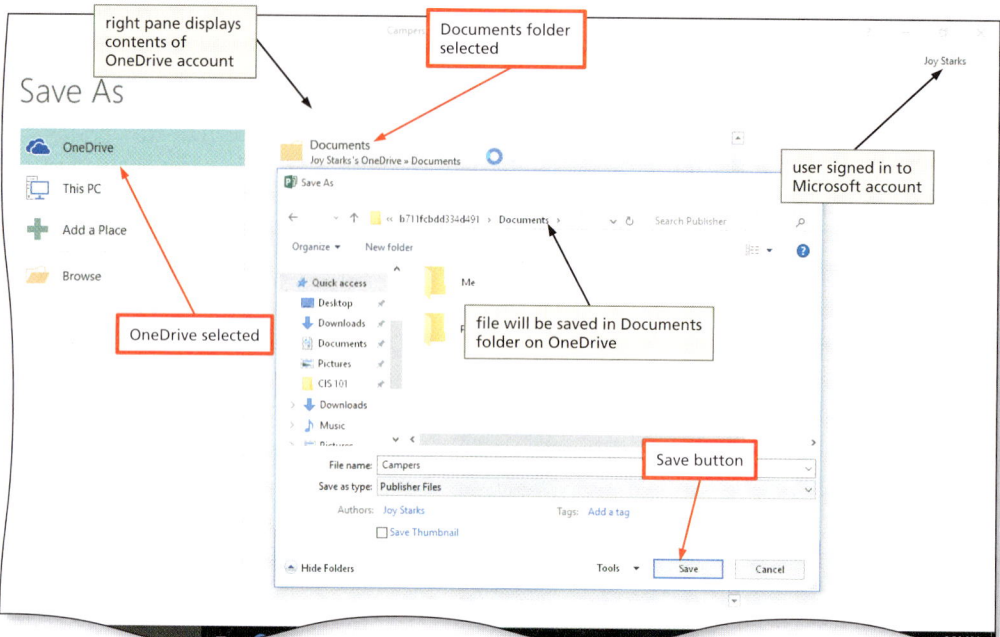

Figure 54

4

- Click the Save button (Save As dialog box) to save the file on OneDrive.

To Sign Out of a Microsoft Account

If you are using a public computer or otherwise wish to sign out of your Microsoft account, you should sign out of the account from the Accounts gallery in the Backstage view. Signing out of the account is the safest way to make sure that nobody else can access online files or settings stored in your Microsoft account. *Why? For security reasons, you should sign out of your Microsoft account when you are finished using a public or shared computer. Staying signed in to your Microsoft account might enable others to access your files.*

The following steps sign out of a Microsoft account from Publisher. You would use the same steps in any Office app. If you do not wish to sign out of your Microsoft account, read these steps without performing them.

1 Click File on the ribbon to open the Backstage view.

2 Click the Account tab to display the Account gallery (Figure 55).

3 Click the Sign out link, which displays the Remove Account dialog box. If a Can't remove Windows accounts dialog box appears instead of the Remove Account dialog box, click the OK button and skip the remaining steps.

Why does a Can't remove Windows accounts dialog box appear? If you signed in to Windows using your Microsoft account, then you also must sign out from Windows, rather than signing out from within Publisher. When you are finished using Windows, be sure to sign out at that time.

4 Click the Yes button (Remove Account dialog box) to sign out of your Microsoft account on this computer or mobile device.

Should I sign out of Windows after removing my Microsoft account? When you are finished using the computer, you should sign out of Windows for maximum security.

5 Click the Back button in the upper-left corner of the Backstage view to return to the publication.

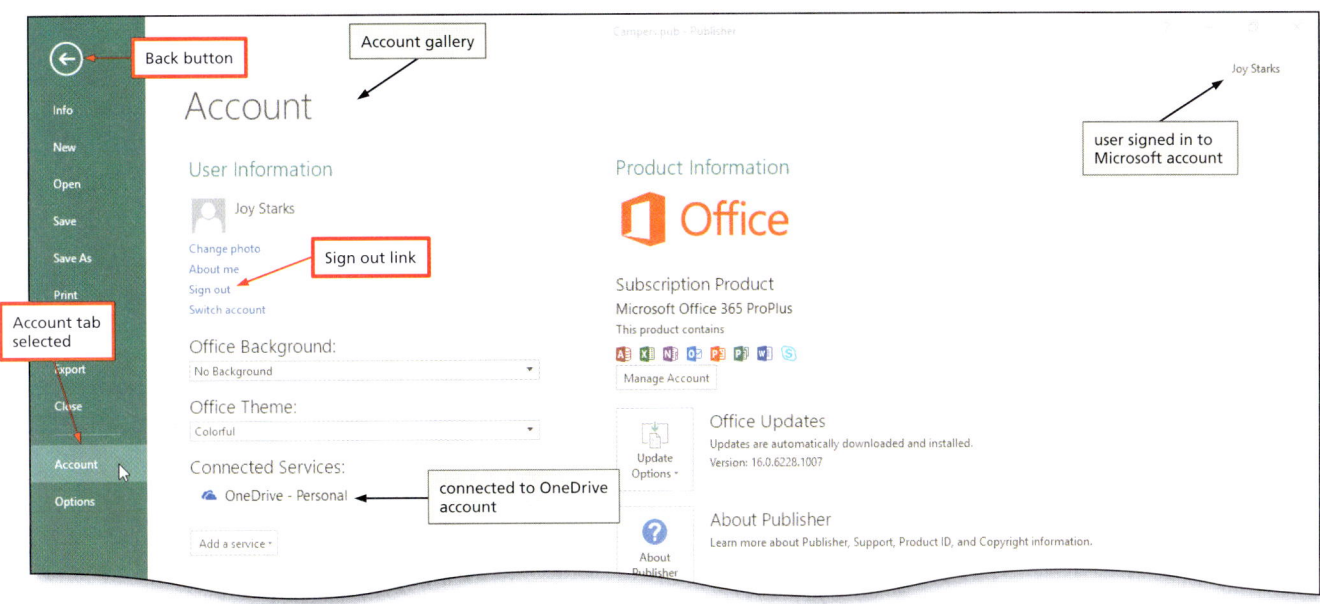

Figure 55

Screen Resolution

Screen resolution indicates the number of pixels (dots) that the computer uses to display the letters, numbers, graphics, and background you see on the screen. When you increase the screen resolution, Windows displays more information on the screen, but the information decreases in size. The reverse also is true: as you decrease the screen resolution, Windows displays less information on the screen, but the information increases in size.

Screen resolution usually is stated as the product of two numbers, such as 1366 × 768 (pronounced "thirteen sixty-six by seven sixty-eight"). A 1366 × 768 screen resolution results in a display of 1366 distinct pixels on each of 768 lines, or about 1,050,624 pixels. Changing the screen resolution affects how the ribbon appears in Office apps and some Windows dialog boxes. Figure 56, for example, shows the Publisher ribbon at screen resolutions of 1366 × 768 and 1024 × 768. All of the same commands are available regardless of screen resolution. The app (Publisher, in this case), however, makes changes to the groups and the buttons within the groups to accommodate the various screen resolutions. The result is that certain commands may need to be accessed differently depending on the resolution chosen. A command that is visible on the ribbon and available by clicking a button at one resolution may not be visible and may need to be accessed using its Dialog Box Launcher at a different resolution.

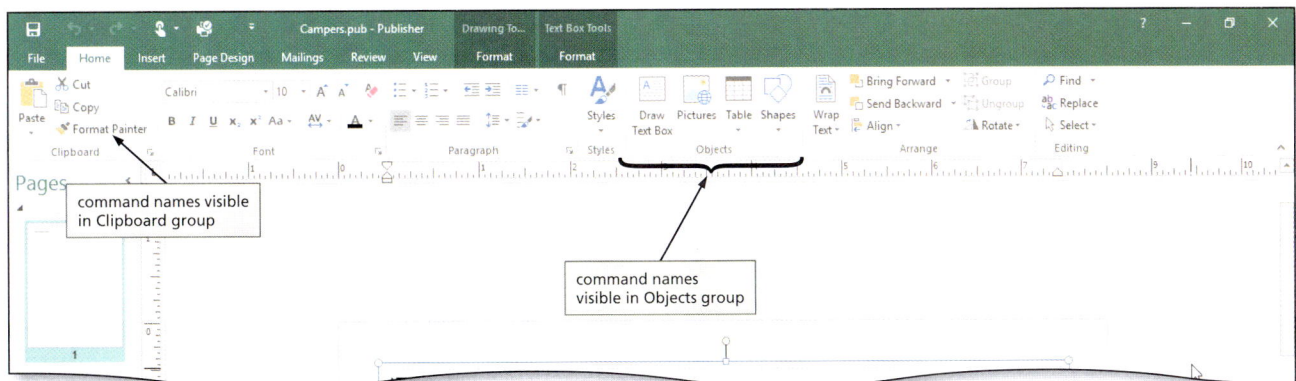

Figure 56a Ribbon at 1366 x 768 Resolution

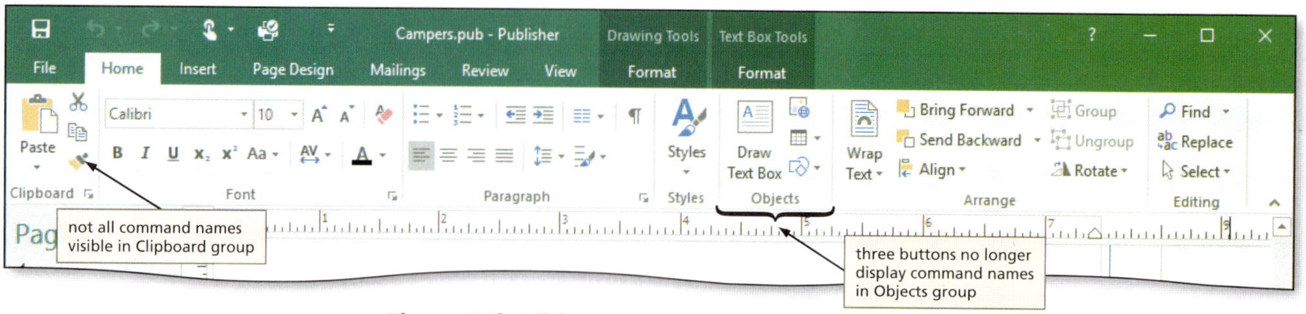

Figure 56b Ribbon at 1024 x 768 Resolution

Comparing the two ribbons in Figure 56, notice the changes in content and layout of the groups and galleries. In some cases, the content of a group is the same in each resolution, but the layout of the group differs. For example, the same gallery and buttons appear in the Objects groups in the two resolutions, but the layouts differ. In other cases, the content and layout are the same across the resolution, but the level of detail differs with the resolution.

To Change the Screen Resolution

1 SIGN IN | 2 USE WINDOWS | 3 USE APPS | 4 FILE MANAGEMENT | 5 SWITCH APPS | 6 SAVE FILES
7 CHANGE SCREEN RESOLUTION | 8 EXIT APPS | 9 USE ADDITIONAL APP FEATURES | 10 USE HELP

If you are using a computer to step through the modules in this book and you want your screen to match the figures, you may need to change your screen's resolution. *Why? The figures in this book use a screen resolution of 1366 × 768.* The following steps change the screen resolution to 1366 × 768. Your computer already may be set to 1366 × 768. Keep in mind that many computer labs prevent users from changing the screen resolution; in that case, read the following steps for illustration purposes.

- Click the Show desktop button, which is located at the far-right edge of the taskbar, to display the Windows desktop.

- Right-click an empty area on the Windows desktop to display a shortcut menu that contains a list of commands related to the desktop (Figure 57).

Q&A

Why does my shortcut menu display different commands?

Depending on your computer's hardware and configuration, different commands might appear on the shortcut menu.

Figure 57

- Click Display settings on the shortcut menu to open the Settings app window. If necessary, scroll to display the 'Advanced display settings' link (Figure 58).

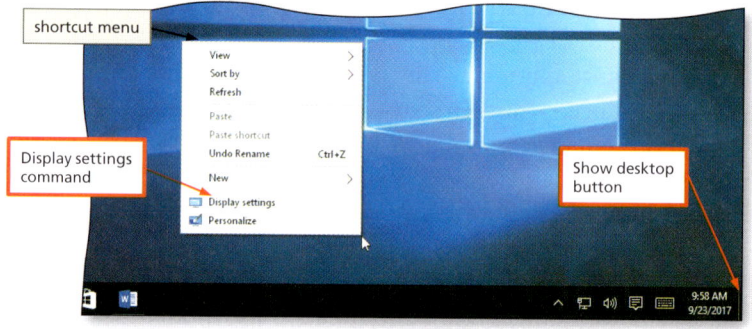

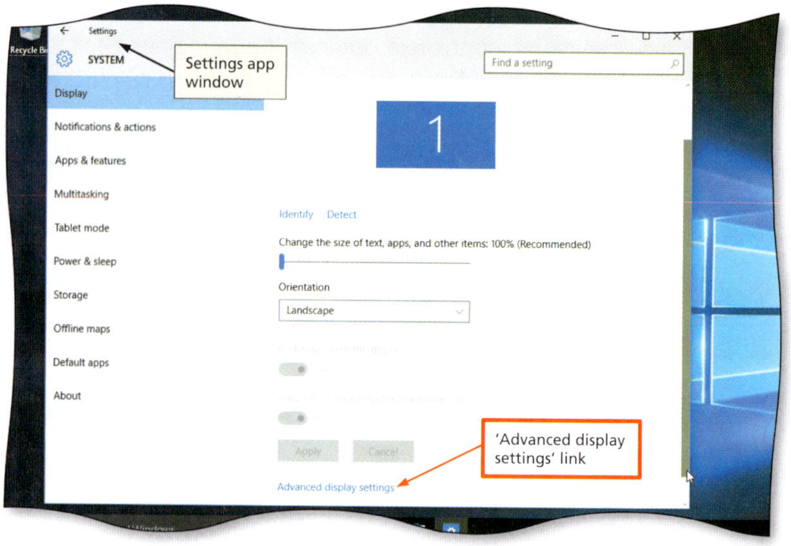

Figure 58

- Click the 'Advanced display settings' link in the Settings app window to display the advanced display settings.
- If necessary, scroll to display the Resolution box (Figure 59).

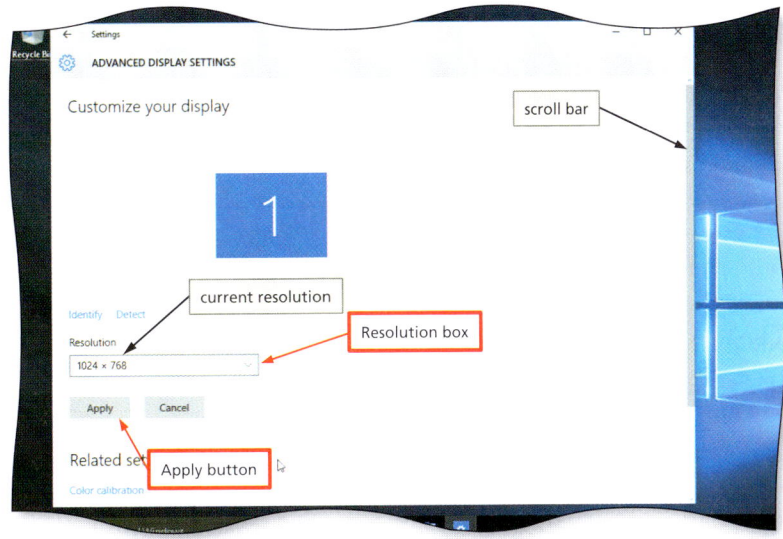

Figure 59

- Click the Resolution box to display a list of available screen resolutions (Figure 60).
- If necessary, scroll to and then click 1366 × 768 to select the screen resolution.

Q&A What if my computer does not support the 1366 × 768 resolution?
Some computers do not support the 1366 × 768 resolution. In this case, select a resolution that is close to the 1366 × 768 resolution.

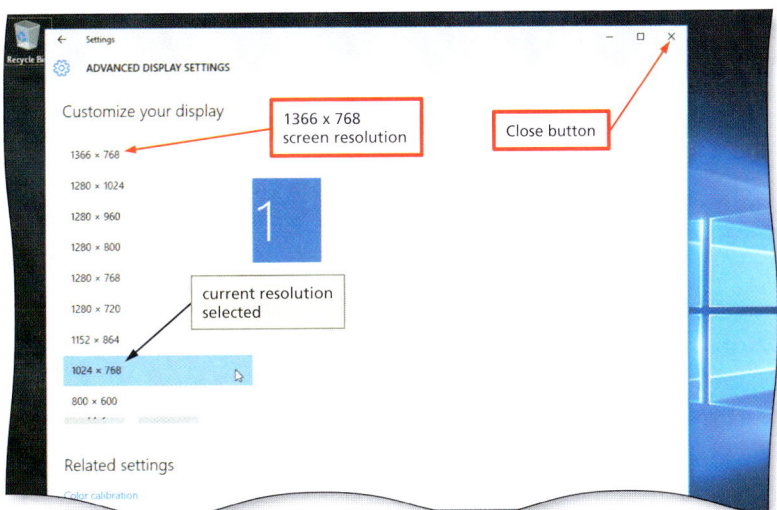

Figure 60

- Click the Apply button (Advanced Display Settings window), shown in Figure 59, to change the screen resolution and a confirmation message (Figure 61).
- Click the Keep changes button to accept the new screen resolution.
- Click the Close button (shown in Figure 60) to close the Settings app window.

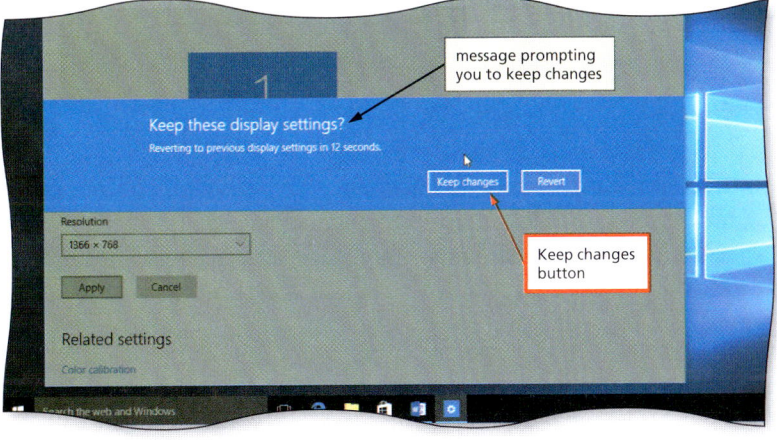

Figure 61

Other Ways

1. Click Start button, click Settings, click System, click Display, click 'Advanced display settings,' select desired resolution in Resolution box, click Apply button, click Keep changes button

2. Type `screen resolution` in search box, click 'Change the screen resolution,' select desired resolution in Resolution box, click Apply button, click Keep changes button

To Exit an App with One Publication Open

When you exit an Office app, such as Publisher, if you have made changes to a file since the last time the file was saved, the app displays a dialog box asking if you want to save the changes you made to the file before it closes the app window. *Why? The dialog box contains three buttons with these resulting actions: the Save button saves the changes and then exits the app, the Don't Save button exits the app without saving changes, and the Cancel button closes the dialog box and redisplays the file without saving the changes.*

If no changes have been made to an open publication since the last time the file was saved, the app will close the window without displaying a dialog box.

The following steps exit Publisher. You would follow similar steps in other Office apps.

- If necessary, click the Publisher app button on the taskbar to display the Publisher window on the desktop (Figure 62).

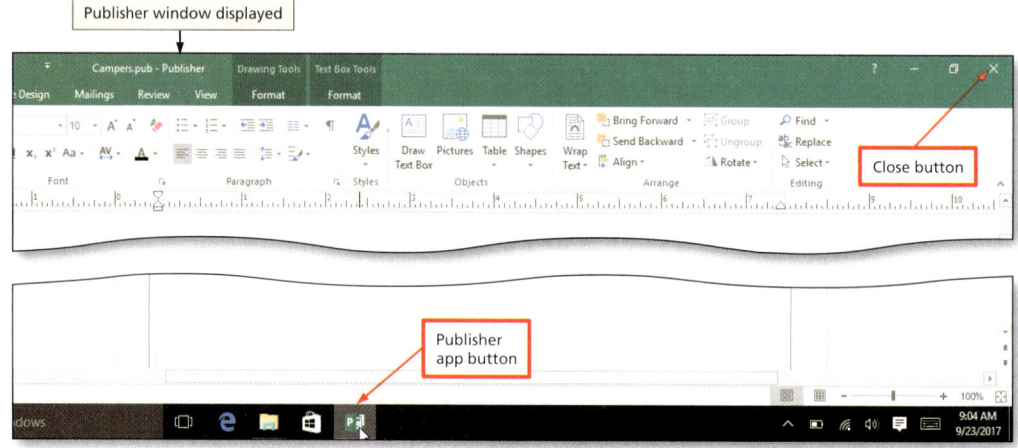

Figure 62

- Click the Close button on the right side of the Publisher window title bar to close the publication and exit Publisher. If a Microsoft Publisher dialog box appears, click the Save button to save any changes made to the publication since the last save.

Q&A

What if I have more than one publication open in Publisher?

You could click the Close button for each open publication. When you click the last open publication's Close button, you also exit Publisher. As an alternative that is more efficient, you could right-click the Publisher app button on the taskbar and then click 'Close all windows' on the shortcut menu to close all open publications and exit Publisher.

Other Ways

1. Right-click Publisher app button on Windows taskbar, click 'Close all windows' on shortcut menu
2. Press ALT+F4

To Copy a Folder to OneDrive

To back up your files or easily make them available on another computer or mobile device, you can copy them to OneDrive. The following steps copy your CIS 101 folder to OneDrive. If you do not have access to a OneDrive account, read the following steps without performing them. *Why? It often is good practice to have a backup of your files so that they are available in case something happens to your original copies.*

- Click the File Explorer button on the taskbar to make the folder window the active window.

- Navigate to the CIS 101 folder (or your class folder) in the Documents folder.

- Click Documents in the This PC area of the navigation pane to display the CIS 101 folder in the file list.

Q&A

What if my CIS 101 folder is stored in a different location? Use the navigation pane to navigate to the location of your CIS 101 folder. The CIS 101 folder should be displayed in the file list once you have located it.

- Click the CIS 101 folder in the file list to select it (Figure 63).

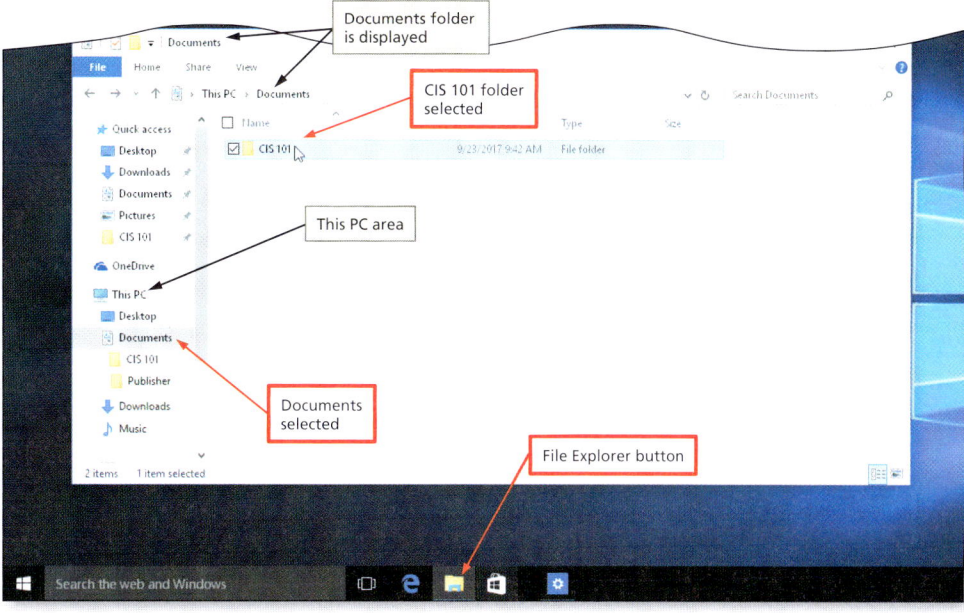

Figure 63

 2

- Click Home on the ribbon to display the Home tab.

- Click the Copy to button (Home tab | Organize group) to display the Copy to menu (Figure 64).

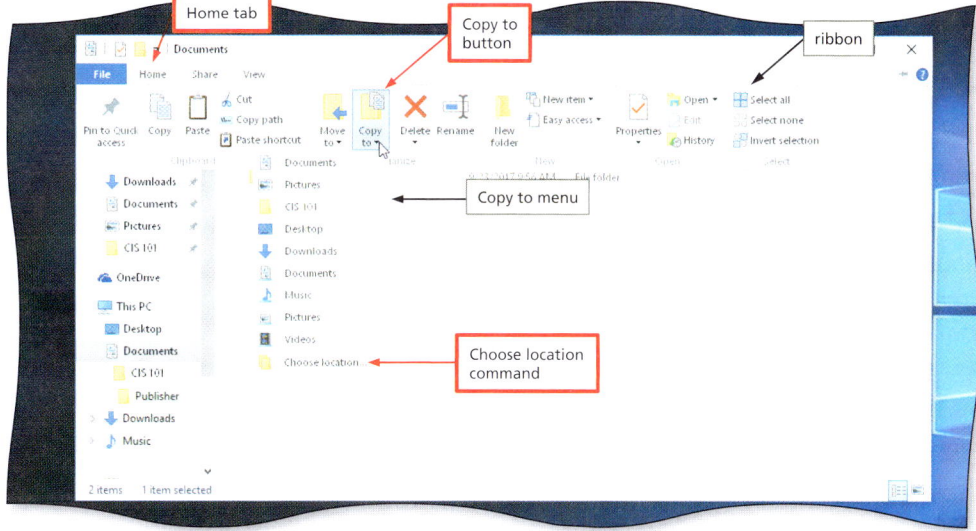

Figure 64

 3

- Click Choose location on the Copy to menu to display the Copy Items dialog box.

- Click OneDrive (Copy Items dialog box) to select it (Figure 65).

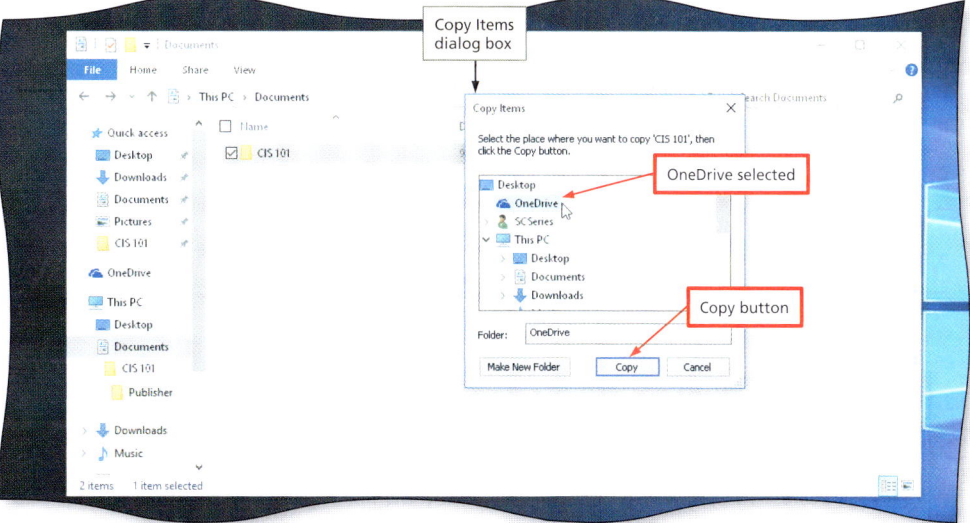

Figure 65

- Click the Copy button (Copy Items dialog box) to copy the selected folder to OneDrive.

- Click OneDrive in the navigation pane to verify the CIS 101 folder displays in the file list (Figure 66).

Q&A Why does a Microsoft OneDrive dialog box appear when I click OneDrive in the navigation pane?
If you are not currently signed in to Windows using a Microsoft account, you will manually need to sign in to a Microsoft account to save files to OneDrive. Follow the instructions on the screen to sign in to your Microsoft account.

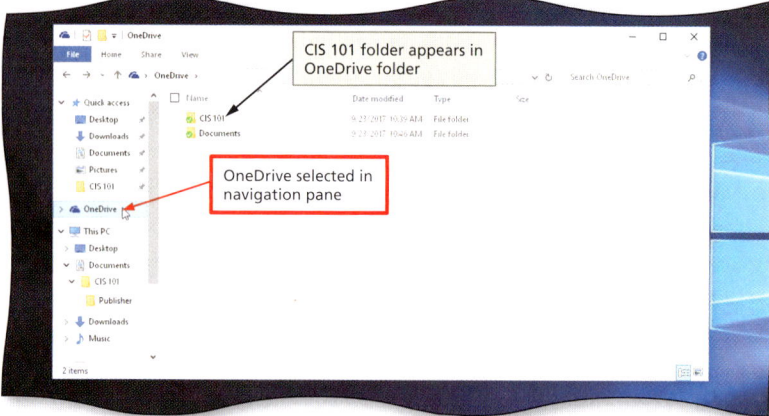

Figure 66

Other Ways

1. In File Explorer, select folder to copy, click Copy button (Home tab | Clipboard group), display contents of OneDrive in file list, click Paste button (Home tab | Clipboard group)

2. In File Explorer, select folder to copy, press CTRL+C, display contents of OneDrive in file list, press CTRL+V

3. Drag folder to copy to OneDrive in navigation pane

To Unlink a OneDrive Account

If you are using a public computer and are not signed in to Windows with a Microsoft account, you should unlink your OneDrive account so that other users cannot access it. **Why?** *If you do not unlink your OneDrive account, other people accessing the same user account on the computer will be able to view, remove, and add to files stored in your OneDrive account.*

The following steps unlink your OneDrive account. If you do not wish to sign out of your Microsoft account, read these steps without performing them.

- Click the 'Show hidden icons' button on the Windows taskbar to show a menu of hidden icons (Figure 67).

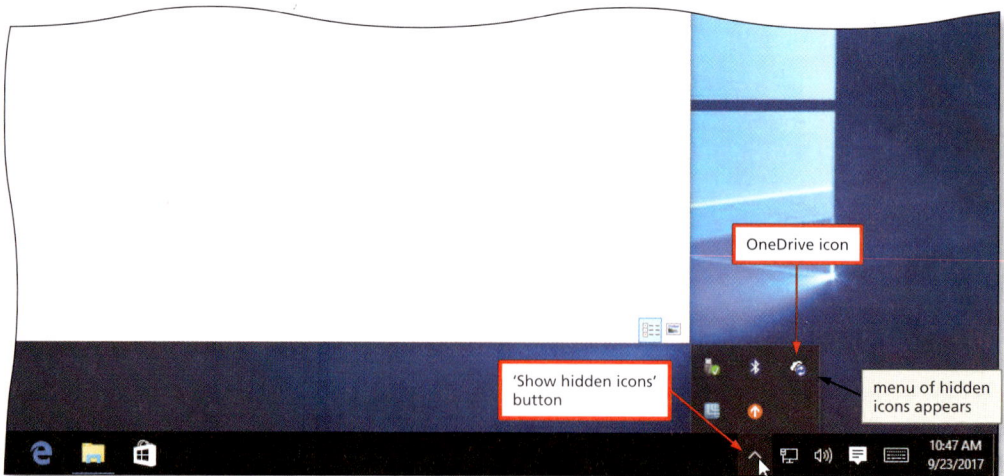

Figure 67

2

- Right-click the OneDrive icon (shown in Figure 67) to display a shortcut menu (Figure 68).

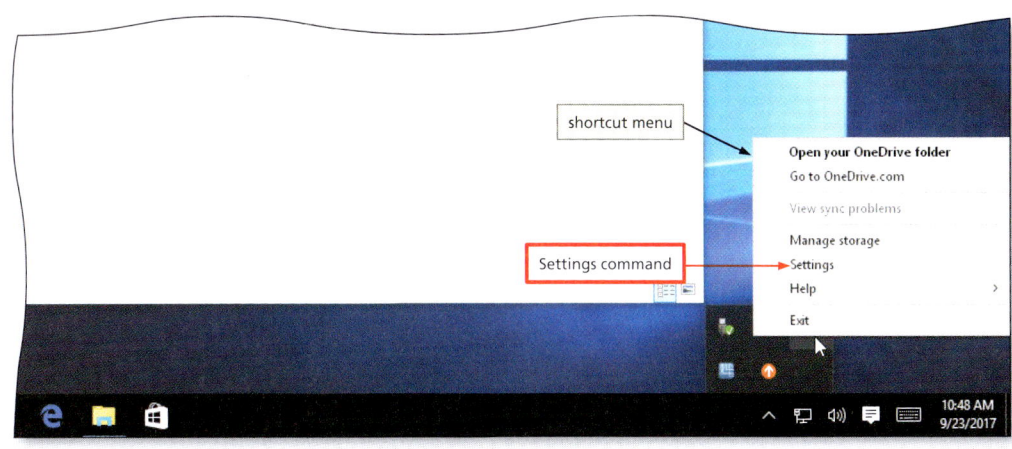

Figure 68

3

- Click Settings on the shortcut menu to display the Microsoft OneDrive dialog box (Figure 69).

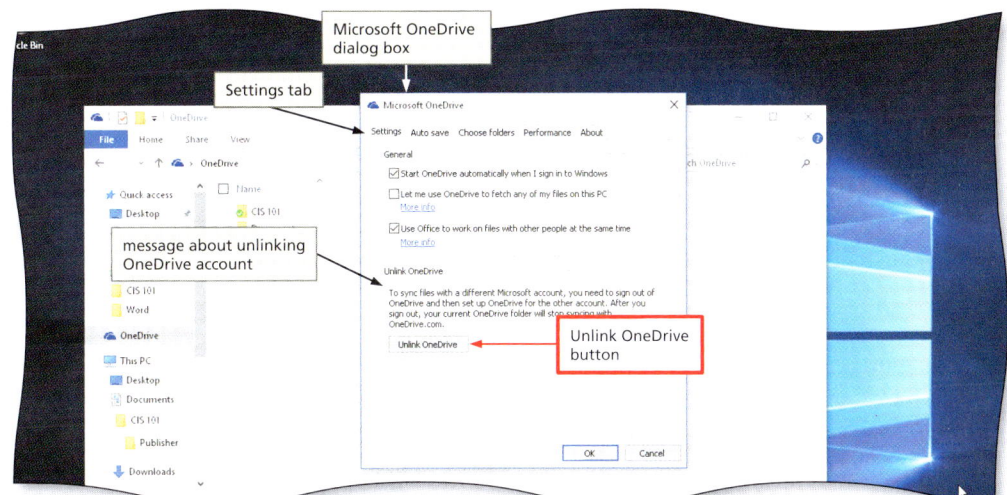

Figure 69

4

- If necessary, click the Settings tab.

- Click the Unlink OneDrive button (Microsoft OneDrive dialog box) to unlink the OneDrive account (Figure 70).

- When the Microsoft OneDrive dialog box appears with a Welcome to OneDrive message, click the Close button.

- Minimize the File Explorer window.

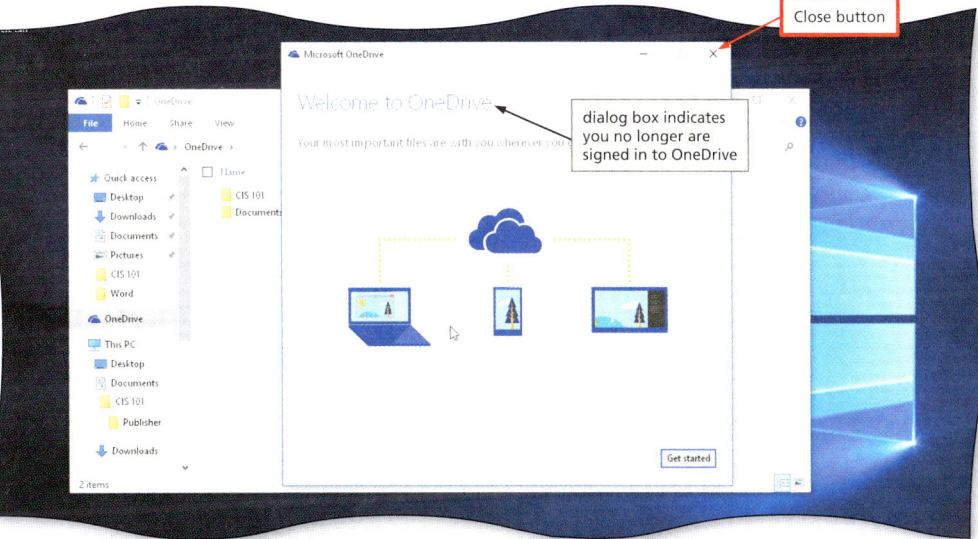

Figure 70

Break Point: If you wish to take a break, this is a good place to do so. To resume at a later time, continue to follow the steps from this location forward.

Additional Common Features of Office Apps

The previous section used Publisher to illustrate common features of Office and some basic elements unique to Publisher. The following sections continue to use Publisher to present additional common features of Office.

In the following pages, you will learn how to do the following:

1. Run Publisher using the search box.
2. Open a publication in Publisher.
3. Close the publication.
4. Reopen the publication just closed.
5. Create a blank Publisher publication from Windows Explorer and then open the file.
6. Save a publication with a new file name.

To Run an App Using the Search Box

1 SIGN IN | 2 USE WINDOWS | 3 USE APPS | 4 FILE MANAGEMENT | 5 SWITCH APPS | 6 SAVE FILES
7 CHANGE SCREEN RESOLUTION | 8 EXIT APPS | 9 USE ADDITIONAL APP FEATURES | 10 USE HELP

The following steps, which assume Windows is running, use the search box to run Publisher based on a typical installation; however, you would follow similar steps to run any app. *Why? Some people prefer to use the search box to locate and run an app, as opposed to searching through a list of all apps on the Start menu.* You may need to ask your instructor how to run Publisher on your computer.

- Type `Publisher 2016` as the search text in the search box and watch the search results appear in the search results (Figure 71).

Q&A

Do I need to type the complete app name or use correct capitalization?
No, you need to type just enough characters of the app name for it to appear in the search results. For example, you may be able to type Publisher or publisher, instead of Publisher 2016.

What if the search does not locate the Publisher app on my computer?
You may need to adjust the Windows search settings. Search for the word, index; click 'Indexing Options Control Panel'; click the Modify button (Indexing Options dialog box); expand the Local Disk, if necessary; place a check mark beside all Program Files entries; and then click the OK button. It may take a few minutes for the index to rebuild. If it still does not work, you may need to click the Advanced button (Indexing Options dialog box) and then click the Rebuild button (Advanced Options dialog box).

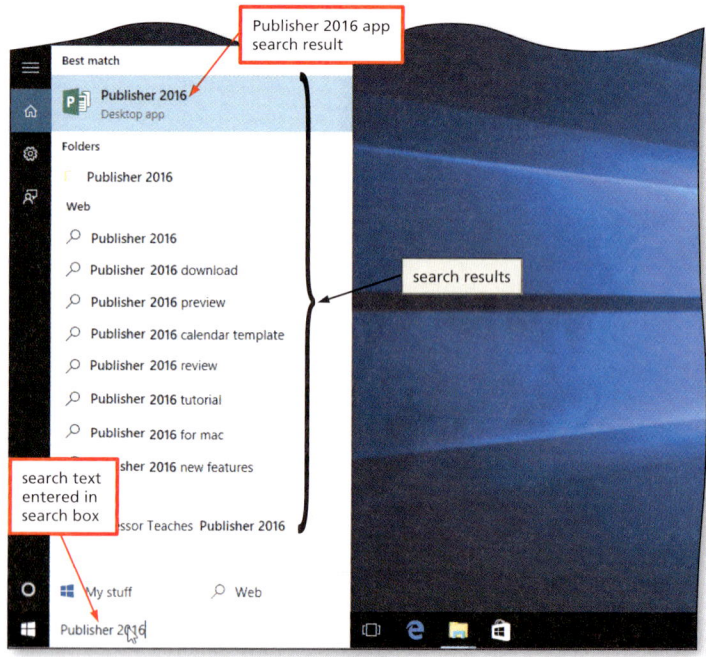

Figure 71

- Click the app name, Publisher 2016 in this case, in the search results to run Publisher and display the Publisher start screen.

- Click the Blank 8.5 × 11" publication thumbnail on the Publisher start screen (shown earlier in this module in Figure 8) to create a blank publication and display it in the Publisher window.

- If the Publisher window is not maximized, click the Maximize button on its title bar to maximize the window (Figure 72).

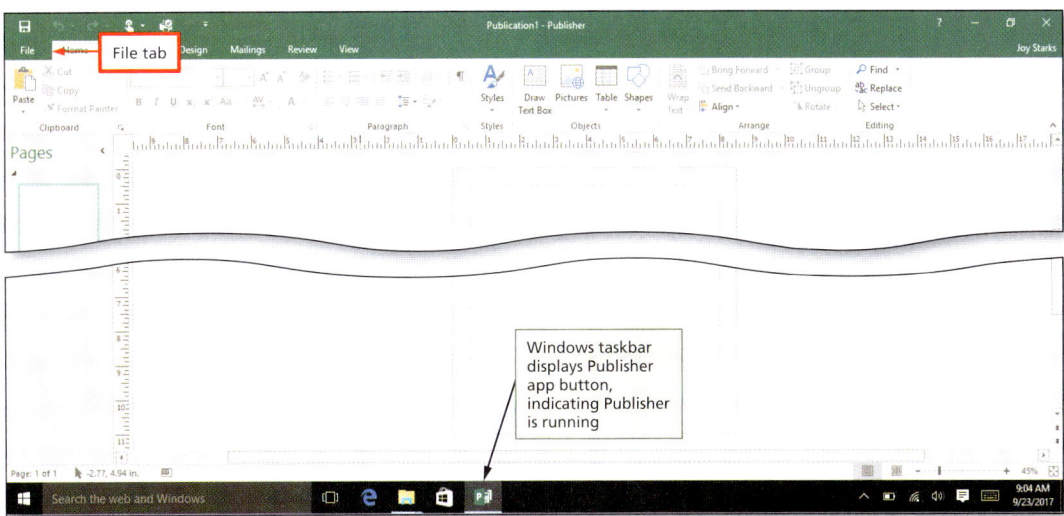

Figure 72

To Open an Existing File

1 SIGN IN | 2 USE WINDOWS | 3 USE APPS | 4 FILE MANAGEMENT | 5 SWITCH APPS | 6 SAVE FILES
7 CHANGE SCREEN RESOLUTION | 8 EXIT APPS | 9 USE ADDITIONAL APP FEATURES | 10 USE HELP

As discussed earlier, the Backstage view contains a set of commands that enable you to manage publications and data about the publications. *Why? From the Backstage view in Publisher, for example, you can create, open, print, and save publications. You also can share publications, manage versions, set permissions, and modify publication properties. In other Office apps, the Backstage view may contain features specific to those apps.* The following steps open a saved file, specifically the Campers file, which recently was saved.

- Click File on the ribbon (shown in Figure 72) to open the Backstage view and then click the Open tab in the Backstage view to display the Open gallery in the Backstage view.

- Click the Browse button to display the Open dialog box.

- If necessary, navigate to the location of the file to open (Publisher folder in the CIS 101 folder).

- Click the file to open, Campers in this case, to select the file (Figure 73).

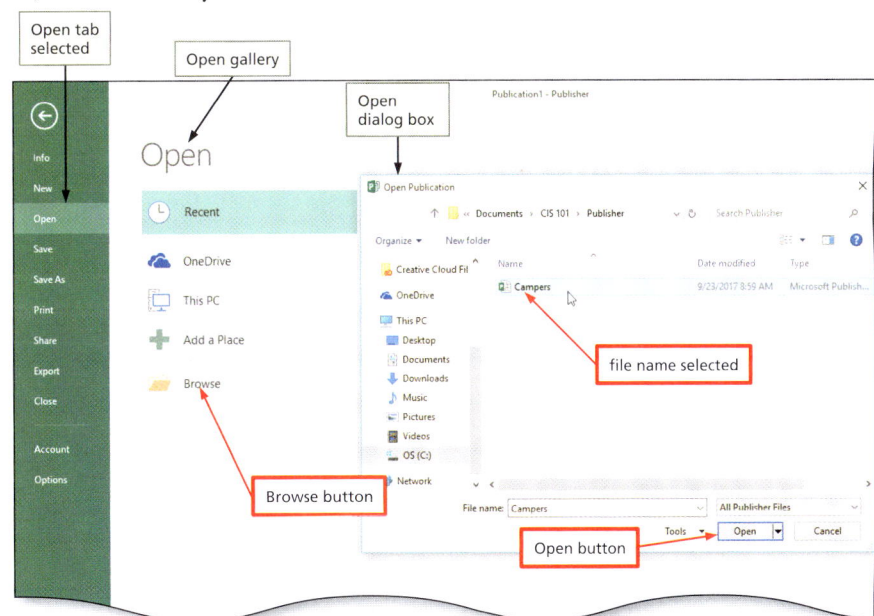

Figure 73

- Click the Open button (Open dialog box) to open the file. If necessary, click the Enable Content button.

Q&A   Why did a Security Warning appear?

The Security Warning appears when you open an Office file that might contain harmful content. The files you create in this module are not harmful, but you should be cautious when opening files from other people.

Other Ways

1. Press CTRL+O	2. Navigate to file in File Explorer window, double-click file name

To Create a New Publication from the Backstage View

You can open multiple publications in an Office program, such as Publisher, so that you can work on the publications at the same time. The following steps create a file, a blank publication in this case, from the Backstage view. *Why? You want to create a new publication while keeping the current publication open.*

- Click File on the ribbon to open the Backstage view.

- Click the New tab in the Backstage view to display the New gallery (Figure 74).

Q&A

Can I create publications through the Backstage view in other Office apps?
Yes. If the Office app has a New tab in the Backstage view, the New gallery displays various options for creating a new file.

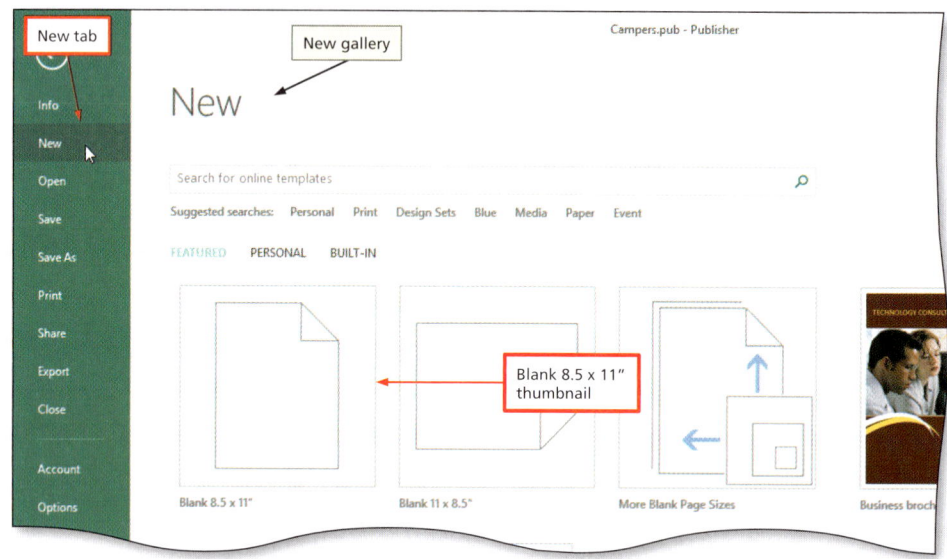

Figure 74

- Click the Blank 8.5 × 11" thumbnail in the New gallery to create a new publication (Figure 75).

Q&A

Why does the title bar now say Publication2?
While Publisher is running, it assigns new files a numbered and temporary file name on the title bar so that you can differentiate among publications. Because the Campers file is open already, this new file becomes the second publication, or Publication2.

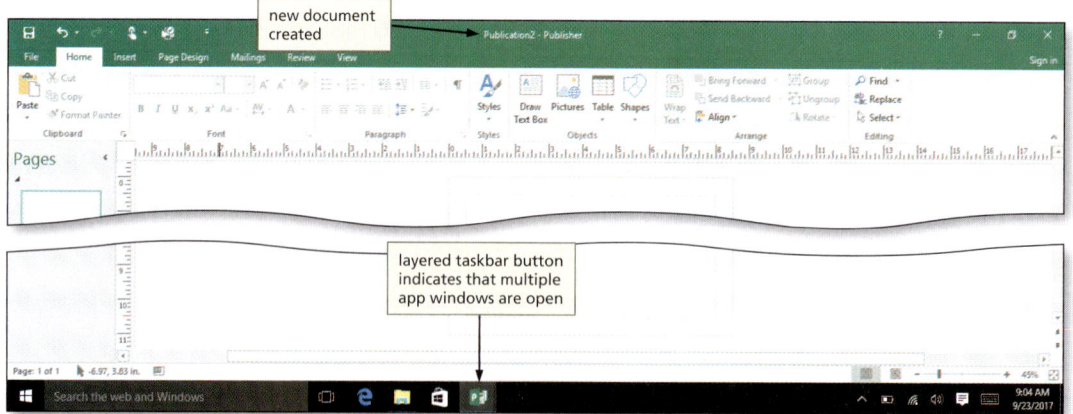

Figure 75

Other Ways

1. Press CTRL+N

To Enter Text in a Publication

The next publication identifies camping rates. The following step enters the first line of text in the new publication.

1 Press the F9 key to zoom to 100%.

2 Type `List of Camping Rates` and then press the ENTER key (Figure 76).

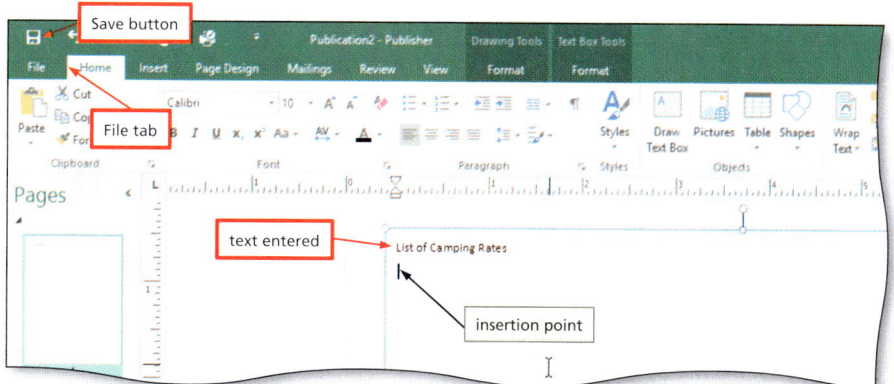

Figure 76

To Save a File in a Folder

The following steps save the second publication in the Publisher folder in the class folder (CIS 101, in this case) in the Documents folder using the file name, Camping Rates.

1 Click the Save button on the Quick Access Toolbar, which depending on settings, will display either the Save As gallery in the Backstage view or the Save As dialog box.

2 If your screen displays the Backstage view, click This PC, if necessary, to display options in the right pane related to saving on your computer; if your screen already displays the Save As dialog box, proceed to Step 4.

3 Click the Browse button in the left pane to display the Save As dialog box.

4 If necessary, type `Camping Rates` in the File name box (Save As dialog box) to change the file name. Do not press the ENTER key after typing the file name because you do not want to close the dialog box at this time.

5 If necessary, navigate to the desired save location (in this case, the Publisher folder in the CIS 101 folder [or your class folder] in the Documents folder). For specific instructions, perform the tasks in Steps 4a and 4b in the previous section in this module titled To Save a File in a Folder.

6 Click the Save button (Save As dialog box) to save the publication in the selected folder on the selected drive with the entered file name.

To Close a File Using the Backstage View

1 SIGN IN | 2 USE WINDOWS | 3 USE APPS | 4 FILE MANAGEMENT | 5 SWITCH APPS | 6 SAVE FILES
7 CHANGE SCREEN RESOLUTION | 8 EXIT APPS | 9 USE ADDITIONAL APP FEATURES | 10 USE HELP

Sometimes, you may want to close an Office file, such as a Publisher publication, entirely and start over with a new file. You also may want to close a file when you are done working with it. *Why? You should close a file when you are done working with it so that you do not make inadvertent changes to it.* The following steps close the current active Publisher file, that is, the Camping Rates publication, without exiting Publisher.

- Click File on the ribbon to open the Backstage view (Figure 77).

- Click Close in the Backstage view to close the open file (Camping Rates, in this case) without exiting the active app (Publisher).

Q&A
What if Publisher displays a dialog box about saving?
Click the Save button if you want to save the changes, click the Don't Save button if you want to ignore the changes since the last time you saved, and click the Cancel button if you do not want to close the publication.

Can I use the Backstage view to close an open file in other Office apps, such as PowerPoint and Excel?
Yes.

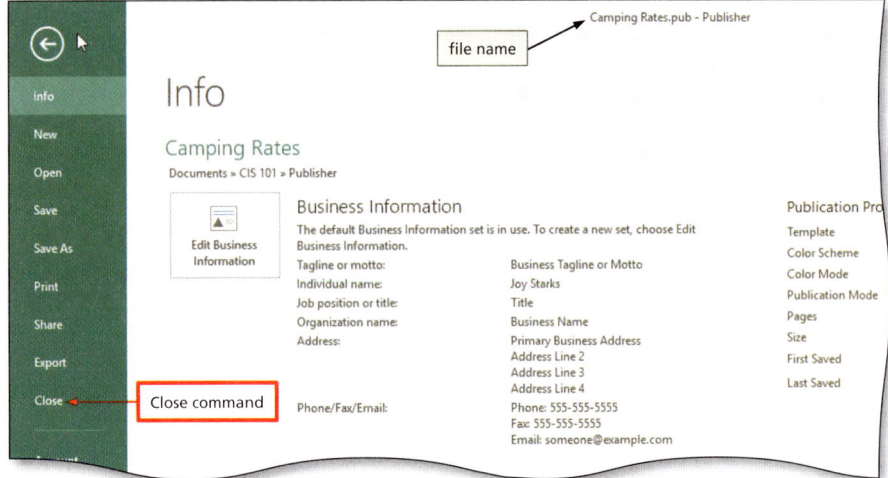

Figure 77

Other Ways

1. Press CTRL+F4

To Open a Recent File Using the Backstage View

You sometimes need to open a file that you recently modified. *Why? You may have more changes to make, such as adding more content or correcting errors.* The Backstage view allows you to access recent files easily. The following steps reopen the Camping Rates file just closed.

- Click File on the ribbon to open the Backstage view.
- Click the Open tab in the Backstage view to display the Open gallery (Figure 78).

- Click the desired file name in the Recent list, Camping Rates in this case, to open the file.

Q&A
Can I use the Backstage view to open a recent file in other Office apps, such as PowerPoint and Excel?
Yes, as long as the file name appears in the list of recent files.

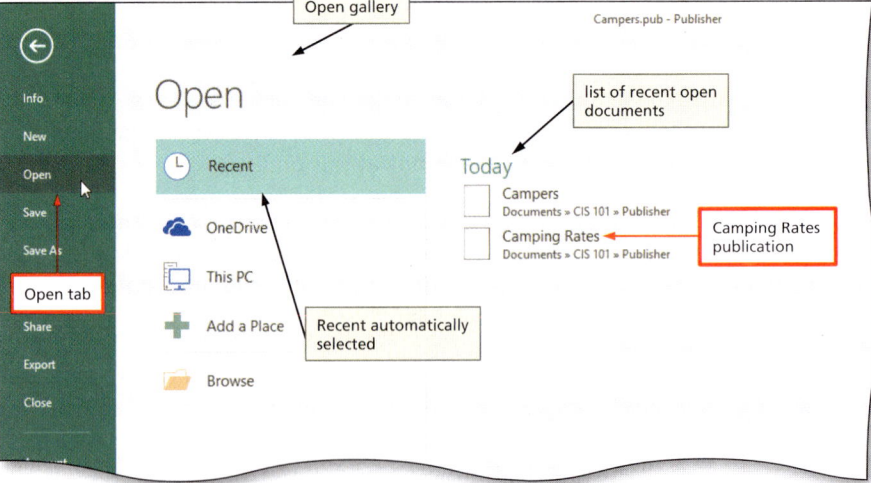

Figure 78

Other Ways

1. Click File on ribbon, click Open in Backstage view, click Browse button, navigate to file (Open dialog box), click Open button

To Create a New Blank Publication from File Explorer

1 SIGN IN | 2 USE WINDOWS | 3 USE APPS | 4 FILE MANAGEMENT | 5 SWITCH APPS | 6 SAVE FILES
7 CHANGE SCREEN RESOLUTION | 8 EXIT APPS | 9 USE ADDITIONAL APP FEATURES | 10 USE HELP

File Explorer provides a means to create a blank Office publication without running an Office app. The following steps use File Explorer to create a blank Publisher publication. *Why? Sometimes you might need to create a blank publication and then return to it later for editing.*

1

- Click the File Explorer button on the taskbar to make the folder window the active window.

- If necessary, double-click the Documents folder in the navigation pane to expand the Documents folder.

- If necessary, double-click your class folder (CIS 101, in this case) in the navigation pane to expand the folder.

- Click the Publisher folder in the navigation pane to display its contents in the file list.

- With the Publisher folder selected, right-click an open area in the file list to display a shortcut menu.

- Point to New on the shortcut menu to display the New submenu (Figure 79).

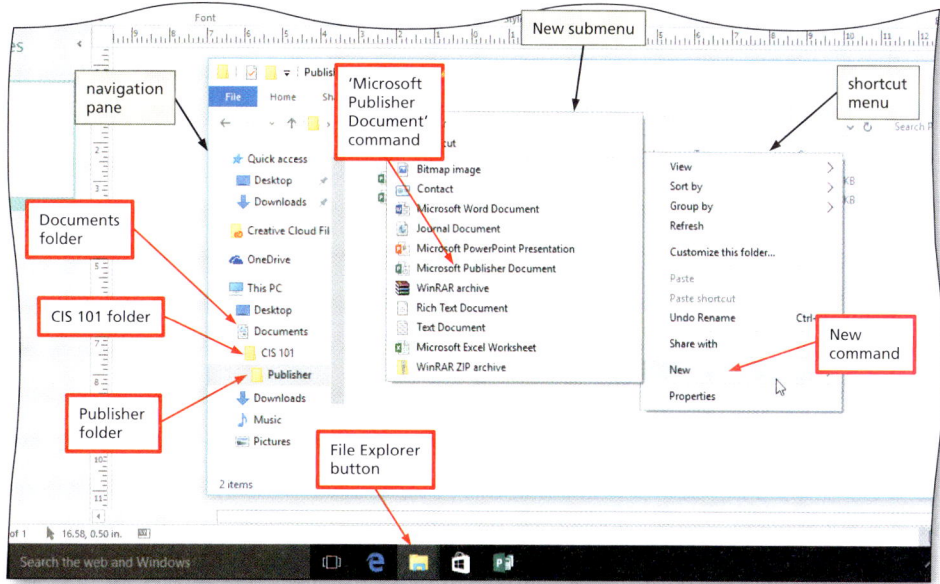

Figure 79

2

- Click 'Microsoft Publisher Document' on the New submenu to display an icon and text box for a new file in the current folder window with the file name, New Microsoft Publisher Document, selected (Figure 80).

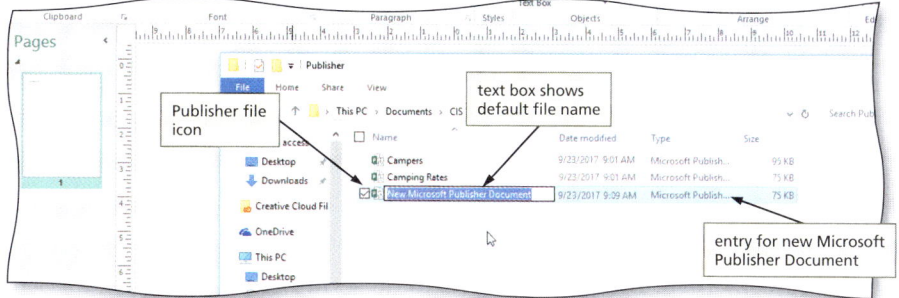

Figure 80

3

- Type `Recommended Campgrounds` in the text box and then press the ENTER key to assign a new file name to the new file in the current folder (Figure 81).

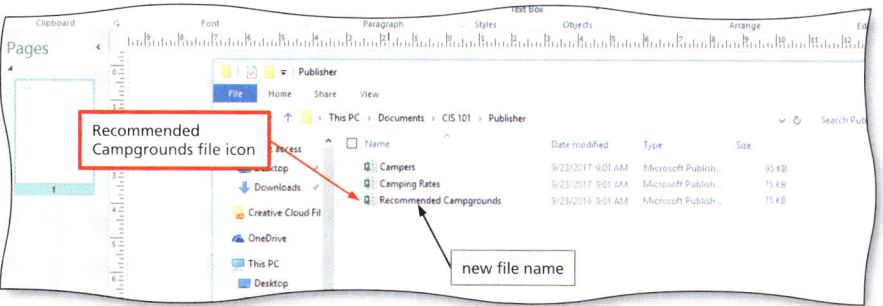

Figure 81

To Run an App from File Explorer and Open a File

Previously in this module, you learned how to run Publisher using the Start menu and the search box. The following steps, which assume Windows is running, use File Explorer to run Publisher based on a typical installation. ***Why?*** *Another way to run an Office app is to open an existing file from File Explorer, which causes the app in which the file was created to run and then open the selected file.* You may need to ask your instructor how to run Publisher for your computer.

- If necessary, display the file to open in the folder window in File Explorer (shown in Figure 81).

- Right-click the file icon or file name you want to open (Recommended Campgrounds, in this case) to display a shortcut menu (Figure 82).

- Click Open on the shortcut menu to open the selected file in the app used to create the file, Publisher in this case (shown in Figure 83).

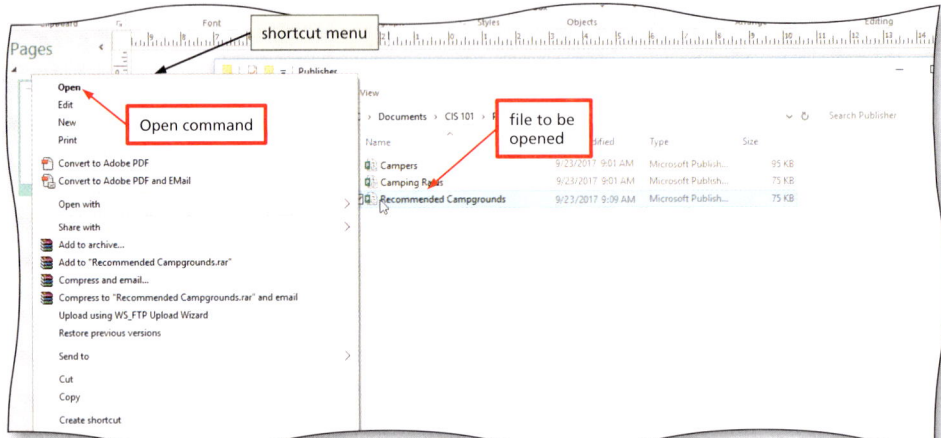

Figure 82

- If the window is not maximized, click the Maximize button on the title bar to maximize the window.

Other Ways
1. Double-click file name in file list

To Enter Text in a Publication

The next step is to enter text in the blank Publisher publication. The following step enters a line of text.

1 Zoom to 100%.

2 Type `List of Recommended Campgrounds` and then press the ENTER key (shown in Figure 83).

To Save an Existing Office File with the Same File Name

Saving frequently cannot be overemphasized. ***Why?*** *You have made modifications to the file (publication) since you created it. Thus, you should save again. Similarly, you should continue saving files frequently so that you do not lose the changes you have made since the time you last saved the file.* You can use the same file name, such as Recommended Campgrounds, to save the changes made to the publication. The following step saves a file again with the same file name.

- Click the Save button on the Quick Access Toolbar to overwrite the previously saved file (Recommended Campgrounds, in this case) in the Publisher folder (Figure 83).

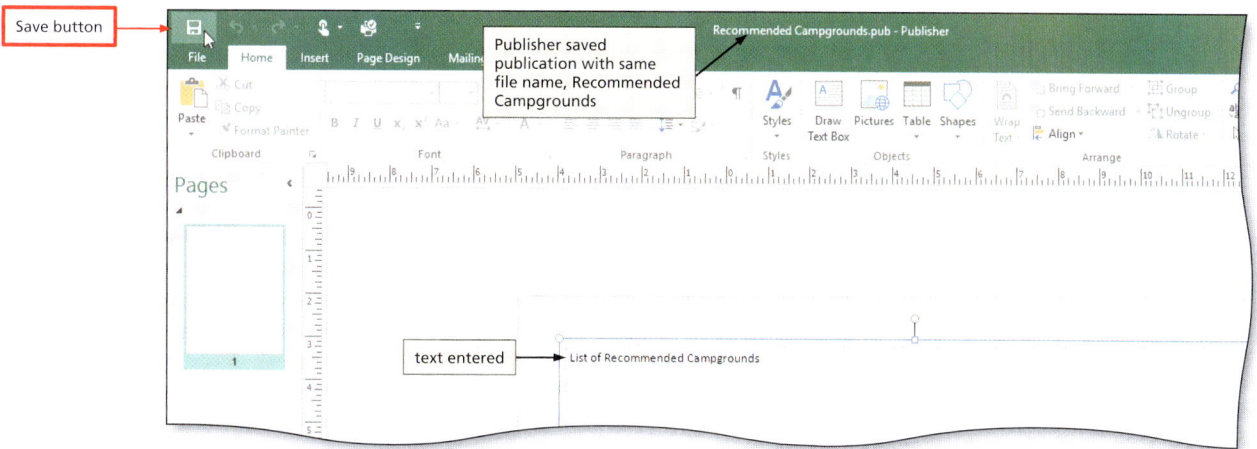

Figure 83

Other Ways

1. Press CTRL+S   2. Press SHIFT+F12

To Save a File with a New File Name

You might want to save a file with a different file name or to a different location. For example, you might start a homework assignment with a data file and then save it with a final file name for submission to your instructor, saving it to a location designated by your instructor. The following steps save a file with a different file name.

1 Click the File tab to open the Backstage view.

2 Click the Save As tab to display the Save As gallery.

3 If necessary, click This PC to display options in the right pane related to saving on your computer.

4 Click the Browse button in the left pane to display the Save As dialog box.

5 Type `Campgrounds` in the File name box (Save As dialog box) to change the file name. Do not press the ENTER key after typing the file name because you do not want to close the dialog box at this time.

6 If necessary, navigate to the desired save location (in this case, the Publisher folder in the CIS 101 folder [or your class folder] in the Documents folder). For specific instructions, perform the tasks in Steps 4a and 4b in the previous section titled To Save a File in a Folder.

7 Click the Save button (Save As dialog box) to save the publication in the selected folder on the selected drive with the entered file name.

To Exit an Office App

You are finished using Publisher. The following steps exit Publisher.

1 Because you have multiple Publisher publications open, right-click the Publisher app button on the taskbar and then click 'Close all windows' on the shortcut menu to close all open publications and exit Publisher.

2 If a dialog box appears, click the Save button to save any changes made to the file since the last save.

Renaming, Moving, and Deleting Files

Earlier in this module, you learned how to organize files in folders, which is part of a process known as **file management**. The following sections cover additional file management topics including renaming, moving, and deleting files.

1 SIGN IN | 2 USE WINDOWS | 3 USE APPS | **4 FILE MANAGEMENT** | 5 SWITCH APPS | 6 SAVE FILES
7 CHANGE SCREEN RESOLUTION | 8 EXIT APPS | 9 USE ADDITIONAL APP FEATURES | **10 USE HELP**

To Rename a File

In some circumstances, you may want to change the name of, or rename, a file or a folder. *Why? You may want to distinguish a file in one folder or drive from a copy of a similar file, or you may decide to rename a file to better identify its contents.* The following steps change the name of the Campers file in the Publisher folder to Campers Flyer.

- If necessary, click the File Explorer button on the taskbar to make the folder window the active window.

- Navigate to the location of the file to be renamed (in this case, the Publisher folder in the CIS 101 [or your class folder] folder in the Documents folder) to display the file(s) it contains in the file list.

- Click the file to be renamed, the Campers icon or file name in the file list in this case, to select it.

- Right-click the selected file to display a shortcut menu that presents a list of commands related to files (Figure 84).

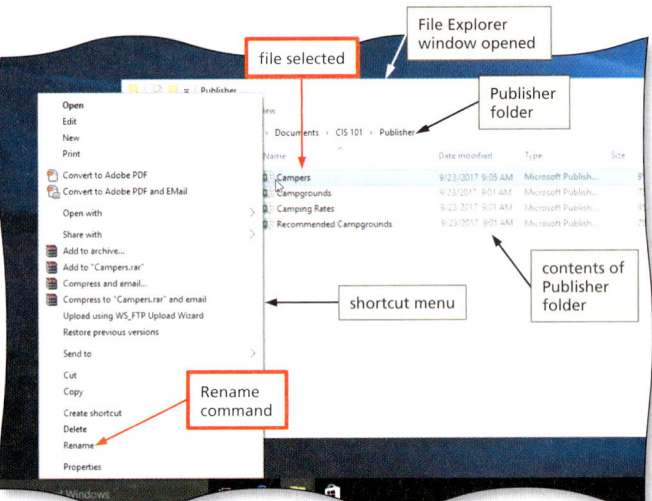

Figure 84

- Click Rename on the shortcut menu to place the current file name in a text box.

- Type `Campers Flyer` in the text box and then press the ENTER key (Figure 85).

Q&A

Are any risks involved in renaming files that are located on a hard drive?
If you inadvertently rename a file that is associated with certain apps, the apps may not be able to find the file and, therefore, may not run properly. Always use caution when renaming files.

Can I rename a file when it is open?
No, a file must be closed to change the file name.

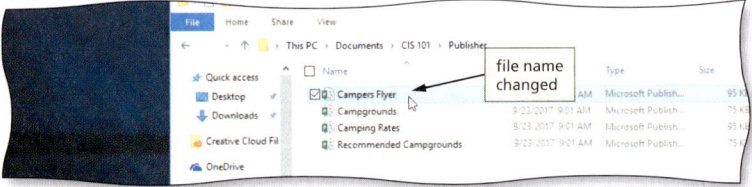

Figure 85

Other Ways

1. Select file, press F2, type new file name, press ENTER

2. Select file, click Rename button (Home tab | Organize group), type new file name, press ENTER

1 SIGN IN | 2 USE WINDOWS | 3 USE APPS | **4 FILE MANAGEMENT** | 5 SWITCH APPS | 6 SAVE FILES
7 CHANGE SCREEN RESOLUTION | 8 EXIT APPS | 9 USE ADDITIONAL APP FEATURES | **10 USE HELP**

To Move a File

Why? At some time, you may want to move a file from one folder, called the source folder, to another, called the destination folder. When you move a file, it no longer appears in the original folder. If the destination and the source folders are on the same media, you can move a file by dragging it. If the folders are on different media, you will need to right-drag the file and then click Move here on the shortcut menu. The following step moves the Recommended Campgrounds file from the Publisher folder to the CIS 101 folder.

- If necessary, in File Explorer, navigate to the location of the file to be moved (in this case, the Publisher folder in the CIS 101 folder [or your class folder] in the Documents folder).

- If necessary, click the Publisher folder in the navigation pane to display the files it contains in the right pane.

- Drag the file to be moved, the Recommended Campgrounds file in the right pane in this case, to the CIS 101 folder in the navigation pane (Figure 86).

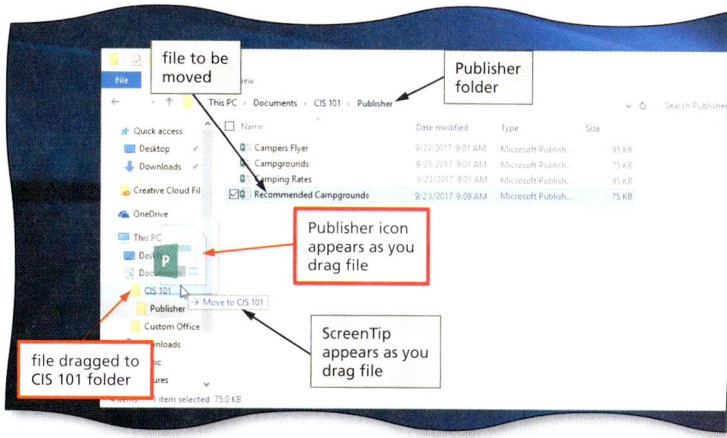

Figure 86

 **Experiment**

- Click the CIS 101 folder in the navigation pane to verify that the file was moved.

Other Ways

1. Right-click file to move, click Cut on shortcut menu, right-click destination folder, click Paste on shortcut menu

2. Select file to move, press CTRL+X, select destination folder, press CTRL+V

To Delete a File

1 SIGN IN | 2 USE WINDOWS | 3 USE APPS | 4 FILE MANAGEMENT | 5 SWITCH APPS | 6 SAVE FILES
7 CHANGE SCREEN RESOLUTION | 8 EXIT APPS | 9 USE ADDITIONAL APP FEATURES | 10 USE HELP

A final task you may want to perform is to delete a file. Exercise extreme caution when deleting a file or files. When you delete a file from a hard drive, the deleted file is stored in the Recycle Bin where you can recover it until you empty the Recycle Bin. If you delete a file from removable media, such as a USB flash drive, the file is deleted permanently. The next steps delete the Recommended Campgrounds file from the CIS 101 folder. *Why? When a file no longer is needed, you can delete it to conserve space on your storage location.*

- If necessary, in File Explorer, navigate to the location of the file to be deleted (in this case, the CIS 101 folder [or your class folder] in the Documents folder).

- Click the file to be deleted, the Recommended Campgrounds icon or file name in the right pane in this case, to select the file.

- Right-click the selected file to display a shortcut menu (Figure 87).

- Click Delete on the shortcut menu to delete the file.

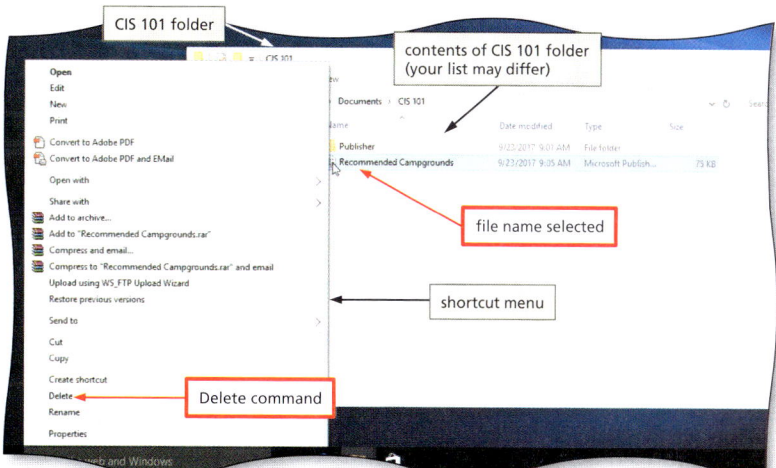

Figure 87

- If a dialog box appears, click the Yes button to delete the file.

Q&A Can I use this same technique to delete a folder?

Yes. Right-click the folder and then click Delete on the shortcut menu. When you delete a folder, all of the files and folders contained in the folder you are deleting, together with any files and folders on lower hierarchical levels, are deleted as well. For example, if you delete the CIS 101 folder, you will delete all folders and files inside the CIS 101 folder.

Other Ways

1. Select file, press DELETE

Microsoft Office and Windows Help

At any time while you are using one of the Office apps, such as Publisher, you can use Office Help to display information about all topics associated with the app. Help in other Office apps operates in a similar fashion.

In Office, Help is presented in a window that has browser-style navigation buttons. Each Office app has its own Help home page, which is the starting Help page that is displayed in the Help window. If your computer is connected to the Internet, the contents of the Help page reflect both the local help files installed on the computer and material from Microsoft's website.

To Open the Help Window in an Office App

1 SIGN IN | 2 USE WINDOWS | 3 USE APPS | 4 FILE MANAGEMENT | 5 SWITCH APPS | 6 SAVE FILES
7 CHANGE SCREEN RESOLUTION | 8 EXIT APPS | 9 USE ADDITIONAL APP FEATURES | 10 USE HELP

The following step opens the Publisher 2016 Help window. *Why? You might not understand how certain commands or operations work in Publisher, so you can obtain the necessary information using help.*

- Run Publisher.

- Click the Blank 8.5 x 11" thumbnail to display a blank publication.

- Press F1 to open the Publisher 2016 Help window (Figure 88).

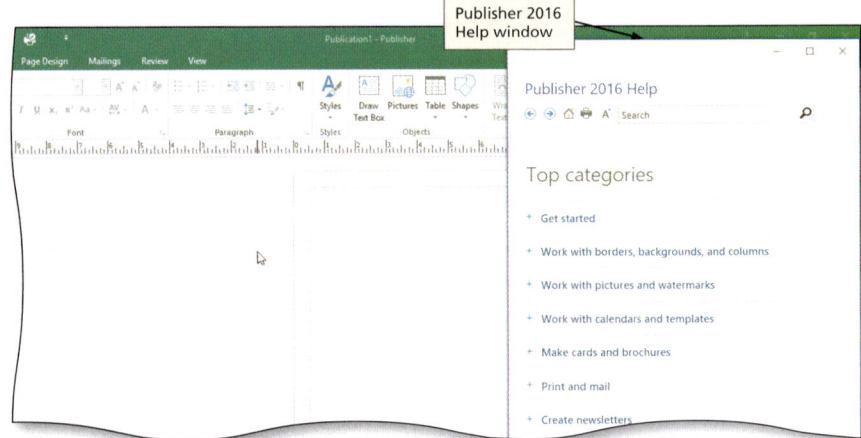

Figure 88

Moving and Resizing Windows

At times, it is useful, or even necessary, to have more than one window open and visible on the screen at the same time. You can resize and move these open windows so that you can view different areas of and elements in the window. In the case of the Publisher 2016 Help window, for example, it could be covering publication text in the Publisher window that you need to see.

To Move a Window by Dragging

1 SIGN IN | 2 USE WINDOWS | 3 USE APPS | 4 FILE MANAGEMENT | 5 SWITCH APPS | 6 SAVE FILES
7 CHANGE SCREEN RESOLUTION | 8 EXIT APPS | 9 USE ADDITIONAL APP FEATURES | 10 USE HELP

You can move any open window that is not maximized to another location on the desktop by dragging the title bar of the window. *Why? You might want to have a better view of what is behind the window or just want to move the window so that you can see it better.* The following step drags the Publisher 2016 Help window to the upper-left corner of the desktop.

- Drag the window title bar (the Publisher 2016 Help window title bar, in this case) so that the window moves to the upper-left corner of the desktop, as shown in Figure 89.

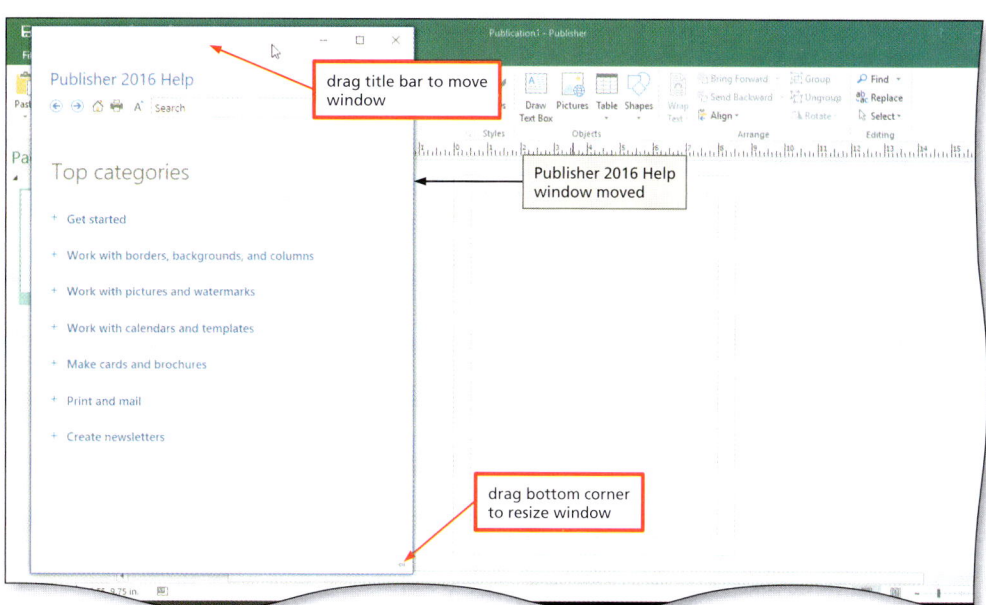

Figure 89

To Resize a Window by Dragging

1 SIGN IN | **2 USE WINDOWS** | 3 USE APPS | 4 FILE MANAGEMENT | 5 SWITCH APPS | 6 SAVE FILES
7 CHANGE SCREEN RESOLUTION | 8 EXIT APPS | 9 USE ADDITIONAL APP FEATURES | 10 USE HELP

A method used to change the size of the window is to drag the window borders. The following step changes the size of the Publisher 2016 Help window by dragging its borders. *Why? Sometimes, information is not visible completely in a window, and you want to increase the size of the window.*

- Point to the lower-right corner of the window (the Publisher 2016 Help window, in this case) until the pointer changes to a two-headed arrow.

- Drag the bottom border as necessary to display more of the active window (Figure 90).

Q&A

Can I drag other borders on the window to enlarge or shrink the window?
Yes, you can drag the left, right, and top borders and any window corner to resize a window.

Will Windows remember the new size of the window after I close it?
Yes. When you reopen the window, Windows will display it at the same size it was when you closed it.

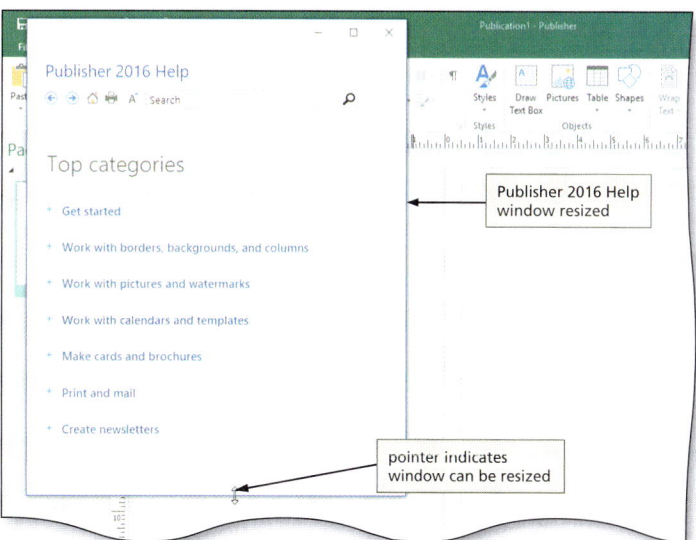

Figure 90

Using Office Help

Once an Office app's Help window is open, several methods exist for navigating Help. You can search for help by using any of the three following methods from the Help window:

1. Enter search text in the Search text box.

2. Click the links in the Help window.

3. Use the Table of Contents.

To Obtain Help Using the Search Text Box

Assume for the following example that you want to know more about fonts. The following steps use the 'Search online help' text box to obtain useful information about fonts by entering the word, fonts, as search text. *Why? You may not know the exact help topic you are looking to find, so using keywords can help narrow your search.*

- Type **fonts** in the Search text box at the top of the Publisher 2016 Help window to enter the search text.

- Press the ENTER key to display the search results (Figure 91).

Q&A

Why do my search results differ?
If you do not have an Internet connection, your results will reflect only the content of the Help files on your computer. When searching for help online, results also can change as content is added, deleted, and updated on the online Help webpages maintained by Microsoft.

Why were my search results not very helpful?
When initiating a search, be sure to check the spelling of the search text; also, keep your search specific to return the most accurate results.

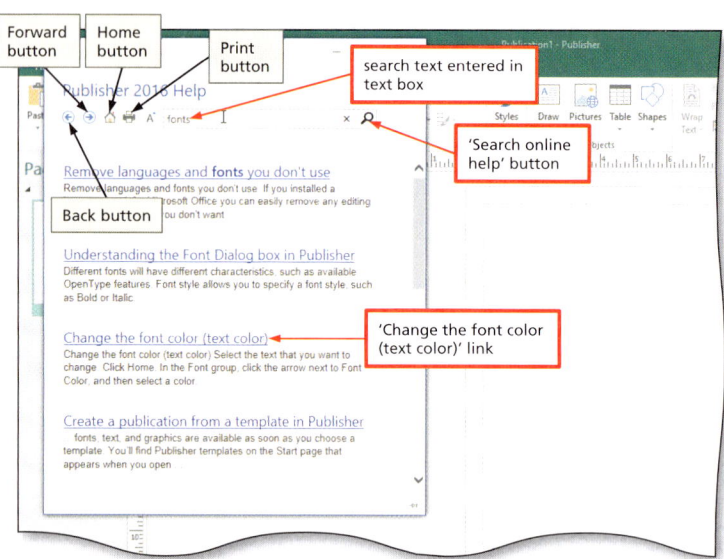

Figure 91

- Click the 'Change the font color (text color)', or a similar, link to display the Help information associated with the selected topic (Figure 92).

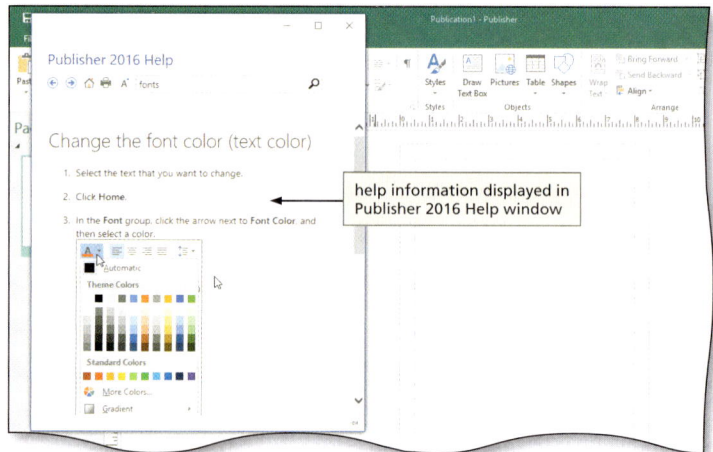

Figure 92

- Click the Home button in the Publisher 2016 Help window to clear the search results and redisplay the Help home page (Figure 93).

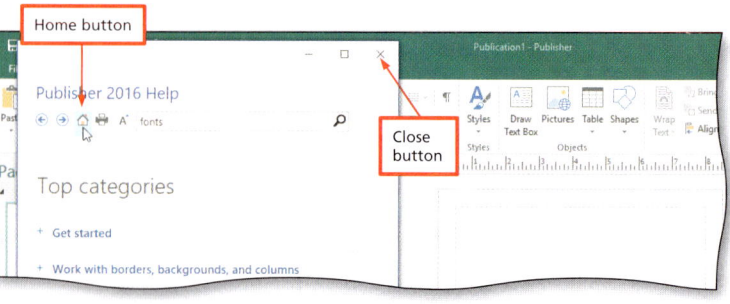

- Click the Close button in the Publisher 2016 Help window to close the window.

- Exit Microsoft Publisher.

Figure 93

Obtaining Help while Working in an Office App

Help in the Office apps, such as Publisher, provides you with the ability to obtain help directly, without opening the Help window and initiating a search. For example, you may be unsure about how a particular command works, or you may be presented with a dialog box that you are not sure how to use.

Figure 94 shows one option for obtaining help while working in an Office app. If you want to learn more about a command, point to its button and wait for the ScreenTip to appear. If the Help icon and 'Tell me more' link appear in the ScreenTip, click the 'Tell me more' link or press the F1 key while pointing to the button to open the Help window associated with that command.

Figure 95 shows a dialog box that contains a Help button. Clicking the Help button or pressing the F1 key while the dialog box is displayed opens a Help window. The Help window contains help about that dialog box, if available. If no help file is available for that particular dialog box, then the main Help window opens.

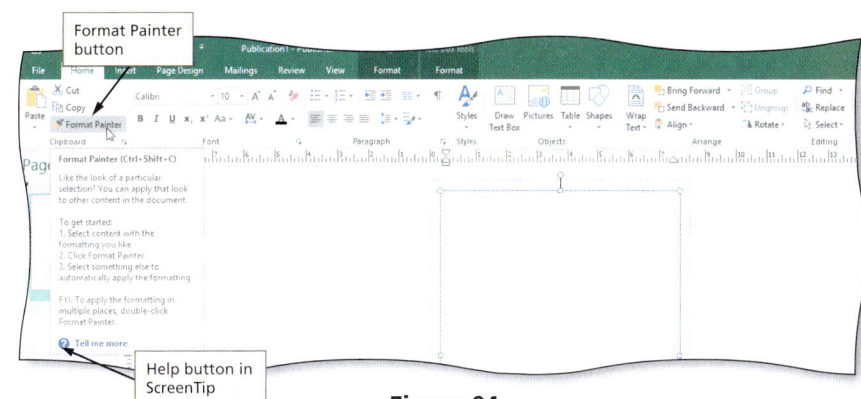

Figure 94

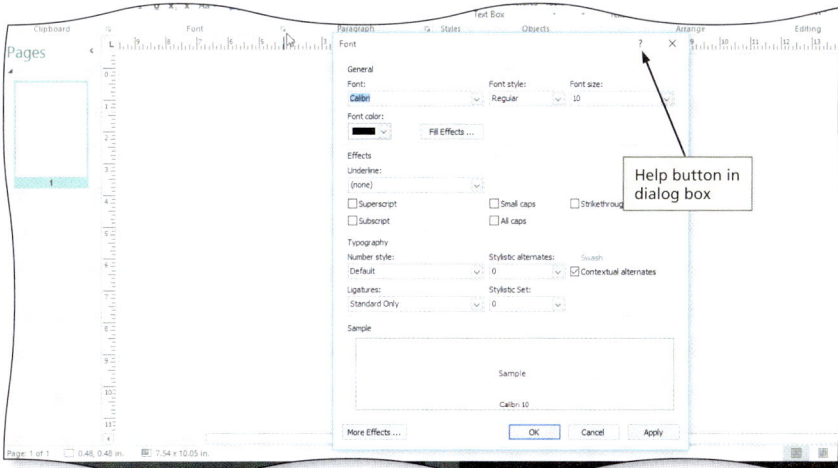

Figure 95

Using the Windows Search Box

One of the more powerful Windows features is the Windows search box. The search box is a central location from where you can type search text and quickly access related Windows commands or web search results. In addition, **Cortana** is a new search tool in Windows that you can access using the search box. It can act as a personal assistant by performing functions such as providing ideas; searching for apps, files, and folders; and setting reminders. In addition to typing search text in the search box, you also can use your computer or mobile device's microphone to give verbal commands.

To Use the Windows Search Box

1 SIGN IN | 2 USE WINDOWS | 3 USE APPS | 4 FILE MANAGEMENT | 5 SWITCH APPS | 6 SAVE FILES
7 CHANGE SCREEN RESOLUTION | 8 EXIT APPS | 9 USE ADDITIONAL APP FEATURES | 10 USE HELP

The following step uses the Windows search box to search for a Windows command. *Why? Using the search box to locate apps, settings, folders, and files can be faster than navigating windows and dialog boxes to search for the desired content.*

1

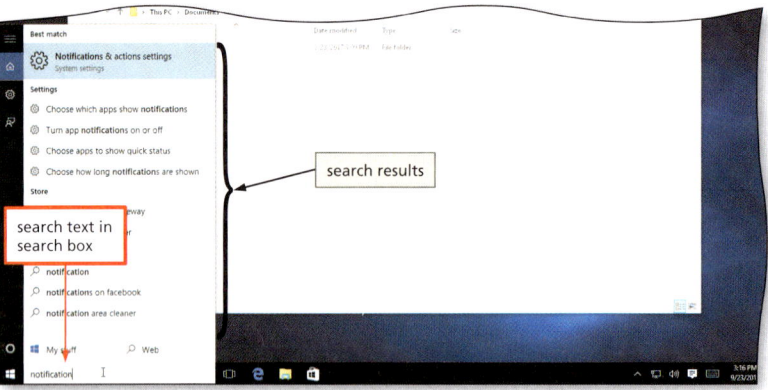

- Type `notification` in the search box to display the search results. The search results include related Windows settings, Windows Store apps, and web search results (Figure 96).

- Click an empty area of the desktop to close the search results.

Figure 96

Summary

In this module, you learned how to use the Windows interface, several touch screen and mouse operations, and file and folder management. You also learned some basic features of Publisher and discovered the common elements that exist among Microsoft Office apps. Topics covered included signing in, using Windows, using apps, file management, switching between apps, saving files, changing screen resolution, exiting apps, using additional app features, and using Help.

What guidelines should you follow to plan your projects?

The process of communicating specific information is a learned, rational skill. Computers and software, especially Microsoft Office 2016, can help you develop ideas and present detailed information to a particular audience and minimize much of the laborious work of drafting and revising projects. No matter what method you use to plan a project, it is beneficial to follow some specific guidelines from the onset to arrive at a final product that is informative, relevant, and effective. Use some aspects of these guidelines every time you undertake a project, and others as needed in specific instances.

1. Determine the project's purpose.
    a) Clearly define why you are undertaking this assignment.
    b) Begin to draft ideas of how best to communicate information by handwriting ideas on paper; composing directly on a laptop, tablet, or mobile device; or developing a strategy that fits your particular thinking and writing style.

2. Analyze your audience.
    a) Learn about the people who will read, analyze, or view your work.
    b) Determine their interests and needs so that you can present the information they need to know and omit the information they already possess.
    c) Form a mental picture of these people or find photos of people who fit this profile so that you can develop a project with the audience in mind.

3. Gather possible content.
    a) Locate existing information that may reside in spreadsheets, databases, or other files.
    b) Conduct a web search to find relevant websites.
    c) Read pamphlets, magazine and newspaper articles, and books to gain insights of how others have approached your topic.
    d) Conduct personal interviews to obtain perspectives not available by any other means.
    e) Consider video and audio clips as potential sources for material that might complement or support the factual data you uncover.

4. Determine what content to present to your audience.
    a) Write three or four major ideas you want an audience member to remember after reading or viewing your project.
    b) Envision your project's endpoint, the key fact you wish to emphasize, so that all project elements lead to this final element.
    c) Determine relevant time factors, such as the length of time to develop the project, how long readers will spend reviewing your project, or the amount of time allocated for your speaking engagement.
    d) Decide whether a graph, photo, or artistic element can express or enhance a particular concept.
    e) Be mindful of the order in which you plan to present the content, and place the most important material at the top or bottom of the page, because readers and audience members generally remember the first and last pieces of information they see and hear.

How should you submit solutions to questions in the assignments identified with a ✳ symbol?

Every assignment in this book contains one or more questions with a ✳ symbol. These questions require you to think beyond the assigned file. Present your solutions to the question in the format required by your instructor. Possible formats may include one or more of these options: write the answer; create a publication that contains the answer; present your answer to the class; discuss your answer in a group; record the answer as audio or video using a webcam, smartphone, or portable media player; or post answers on a blog, wiki, or website.

Apply Your Knowledge

Reinforce the skills and apply the concepts you learned in this module.

Creating a Folder and a Publication

Instructions: You will create a Publisher Assignments folder and then create a publication and save it in the folder.

Perform the following tasks:

1. Open the File Explorer window and then double-click to open the Documents folder.

2. Click the New folder button on the Quick Access Toolbar to display a new folder icon and text box for the folder name.

3. Type **Publisher Assignments** in the text box to name the folder. Press the ENTER key to create the folder in the Documents folder.

4. Run Publisher and create a new blank publication.

5. Press the F9 key to zoom to 100%.

6. Type **Contact Information** and then press then ENTER key to enter a line of text (Figure 97).

7. If requested by your instructor, enter your name, phone number, and email address in the Publisher publication.

8. Click the Save button on the Quick Access Toolbar. Navigate to the Publisher Assignments folder in the Documents folder and then save the publication using the file name, Apply 1 Publication.

9. If your Quick Access Toolbar does not show the Quick Print button, add the Quick Print button to the Quick Access Toolbar. Print the publication using the Quick Print button on the Quick Access Toolbar. When you are finished printing, remove the Quick Print button from the Quick Access Toolbar.

10. Submit the printout to your instructor.

11. Exit Publisher.

12. ✳ What other commands might you find useful to include on the Quick Access Toolbar?

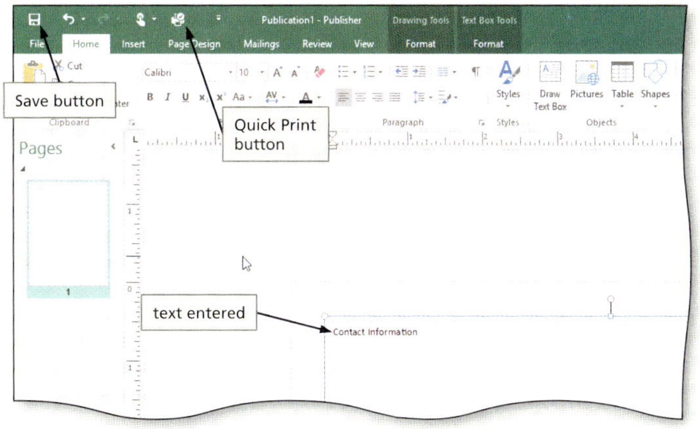

Figure 97

Extend Your Knowledge

Extend the skills you learned in this module and experiment with new skills. You will use Help to complete the assignment.

Using Help

Instructions: Use Publisher 2016 Help to perform the following tasks.

Perform the following tasks:

1. Run Publisher.
2. Press the F1 key to open the Publisher 2016 Help window (shown in Figure 88).
3. Search Publisher 2016 Help to answer the following questions.
   a. What are three new features of Publisher 2016?
   b. What type of training is available through Publisher 2016 Help?
   c. What are the steps to customize the ribbon?
   d. What is the purpose of the Office Clipboard?
   e. How do you cascade Publisher windows?
   f. Why would you use mail merge?
   g. How do you insert pictures?
   h. How do you change the size of text?
   i. What are the steps to zoom in and out of a publication?
   j. What is the purpose of the Design Checker pane? How do you display it?
4. Type the answers from your searches in a new blank Publisher publication. Save the publication with a new file name and then submit it in the format specified by your instructor.
5. If requested by your instructor, enter your name in the Publisher publication.
6. Exit Publisher.
7. ✴ What search text did you use to perform the searches above? Did it take multiple attempts to search and locate the exact information for which you were searching?

Expand Your World

Create a solution that uses cloud or web technologies by learning and investigating on your own from general guidance.

Creating Folders on OneDrive and Using the Publisher Online App

Instructions: You will create the folders shown in Figure 98 on OneDrive. Then, you will use the Publisher Online app to create a small file and save it in a folder on OneDrive.

Perform the following tasks:

1. Sign in to OneDrive in your browser.
2. Use the New button to create the folder structure shown in Figure 98.
3. In the Upcoming Events folder, use the New button to create a Publisher publication with the file name, Extend 1 Task List, that contains the text, Prepare agenda for Tuesday's meeting.

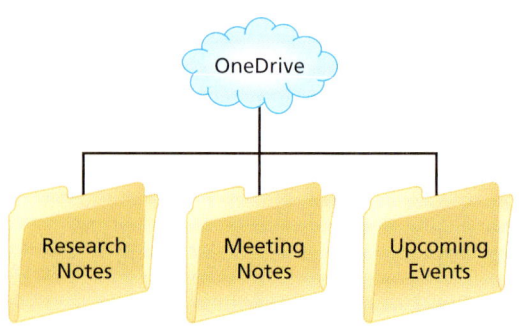

Figure 98

4. If requested by your instructor, add your name to the publication.

5. Save the publication in the Upcoming Events folder.

6. Submit the assignment in the format specified by your instructor.

7. ✴ Based on your current knowledge of OneDrive, do you think you will use it? What about the Publisher Online app?

In the Labs

Design, create, modify, and/or use files following the guidelines, concepts, and skills presented in this module. Labs 1 and 2, which increase in difficulty, require you to create solutions based on what you learned in the module; Lab 3 requires you to apply your creative thinking and problem-solving skills to design and implement a solution.

Lab 1: **Creating Folders for a Bookstore**

Problem: Your friend works for a local bookstore. He would like to organize his files in relation to the types of books available in the store. He has seven main categories: fiction, biography, children, humor, social science, nonfiction, and medical. You are to create a folder structure similar to Figure 99.

Perform the following tasks:

1. Click the File Explorer button on the taskbar and display the contents of the Documents folder.

2. In the Documents folder, create the main folder and name it Book Categories.

3. Navigate to the Book Categories folder.

4. Within the Book Categories folder, create a folder for each of the following: Fiction, Biography, Children, Humor, Social Science, Nonfiction, and Medical.

5. Within the Fiction folder, create two additional folders: Science Fiction and Western.

6. If requested by your instructor, add another folder using your last name as the folder name.

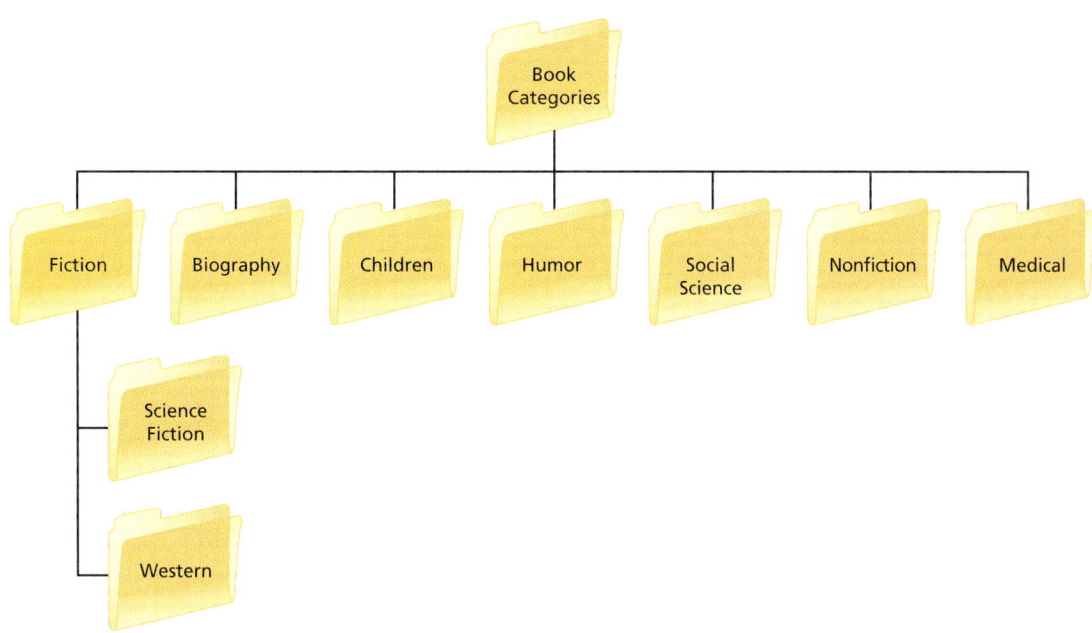

Figure 99

Continued >

In the Labs *continued*

7. Submit the assignment in the format specified by your instructor.

8. ✳ Think about how you use your computer for various tasks (personal, professional, and academic). What folders might be required on your computer to store the files you save?

Lab 2: **Creating Publisher Publications and Saving Them in Appropriate Folders**

Problem: You are taking a class that requires you to complete three Publisher modules. You will save the work completed in each module in a different folder (Figure 100).

Perform the following tasks:

1. Create the folders shown in Figure 100.

2. Create a Publisher publication containing the text, Module 1 Notes.

3. In the Backstage view, click Save As and then click This PC.

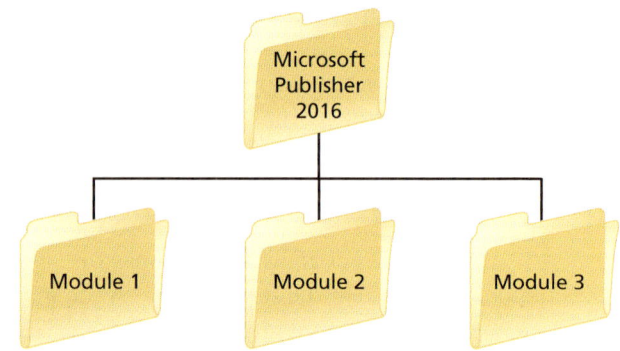

Figure 100

4. Click the Browse button to display the Save As dialog box. Click Documents to open the Documents folder. Navigate to the Module 1 folder and then save the file in the Publisher folder using the file name, Lab 2 Module 1 Notes.

5. Create another publication containing the text, Module 2 Notes, and then save it in the Module 2 folder using the file name, Lab 2 Module 2 Notes.

6. Create a third publication containing the text, Module 3 Notes, and then save it in the Module 3 folder using the file name, Lab 2 Module 3 Notes.

7. If requested by your instructor, add your name to each of the three Publisher publications.

8. Submit the assignment in the format specified by your instructor.

9. ✳ Based on your current knowledge of Windows and Publisher, how will you organize folders for assignments in this class? Why?

Lab 3: **Consider This: Your Turn**

Performing Research about Malware

Problem: You have just installed a new computer with the Windows 10 operating system. Because you want to be sure that it is protected from the threat of malware, you decide to research malware, malware protection, and removing malware.

Perform the following tasks:

Part 1: Research the following three topics: malware, malware protection, and removing malware. Use the concepts and techniques presented in this module to use the search box to find information regarding these topics. Create a publication that contains steps to safeguard a computer properly from malware, ways to prevent malware, as well as different ways to remove malware or a virus should your computer become infected. Submit your assignment in the format specified by your instructor.

Part 2: ✳ You made several decisions while searching for this assignment. What decisions did you make? What was the rationale behind these decisions? How did you locate the required information about malware?

Microsoft Office 365 & Publisher 2016

1 Creating a Flyer

Objectives

You will have mastered the material in this module when you can:

- Choose Publisher template options
- Describe the Publisher window
- Select objects and zoom
- Replace Publisher placeholder and default text
- Delete objects
- Check spelling as you type
- Format text and autofit

- Use graphics
- Insert a photo
- Move, align, and resize objects
- Print a publication
- Open and modify a publication
- Create a hyperlink
- Save a print publication as a web publication

Introduction

To publicize an event, advertise a sale or service, promote a business, or convey a message to the community, you may want to create a flyer and post it in a public location. A **flyer** is a single-page publication, which may be printed on various sizes of paper, announcing personal items for sale or rent (car, boat, apartment); garage or block sales; services being offered (housecleaning, lessons, carpooling); membership, sponsorship, or charity events (religious organization, club); and other messages. Flyers are an inexpensive means of reaching the community, yet many go unnoticed because they are designed poorly. A good flyer, or any publication, must deliver a message in the clearest, most attractive and effective way possible. You must clarify your purpose and know your target audience. You need to gather ideas and plan for the printing. Finally, you must edit, proofread, and then publish your flyer. Flyers must stand out to be noticed.

Flyers also can be posted on the web. Electronic bulletin boards, social networking sites, and online auction websites are good places to reach people with flyers, advertising everything from a bake sale to a part-time job.

To illustrate the features of Publisher, this book presents a series of projects that create publications similar to those you will encounter in academic and business environments.

Project — 5K Flyer

The project in this module uses Publisher and a template to create the flyer shown in Figure 1–1. This attractive flyer advertises a local 5K walk/run for charity. The date of the event appears in the upper-right corner. The title runs across the center and clearly identifies the purpose of the flyer, using large, bold letters. Below the title, to maintain consistency, the same font is used for the description of the event. The shoe graphic is placed to be eye-catching; it entices people to stop and look at the flyer. The QR code graphic allows mobile devices to access the event's webpage quickly. The tear-offs, aligned at the bottom of the flyer, include the phone number for more information. Finally, the font and color schemes support the topic and make the text stand out.

The following roadmap identifies general activities you will perform as you progress through this module:

1. CUSTOMIZE the TEMPLATE options such as choice, color scheme, and font scheme.
2. NAVIGATE the interface and SELECT objects.
3. REPLACE placeholder TEXT.
4. DELETE OBJECTS you do not plan to use in the publication, if any.
5. FORMAT the TEXT in the flyer.
6. INSERT GRAPHICS in placeholders and in other locations, as necessary.
7. ENHANCE the PAGE by repositioning and aligning objects.
8. After saving, OPEN and REVISE the publication.

Creating a Flyer

Publisher provides many ways to begin the process of creating and editing a publication. You can:

- Create a new publication from a template.
- Create a new publication from scratch.
- Create a new publication based on an existing one.
- Open an existing publication.

Choosing the appropriate method depends on your experience with desktop publishing and on how you have used Publisher in the past.

BTW
Featured Template Gallery
You may have to wait a few minutes for Publisher to populate the FEATURED template gallery, because Microsoft updates the gallery every day.

Templates

Because many people find that composing and designing from scratch is a difficult process, Publisher provides templates to assist in publication preparation. Publisher has hundreds of templates to create professionally designed and unique publications. A **template** is a tool that helps you through the design process by offering you publication options — changing your publication accordingly — and preset objects placed in an attractive layout. A template is similar to a blueprint you can use over and over, filling in the blanks, replacing prewritten text as necessary, and changing the art to fit your needs.

BTW
Templates
Choose a template that suits the purpose of the publication, with headline and graphic placement that attracts your audience. Choose a style that complements the topic.

April 8, 2017

5K Family Walk/Run for Children's Hospital

Friends of Children's Hospital

Support **Children's Hospital** by bringing your family out for the 5K Family Walk/Run on April 8. Check-in begins at 7:00 a.m. Race begins at 8:30 a.m. Register by phone or on the web at 5Kwalkrun.org. The first 50 people to register online receive a <u>free T-shirt</u>.

Call: (214) 555-1306

For more information, call:
(214) 555-1306

For more information, call:
(214) 555-1306

For more information, call:
(214) 555-1306

For more information, call:
(214) 555-1306

For more information, call:
(214) 555-1306

For more information, call:
(214) 555-1306

For more information, call:
(214) 555-1306

For more information, call:
(214) 555-1306

For more information, call:
(214) 555-1306

For more information, call:
(214) 555-1306

For more information, call:
(214) 555-1306

For more information, call:
(214) 555-1306

Figure 1–1

Publisher provides two kinds of templates. **Featured templates** (shown in Figure 1–2) are downloaded from Office.com and customized for specific situations. **Built-in templates** are more generic and require no downloading. In this first project, as you begin to learn about the features of Publisher, a series of steps is presented to create a publication using a built-in template.

To Run Publisher and View Built-In Templates

1 CUSTOMIZE TEMPLATES | 2 NAVIGATE & SELECT | 3 REPLACE TEXT | 4 DELETE OBJECTS
5 FORMAT TEXT | 6 INSERT GRAPHICS | 7 ENHANCE PAGE | 8 OPEN & REVISE

The following steps run Publisher and view the built-in templates.

1

- Run Publisher. If the Publisher window is not maximized, click the Maximize button on its title bar to maximize the window (Figure 1–2).

Q&A Why does my list of templates look different?
It may be that someone has downloaded additional templates on your system. Or, the resolution on your screen may be different. Thus, the size and number of displayed templates may vary.

Figure 1–2

2

- In the Publisher start screen, click BUILT-IN to display the built-in templates (Figure 1–3).

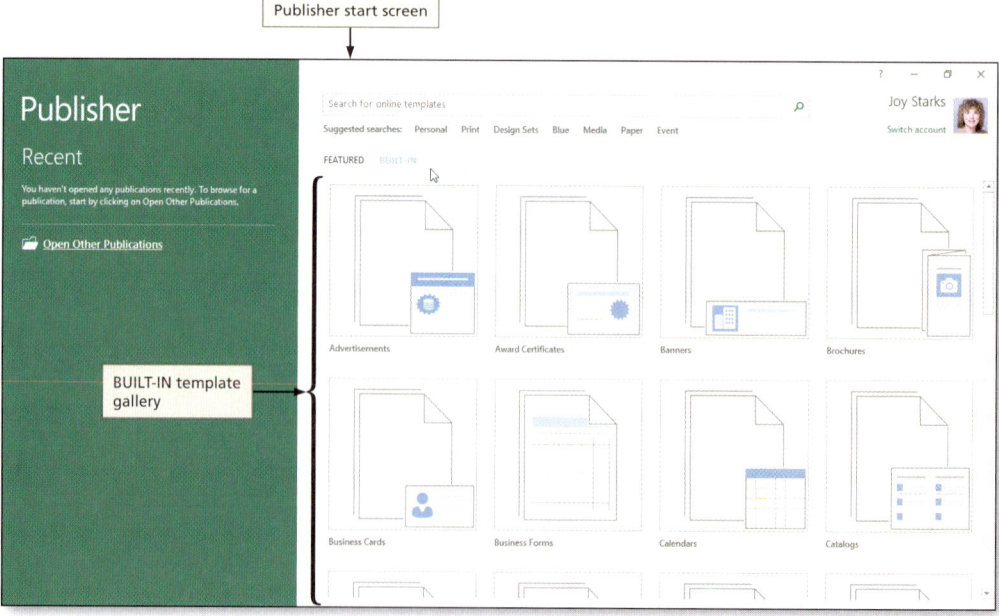

Figure 1–3

1 CUSTOMIZE TEMPLATES | 2 NAVIGATE & SELECT | 3 REPLACE TEXT | 4 DELETE OBJECTS
5 FORMAT TEXT | 6 INSERT GRAPHICS | 7 ENHANCE PAGE | 8 OPEN & REVISE

To Select a Built-In Template

Built-in templates are organized by publication type (for example, Flyers); within publication type, they are organized by purpose or category (for example, Marketing) and then alphabetically by design type. Publisher groups additional templates into folders. Once you select a built-in template, Publisher displays the **template information pane** on the right with a larger preview of the selected template, along with some customization options.

The following steps select an event flyer template. ***Why?*** *An event flyer template contains many of the objects needed to create the desired flyer.*

1

- If necessary, scroll down to display the desired publication type (in this case, Flyers) (Figure 1–4).

🔍 **Experiment**

- Scroll through the available template types.

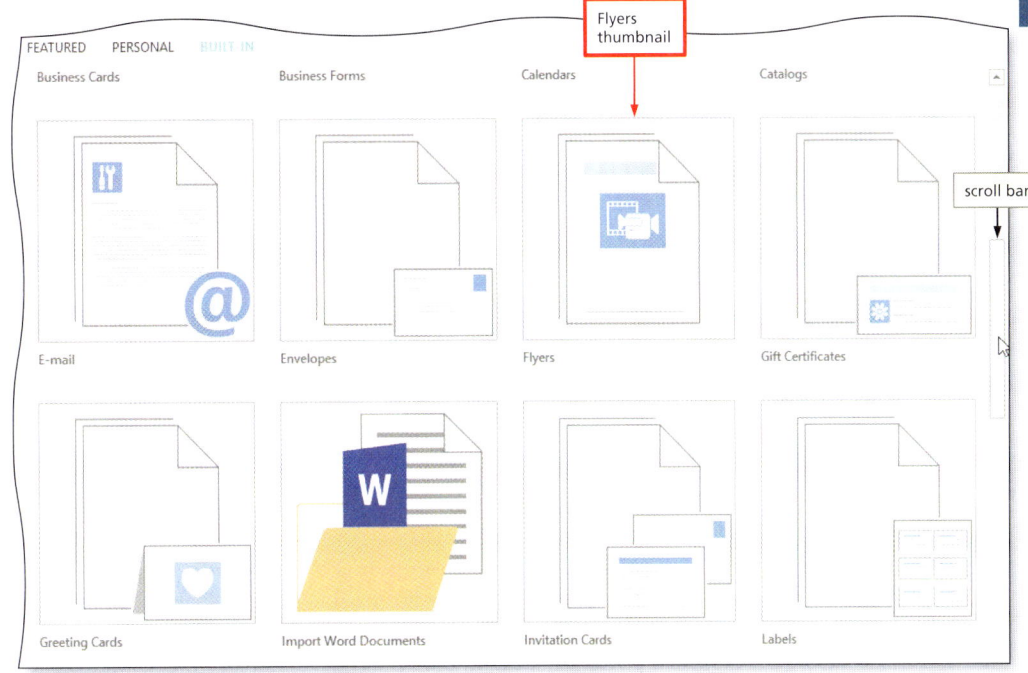

Figure 1–4

2

- Click the Flyers thumbnail to display the Flyer templates and folders of additional templates (Figure 1–5).

Q&A Can I go back and choose a different category of templates?
Yes, you can click the Back button in the upper-left corner of the template gallery, or you can click Home or Flyers in the navigation trail to move back to those previous locations.

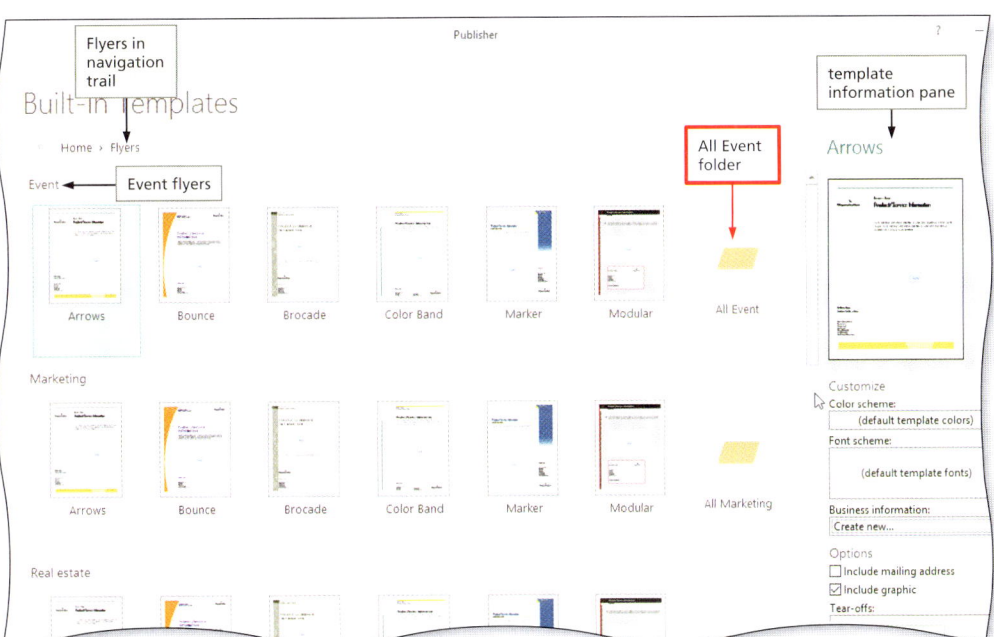

Figure 1–5

3

- Click the All Event folder to open it.
- Scroll down to display the Informational templates in the More Installed Templates area.
- Click the Capsules thumbnail to select it (Figure 1–6).

Could I use a different template? You could, but it does not have the same features as the template used in this module.

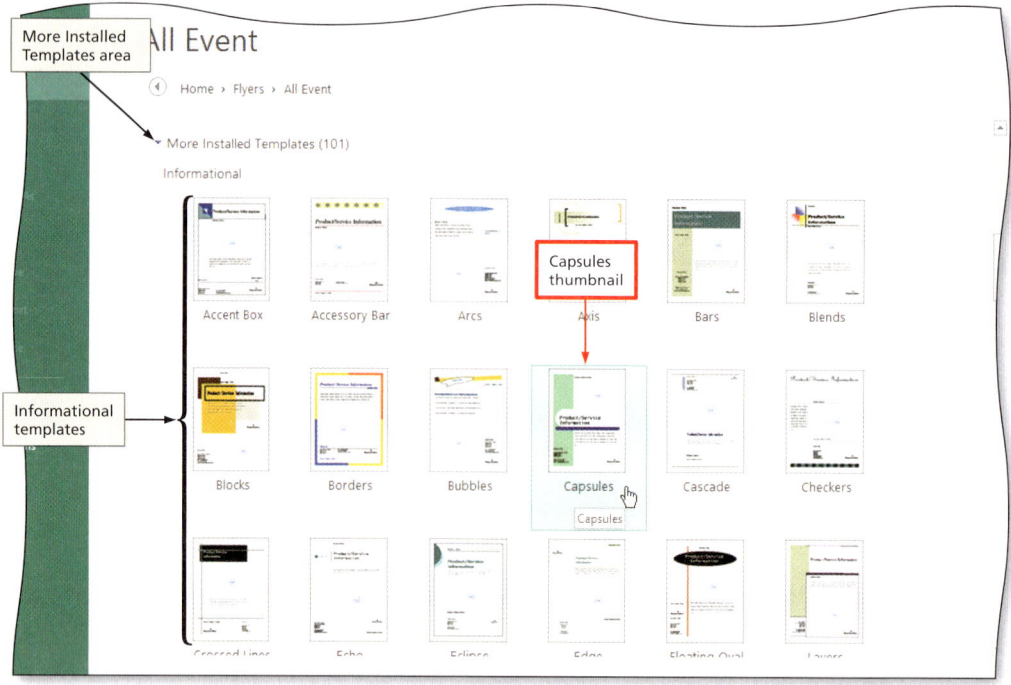

Figure 1–6

Does it make any difference which color scheme and font scheme you use?
Yes. The choice of an appropriate template, font, and color scheme is determined by the flyer's purpose and intended audience. For example, in this 5K Flyer about a walk/run, the Sagebrush color scheme helps connect the audience with the outdoor nature of the event. The Online font scheme uses a Verdana Bold font for the heading. Verdana Bold is a sans serif font, meaning it has no flourishes on individual letters and is suitable for print publications.

BTW

Font Schemes

Choose a font scheme that gives your flyer a consistent, professional appearance and that characterizes your subject. Make intentional decisions about the font style and type. Avoid common reading fonts such as Arial, Times New Roman, and Helvetica that are used in other kinds of print publications. Flyers are more effective with stronger or unusual font schemes.

Customizing Templates

Once you choose a template, you should make choices about the color scheme, font scheme, and other components of the publication. A **color scheme** is a defined set of colors that complement each other when used in the same publication. Each Publisher color scheme provides four complementary colors. A **font scheme** is a defined set of fonts associated with a publication. A **font**, or typeface, defines the appearance and shape of the letters, numbers, and special characters. A font scheme contains one font for headings and another font for body text and captions. Font schemes make it easy to change all the fonts in a publication to give it a new look. Other customization options allow you to choose to include business information, a mailing address, a graphic, or tear-offs.

To Choose Publication Options

The following steps choose customization options for the template. *Why? You typically will want to customize a template with an appropriate font and color scheme, determined by the flyer's purpose and intended audience.*

1

• Click the Color scheme button in the Customize area to display the Color scheme gallery (Figure 1–7).

Q&A

What are the individual colors used for in each scheme?

By default, the text will be black and the background will be white in each color scheme. Publisher uses the first and second scheme colors for major color accents within a publication. The third and fourth colors are used for shading and secondary accents.

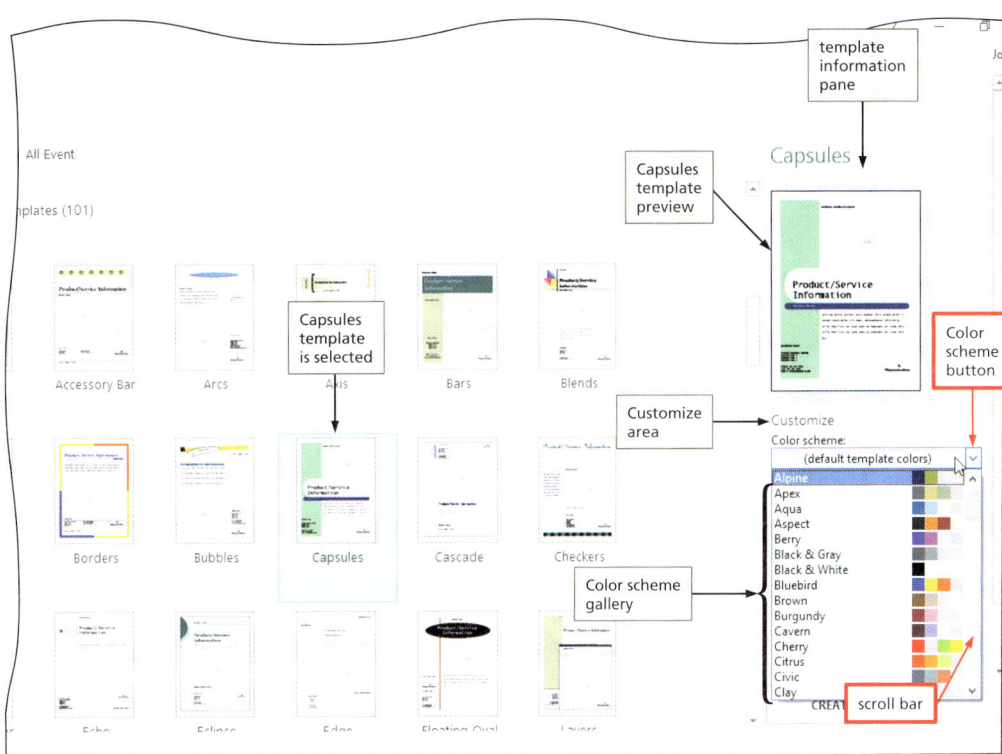

Figure 1–7

2

• Scroll as necessary and then click Sagebrush in the Color scheme gallery to select it (Figure 1–8).

 Experiment

• Click various color schemes and watch the changes in all of the thumbnails. When you finish experimenting, click Sagebrush in the Color scheme gallery.

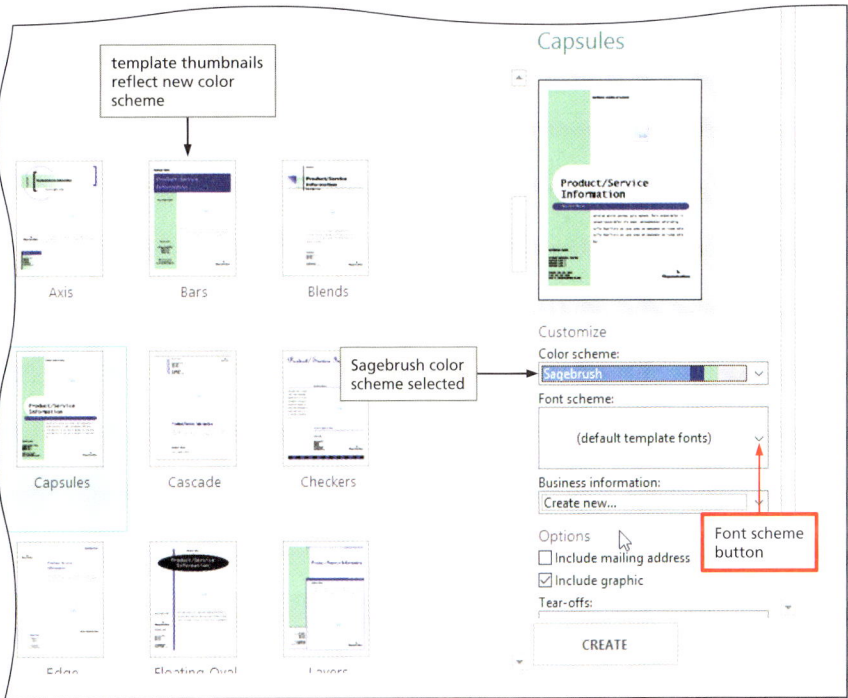

Figure 1–8

3

- Click the Font scheme button in the Customize area to display the Font scheme gallery (Figure 1–9).

◀ | How are the font schemes
Q&A | organized?

The font schemes are organized alphabetically by the generic name of the scheme that appears above the major font in the list.

🔍 **Experiment**

- Click various font schemes and watch the changes in all of the thumbnails.

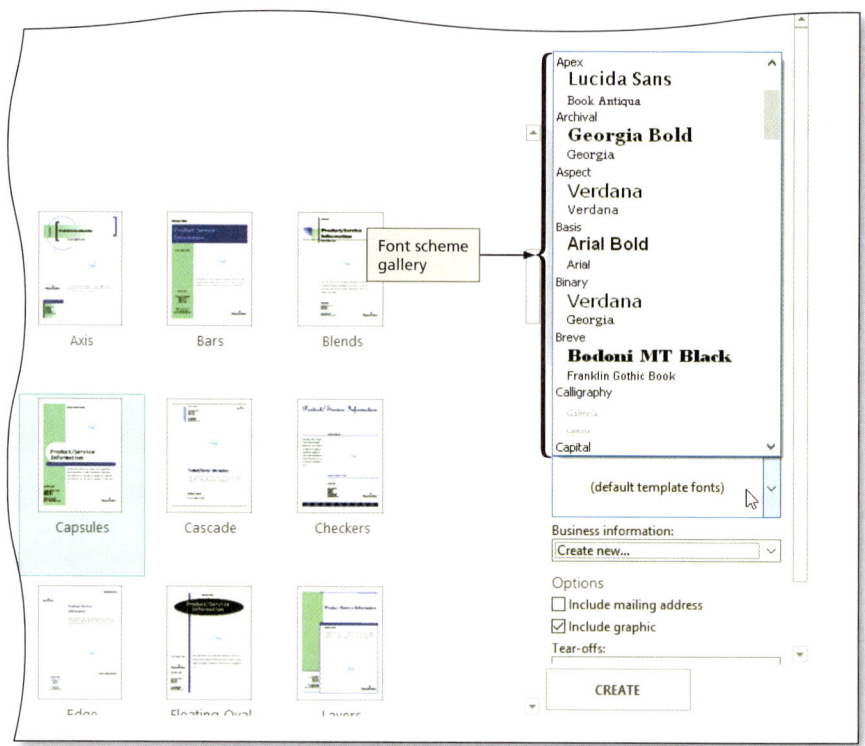

Figure 1–9

4

- Scroll as necessary and then click the Online font scheme in the Font scheme gallery to select it.

- If necessary, scroll to display the Options area of the template information pane (Figure 1–10).

◀ | What are the three items listed in
Q&A | each scheme?

The first line is the generic name of the scheme. Below that, both a major font and a minor font are specified. Generally, a major font is used for titles and headings, and a minor font is used for body text. In the Online font scheme, for example, Online is the generic name of the scheme, Verdana Bold is the major font, and Verdana is the minor font.

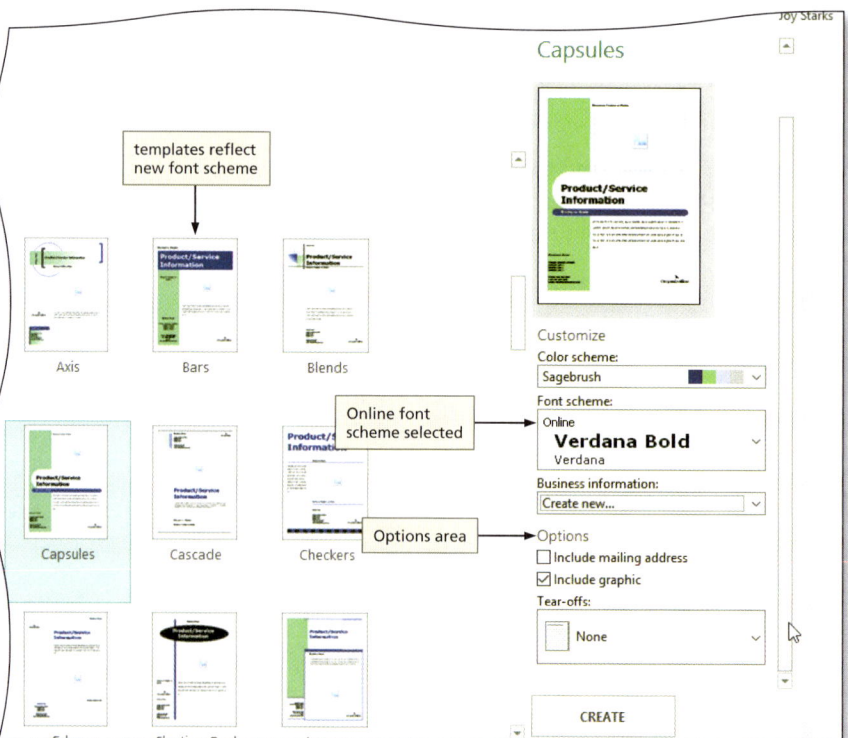

Figure 1–10

5

- Click the Tear-offs button in the Options area to display the Tear-offs gallery (Figure 1–11).

What are the other kinds of tear-offs?
You can choose to display tear-offs for coupons, order forms, response forms, and sign-up forms.

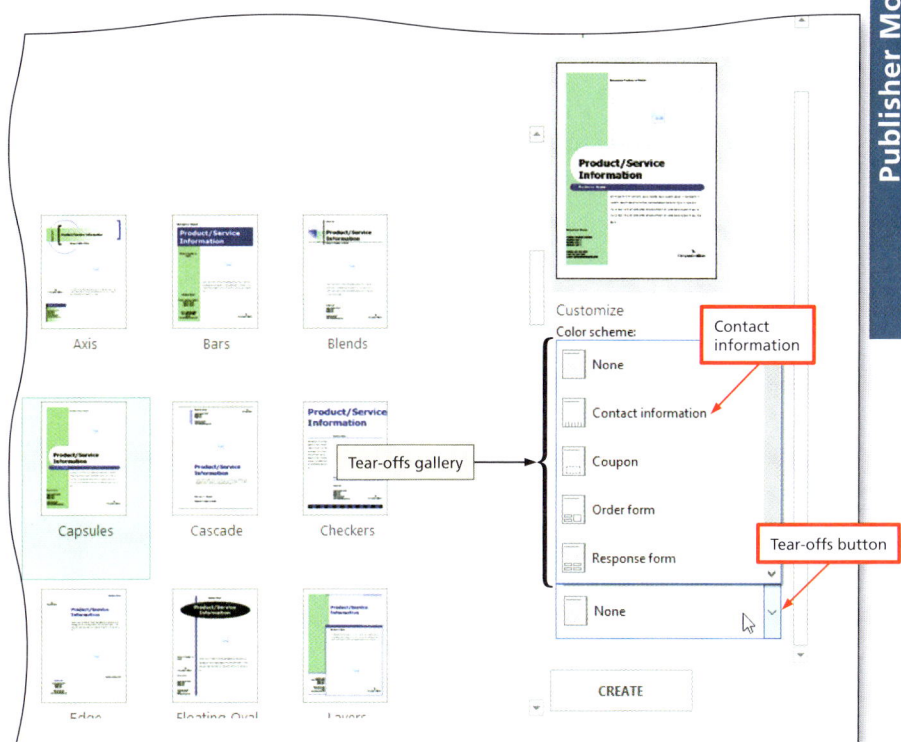

Figure 1–11

6

- Click Contact information in the Tear-offs gallery to select tear-offs that will display contact information (Figure 1–12).

Should I change the check boxes?
No, the flyer you create in this module uses the default value of no mailing address, but includes a graphic.

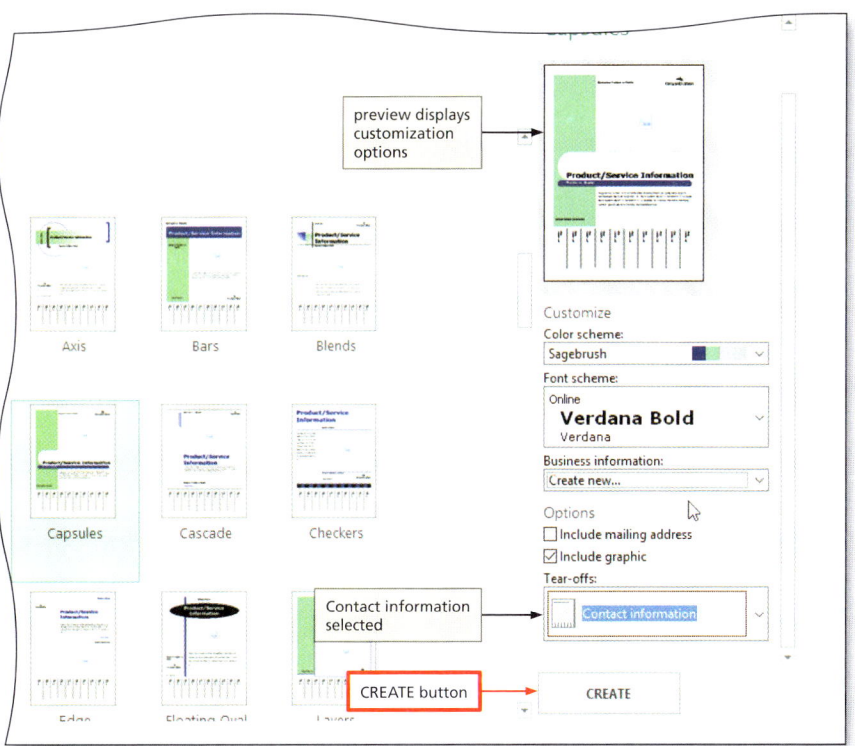

Figure 1–12

7

● Click the CREATE button to create the publication using the selected template and options (Figure 1–13).

Q&A How can I go back if I change my mind?
You can click File on the ribbon and start a new publication, or you can make changes to the template, font scheme, color scheme, and other options using the ribbon, as you will see in this and subsequent modules.

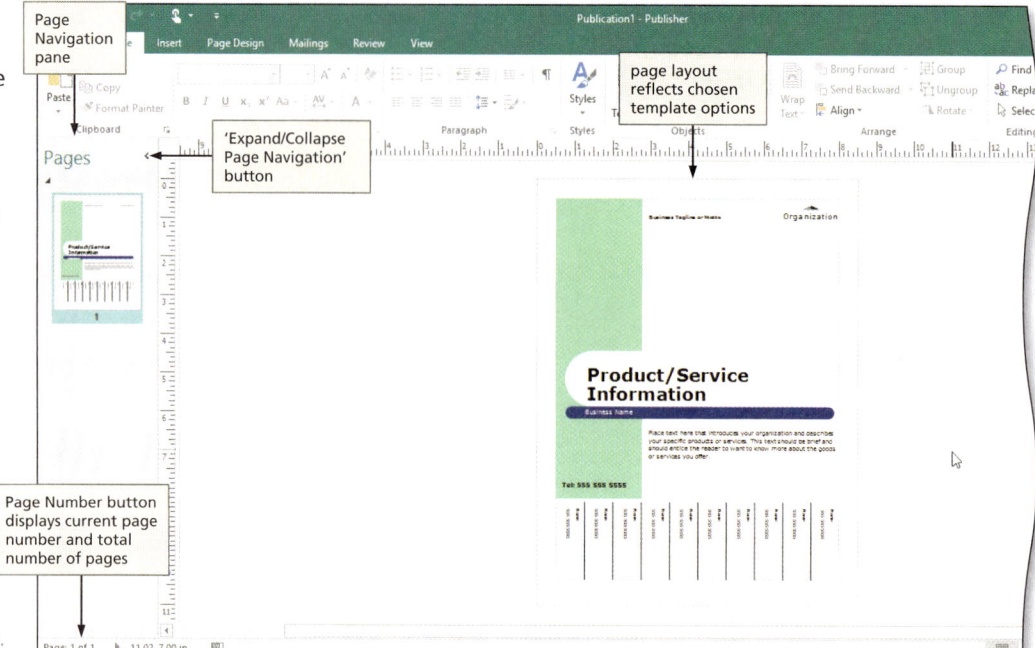

Figure 1–13

The Publisher Window

The Publisher window consists of a variety of components to make your work more efficient and your publications more professional. The following sections discuss these components.

The Workspace

The **workspace** contains several elements similar to the document windows of other applications, as well as some elements unique to Publisher. In Publisher, as you create a publication, the page layout, rulers, scroll bars, guides, the Page Navigation pane, and the status bar are displayed in the workspace (Figure 1–14). Objects can be placed on the page layout or in the gray scratch area.

Page Layout The **page layout** contains a view of the publication page, all the objects contained therein, plus the guides and boundaries for the page and its objects. The page layout can be changed to accommodate multipage spreads. You also can use the Special Paper command to view your page layout as it will appear when printed on special paper or see the final copy after preparing your publication for a printing service.

Rulers Two rulers outline the workspace at the top and left. A **ruler** is used to measure and place objects on the page. Although the vertical and horizontal rulers are displayed at the left and top of the workspace, they can be moved and placed anywhere you need them. You use the rulers to measure and align objects on the page, set tab stops, adjust text frames, and change margins. Additionally, the rulers can be hidden to show more of the workspace. You will learn more about rulers in a later module.

Objects The elements you want to place in your publication are called **objects**, which include text, WordArt, tear-offs, graphics, pictures, bookmarks, bullets, lines, and web tools.

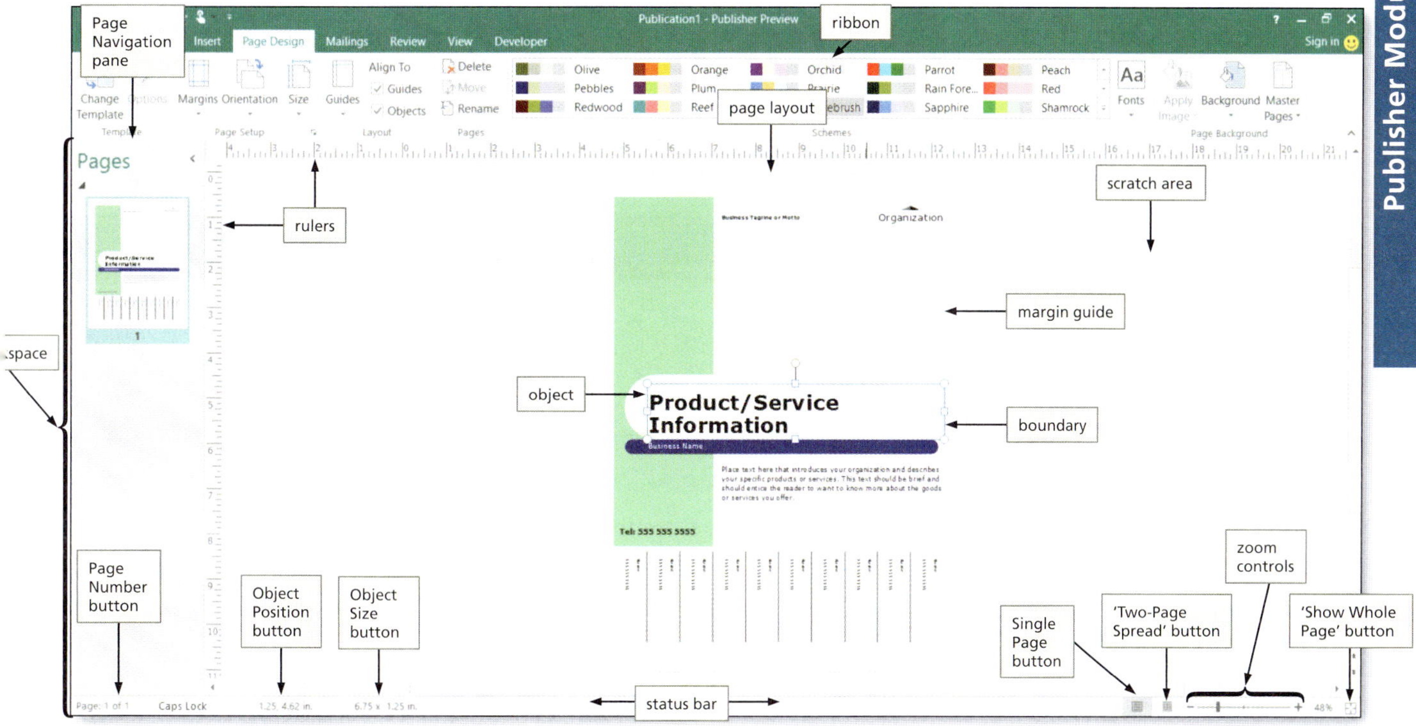

Figure 1–14

Guides and Boundaries Publisher's page layout displays guides and boundaries of the page and selected objects. A **boundary** is the gray, dotted line surrounding an object. Boundaries are useful when you want to move or resize objects on the page. Boundaries and guides can be turned on and off using the View tab. They do not display on printed copies. **Margin guides** automatically are displayed in blue at all four margins. Other guides include grid guides, which you can turn on to help organize objects in rows and columns, pink visual layout guides that display as you move objects, and baseline guides that help you align text horizontally across text boxes.

Status Bar As you learned in the Office and Windows module, the Publisher status bar contains buttons and controls you can use to view the position and size of objects, change the view of a publication, and adjust the size of the displayed publication.

The **Page Number button** allows you to show or hide the Page Navigation button, and also displays the current page and number of pages in the publication. A Caps Lock notification will appear next to the Page Number button in the status bar when the Caps Lock button is engaged on the keyboard. The **Object Position button** and **Object Size button** serve as guidelines for lining up objects from the left and top margins. The exact position and size of a selected object is displayed in inches as you create or move it. You may choose to have the measurement displayed in pixels, picas, points, or centimeters. If no object is selected, the Object Position button displays the location of the pointer. Clicking either button will display the Measurements toolbar. You will learn more about the Measurements toolbar in a later module.

The right side of the status bar includes the Single Page, 'Two-Page Spread', and 'Show Whole Page' buttons, as well as the zoom controls. If you right-click the status bar, you can choose which controls to display.

Page Navigation Pane The Page Navigation pane displays all of the current pages in the publication as thumbnails in a panel on the left side of the workspace. Clicking a thumbnail displays that page in the workspace.

BTW

Screen Resolution

If you are using a computer or mobile device to step through the project in this module and you want your screens to match the figures in this book, you should change your screen's resolution to 1366 × 768. For information about how to change a computer's resolution, refer to the Office and Windows module at the beginning of this book.

BTW

The Ribbon and Screen Resolution

Publisher may change how the groups and buttons within the groups appear on the ribbon, depending on the computer or mobile device's screen resolution. Thus, your ribbon may look different from the ones in this book if you are using a screen resolution other than 1366 × 768.

To Hide the Page Navigation Pane

Because the flyer contains only one page, you will hide the Page Navigation pane using the Page Number button on the status bar. *Why? Hiding the pane gives you more room on the screen for viewing and editing the flyer.* The following step hides the Page Navigation pane.

1

- Click the Page Number button on the status bar to hide the Page Navigation pane (Figure 1–15).

Q&A

I do not see the Page Navigation pane. What did I do wrong?

It may be that someone has hidden the Page Navigation pane already. The Page Number button opens and closes the Page Navigation pane. Click it again.

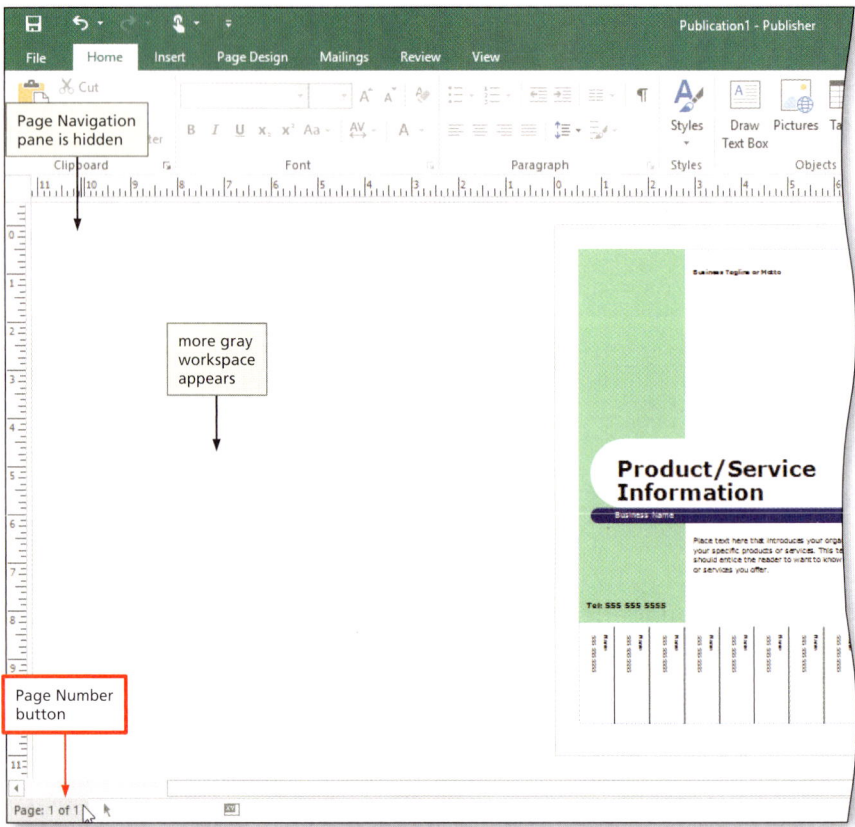

Figure 1–15

Other Ways

1. Click Page Navigation check box (View tab | Show group)

TO COLLAPSE AND EXPAND THE PAGE NAVIGATION PANE

An alternative to hiding the Page Navigation pane is to collapse or minimize it. If you wanted to collapse the Page Navigation pane, you would perform the following steps.

1. If the Page Navigation pane is not open, click the Page Number button on the status bar to display the Page Navigation pane.

2. Click the 'Collapse Page Navigation Pane' button in the upper-right corner of the pane.

3. If you want to expand a collapsed Page Navigation pane, click the 'Expand Page Navigation Pane' button in the upper-right corner of the pane.

BTW

Selecting

If your screen normally displays dark letters on a light background, which is the default setting in Publisher, then selected text displays as light letters on a dark background.

Selecting Objects and Zooming

Pointing to an object in Publisher causes the object to display its boundary, helping you to determine the edges and general shape of the object. When you **select** an object by clicking it, the object appears surrounded by a solid **selection rectangle**, which has small squares and circles, called **handles**, at each corner and middle location. Many objects also display a **rotation handle** connected to the top of the object or a yellow **adjustment handle** diamond used to change the shape of some objects. A selected object can be resized, rotated, moved, deleted, or grouped with other objects.

Objects such as photos, clip art, and shapes are easy to select. You simply click them. With other objects such as text boxes, logos, and placeholders, you first must point to them — to display their boundaries — and then click the boundary. Selecting text does not necessarily select the text box object that holds the text; rather, it may select the text itself. Clicking the boundary is the best way to select a text box object.

To Select

1 CUSTOMIZE TEMPLATES | **2 NAVIGATE & SELECT** | 3 REPLACE TEXT | 4 DELETE OBJECTS
5 FORMAT TEXT | 6 INSERT GRAPHICS | 7 ENHANCE PAGE | 8 OPEN & REVISE

The following step selects the box that surrounds the title in the flyer. *Why? Before you can edit an object, you first must select it.*

- Point near the desired object or click the boundary of the desired object (in this case, the title text box) to select the object rather than the text (Figure 1–16).

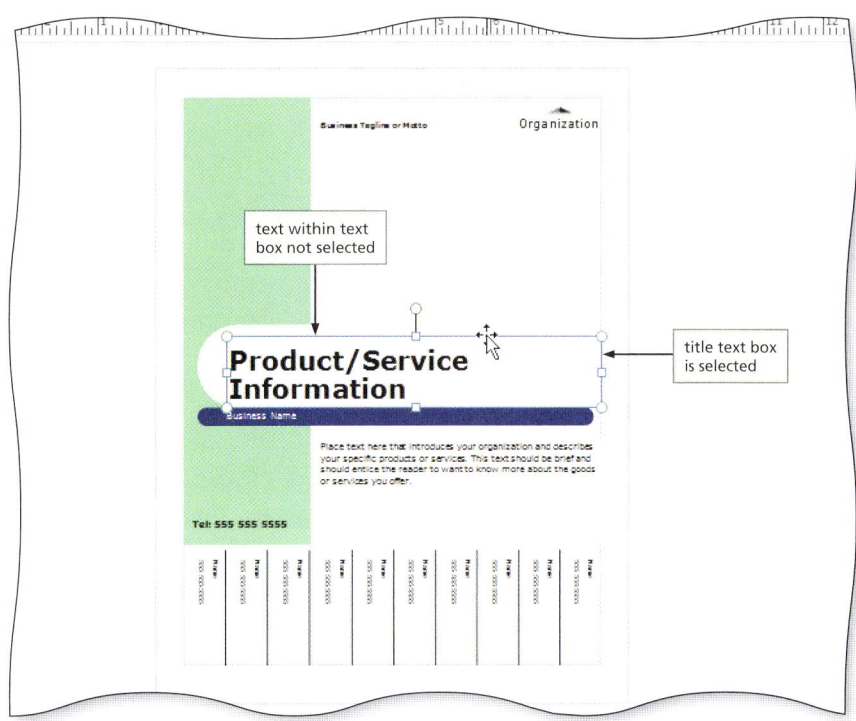

text within text box not selected

title text box is selected

Figure 1–16

Other Ways

1. With no object selected, press TAB key until desired object is selected

Zooming

Once selected, the size of the object might be small and, therefore, difficult to edit. Publisher provides several ways to **zoom**, or change the magnification of an object, to facilitate viewing and editing.

Table 1–1 shows several zoom methods.

Tool	Method	Result
Table 1–1 Zoom Methods		
Function key	To zoom in on an object, press the F9 key on the keyboard, press the F9 key again to return to the previous magnification.	Selected object appears centered in the workspace at 100% magnification.
Keyboard shortcut	To zoom to page width, press CTRL+SHIFT+L.	Page layout is magnified as large as possible in the workspace.
Mouse wheel	To change the magnification, press and hold the CTRL key and then move the mouse wheel down or up.	Page layout appears 20% smaller or larger.
Page Width button	To zoom to page width, click the Page Width button (View tab | Zoom group).	Page layout expands to fill the workspace horizontally.
Ribbon	To use the ribbon, click the View tab. In the Zoom group, click the desired button.	Page layout appears at selected magnification.
Selected Objects button	To zoom to objects, click the Selected Objects button (View tab | Zoom group).	Selected object is magnified as large as possible to fit on the screen.
Shortcut menu	To zoom in on an object, right-click the object, point to Zoom on the shortcut menu, click the desired magnification.	Object appears at selected magnification.
'Show Whole Page' button	To zoom to whole page, click the 'Show Whole Page' button on the status bar.	Page layout is magnified as large as possible in the workspace.
Whole Page button	To zoom to whole page, click the Whole Page button (View tab | Zoom group).	Page layout is magnified as large as possible in the workspace.
Zoom box	To change the magnification, enter a magnification percentage in the Zoom box (View tab | Zoom group).	Page layout appears at entered magnification.
Zoom arrow	To change the magnification, click Zoom arrow (View tab | Zoom group) and then click desired magnification.	Page layout appears at selected magnification.
Zoom Out button Zoom In button	To increment or decrement magnification, click the Zoom Out or Zoom In button on the status bar.	Page layout appears 10% smaller or larger with each click.
Zoom slider	To change the magnification of the entire page, drag the Zoom slider on the status bar.	Objects appear at selected magnification.
100% button	To zoom to page width, click the 100% button (View tab | Zoom group).	Page layout is magnified to 100%.

1 CUSTOMIZE TEMPLATES | **2 NAVIGATE & SELECT** | 3 REPLACE TEXT | 4 DELETE OBJECTS
5 FORMAT TEXT | 6 INSERT GRAPHICS | 7 ENHANCE PAGE | 8 OPEN & REVISE

To Zoom

When viewing an entire printed page, 8½ × 11 inches, the magnification is approximately 48%, which makes reading small text difficult. If your keyboard has function keys, you can press the F9 key to enlarge selected objects to 100% and center them in the Publisher window. Pressing the F9 key a second time returns the layout to its previous magnification. If you are using touch gestures, you can stretch to zoom in. Alternately, Publisher has several zoom controls on the status bar and on the View tab. The following step zooms in on the title. *Why? Editing small areas of text is easier if you use zooming techniques to enlarge the view of the publication.*

- Press the F9 key to zoom the selected object to approximately 100% (Figure 1–17).

Q&A What is the best way to zoom?
It really is your personal preference. The Zoom controls on the status bar allow you to change the magnification percentage in 10% increments. The Zoom group on the View tab contains some preset sizes as well as custom size text boxes.

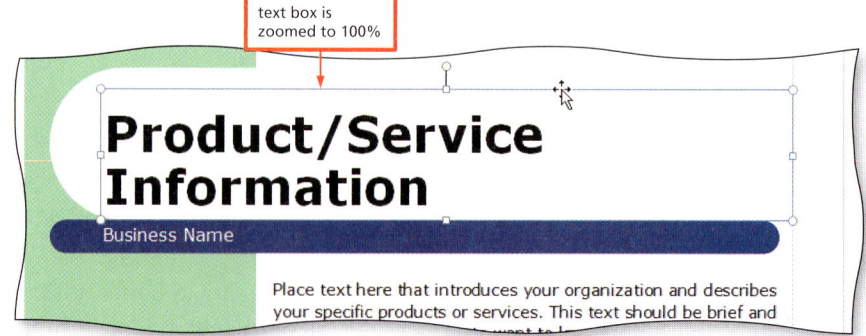

Figure 1–17

Other Ways

1. Click Zoom arrow (View tab \| Zoom group), click desired magnification
2. Click Selected Objects button (View tab \| Zoom group)
3. Right-click object, point to Zoom on shortcut menu, click desired magnification on Zoom menu
4. Drag Zoom slider on status bar
5. Click Zoom In button or Zoom Out button on status bar

Selecting and Entering Text

The first step in editing a publication template is to replace its text by typing on the keyboard. You may have to scroll and zoom in the page layout to make careful edits. In a later section of this module, you will learn how to format, or change the appearance of, the entered text.

Text Boxes

Most of Publisher's templates come with text already inserted into text boxes. A **text box** is an object in a publication designed to hold text in a specific shape, size, and style. Text boxes also can be drawn on the page using the 'Draw a Text Box' button (Home tab | Objects group). Text boxes can be formatted using the ribbon, the mini toolbar, or the shortcut menu. A text box has changeable properties. A **property** is an attribute or characteristic of an object. Within text boxes, you can **edit**, or make changes to, many properties such as font, spacing, alignment, line/border style, fill color, and margins, among others.

As you type, if you make a mistake you can backspace or use the DELETE key as you do in word processing. You also can **undo** typing by clicking the Undo button on the Quick Access Toolbar or by pressing CTRL+Z.

When you create a new text box, it is empty, ready for you to type. In the templates, however, Publisher insert two types of text in template text boxes. As you will see in the next steps, placeholder text and default text are selected differently, and used for different purposes.

BTW

Selected Objects Button
When you click the Selected Objects button (View tab | Zoom group), the selected object is magnified to fill the window, even if that is more than 100 percent.

BTW

Organizing Files and Folders
You should organize and store files in folders so that you easily can find the files later. For example, if you are taking an introductory technology class called CIS 101, a good practice would be to save all Publisher files in a Publisher folder in a CIS 101 folder. For a discussion of folders and detailed examples of creating folders, refer to the Office and Windows module at the beginning of this book.

To Replace Placeholder Text

1 CUSTOMIZE TEMPLATES | 2 NAVIGATE & SELECT | **3 REPLACE TEXT** | **4 DELETE OBJECTS**
5 FORMAT TEXT | **6 INSERT GRAPHICS** | **7 ENHANCE PAGE** | **8 OPEN & REVISE**

You select **placeholder text**, such as that in the flyer title, with a single click. *Why? Clicking once to select text allows you to begin typing immediately without having to select the text or press the DELETE key.*

The following steps select and replace placeholder text.

- Click the title text to select it (Figure 1–18).

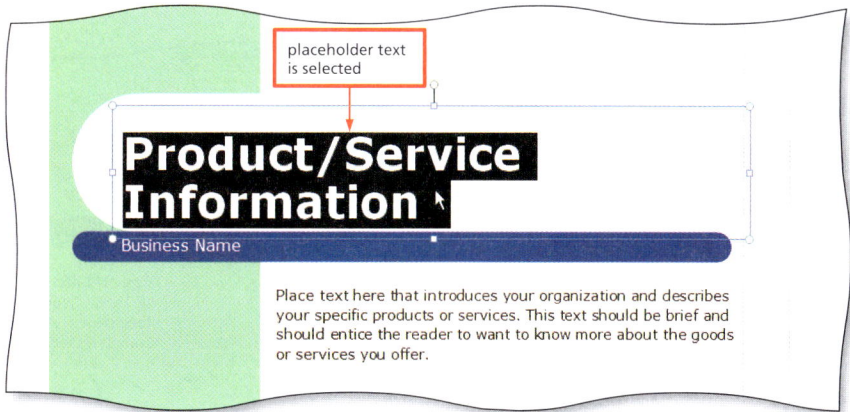

Figure 1–18

2

- Type `5K Family Walk/Run for Children's Hospital` (Figure 1–19).

Q&A What if I make an error while typing?

Common word processing techniques work in Publisher text boxes. For example, you can press the BACKSPACE key until you have deleted the text in error and then retype the text correctly.

Figure 1–19

3

- Below the Business Name box, click the text in the description text box to select the placeholder text (Figure 1–20).

Q&A Am I skipping the Business Name text box?

The text in the Business Name text box is not selected with a single click. You will edit that text later in the module.

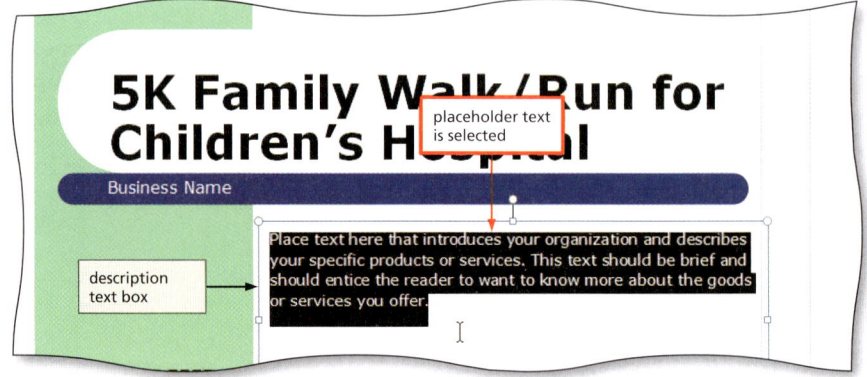

Figure 1–20

4

- Type `Support Children's Hospital by bringing your family out for the 5K Family Walk/Run on April 8. Check-in begins at 7:00 a.m. Race begins at 8:30 a.m. Register by phone or on the web at 5kwalkrun.org. The first 50 people to register online receive a free T-shirt.` to complete the text (Figure 1–21).

Figure 1–21

- On the left side of the flyer, click the text in the phone number text box to select the placeholder text.
- Type `Call: (214) 555-1306` to replace the text (Figure 1–22).

Figure 1–22

To Replace Default Text

1 CUSTOMIZE TEMPLATES | 2 NAVIGATE & SELECT | 3 REPLACE TEXT | 4 DELETE OBJECTS
5 FORMAT TEXT | 6 INSERT GRAPHICS | 7 ENHANCE PAGE | 8 OPEN & REVISE

In the following steps, you replace the **default text**, or preset text, in other template text boxes. Text, such as the business name, address, or tag line, is selected by dragging through the text, double-clicking specific words, or by pressing CTRL+A to select all of the text in the text box. Then, you simply type to replace the text. *Why? Default text is different from placeholder text that is selected with a single click.* In a future module, you will learn that default text also may be edited by changing the business information set.

1

- Click the text in the Business Name text box to position the insertion point inside the text box (Figure 1–23).

Q&A What is the button that displays the letter, i?
It is the smart tag button. If you click it, Publisher offers to fill in the text for you with various options. **Smart tag buttons** appear when you point to certain text boxes that are part of the business information set or when you click a logo.

My business name is different. Did I do something wrong?
No. Someone may have changed the business name during installation. You will replace it in the next steps.

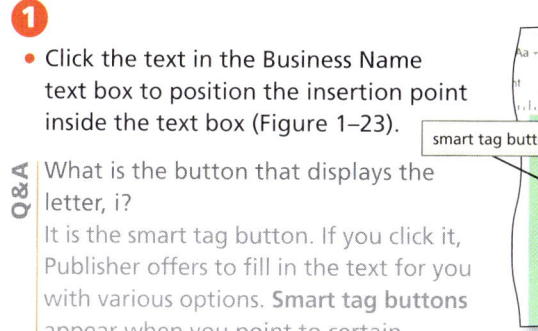

Figure 1–23

2

- Drag through the text in the Business Name text box to select all of the text in the text box (Figure 1–24).

Q&A Could I press CTRL+A?
Yes, as long as the insertion point is positioned inside the text box, CTRL+A will select all of the text in the text box.

Figure 1–24

3

- Type `Friends of Children's Hospital` to complete the text (Figure 1–25).

Q&A Should I press the DELETE key before typing?
It is not necessary to press the DELETE key; the text you type deletes the selected text automatically.

Figure 1–25

Other Ways

1. Select text box, click Select button (Home tab | Editing group), click 'Select All Text in Text Box', type new text

2. Position insertion point in text box, press CTRL+A, type new text

1 CUSTOMIZE TEMPLATES | 2 NAVIGATE & SELECT | **3 REPLACE TEXT** | 4 DELETE OBJECTS
5 FORMAT TEXT | 6 INSERT GRAPHICS | 7 ENHANCE PAGE | 8 OPEN & REVISE

To Deselect an Object

For various reasons, you may want to deselect or remove the selection from an object. For example, when a Publisher object is selected, scrolling is limited. **Why?** *Publisher assumes you would not want to scroll past the end of the object.* The following step deselects the object by clicking outside of its boundaries.

1

- Click outside of the selected object (in this case, the text box) to deselect it (Figure 1–26).

Q&A Exactly where should I click?
As long as you do not select another object, anywhere in the workspace is fine. You may want to click just to the left of the selection rectangle or in the scratch area.

Figure 1–26

Other Ways

1. Press ESC

Tear-Offs

Across the lower portion of the flyer are contact information tear-offs. **Tear-offs** are small, ready-to-be scored text boxes with some combination of name, phone number, fax, email, or address information. Designed for customer use, tear-offs typically are perforated so that a person walking by can tear off a tab to keep, rather than having to stop, find a pen and paper, and write down the name and phone number. Traditionally, small businesses or individuals wanting to advertise something locally used tear-offs, but more recently, large companies are mass-producing advertising flyers with tear-offs to post at shopping centers, display in offices, and advertise on college campuses.

Publisher tear-offs contain placeholder text and are **synchronized**, which means when you finish editing one of the tear-off text boxes, the others change to match it automatically.

1 CUSTOMIZE TEMPLATES | 2 NAVIGATE & SELECT | **3 REPLACE TEXT** | 4 DELETE OBJECTS
5 FORMAT TEXT | 6 INSERT GRAPHICS | 7 ENHANCE PAGE | 8 OPEN & REVISE

To Enter Tear-Off Text

The following steps edit the tear-off text boxes. **Why?** *The tear-offs must contain information to contact the flyer's creator or to request more information.*

1

- Scroll to display the lower portion of the flyer.
- Click the text in one of the tear-off text boxes to select it (Figure 1–27).

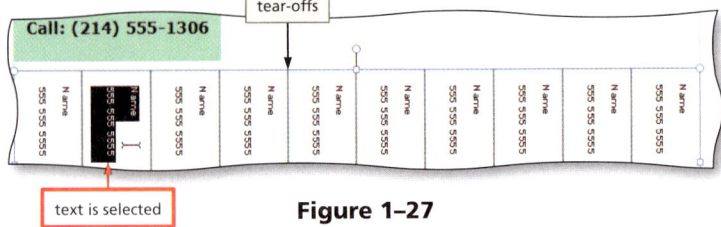

Figure 1–27

2

- Type `For more information, call:` and then press the ENTER key.

- Type `(214) 555-1306` to complete the tear-off text (Figure 1–28).

- If requested by your instructor, enter your phone number instead of (214) 555-1306 in the tear-off.

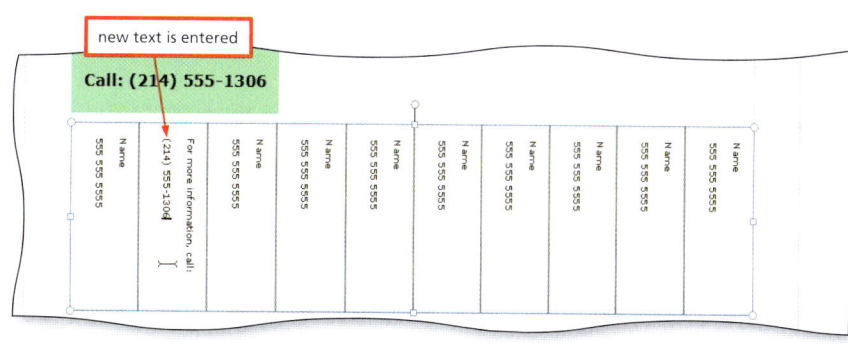

Figure 1–28

3

- Click outside of the text box to synchronize the other tear-offs (Figure 1–29).

Q&A What if I want to make each tear-off different?

Typically, all of the tear-offs are the same, but you can undo synchronization by clicking the Undo button on the Quick Access Toolbar and then entering the text for other tear-offs.

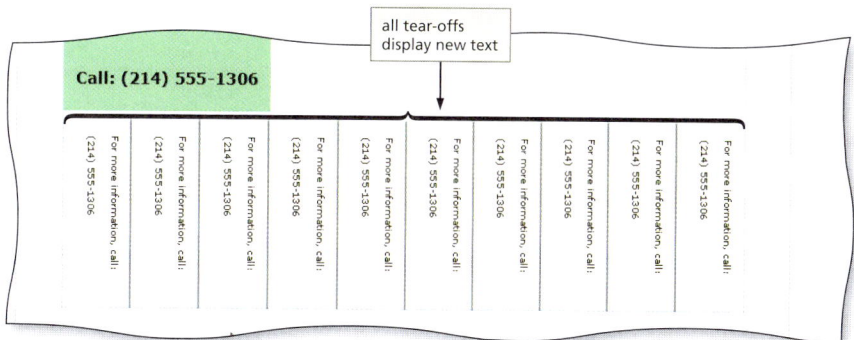

Figure 1–29

Deleting Objects

Templates may display objects in the page layout that you do not wish to use. In those cases, or when you change your mind about including an inserted object, you must delete objects.

To Delete Objects

1 CUSTOMIZE TEMPLATES | 2 NAVIGATE & SELECT | 3 REPLACE TEXT | 4 **DELETE OBJECTS**
5 FORMAT TEXT | 6 INSERT GRAPHICS | 7 ENHANCE PAGE | 8 OPEN & REVISE

In order to delete an object, it must be selected. In the following steps, you delete the organization logo. *Why? The logo is not used in this flyer.*

1

- Scroll to the top of the flyer to display the organization logo. Click the Zoom In button on the status bar several times to increase the magnification.

- Point to the logo to display the boundary and then click the boundary to select the object. Avoid clicking the text in the logo (Figure 1–30).

Q&A What if I want to delete just part of the logo?

The template logo is a small picture and the word, Organization, grouped together. To delete one or the other, select the logo first, and then click only the part of the object you wish to delete. Press the DELETE key to delete that part of the grouped object.

Figure 1–30

2

- Press the DELETE key to delete the selected object (Figure 1–31).

Q&A

Why did only the text disappear?
You may have selected the text or the boundary of the text box instead of the boundary of the entire logo. Select the remaining object and then press the DELETE key.

What if I delete an object accidentally?
Press CTRL+Z to undo the most recent step, or click the Undo button on the Quick Access Toolbar. The object will reappear in the original location.

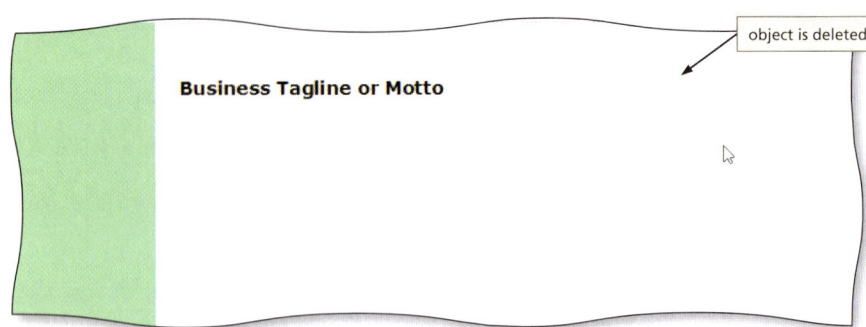

Business Tagline or Motto

object is deleted

Figure 1–31

Other Ways

1. Right-click object, click Delete Object on shortcut menu
2. Select object, press BACKSPACE

TO DELETE A TEXT BOX

If you wanted to delete a text box, you would follow these steps.

1. Point to the text box until the dotted border is displayed and the pointer changes to a double two-headed arrow.
2. Click the border to select the text box rather than the text.
3. Press the DELETE key to delete the text box.

BTW

Automatic Spelling Correction

As you type, Publisher automatically corrects some misspelled words. For example, if you type, recieve, Publisher automatically corrects the misspelling and displays the word, receive, when you press the SPACEBAR or type a punctuation mark.

BTW

Automatically Corrected Words

To see a complete list of automatically corrected words, click File on the ribbon to open the Backstage view, click the Options tab in the Backstage view, click Proofing in the left pane (Publisher Options dialog box), click the AutoCorrect Options button, and then scroll through the list near the bottom of the dialog box.

Checking the Spelling

As you type text in a publication, Publisher checks your typing for possible spelling errors. Publisher **flags** any potential error in the publication window with a red wavy underline. A red wavy underline means the flagged text is not in Publisher's dictionary (because it is a proper name, a slang term, or misspelled). Although you can check the entire publication for spelling errors at once, you also can check these flagged errors as they appear on the screen.

To display a list of corrections for flagged text, right-click the flagged text. Publisher displays a list of suggested spelling corrections on the shortcut menu. A flagged word, however, is not necessarily misspelled. For example, many names, abbreviations, and specialized terms are not in Publisher's main dictionary. In these cases, you instruct Publisher to ignore the flagged word. As you type, Publisher also detects duplicate words while checking for spelling errors. For example, if your publication contains the phrase, to the the store, Publisher places a red wavy underline below the second occurrence of the word, the.

1 CUSTOMIZE TEMPLATES | 2 NAVIGATE & SELECT | 3 REPLACE TEXT | **4 DELETE OBJECTS**
5 FORMAT TEXT | 6 INSERT GRAPHICS | 7 ENHANCE PAGE | 8 OPEN & REVISE

To Check Spelling as You Type

In the following steps, the word, April, is misspelled intentionally as Aprl to illustrate Publisher's check spelling as you type feature. If you are doing this project on a computer, your flyer may contain different misspelled words. ***Why?*** *You may have made spelling or typographical errors, if your typing was not accurate.*

1

- Click the text in the 'Business Tagline or Motto' text box to position the insertion point inside the text box.

- Drag through the text or press CTRL+A to select all of the text in the text box (Figure 1–32).

Why does my template list a different business name?

The person who installed Microsoft Office on your computer or network may have set or customized the field.

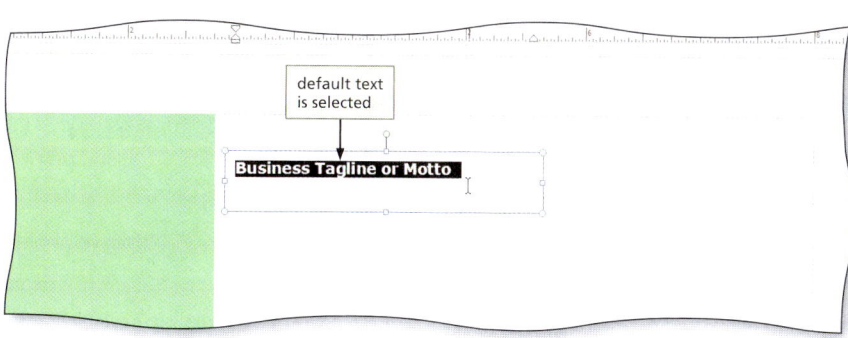

Figure 1–32

2

- Type Aprl 8, 2017, misspelling the word, April, so that a red wavy underline appears (Figure 1–33).

What if Publisher does not flag my spelling errors with wavy underlines?

To verify that the check spelling as you type features are enabled, click File on the ribbon to open the Backstage view and then click the Options tab. Click Proofing in the left pane and then ensure that the 'Check spelling as you type' check box contains a check mark. Also, ensure the 'Hide spelling and grammar errors' check box does not have a check mark.

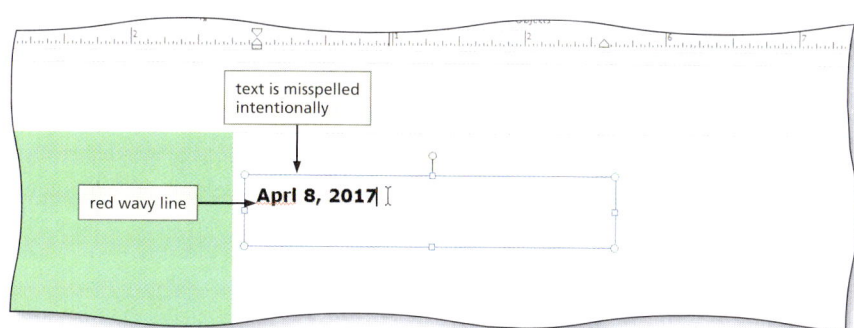

Figure 1–33

3

- Right-click the flagged word (Aprl, in this case) to display a shortcut menu that presents a list of suggested spelling corrections for the flagged word (Figure 1–34).

What if, when I right-click the misspelled word, my desired correction is not in the list on the shortcut menu?

You can click outside the shortcut menu to close the shortcut menu and then retype the correct word.

What toolbar was displayed when I selected the text?

Recall from the Office and Windows module that the mini toolbar appears automatically and contains commands related to changing the appearance of text in a publication. If you do not use the mini toolbar, it disappears from the screen.

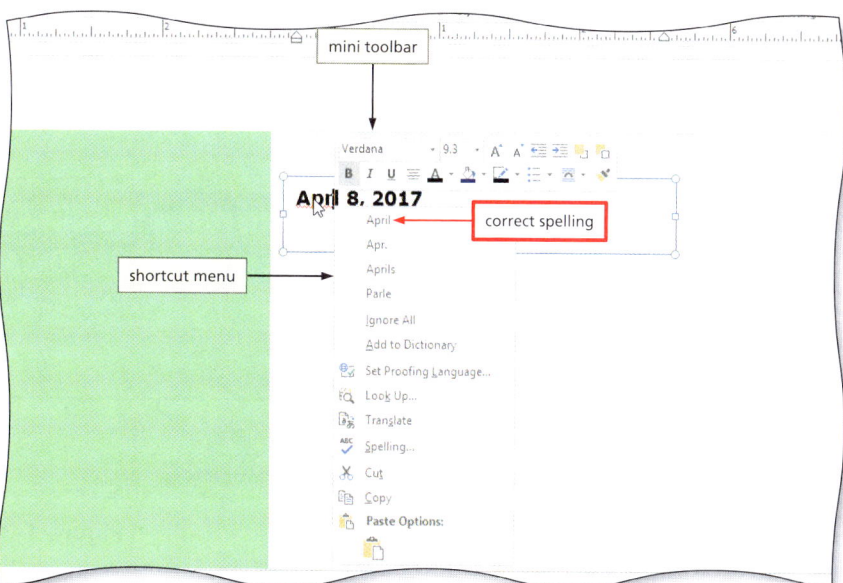

Figure 1–34

4

- Click the correct spelling (in this case, April) on the shortcut menu to replace the misspelled word with a correctly spelled word (Figure 1–35).

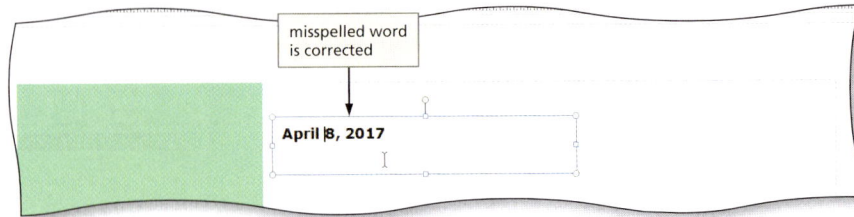

Q&A What if a flagged word actually is a proper name and spelled correctly?

Right-click the word, and then click Ignore All on the shortcut menu to instruct Publisher not to flag future occurrences of the same word in this publication.

Figure 1–35

5

- Save the publication on your hard drive, OneDrive, or other storage location using the file name, 5K Flyer.

Q&A Why should I save the publication at this time?

You have performed many tasks while creating this publication and do not want to risk losing work completed thus far.

Break Point: If you wish to take a break, this is a good place to do so. Exit Publisher. To resume at a later time, run Publisher, open the file named 5K Flyer, and continue following the steps from this location forward.

BTW
Touch Screen Differences
The Office and Windows interfaces may vary if you are using a touch screen. For this reason, you might notice that the function or appearance of your touch screen differs slightly from this module's presentation.

Formatting Text

Although you can format text before you type, many Publisher users enter text first and then format the existing text. Publisher provides many ways to modify the appearance, or **format**, of selected text. Some formatting options include editing the font, paragraph, alignment, typography, copy fitting, and text effects. The more common formatting commands are shown in the Font group on the Home tab on the ribbon (Figure 1–36) or on the Text Box Tools Format tab. Many of these formatting tools also appear on a mini toolbar when you point to text. These include the capability to change the font size, color, style, and effects. You will learn more about each of the formatting options in the Font group as you use them.

BTW
Exiting Publisher
If you have one Publisher publication open, click the Close button on the right side of the title bar to close the open publication and exit Publisher. If you have multiple Publisher publications open, right-click the Publisher app button on the taskbar and then click 'Close all windows' on the shortcut menu, or press ALT+F4 to close all open publications and exit Publisher. You also could click the Close button to close all open publications and exit Publisher.

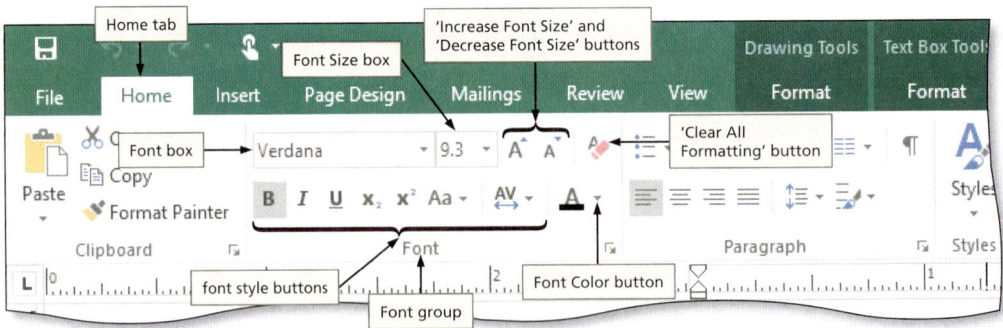

Figure 1–36

A third way to format text involves using the shortcut menu, which appears when you right-click an object, or when you press SHIFT+F10. The shortcut menu is a list of frequently used commands that relate to the selected object. If you right-click some items, Publisher displays both the mini toolbar and a shortcut menu.

Fonts

Characters that appear on the screen are a specific shape and size, determined by the template you choose or the settings you apply. Recall that the font, or typeface, defines the appearance and shape of the letters, numbers, and special characters. The name of the font appears in the Font box (Home tab | Font group). You can leave characters in the default font or change them to a different font. **Font size** specifies the size of the characters and is determined by a measurement system called points. A single **point** is about 1/72 of one inch in height. Thus, a character with a font size of 12 is about 12/72 or 1/6 of one inch in height. You can increase or decrease the font size of characters in a publication, as well as change the capitalization.

In addition to the common bold, italic, and underline formatting options, Publisher also allows you to apply special text effects and highlights.

Formatting Single versus Multiple Characters and Words

To format a single character, the character must be selected. To format a word, however, you simply can position the insertion point in the word, to make it the current word, and then format the word. You will learn in a later module that paragraph formatting, such as alignment and bullets, also can be applied without first selecting it; however, if you want to format multiple characters or words, you first must select the words you want to format and then format the selection.

To Bold Text

1 CUSTOMIZE TEMPLATES | 2 NAVIGATE & SELECT | 3 REPLACE TEXT | 4 DELETE OBJECTS
5 FORMAT TEXT | 6 INSERT GRAPHICS | 7 ENHANCE PAGE | 8 OPEN & REVISE

Bold characters appear somewhat thicker and darker than those that are not bold. To format the name of the hospital, you first will select the text. *Why? Multiple words must be selected in order to apply formatting.* The following step adds bold formatting to the name of the hospital.

①

- Click Home on the ribbon to display the Home tab.
- In the publication, scroll to the description text box and then drag through the text you wish to format (in this case, Children's Hospital) to select it.
- With the text selected, click the Bold button (Home tab | Font group) to bold the selected text (Figure 1–37).

Q&A How would I remove a bold format?

You would click the Bold button a second time, or you immediately could click the Undo button on the Quick Access Toolbar, or press CTRL+Z.

Figure 1–37

Other Ways

1. Click Font Dialog Box Launcher (Home tab | Font group), click Bold in Font style list (Font dialog box), click OK button
2. Click Bold button on mini toolbar
3. Right-click text, point to Change Text on shortcut menu, click Font, click Bold in Font style list (Font dialog box), click OK button
4. Press CTRL+B

To Underline Text

Underlines are used to emphasize or draw attention to specific text. **Underlined** text prints with an underscore (_) below each character including spaces. *Why? Underlining the spaces between words provides continuity.* The following step selects the text, free T-shirt, and formats it with an underline.

- Drag through the text, free T-shirt, to select it.
- With the text selected, click the Underline button (Home tab | Font group) to underline the selected text (Figure 1–38).

Q&A How can I tell what formatting has been applied to text?
The selected buttons and boxes on the Home tab show formatting characteristics of the location of the insertion point.

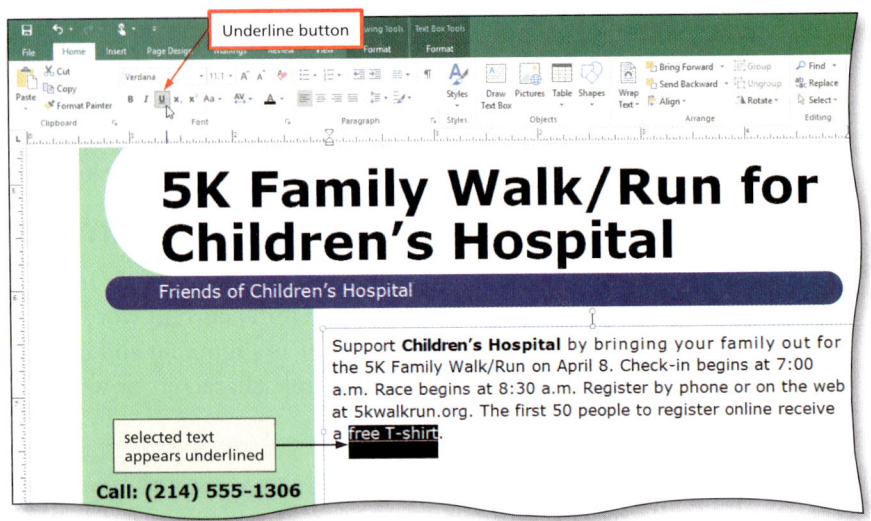

Figure 1–38

Other Ways

1. Click Font Dialog Box Launcher (Home tab | Font group), click Underline in Font style list (Font dialog box), click OK button

2. Click Underline button on mini toolbar

3. Right-click text, point to Change Text on shortcut menu, click Font, click Underline in Font Style list (Font dialog box), click OK button

4. Press CTRL+U

To Italicize Text

Italic text has a slanted appearance. The following step formats the phone number in italics. *Why? The italicized text draws attention and makes the text stand out.*

- Select the text in the phone number text box.
- With the text selected, click the Italic button (Home tab | Font group) to italicize the selected text (Figure 1–39).

Q&A Why is the Bold button enabled?
The Capsules template displayed the phone number in bold. You are adding italics to the formatting.

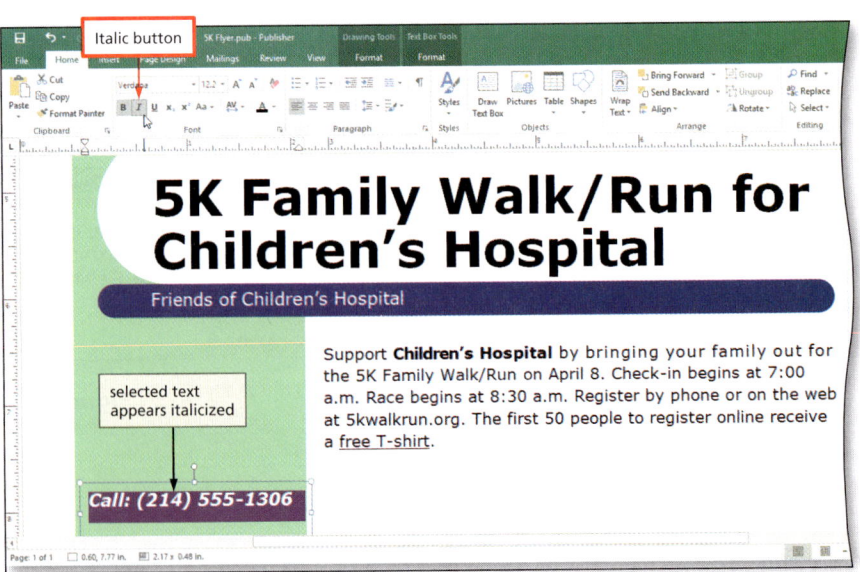

Figure 1–39

Other Ways

1. Click Font Dialog Box Launcher (Home tab | Font group), click Italic in Font style list (Font dialog box), click OK button

2. Click Italic button on mini toolbar

3. Right-click text, point to Change Text on shortcut menu, click Font on Change Text submenu, click Italic in Font Style list (Font dialog box), click OK button

4. Press CTRL+I

Autofitting Text

Other advanced text formatting commands are located on the Text Box Tools Format tab that is displayed when a text box is selected. You can autofit text, change the text direction, and hyphenate, as well as make changes to the alignment, styles, and typography.

Sometimes, the replacement text that you enter into a template does not fit the same way as the original template text — you might have too much text to fit, or too little text to fill the box. In those cases, you may want **autofit**, or **copy fit**, the text to adjust the way the text fits into the text box. Publisher autofitting choices are listed in Table 1–2.

Table 1–2 Types of Autofitting	
Type of Autofitting	**Result**
Best Fit	Shrinks or expands text to fit in the text box, even when the text box is resized
Shrink Text On Overflow	Reduces the point size of text until no text is in overflow
Grow Text Box to Fit	Enlarges text box to fit all of the text at its current size
Do Not Autofit	Text appears at its original size

To Autofit Text

1 CUSTOMIZE TEMPLATES | 2 NAVIGATE & SELECT | 3 REPLACE TEXT | 4 DELETE OBJECTS

5 FORMAT TEXT | 6 INSERT GRAPHICS | 7 ENHANCE PAGE | 8 OPEN & REVISE

The following steps autofit the text in the description text box. *Why? You want the text to appear as large as possible.*

1

- Click the description text and then click Text Box Tools Format on the ribbon to display the Text Box Tools Format tab.

- Click the Text Fit button (Text Box Tools Format tab | Text group) to display the Text Fit menu (Figure 1–40).

Q&A
Do I have to select all of the text in a text box in order to autofit it?
No. Because all of the text in the text box is included automatically in autofitting, you do not need to select the text in order to autofit it.

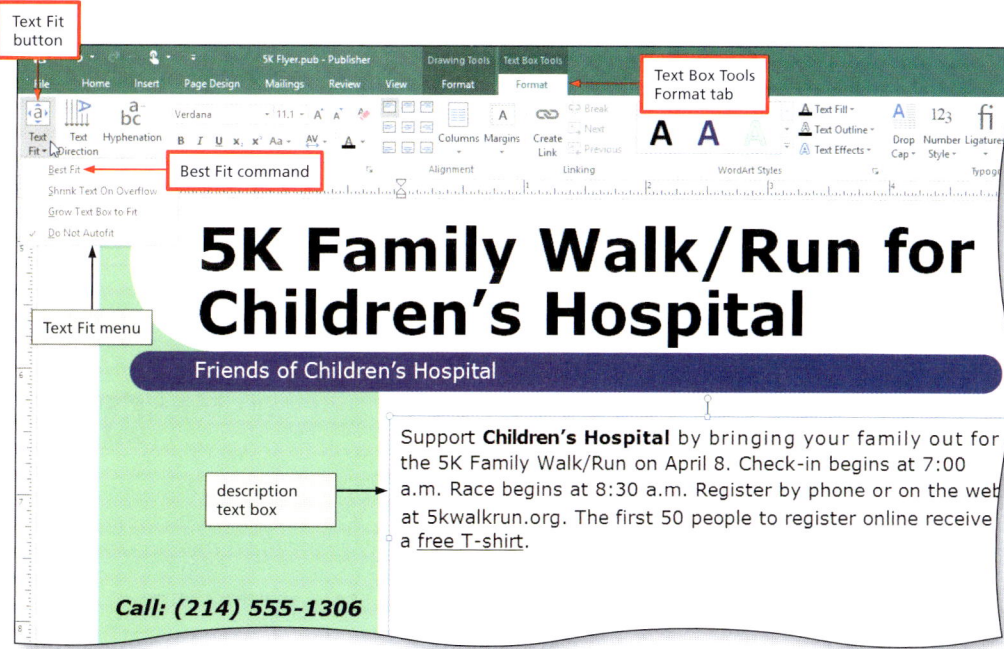

Figure 1–40

2

- Click Best Fit on the Text Fit menu to autofit the text in the text box (Figure 1–41).

Q&A

Could I use the 'Increase Font Size' button to make the title larger?

Yes, but you would have to estimate how big to make the text, and future editing might be displayed incorrectly. Autofitting is different from using the 'Increase Font Size' button. With autofitting, the text and any future text is increased or decreased to fit the given size of the text box automatically.

Figure 1–41

Other Ways

1. Right-click text, click Best Fit on shortcut menu

To Increase the Font Size

1 CUSTOMIZE TEMPLATES | 2 NAVIGATE & SELECT | 3 REPLACE TEXT | 4 DELETE OBJECTS
5 FORMAT TEXT | 6 INSERT GRAPHICS | 7 ENHANCE PAGE | 8 OPEN & REVISE

The following step uses the 'Increase Font Size' button to enlarge the date text to make it easier to read. *Why? The organization wants to be sure viewers know about the event.* If no text is selected, the current word will be increased.

1

- Scroll as necessary to display the text in the date text box.

- Click the text and then press CTRL+A to select all of the text in the text box.

- Click the 'Increase Font Size' button (Home tab | Font group) several times until the text fills the text box without wrapping to a second line, to approximately a font size of 24. If the line wraps, click the 'Decrease Font Size' button (Home tab | Font group) one time (Figure 1–42).

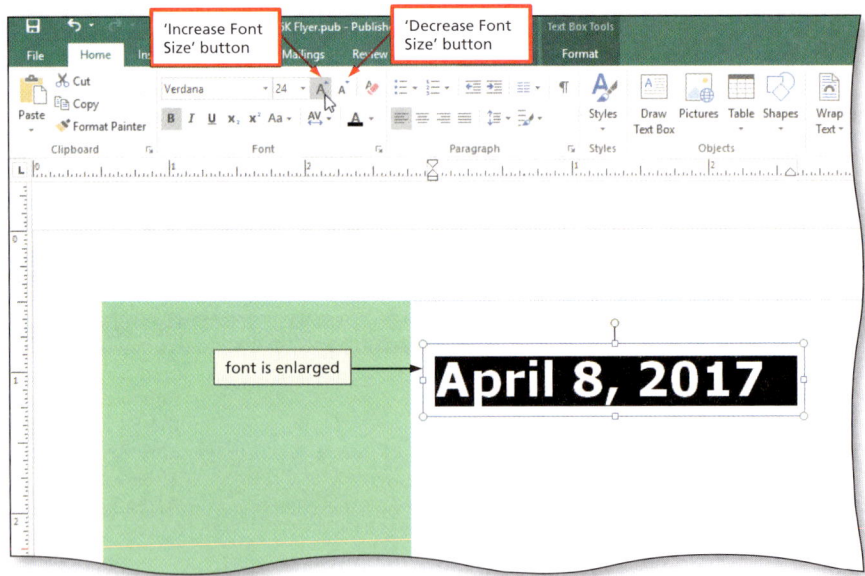

Q&A

Do I have to select the text first?

If no text is selected, only the current word will be increased when you click the 'Increase Font Size' button.

Figure 1–42

Other Ways

1. Select text, click Font Size arrow (Home tab | Font group), click larger font size   2. Press CTRL+>

Using Graphics

Files containing graphical images, also called **graphics**, are available from a variety of sources. For example, a **clip** is a single media file, such as art, sound, or animation that you can insert and use in print publications, web publications, and other Microsoft Office documents. You also can insert pictures stored on your computer or storage location or search for pictures on the web. You will learn about other kinds of graphics in future modules.

Many templates have picture placeholders that provide a size and shape to hold selected pictures. A **picture placeholder** has boundaries called the picture frame and a picture icon that is displayed only when you point to it. You can click the picture icon in a template to access the Insert Pictures dialog box; Publisher offers you three choices to locate a picture or graphic: from a file, from an online search, or from your OneDrive account, if you are signed in. In this module, you will insert a picture from a file. In a future module, you will use the online search. You also can insert an empty picture placeholder to reserve space for pictures you want to add later.

BTW

Using Graphics
When you insert a graphic, Publisher automatically displays the Picture Tools Format tab that contains buttons and tools to help you format the picture.

How do you choose appropriate graphics?

If your client or business has not provided you with a graphic, you should look for a graphic that enhances your topic with strong bright colors. Try to coordinate graphic colors and the Publisher color scheme. Perhaps the most important consideration, however, is ownership. Photos and clip art are not always free. Some web clip art galleries might specify royalty-free images for one-time use, but not for commercial use intended to generate profit. For other uses, you must purchase clip art. It is important to read all licensing agreements carefully. The usage of some artwork requires written permission. Copyright laws apply to all images equally — the right of legal use depends on the intended use and conditions of the copyright owner. All images are copyrighted, regardless of whether they are marked as copyrighted.

CONSIDER THIS

To Use the Picture Placeholder

1 CUSTOMIZE TEMPLATES | 2 NAVIGATE & SELECT | 3 REPLACE TEXT | 4 DELETE OBJECTS
5 FORMAT TEXT | **6 INSERT GRAPHICS** | **7 ENHANCE PAGE** | **8 OPEN & REVISE**

Many templates contain picture placeholders whose size and shape fit in with the template style. *Why? Publications with pictures attract attention and add a sense of realism; most users want pictures in their publications.* The following steps use the picture placeholder to place a photo that is located in the Data Files. Please contact your instructor for information about accessing the Data Files.

1

- Click the area above the title to display the boundary of the picture placeholder and the picture icon (Figure 1–43).

Q&A

I am not using a mouse. Can I make the boundary visible so that I can see it without pointing to it?
Yes. Tap the Boundaries check box (View tab | Show group), which will display the boundaries on all objects.

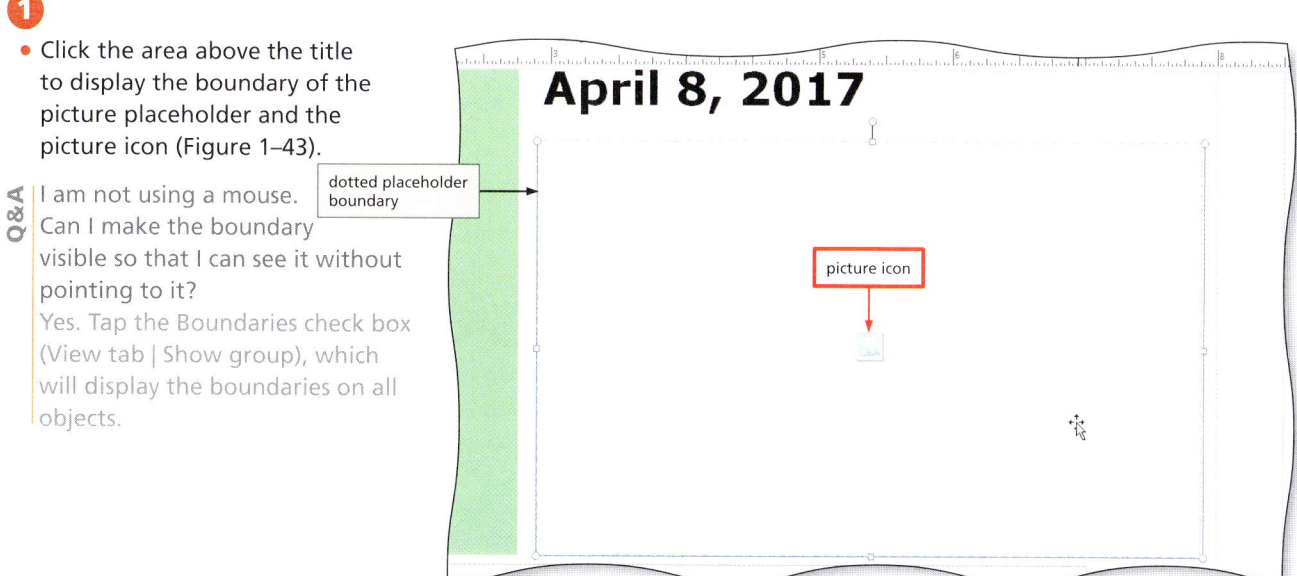

Figure 1–43

- Click the picture icon to display the Insert Pictures dialog box (Figure 1–44).

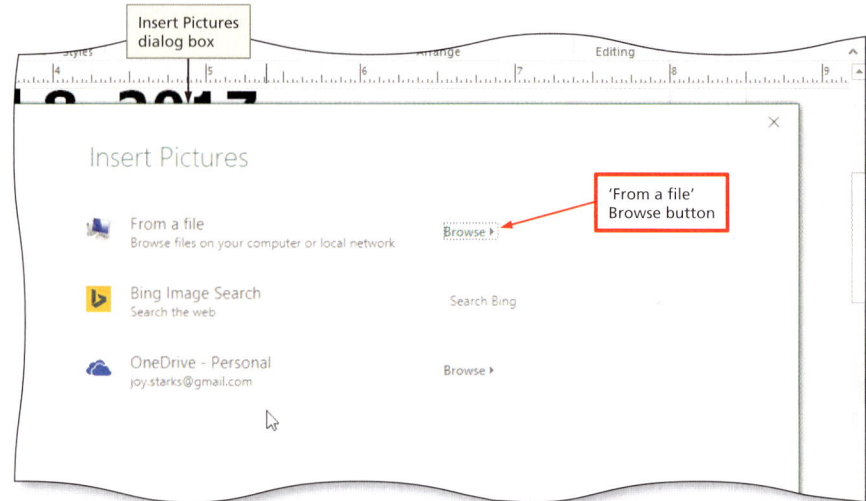

Figure 1–44

- Click the 'From a file' Browse button to display the Insert Picture dialog box.
- Navigate to the Data Files and the Module 01 folder. Scroll down in the list, as necessary, to display the file named, Shoes (Figure 1–45).

Q&A

If I decide not to add a picture, will the placeholder print?
No. Graphic placeholders do not print. Placeholder text will print, however.

Why is my view different?
The default view for graphic files is to display a medium icon. To change the view, click the More options arrow.

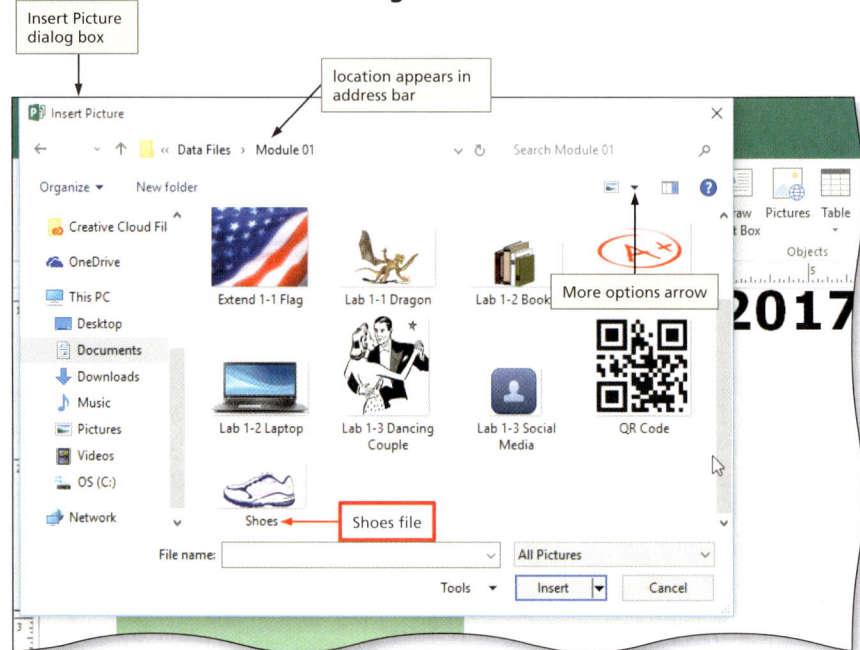

Figure 1–45

4

- Double-click the file named Shoes to insert the chosen picture into the publication (Figure 1–46).

Figure 1–46

To Insert a Picture

You do not have to have a picture placeholder to insert pictures into a publication. *Why? You may want to use a picture as is and not have it conform to the size of the placeholder.* You can insert both online pictures and those from storage, using the Publisher ribbon.

The following steps insert a picture without the use of a picture placeholder. To complete this assignment, you will be required to use the Data Files. Please contact your instructor for information about accessing the Data Files.

- Click outside the page layout so that no object is selected.
- Click Insert on the ribbon to display the Insert tab (Figure 1–47).

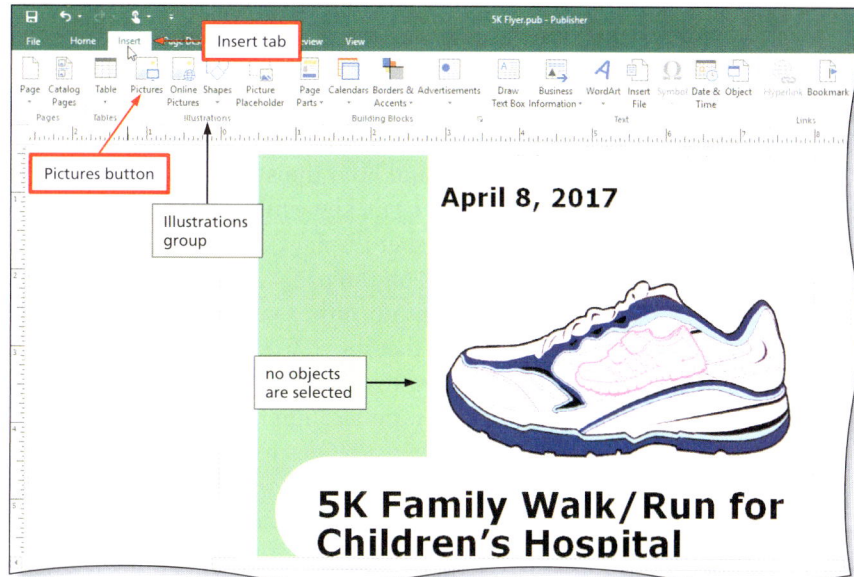

Figure 1–47

- Click the Pictures button (Insert tab | Illustrations group) to display the Insert Picture dialog box.
- Navigate to the location of the Data Files and the Module 01 folder.
- Double-click the desired picture (in this case, the QR Code file) to insert the graphic into the publication (Figure 1–48).

Q&A
How did Publisher decide where to place the picture?
Publisher inserts the picture in the middle of the screen, regardless of the magnification or scrolled area. You will resize and move it in the next series of steps.

Figure 1–48

Resizing, Moving, and Aligning Objects

BTW
QR Codes
A QR code, or quick response code, can be generated by a variety of programs on the web. If a company wants to include a graphic in its QR code, the graphic designer needs to maintain the integrity of the code by inserting a graphic that covers less than 30 percent of the space.

Many times, even when using a template, you will want to enhance the page by resizing objects, moving objects around on the page layout, and aligning them with other objects.

Sometimes pictures and graphics are not the right size. In that case, you need to resize them. To **resize** any object in Publisher, select the object and then drag a handle. Recall that a handle is one of several small shapes displayed around an object when the object is selected. Pressing the CTRL key while dragging (CTRL+drag) keeps the center of the graphic in the same place while resizing. Pressing the SHIFT key while dragging (SHIFT+drag) maintains the graphic's proportions while resizing. Finally, pressing the SHIFT and CTRL keys while dragging (SHIFT+CTRL+drag) maintains the proportions and keeps the center in the same place.

To **move** an object, it must be selected. The pointer changes to a double two-headed arrow, and you then drag the object to the new location or to the scratch area. If you press and hold the SHIFT key while dragging, the object moves in a straight line. Pressing the CTRL key while dragging creates a copy of the object. As you move an object, Publisher displays visual **layout guides** to help you place and align the object to other objects on the page layout. When you **align** an object to another object, its edge or center lines up, either vertically or horizontally. The visual layout guides display as pink lines that move from object to object as you drag. Visual layout guides appear when aligning to the left, right, top, bottom, or middle of objects.

If you want to align the text within a text box rather than aligning the text box itself, Publisher provides four alignment options: Align Right, Center, Align Left, and Justify. Justify aligns text on both the left and right, padding it with extra spaces if necessary. The align tools are on the Home tab, in the Paragraph group. You will learn more about paragraph options in a later module.

To Resize an Object

1 CUSTOMIZE TEMPLATES | 2 NAVIGATE & SELECT | 3 REPLACE TEXT | 4 DELETE OBJECTS
5 FORMAT TEXT | 6 INSERT GRAPHICS | **7 ENHANCE PAGE** | 8 OPEN & REVISE

The next step resizes the QR code to make it smaller. *Why? The QR code eventually will need to fit in a smaller space.*

①

- Scroll as necessary and then select the object to be resized (in this case, the QR code).
- SHIFT+drag the lower-right sizing handle up and left, until the status bar displays a size of approximately 1.33 by 1.33 inches (Figure 1–49).

Q&A Why do I have to use the SHIFT key?
Using the SHIFT key keeps the QR code proportional in size.

picture is resized

pointer displays a double-headed arrow as sizing handle is moved

size reflected on status bar

April 8, 2017

5K Family Walk/Run for Children's Hospital

Page: 1 of 1   2.89, 1.61 in.   1.33 x 1.33 in.

Figure 1–49

Other Ways

1. Enter new width and height on Measurement toolbar

2. Enter new width and height (Drawing Tools Format tab | Size group)

3. Enter new width and height (Picture Tools Format tab | Size group)

To Move a Graphic

1 CUSTOMIZE TEMPLATES | 2 NAVIGATE & SELECT | 3 REPLACE TEXT | 4 DELETE OBJECTS
5 FORMAT TEXT | 6 INSERT GRAPHICS | **7 ENHANCE PAGE** | **8 OPEN & REVISE**

The following steps move the QR code from its current centered location to a location to the left of and aligned with the date. ***Why?*** *Moving the graphic up gives it a more prominent place in the flyer and aligns it for consistency.*

 1

- If necessary, select the graphic (in this case, the QR code).

- Drag the graphic up and to the left side of the flyer, until the pink layout guide appears and is aligned horizontally with the date (Figure 1–50).

Q&A | When do the layout guides appear?

As you drag an object, when one of its borders or its center aligns with another object on the page, Publisher displays a pink guide showing you the possible alignment.

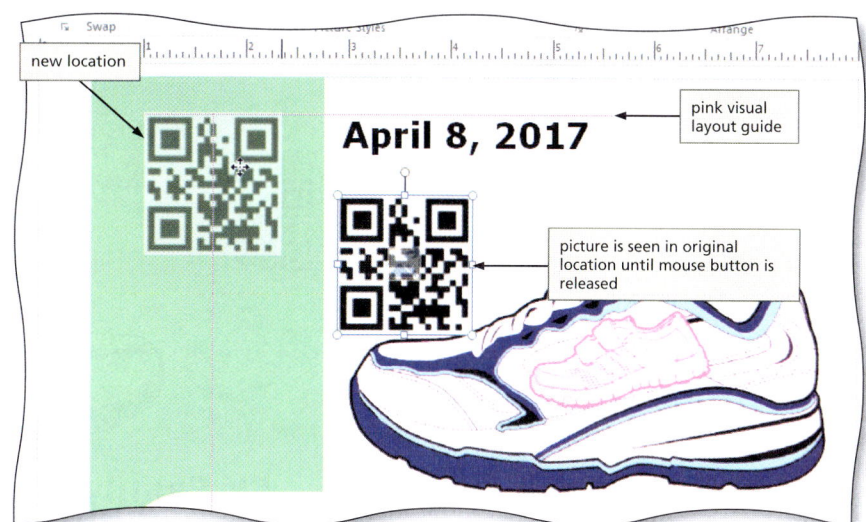

Figure 1–50

 2

- Release the mouse button, if necessary, to finish moving the object.

Other Ways

1. Select object, press ARROW key

2. Select object, click Object Position button on status bar, enter new *x* and *y* coordinates on Measurement toolbar

To Move a Text Box

1 CUSTOMIZE TEMPLATES | 2 NAVIGATE & SELECT | 3 REPLACE TEXT | 4 DELETE OBJECTS
5 FORMAT TEXT | 6 INSERT GRAPHICS | **7 ENHANCE PAGE** | **8 OPEN & REVISE**

The following step moves the date text box and aligns it with the right margin by dragging its border. ***Why?*** *If you drag the text inside a text box, you may move the text, rather than the entire text box object.* In the overall design of the flyer, aligning the date on the right provides a tiered effect among central objects to infer movement from right to left in the flyer.

1

- Select the text box you wish to move (in this case, the date text box) by clicking its border.

- SHIFT+drag the text box to move it in a straight line until it aligns with the right margin as noted by the pink vertical layout guide (Figure 1–51).

Q&A | Why did Publisher change to the Home tab?

The Publisher ribbon is context-sensitive, which means it senses whether you are working with text, graphics, tables, etc., and displays the appropriate ribbon with the tools you might need.

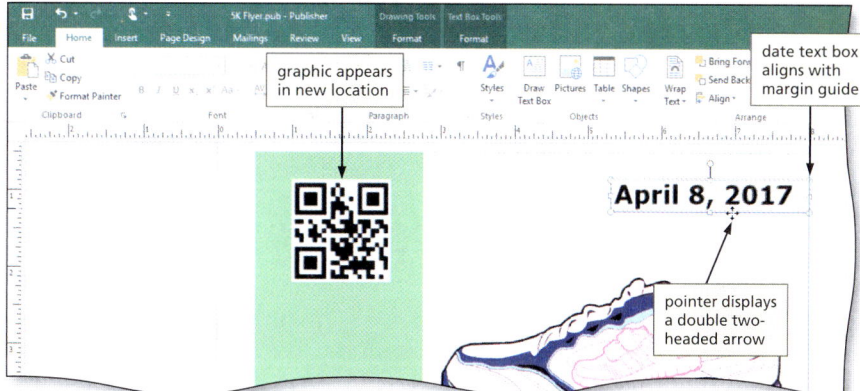

Figure 1–51

Other Ways

1. Select text box border, press ARROW key

2. Select text box, click Object Position button on status bar, enter new *x* and *y* coordinates on Measurement toolbar

To Align Text

The following step right-aligns the text in the title. *Why? Aligning the title text on the right will match the general alignment of the top half of the flyer.*

- Click the text in the title.
- Click the Align Right button (Home tab | Paragraph group) to align the text on the right (Figure 1–52).

Q&A Will it align both lines? Yes, the align buttons are paragraph-based.

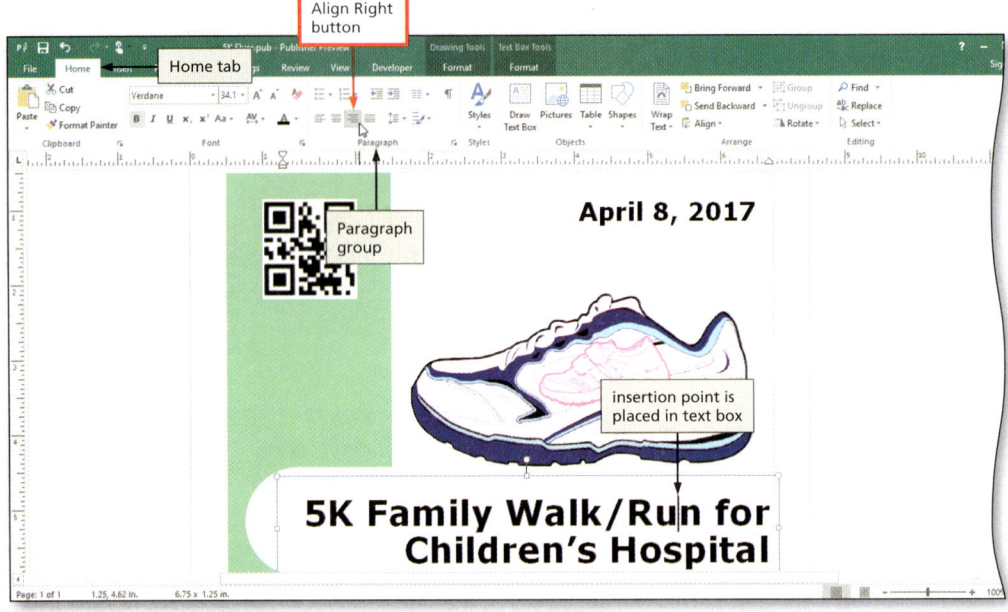

Figure 1–52

Other Ways

1. Click Paragraph Spacing button (Home tab | Paragraph group), click 'Paragraph Spacing Options' on Paragraph Spacing menu, click Alignment button (Paragraph dialog box), click Right, click OK button
2. Press CTRL+R

To View Whole Page

The following steps view the entire page layout. *Why? Before you save the publication again, you may want to see how it looks so far.*

- Click outside of any selected object to deselect it.
- Click the 'Show Whole Page' button on the status bar to view the entire page (Figure 1–53).

- Click the Save button on the Quick Access Toolbar to save the file with the same file name and to overwrite the previously saved file.

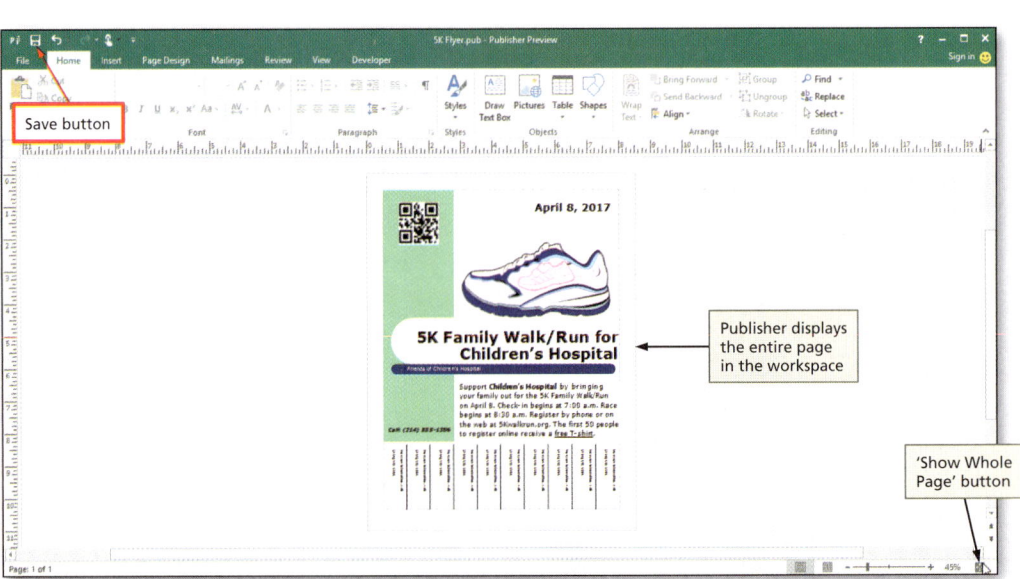

Figure 1–53

Other Ways

1. Click Whole Page button (View tab | Zoom group)
2. Press SHIFT+CTRL+L

CONSIDER THIS

What is the best method for distributing a publication?
The traditional method of distributing a publication uses a printer to produce a hard copy. A **hard copy** or **printout** is information that exists on a physical medium such as paper. Hard copies can be useful for the following reasons:

• Some people prefer proofreading a hard copy of a publication rather than viewing it on the screen to check for errors and readability.

• Hard copies can serve as a backup reference if your storage medium is lost or becomes corrupted and you need to recreate the publication.

Instead of distributing a hard copy of a publication, users can distribute the publication as an electronic image that mirrors the original publication's appearance. The electronic image of the publication can be sent as an email attachment, posted on a website, or copied to a portable storage medium such as a USB flash drive. Two popular electronic image formats, sometimes called fixed formats, are PDF by Adobe Systems and XPS by Microsoft. In Publisher, you can create electronic image files through the Save As dialog box and the Export, Share, and Print tabs in the Backstage view. Electronic images of publications, such as PDF and XPS, can be useful, as users can view electronic images of publications without the software that created the original publication (e.g., Publisher). Specifically, to view a PDF file, you use a program called Adobe Reader, which can be downloaded free from Adobe's website. Similarly, to view an XPS file, you use a program called XPS Viewer, which is included in the latest versions of Windows and Internet Explorer.

Sending electronic publications saves paper and printer supplies. Society encourages users to contribute to **green computing**, which involves reducing the electricity consumed and environmental waste generated when using computers, mobile devices, and related technologies, as well as saving paper.

To Print a Publication

After creating a publication, you may want to print it. Printing a publication enables you to distribute it to others in a form that can be read or viewed, but typically not edited. It is a good practice to save a publication before printing it, in case you experience difficulties printing.

The following steps print a hard copy of the contents of the saved 5K Flyer publication.

1 Click File on the ribbon to open the Backstage view.

2 Click the Print tab in the Backstage view to display the Print gallery.

3 Verify the printer name listed on the Printer Status button will print a hard copy of the publication. If necessary, click the Printer Status button to display a list of available printer options and then click the desired printer to change the currently selected printer.

4 Click the Print button in the Print gallery to print the publication on the currently selected printer.

5 When the printer stops, retrieve the hard copy.

6 Exit Publisher. If a Microsoft Publisher dialog box appears, click the Save button to save any changes made to the publication since the last save.

Break Point: If you wish to take a break, this is a good place to do so. To resume at a later time, continue following the steps from this location forward.

Changing a Publication

After creating a publication, you often will find that you must make changes to it. Changes can be required because the publication contains an error or because of new circumstances. The types of changes made to publications normally fall into one of the three following categories: deletions, additions, or modifications.

BTW

Conserving Ink and Toner
If you want to conserve ink or toner, you can instruct Publisher to print draft quality documents by clicking Print in the Backstage view to display the Print gallery, clicking the Printer Properties link, and then, depending on your printer, click the Print Quality button and choose Draft in the list.

BTW
Pinned Files
Files that appear in the Recent list can be unpinned from the list. Right-click the file and then click 'Remove from list' on the shortcut menu.

BTW
Recent List
A list of recently used files also appears in the Backstage view when you click Open.

Deletions Sometimes deletions are necessary in a publication because objects are incorrect or no longer are needed. For example, to place this advertising flyer on a website, the tear-offs no longer are needed. In that case, you would delete them from the page layout.

Additions Additional text, objects, or formatting may be required in the publication. For example, in the 5K Flyer you may want to insert a text box that could be displayed when the flyer is published on the web.

Modifications If you make modifications to text or graphics, normal techniques of inserting, deleting, editing, and formatting apply. Publisher provides several methods for detecting problems in a publication and making modifications, including spell checking and design checking.

In the following sections, you will make changes to the flyer to prepare it for publishing to the web.

To Open a Recent Publication

1 CUSTOMIZE TEMPLATES | 2 NAVIGATE & SELECT | 3 REPLACE TEXT | 4 DELETE OBJECTS
5 FORMAT TEXT | 6 INSERT GRAPHICS | 7 ENHANCE PAGE | **8 OPEN & REVISE**

Earlier in this module, you saved your publication using the file name, 5K Flyer. Publisher maintains a list of the last few publications that have been opened or saved on your computer. The **Recent list** allows you to click the name of the publication to open it, without browsing to the location. The following steps run Publisher and open the 5K Flyer file from the Recent Publication list.

• Run Publisher (Figure 1–54).

Q&A My list of recent publications is different. Did I do something wrong?
No, your list will differ depending on what publications you have opened in the past.

The file does not appear in the Recent list. What should I do?
If the file you wish to open does not appear in the Recent list, click 'Open Other Publications' and then navigate to the location of the file to be opened. Double-click the file name to open it.

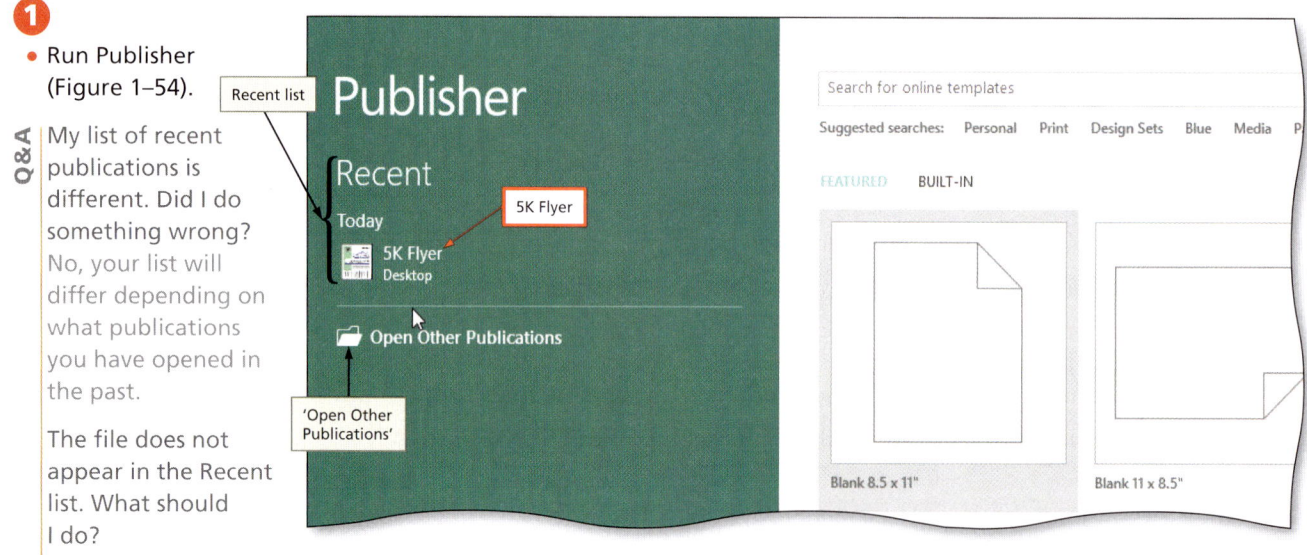

Figure 1–54

• In the Recent list, click 5K Flyer to open the publication.

Q&A Can I change the total number of publications listed in the Recent list?
Yes. In the Backstage view, click the Options tab, click Advanced (Publisher Options dialog box), and then in the Display area, change the number in the 'Show this number of Recent Publications' text box.

To Insert a Hyperlink

A **hyperlink**, or link, is a clickable link or reference to another location. A hyperlink can link to a page on the web, to an email address, to a location on a storage device, or another location within a publication. The following steps create a link to the event website. *Why? This version of the flyer will be seen on the web, where users may want to click to register.*

- Select the text you wish to make a hyperlink (in this case, the web address in the description text box) and then zoom to 100% (Figure 1–55).

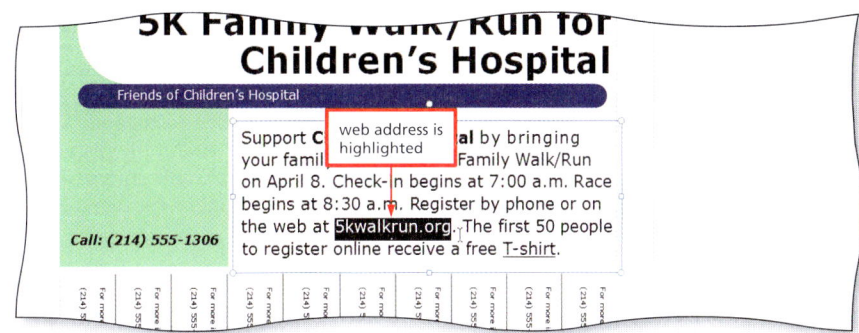

Figure 1–55

- Click Insert on the ribbon to display the Insert tab.

- Click the 'Add a Hyperlink' button (Insert tab | Links group) to display the Insert Hyperlink dialog box.

- If necessary, click the Address text box to position the insertion point and then type **www.5Kwalkrun.org** to enter the web address. Publisher will add the http:// protocol to your web address (Figure 1–56).

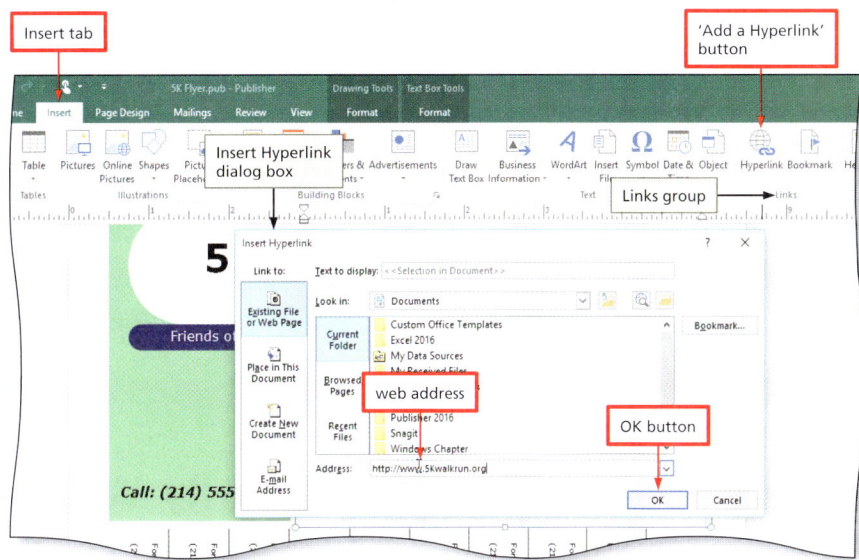

Figure 1–56

- Click the OK button (Insert Hyperlink dialog box) to assign the hyperlink (Figure 1–57).

Q&A

How can I tell if it is a hyperlink? Publisher will underline a hyperlink and use a purple or blue font. When a user hovers over a hyperlink, the pointer will appear as a hand.

Figure 1–57

Other Ways

1. Right-click text, click Hyperlink on shortcut menu, enter web address in Address text box (Insert Hyperlink dialog box), click OK button

2. Press CTRL+K, enter web address in Address text box (Insert Hyperlink dialog box), click OK button

To Delete Using a Shortcut Menu

If this flyer is displayed on a website, the tear-offs are unnecessary and should be deleted. The following steps delete the tear-offs using the shortcut menu. *Why? In many cases, executing a command from the shortcut menu is faster because you do not have to move the pointer.*

1

- Scroll to the lower portion of the flyer.

- Right-click any one of the tear-offs to display the shortcut menu (Figure 1–58).

Q&A My shortcut menu is different. Did I do something wrong? No. Shortcut menus are context-sensitive, so they are displayed slightly different if you click the text versus the border of the text box.

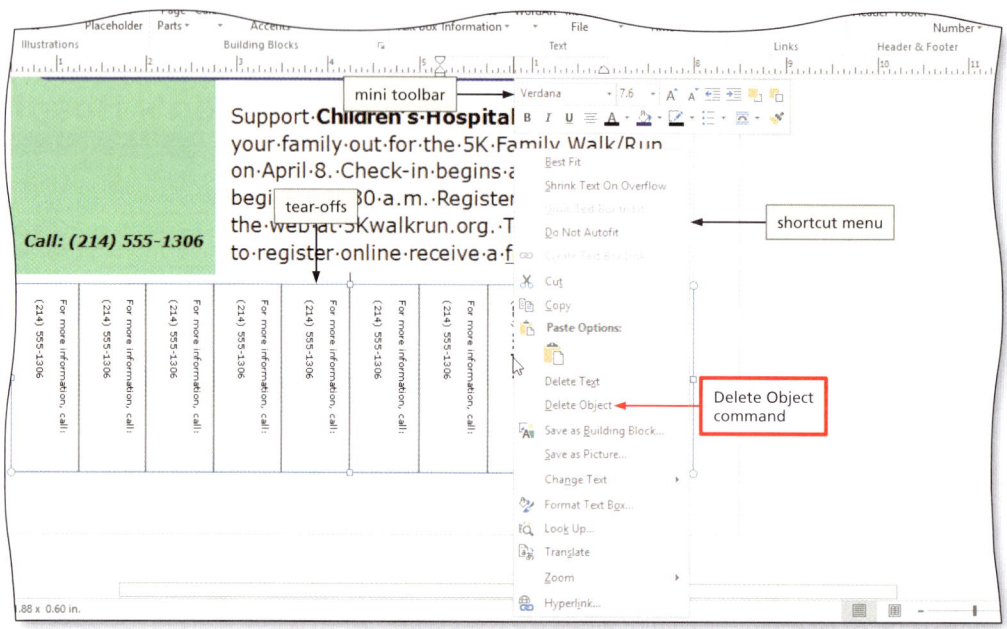

Figure 1–58

2

- Click Delete Object on the shortcut menu to delete the tear-offs (Figure 1–59).

Q&A What do I do if my shortcut menu does not display a Delete Object command? Click in a slightly different location within the tear-offs.

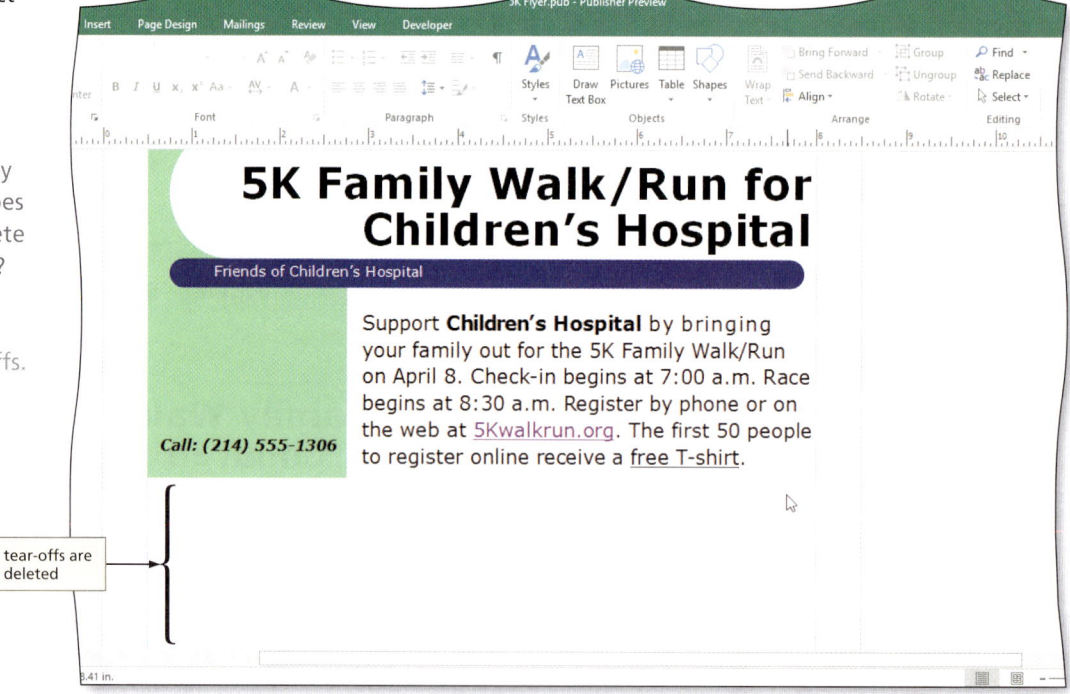

Figure 1–59

Creating a Webpage from a Publication

You can create several types of publications with Microsoft Publisher, other than standard print publications. A **web publication** is one suitable for publishing to the web, containing certain objects, formatting options, hyperlinks, and other features specific to webpages. You can create a web publication from scratch, or you can save the print publication as a web publication. The following sections create a web version of the flyer that might be posted on a campus website or social networking site.

BTW

Web Publications
When converting to a web publication, determine which objects will work effectively on the web and which ones will not, modifying the publication as necessary. Will the publication be accessible on the web? Is the target audience common web users? If so, determine whether an email or website would be the most efficient means of communication.

To Save a Print Publication as a Web Publication

1 CUSTOMIZE TEMPLATES | 2 NAVIGATE & SELECT | 3 REPLACE TEXT | 4 DELETE OBJECTS
5 FORMAT TEXT | 6 INSERT GRAPHICS | 7 ENHANCE PAGE | **8 OPEN & REVISE**

The Export tab in the Backstage view includes a group of commands that allow you to save publications as different file types or to package publications for sending to other users. In the following steps, you will export the publication by publishing it to the web. **Publishing HTML** or **publishing to the web** is the process of making webpages available to others, for example, on the World Wide Web or on a company's intranet.

A **Hypertext Markup Language** (**HTML**) file is a file capable of being stored and transferred electronically on a file server in order to display on the web.

The **Mime Hypertext Markup Language** (**MHTML**) is a small, single-file format that does not create a supporting folder of resources. The following steps save the publication as a web flyer in the MHTML format. *Why?* *The MHTML file can be published to and downloaded from the web quickly.*

1

- Click File on the ribbon to open the Backstage view.

- Click the Export tab in the Backstage view to display the Export gallery.

- Click the Publish HTML tab to display its options.

- Click the 'Web Page (HTML)' button to display options for publishing HTML (Figure 1–60).

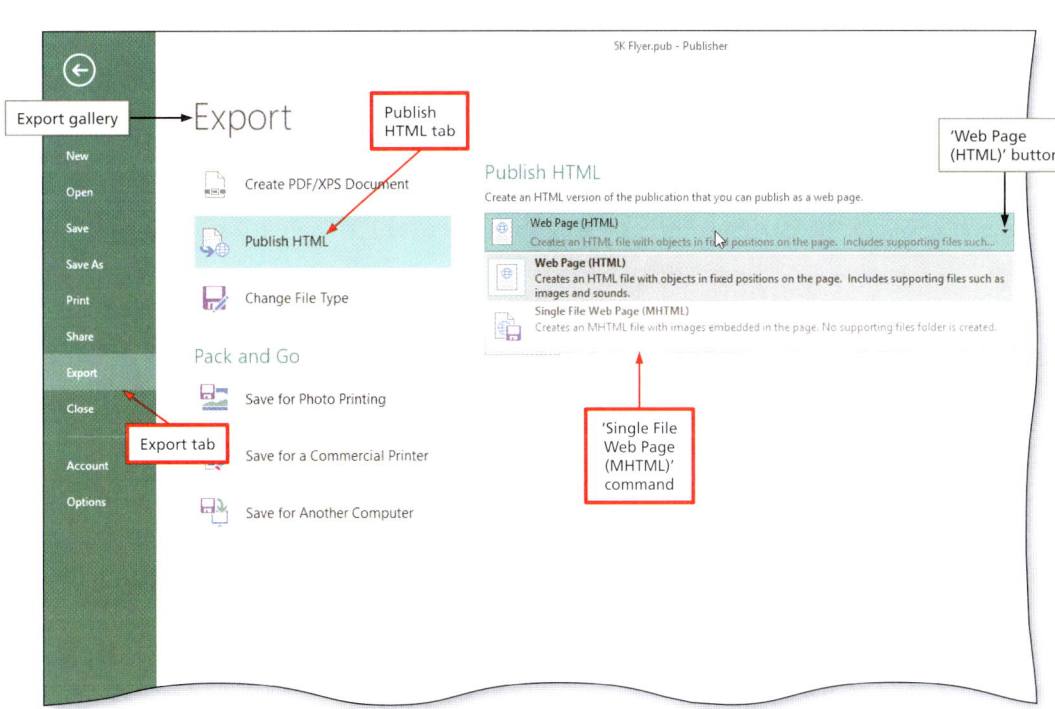

Figure 1–60

- Click 'Single File Web Page (MHTML)' to select it.

- Click the Publish HTML button in the Backstage view to display the Save As dialog box.

- Type **5K Web Flyer** in the File name text box (Save As dialog box). Do not press the ENTER key after typing the file name.

- Navigate to your storage location (Figure 1–61).

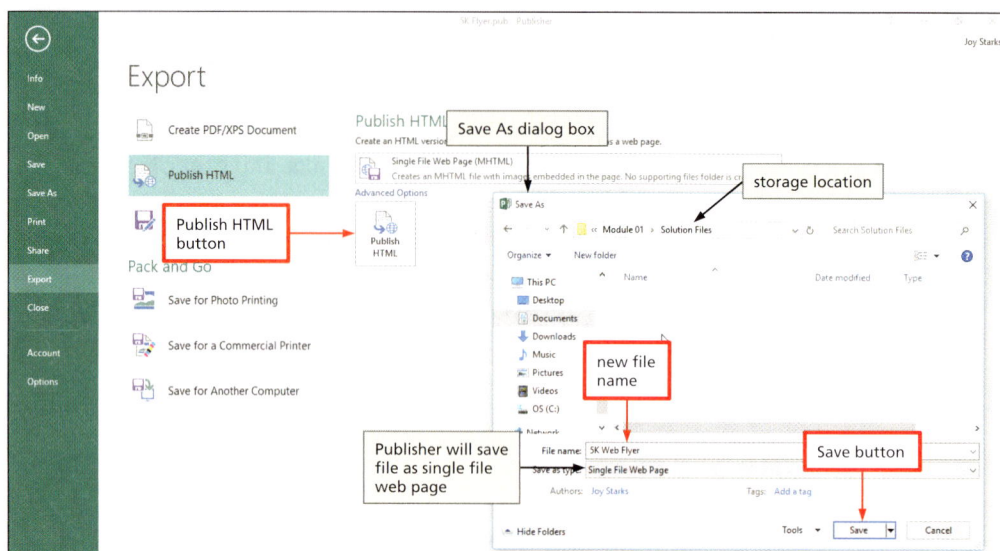

Figure 1–61

Q&A How do I move the the dialog box out of the way?
In general, you can move dialog boxes by dragging the title bar. You also can resize them to view different parts of your screen.

- Click the Save button (Save As dialog box) to save the publication as a single file web page.

Other Ways

1. Click Save As in Backstage view, click storage location, enter file name, click 'Save as type' button, click 'Single File Web Page (*.mht;*.mhtml)', click Save button (Save As dialog box)

To Preview the Web Publication in a Browser

1 CUSTOMIZE TEMPLATES | 2 NAVIGATE & SELECT | 3 REPLACE TEXT | 4 DELETE OBJECTS
5 FORMAT TEXT | 6 INSERT GRAPHICS | 7 ENHANCE PAGE | **8 OPEN & REVISE**

The following steps preview the web publication. **Why?** *Previewing is the best way to test the look and feel of the webpage and to test the hyperlink.* You will open the MHTML file from its storage location.

1

- Click the folder icon on your taskbar to run the File Explorer. When the File Explorer window opens, navigate to your storage location (Figure 1–62).

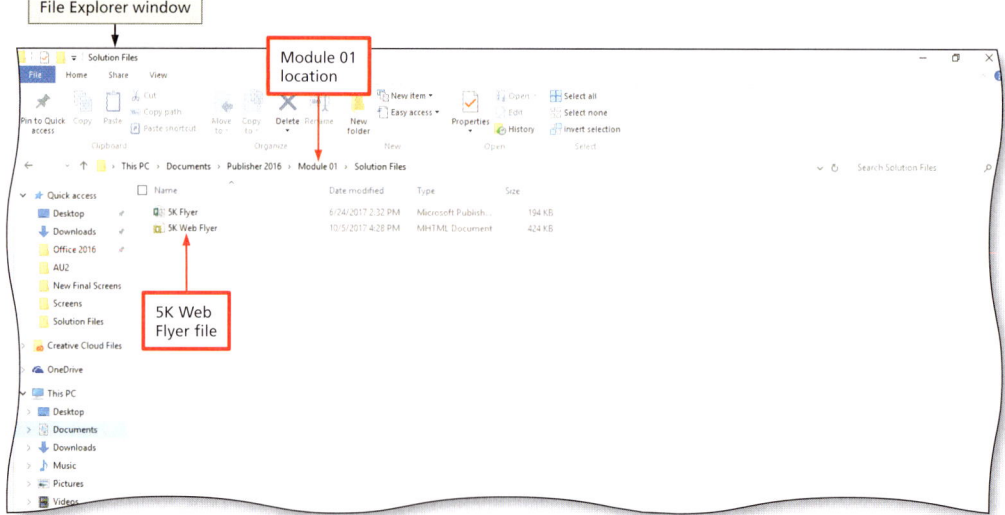

Figure 1–62

- Double-click the 5K Web Flyer file.
- When the browser window opens, if necessary, maximize the window and scroll to display the hyperlink (Figure 1–63).

Q&A

Why does my display look different?
Each brand and version of browser software displays information in a slightly different manner.

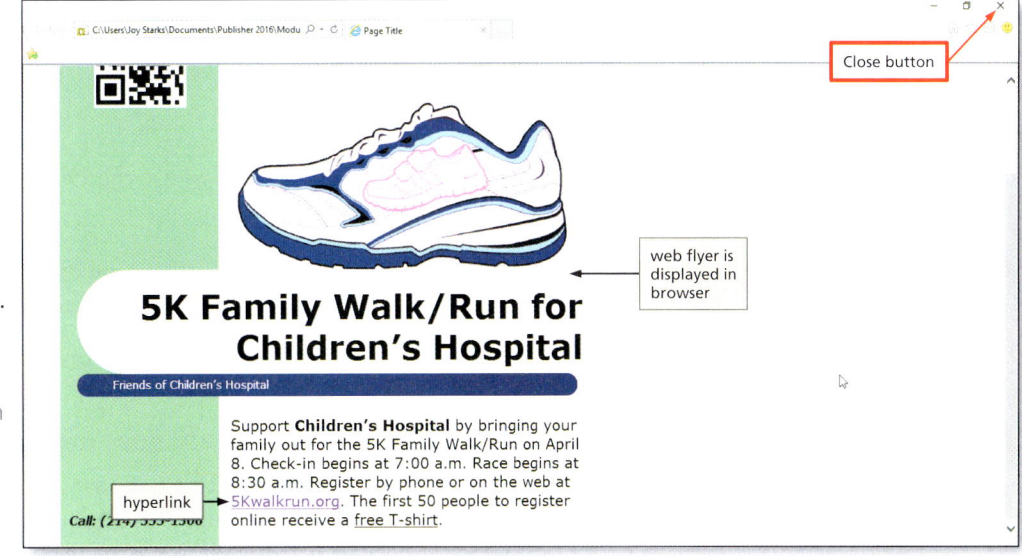

Figure 1–63

- Click the Close button on the browser window's title bar and then click the Close button on the File Explorer window's title bar.
- Exit Publisher. If a Microsoft Publisher dialog box appears, click the Don't Save button to exit Publisher.
- Sign out of your Microsoft Account if necessary.

Summary

In this module, you learned some basic Publisher techniques as you created a flyer from a template. You learned how to choose a publication template and set font and color schemes. You learned how to enter and edit both placeholder and default text. After creating synchronized tear-offs, you formatted text with bold, underline, and italics. You added a graphic using a picture placeholder and then inserted a picture without a placeholder. You learned how to delete, resize, move, and align objects. After checking the spelling, you saved the file and reopened it for revisions, such as creating a hyperlink and removing tear-offs in the publication. Finally, you saved a print publication as a web publication.

CONSIDER THIS

What decisions will you need to make when creating your next publication?
Use these guidelines as you complete the assignments in this module and create your own publications outside of this class.

1. Select template options.
   a) Select a template that matches your need.
   b) Choose font and color schemes determined by the flyer's purpose and audience.
2. Choose words for the text.
   a) Replace all placeholder and default text.
   b) Add other objects as necessary; delete unused items.
3. Identify how to format various objects in the flyer.
   a) Use bold, underline, and italics for emphasis.
   b) Autofit the text to make the flyer easy to read.
4. Find and insert the appropriate graphic(s).
   a) Resize, move, and align as necessary.
5. Determine whether the flyer will be more effective as a print publication, web publication, or both.
   a) Insert any necessary hyperlinks.
   b) Consider creating a background for a web publication.

Apply Your Knowledge

Reinforce the skills and apply the concepts you learned in this module.

Editing a Flyer with Text and Graphics

Note: To complete this assignment, you will be required to use the Data Files. Please contact your instructor for information about accessing the Data Files.

Instructions: Run Publisher and open the file named Apply 1-1 Sale Flyer from the Data Files. The document contains a flyer to advertise a home for sale that you are to modify. The modified flyer is shown in Figure 1–64.

Perform the following tasks:

1. Select the default text in the Price text box. Type `$239,900` to replace the text.
2. Select the default text in the address text box. Type `1217 81st Terrace` and then press the ENTER key. Type `Gladstone, Indiana 46109` to replace the text.
3. With the insertion point still positioned in the address text box, click the Text Box Tools Format tab. Click the Text Fit button (Text Box Tools Format tab | Text group) and then click Best Fit on the Text Fit menu.
4. Select the default text in the phone number text box. Type `Call: 317-555-6628` to replace the text.

Courtesy of Joy Starks

Figure 1–64

5. If instructed to do so, change the phone number in Step 4 to your phone number.

6. Select the default text in the description text box. Type `2500 sq. ft.` and then press the TAB key 3 times. Type `4 bedrooms & 2 baths` and then press the ENTER key.

7. Type `Central air` and then press the TAB key four times. Type `Newly renovated kitchen` and then press the ENTER key.

8. Type `New roof` and then press the TAB key four times. Type `Pool` to complete the description text.

9. Delete the More Information text box.

10. On the right side of the flyer, select the picture placeholder. In the picture placeholder, click the picture icon to display the Insert Pictures dialog box. Browse to the Data Files and the Module 1 folder. Insert the picture called Apply 1-1 Home. Deselect the picture.

11. Click the Pictures button (Insert tab | Illustrations group). Browse to the Data Files and the Module 1 folder. Insert the picture Apply 1-1 Pool. Move the picture to a location below and slightly overlapping the picture of the house, as shown in Figure 1–64.

12. Save the flyer on your storage location with the file name, Apply 1-1 Sale Flyer Complete.

13. Submit the completed publication in the format specified by your instructor, which may involve printing a hard copy.

14. ✳ What would you add or delete if you were to publish this flyer in the MHTML format on the web? Why?

Extend Your Knowledge

Extend the skills you learned in this module and experiment with new skills. You may need to use Help to complete the assignment.

Creating a Flyer from Scratch

Note: To complete this assignment, you will be required to use the Data Files. Please contact your instructor for information about accessing the Data Files.

Instructions: Run Publisher and open a blank 8.5 × 11" template. Use Publisher to create the flyer shown in Figure 1–65 by inserting graphics, drawing text boxes, applying picture styles, and formatting the text.

Perform the following tasks:

1. Click the Pictures button (Insert tab | Illustrations group). Insert the graphic named, Extend 1-1 Decorative Rectangle, which is located in the Data Files. Move it as necessary to approximately the center of the page.

2. Insert a second picture named, Extend 1-1 Blue Rectangle, which is located in the Data Files. Move it to the upper-center as shown in Figure 1–65.

3. Insert a third picture named, Extend 1-1 Flag, which is located in the Data Files. Move it above the blue rectangle as shown in Figure 1–65.

4. Use Help to read about applying picture styles. Use the More button (Picture Tools Format | Picture styles group) to apply a picture style, such as Relaxed Perspective, White, to the flag graphic.

5. Use Help to read about drawing text boxes and then perform the following tasks, zooming as necessary:

   a. Use the 'Draw a Text Box' button (Home tab | Objects group) to create a text box on top of the blue rectangle, filling the area below the flag graphic.

   b. Before typing the text, return to the Home tab. Click the Font Color arrow (Home tab | Font group) and then choose a white color. Type the text, `Register to Vote!` and then autofit it. *Continued >*

Extend Your Knowledge *continued*

first text box is bold

second text box is italicized

third text box is underlined

Figure 1–65

c. Draw another text box below the first one. Return to the Home tab. Click the Font Color arrow (Home tab | Font group) and then choose a black color. Click the Center button (Home tab | Paragraph group).

d. Click the Bold button (Home tab | Font group) and then type the text shown in Figure 1–65. Use the 'Increase Font Size' button (Home tab | Font group) to change the font size to approximately 24 pt.

e. Repeat Step 5c for the next text box and format the text italic. Increase the font size to approximately 20 pt. Type the text as shown in Figure 1-65. If Publisher automatically capitalizes some letters, fix them as necessary.

f. Repeat Step 5c for the last text box and format the text underlined. Increase the font size to approximately 16 pt. Type the text as shown in Figure 1-65.

g. If requested to do so by your instructor, add the name of your voting location to the flyer.

6. Save the file with the file name, Extend 1-1 Vote Flyer Complete.

7. Submit the file in the format specified by your instructor.

8. ✳ When would you use a template instead of creating a flyer from scratch that contains only the objects you need? Was formatting the font before you typed easier than selecting text and formatting it afterward? Why?

Expand Your World

Create a solution that uses cloud and web technologies by learning and investigating on your own from general guidance.

Modifying and Exporting a Publication

Note: To complete this assignment, you will be required to use the Data Files. Please contact your instructor for information about accessing the Data Files.

Instructions: Run Publisher and open the file Expand 1-1 Spring Break Ad from the Data Files. The file contains a flyer to advertise a spring break trip that you are to modify and post on OneDrive. The modified flyer is shown in Figure 1–66.

Figure 1–66

Continued >

Expand Your World *continued*

Perform the following tasks:

1. Replace the placeholder text, Attention Grabber, with the name of your school. Replace the Date placeholder text with the date of your school's spring break.

2. If requested to do so by your instructor, change the phone number to your phone number.

3. Save the presentation on OneDrive using the file name, Expand 1-1 Spring Break Ad Complete.

4. Submit the assignment in the format specified by your instructor.

5. ✹ On what occasions might you save one of your files for school or your job on OneDrive? Do you think using OneDrive enhances collaboration efforts? Why?

In the Labs

Design, create, modify, and/or use a publication following the guidelines, concepts, and skills presented in this module. Labs 1 and 2, which increase in difficulty, require you to create solutions based on what you learned in the module; Lab 3 requires you to apply your creative thinking and problem-solving skills to design and implement a solution.

Lab 1: **Creating a Multipurpose Flyer**

Note: To complete this assignment, you will be required to use the Data Files. Please contact your instructor for information about accessing the Data Files.

Problem: The Computer Club on campus is sponsoring a video game tournament and would like you to create a flyer for print and web posting. You decide to look through Publisher's templates for an appropriate flyer to use as a starting point. You create the flyer shown in Figure 1–67.

Perform the following tasks:

1. Run Publisher.

2. Click BUILT-IN templates.

3. Click the Flyers thumbnail to display the Flyer templates and folders of additional templates. Click the All Event folder to open it. Scroll down to display the 'More Installed Templates' area and the Special Offer flyers. Click the Blocks thumbnail to select it.

4. Customize the template with the Mountain color scheme and the Etched font scheme. If necessary, in the Options area, click the Tear-offs button and then click None.

5. Click the OK button to create the publication.

6. At the top of the flyer, zoom in to make the following changes:

   a. Select the Business Name text. Type `Computer Club`. Right-click the text box to display the shortcut menu, and then click Best Fit to autofit the text.

   b. If instructed to do so, change the name of the club in Step 6a to the name of a club or group of which you are a member.

   c. Click the border of the 'Business Tagline or Motto' text box to select it. Press the DELETE key to delete the text box.

   d. Select all of the text in the Date text box. Type `October 7, 2017` to replace the text. Autofit the text.

   e. Change the Time text to `Start: 10:00 a.m.` Autofit the text.

   f. Delete the logo.

Figure 1–67

7. Scroll to the center of the flyer and make the following changes.

a. Click the Promotion Title placeholder text to select it. Type `Dragon Tournament` to replace the text.

b. Click the description placeholder text to select it. Press the F9 key to zoom to 100%. Type the following text, pressing the ENTER key at the end of each line.

```
Dragons: 12-player maximum

Event Format: League rules

Cost: Free! You may preregister your spot online for $3.00.
```

c. In the same box, type the following text that purposefully has a misspelled word (in this case, acheivements).

```
Event Details: Players will be assigned a character. Play in
each pod lasts 4 hours. Prizes will be awarded for outstanding
acheivements and good play!
```

d. Right-click the misspelled word and choose the correct spelling from the list.

Continued >

In the Labs *continued*

   e. Autofit the description text box.

   f. Click the border of the bulleted list text box to select it. Press the DELETE key to delete the text box.

   g. Resize the description text box by selecting it and dragging the center-right handle to the right to fill in the space left by the bulleted list.

8. Scroll to the lower portion of the flyer and make the following changes:

   a. Delete the organization logo.

   b. Click the lower-right area in the flyer to display the boundary of the picture placeholder and the picture icon. Click the picture icon to display the Insert Pictures dialog box. Click the 'From a file' Browse button to display the Insert Picture dialog box. Navigate to the Data Files and the Module 01 folder. Double-click the file named, Lab 1-1 Dragon, to insert the chosen picture into the publication. Deselect the graphic.

   c. Click the Pictures button (Insert tab | Illustrations group) to display the Insert Picture dialog box. Navigate to the location of the Data Files and the Module 01 folder. Double-click the desired picture (in this case, the QR Code file) to insert the file into the publication. Resize the picture to approximately 1.33 × 1.33 inches. Move the QR code to the lower-left corner of the flyer.

9. Save the flyer on your storage location with the file name, Lab 1-1 Tournament Flyer.

10. Print a hardcopy of the flyer.

11. To convert the flyer to a web flyer, perform the following steps.

   a. At the top of the flyer, select the text, Computer Club.

   b. Click the 'Add a Hyperlink' button (Insert tab | Links group) to display the Insert Hyperlink dialog box. If necessary, click the Address text box to position the insertion point, and then type **www.cengagecomputerclub.org** to enter the web address.

   c. Click the OK button (Insert Hyperlink dialog box) to assign the hyperlink.

   d. Delete the QR code.

   e. Click File on the ribbon to open the Backstage view and then click the Export tab to display the Export gallery.

   f. Click Publish HTML to display its options.

   g. Click the 'Web Page (HTML)' button to display options for publishing HTML. Click 'Single File Web Page (MHTML)' to select it.

   h. Click the Publish HTML button to display the Save As dialog box.

   i. Type **Lab 1-1 Web Flyer** in the File name text box. Do not press the ENTER key after typing the file name. Navigate to your storage location. Click the Save button (Save As dialog box) to save the publication as a single file web page.

   j. Preview the web flyer in a browser.

12. Submit the file as directed by your instructor.

13. ✳ As you see QR codes in public places, where are they normally placed on the object? How are they placed differently on products versus advertisements? Why do you think that is true?

Lab 2: **Customizing a Flyer**

Note: To complete this assignment, you will be required to use the Data Files. Please contact your instructor for information about accessing the Data Files.

Problem: Your friend wants to earn some extra money by tutoring. He wants you to create a flyer that he can post on dormitory bulletin boards. You create the flyer shown in Figure 1–68.

Courtesy of OpenClipArt.org

Figure 1–68

Perform the following tasks:

1. Run Publisher. Open the flyer named Lab 1-2 Tutoring Flyer, which is located in the Data Files.

2. Select the description placeholder text in the bulleted list. Press the F9 key to zoom to 100%. Type the following lines, pressing the ENTER key after each one.

```
Computer Concepts
Intro to Database
Desktop Publishing
Office Applications
```

Continued >

In the Labs *continued*

3. If instructed to do so, change the four tutoring topics in Step 2 to the name of four classes you have taken.

4. Click a single tear-off. Press CTRL+A to select all of the text in the tear-off. Type `Call Ben at:` and then press the ENTER key. Type `303-555-8606` to complete the tear-off. If requested by your instructor, use your name and phone number in the tear-offs. Click outside the tear-offs to synchronize them.

5. Locate the picture placeholder on the upper-right. Insert the picture named Lab 1-2 Laptop, which is located in the Data Files.

6. Locate the picture placeholder on the left. Insert the picture named Lab 1-2 Grade, which is located in the Data Files.

7. Insert the picture named QR Code, which is located in the Data Files. Resize it and place it in the lower-right corner of the flyer.

8. Save the flyer on your storage location with the file name, Lab 1-2 Tutoring Flyer Complete.

9. Print a hardcopy of the flyer.

10. Submit the file as directed by your instructor.

11. ✳ Which elements would you change if this were a flyer on the web? Why?

Lab 3: **Consider This: Your Turn**

Creating an Advertisement

Note: To complete this assignment, you will be required to use the Data Files. Please contact your instructor for information about accessing the Data Files.

Problem: You attend a college that is famous for its Department of Dance. Students who major in dance are required to complete internships as dance instructors. Because you are a computer technology major, they have asked you to create a flyer that advertises the lessons and includes a social media logo.

Perform the following tasks:

Part 1: Use the concepts and techniques presented in this module to design and create an advertising flyer. Use an appropriate template, font scheme, and color scheme. Replace placeholder text. Include wording such as, "The graduate students from the Department of Dance will teach Ballroom Dancing. No prior dance experience is necessary. Come and have a great time — it is a great date night, guys!!" Include the date and time of the dance lessons. Choose text for a hyperlink and your email address as the hyperlink address. In the picture placeholder, click the picture icon for the template graphic, and insert the Lab 1-3 Dancing Couple file from the Data Files. Insert the Lab 1-3 Social Media logo from the Data Files and use an appropriate text reference. Submit your assignment in the format specified by your instructor.

Part 2: ✳ You made several decisions while determining the appropriate template, schemes, text, and graphics. How did you choose the template? What did you consider when choosing the color and font schemes? How did you decide on graphic placement?

2 Publishing a Trifold Brochure

Objectives

You will have mastered the material in this module when you can:

- Discuss advantages of the brochure medium
- Choose brochure options
- Copy and paste with paste options
- Wordwrap text
- Swap pictures using the scratch area
- Use a picture as a background
- Insert and format a shape
- Use stylistic sets

- Search for online pictures
- Arrange thumbnails
- Edit captions and caption styles
- Check the spelling of the entire publication
- Run the Design Checker
- Choose appropriate printing services, paper, and color libraries
- Package a publication for a printing service

Introduction

Whether you want to advertise a service, an event, or a product, or merely want to inform the public about a current topic of interest, brochures are a popular type of promotional publication. A **brochure**, or pamphlet, usually is a high-quality publication with lots of color and graphics, created for advertising purposes. Businesses that may not be able to reach potential clientele effectively through traditional advertising, such as web, newspapers, and radio, can create a long-lasting advertisement with a well-designed brochure.

Brochures come in all shapes and sizes. Colleges and universities produce brochures about their programs. The travel industry uses brochures to entice tourists. Service industries and manufacturers display their products using this visual, hands-on medium.

Project — Park Brochure

The project in this module shows you how to build the two-page, trifold brochure shown in Figure 2–1. The brochure informs potential visitors about activities at a state park. Each side of the brochure has three panels. Page 1 (Figure 2–1a) contains the front and back panels, as well as the inside fold. Page 2 (Figure 2–1b) contains a three-panel display that, when opened completely, provides the reader with more details about the park and a response form.

On page 1, the front panel contains shapes, text boxes, graphics, and a background designed to draw the reader's attention and inform the reader of the intent of the brochure. The back panel, which displays in the middle of page 1, contains the name of the park, the address, phone and fax numbers, and an email address. The inside fold, on the left, contains a map and information about camping and hiking.

The three inside panels on page 2 contain more information about the park and a form the reader may use to request more information.

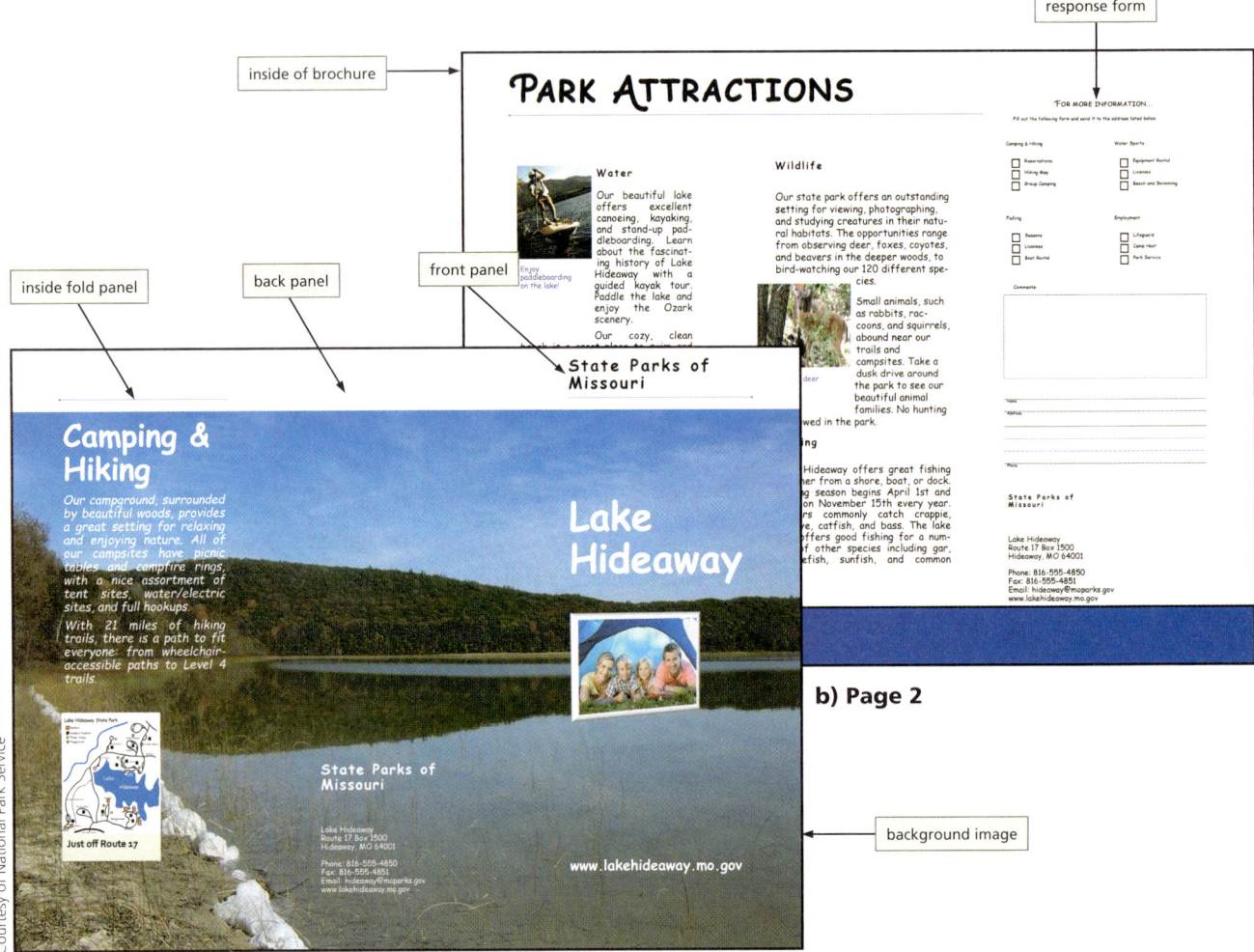

a) Page 1

Figure 2–1

The following roadmap identifies general activities you will perform as you progress through this module:

1. CUSTOMIZE the BROCHURE template options such as page size, color scheme, and font scheme.
2. EDIT template TEXT and OBJECTS.
3. SWAP PICTURES and use picture backgrounds.
4. CREATE PICTURE STYLES and SHAPES.
5. USE STYLISTIC SETS to enhance brochure text.
6. SEARCH for ONLINE PICTURES.

7. **INSERT CAPTIONS** for each photo.
8. **CHECK** the **PUBLICATION** for errors.
9. **PACK** the publication for a printing service.

The Brochure Medium

Professionals commonly print brochures on special paper to provide long-lasting documents and to enhance the graphics. The brochure medium intentionally is tactile; brochures are meant to be touched, carried home, passed along, and looked at, again and again. Newspapers and flyers usually have short-term readership and are printed on paper that readers throw away or recycle. Brochures, on the other hand, frequently use a heavier stock of paper so that they can stand better in a display rack.

How do you decide on the purpose, shelf life, and layout of a brochure?

Spend time brainstorming ideas for the brochure. Think about why you want to create one. Decide on the purpose of the brochure. Is it to inform, sell, attract, or advertise an event? Adjust your template, fonts, colors, and graphics to match that purpose. Brochures commonly have a wider audience than flyers. They need to last longer, so carefully consider whether to add dated material or prices. Create a timeline of effectiveness and plan to have the brochure ready far in advance. Decide how many panels your brochure should be and how often you are going to produce it. If you are working for someone, draw a storyboard and get it approved before you begin. Think about alignment of objects, proximity of similar data, contrast, and repetition.

The content of a brochure needs to last longer, too. On occasion, the intent of a brochure is to educate, such as a brochure on health issues in a doctor's office. More commonly, though, the intent is to market a product or sell a service. Prices and dated materials that are subject to frequent change affect the usable life of a brochure.

Typically, brochures use a great deal of color, and they include actual photos instead of drawings or clip art. Photos give a sense of realism to a publication and show people, places, or objects that are real, whereas images or drawings more appropriately are used to convey concepts or ideas.

Brochures, designed to be in circulation for longer periods as a type of advertising, ordinarily are published in greater quantities and on more expensive paper than other single-page publications, so they can be more costly. The cost, however, is less prohibitive when produced **in-house** using desktop publishing software rather than hiring an outside service. The cost per copy is lower when producing brochures in mass quantities.

Table 2–1 lists some benefits and advantages of using the brochure medium.

BTW

How Brochures Differ
Each brochure template produces two pages of graphics, business information text boxes, and story boxes. Brochures are differentiated by the look and feel of the front panel, the location and style of the shapes and graphics, the design of any panel dividers, and the specific kind of decorations unique to each publication set.

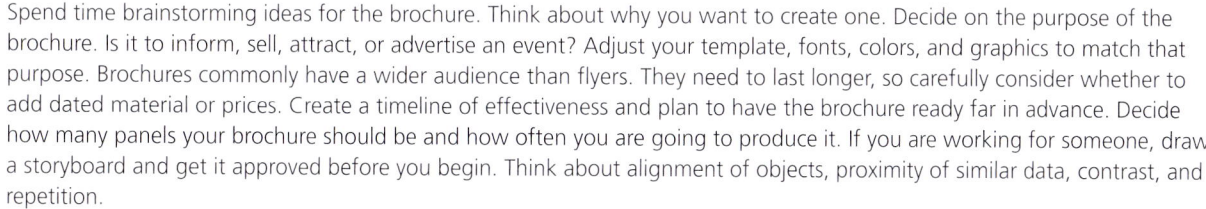

Table 2–1 Benefits and Advantages of Using the Brochure Medium	
Exposure	An attention-getter in displays
	A take-along document encouraging second looks
	A long-lasting publication due to paper and content
	An easily distributed publication — mass mailings, advertising sites
Information	An in-depth look at a product or service
	An opportunity to inform in a nonrestrictive environment
	An opportunity for focused feedback using forms
Audience	Interested clientele and potential customers
Communication	An effective medium to highlight products and services
	A source of free information to build credibility
	An easier method to disseminate information than a magazine

BTW

Gatefolds
A gatefold is a four-panel brochure where both ends fold toward the center. Gatefolds, also called foldouts, commonly are used in advertising, for menus, or as inserts in magazines.

BTW
Brochure Page Size
In addition to the intent and content of the brochure, you must consider the shape and size of the page when designing a brochure. Publisher can incorporate a variety of paper sizes; the most common are 8½ × 11 inches and 11 × 17 inches. You also can design smaller brochures, such as those used as liner notes for CD jewel cases or inserts for videotapes.

BTW
Color Scheme
Choose a color scheme that is consistent with your company, client, or purpose. Do you need color, or black and white? Think about the plan for printing and the number of copies in order to select a manageable color scheme. Remember that you can add more visual interest and contrast by bolding the color of text in the scheme.

Creating a Trifold Brochure

Publisher-supplied templates use proven design strategies and combinations of objects, which are placed to attract attention and disseminate information effectively. The options for brochures differ from other publications in that they allow you to choose from page sizes, special kinds of forms, and panel/page layout options.

Making Choices about Brochure Options

For the park brochure publication, you will use an informational brochure template, making changes to its color scheme, font scheme, page size, and forms. When choosing a template, **page size** refers to the number of panels in the brochure. **Form options**, which appear on page 2 of the brochure, include an order form, response form, and sign-up form, or no form at all. The **order form** displays fields for the description of items ordered, as well as types of payment information, including blank fields for entering items, quantities, and prices. The **response form** displays check box choices for up to four multiple-choice questions and a comment section. The **sign-up form** displays check box choices, fields for time and price, and payment information. Each form contains blanks for the name and address of prospective customers or clients. A company not only verifies the marketing power of its brochure, it also is able to create a customer database with the information. All three forms are meant to be detached as turnaround documents.

To Select a Brochure Template

1 CUSTOMIZE BROCHURE | 2 EDIT TEXT & OBJECTS | 3 SWAP PICTURES | 4 CREATE PICTURE STYLES & SHAPES
5 USE STYLISTIC SETS | 6 SEARCH ONLINE PICTURES | 7 INSERT CAPTIONS | 8 CHECK PUBLICATION | 9 PACK

The following steps select a brochure template. *Why? You should use a template until you are more experienced in designing brochures.*

1

- Run Publisher and then click BUILT-IN to display the built-in templates.
- Click Brochures and then click Simple Divider in the Informational area to select the template.
- Click the Color scheme button and then select the Pebbles color scheme.
- Click the Font scheme button and then select the Casual font scheme.
- Click the Page size button in the Options area and then, if necessary, click 3-panel to choose the number of panels. If necessary, click to remove the check mark in the 'Include customer address' check box.
- Scroll down and then click the Form button in the Options area. Click Response form to choose the type of form (Figure 2–2).

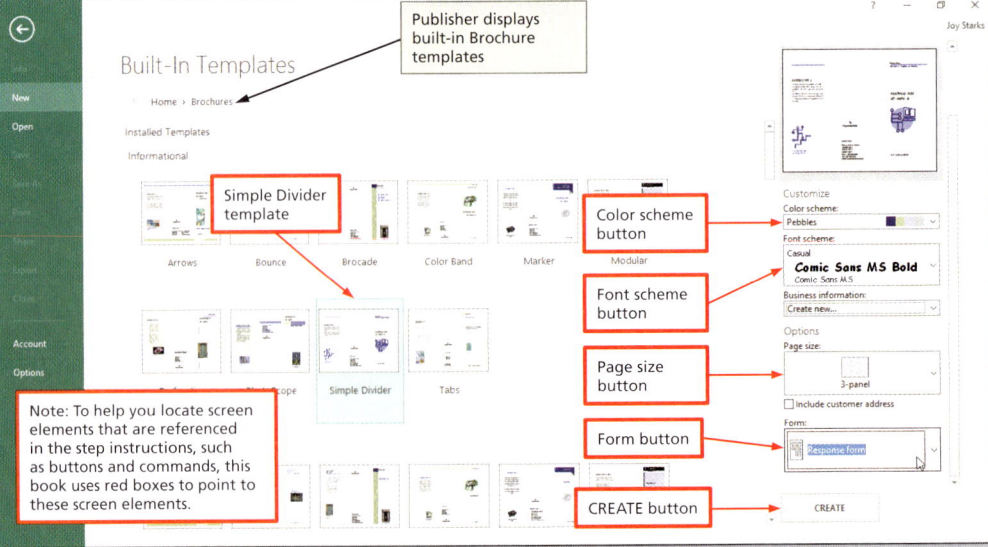

Figure 2–2

2

• Click the CREATE button to create the publication using the selected template and options.

What if I change my mind about the brochure options? You can choose a different template by using the Change Template button (Page Design tab | Template group) or change the color and fonts schemes using buttons in the Schemes group on the Page Design tab.

3

• Save the publication on your hard drive, OneDrive, or other storage location using the file name, Lake Hideaway Brochure (Figure 2–3).

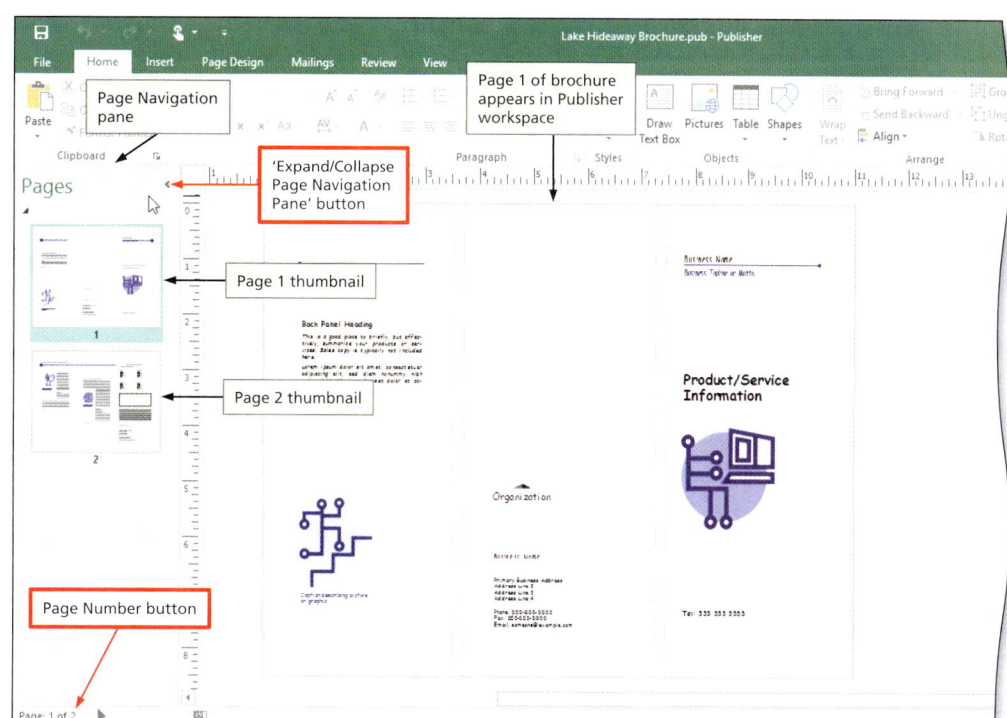

Figure 2–3

To Open and Maximize the Page Navigation Pane

The following step opens the Page Navigation pane to display both pages of the brochure.

1 If the Page Navigation pane is not displayed, click the Page Number button on the status bar to open the Page Navigation pane. If the Page Navigation pane is minimized, click the 'Expand Page Navigation Pane' button to maximize it.

To Edit Objects in the Right Panel

The front of the brochure displays in the right panel of page 1 and contains default text, placeholder text, and some synchronized text boxes. Recall that default text must be selected by dragging or pressing CTRL+A. Placeholder text is selected with a single click. You may want to zoom and scroll to make careful edits. The Business Name text box is a synchronized object that appears in both the right and middle panels. Recall that changing synchronized text in one location will change the text in other locations. The following steps edit objects in the publication's right panel.

1 In the right panel, select the default text, Business Name, by dragging through the text. Use the Zoom In button on the status bar to zoom to approximately 130%.

2 Type `State Parks of` and then press the ENTER key. Type `Missouri` to finish the text.

3 Select the border of the 'Business Tagline or Motto' text box. Delete the text box.

4 Click the Product/Service Information placeholder text to select it. Type `Lake Hideaway` to replace the text (Figure 2–4).

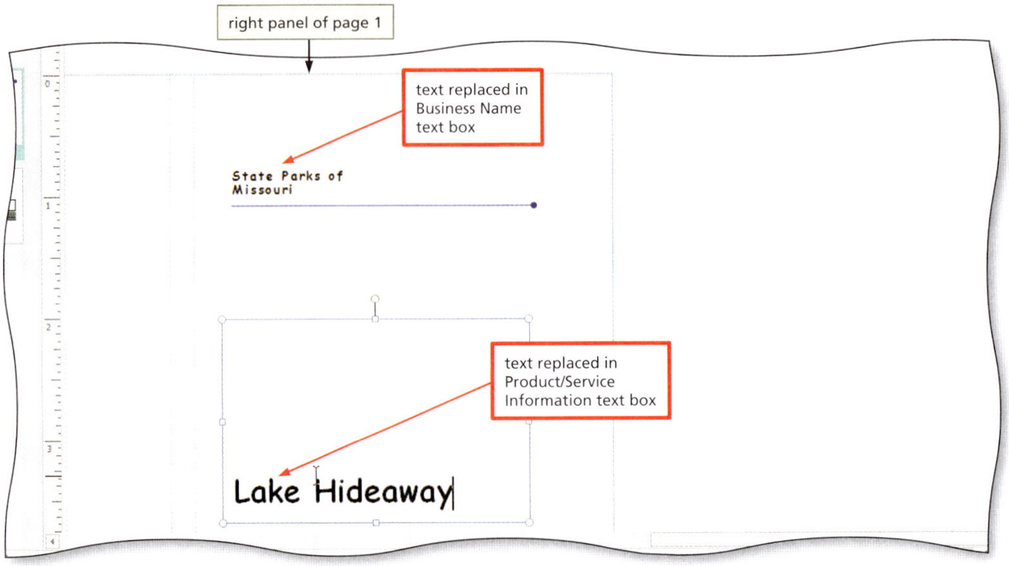

right panel of page 1

text replaced in
Business Name
text box

State Parks of
Missouri

text replaced in
Product/Service
Information text box

Lake Hideaway

Figure 2–4

To Use the AutoCorrect Options Button

1 CUSTOMIZE BROCHURE │ 2 EDIT TEXT & OBJECTS │ 3 SWAP PICTURES │ 4 CREATE PICTURE STYLES & SHAPES
5 USE STYLISTIC SETS │ 6 SEARCH ONLINE PICTURES │ 7 INSERT CAPTIONS │ 8 CHECK PUBLICATION │ 9 PACK

Sometimes, Publisher changes a word or letter for you, trying to interpret your meaning or to help you with sentence structure and spelling. When you position the pointer near text that Publisher has corrected automatically, a small blue box appears below the text. It is a minimized AutoCorrect Options button. If you point to the button, Publisher displays the maximized AutoCorrect Options button. When you click the AutoCorrect Options button, Publisher displays a menu. *Why? The menu allows you to undo a correction or change how Publisher handles future automatic corrections of this type.* The following steps use the AutoCorrect Options button and menu.

1

- Scroll to the lower portion of the right panel. Select the phone number default text by dragging through the text.

- Type **www.lakehideaway.mo.gov** to replace the text, and watch Publisher capitalize the first letter automatically.

- Move the mouse pointer close to the capital W to display the minimized AutoCorrect Options button (Figure 2–5).

Q&A Why did Publisher change this to a capital W? Publisher interprets the web address as the beginning of a sentence and capitalizes the first letter.

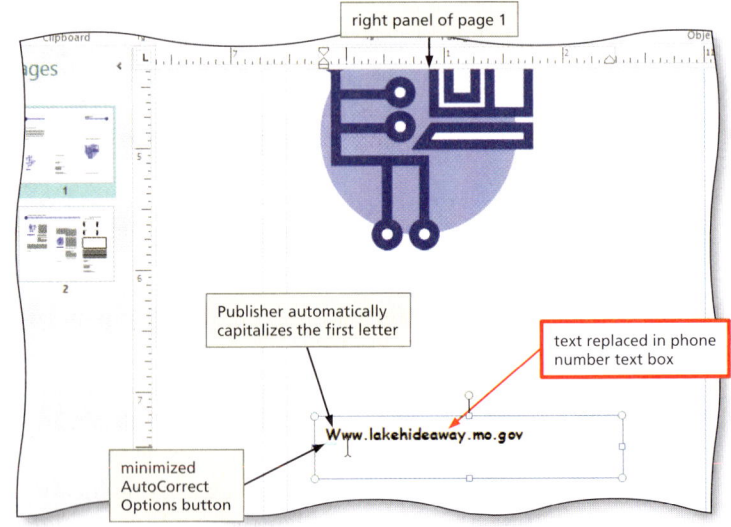

right panel of page 1

Publisher automatically
capitalizes the first letter

text replaced in phone
number text box

Www.lakehideaway.mo.gov

minimized
AutoCorrect
Options button

Figure 2–5

2

- Point to the minimized AutoCorrect Options button. When it appears maximized, click it to display the AutoCorrect Options menu (Figure 2–6).

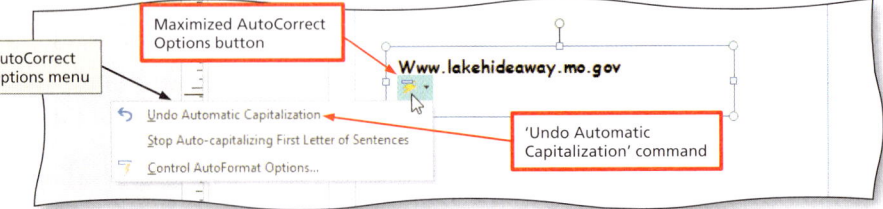

Maximized AutoCorrect
Options button

AutoCorrect
Options menu

Www.lakehideaway.mo.gov

↩ Undo Automatic Capitalization
   Stop Auto-capitalizing First Letter of Sentences
▭ Control AutoFormat Options...

'Undo Automatic
Capitalization' command

Figure 2–6

3

- Click 'Undo Automatic Capitalization' to cause the text to revert to lowercase (Figure 2–7).

Q&A How do I remove the AutoCorrect Options button from the screen?
When you move the mouse pointer, the AutoCorrect Options button will disappear from the screen. Alternatively, you can press the ESCAPE key twice. It does not print.

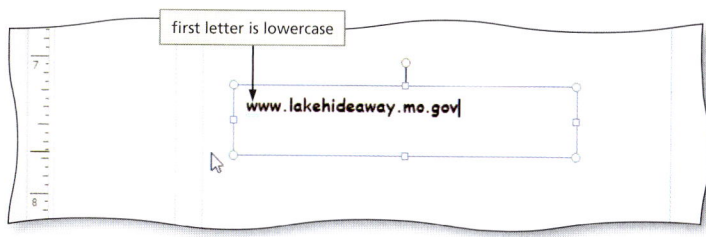

first letter is lowercase

www.lakehideaway.mo.gov

Figure 2–7

To Edit Objects in the Middle Panel

When folded, the middle panel will display on the back of the trifold brochure. It contains text boxes for the business address, phone numbers, and email address. The following steps edit the text in the middle panel.

1 Scroll as necessary to display the middle panel. Zoom to approximately 150%.

2 Delete the organization logo. Note that the business name text has been replaced already.

3 Drag to select all of the text in the Primary Business Address text box. Type `Lake Hideaway` and then press the ENTER key to finish the first line of the address and advance to the next address line.

4 Type `Route 17 Box 1500` and then press the ENTER key to finish the second line. Type `Hideaway, MO 64001` to finish entering the address text. Do not press the ENTER key after the last line.

If requested by your instructor, enter your name, address, city, and state instead of those in Steps 3 and 4. Do not press the ENTER key after the last line.

5 Drag to select the phone and fax numbers and the email address text. Type `Phone: 816-555-4850` and then press the ENTER key to finish entering the first line. Type `Fax: 816-555-4851` and then press the ENTER key to finish entering the second line. Type `Email: hideaway@moparks.gov` and then press the ENTER key to create a new line for future text (Figure 2–8).

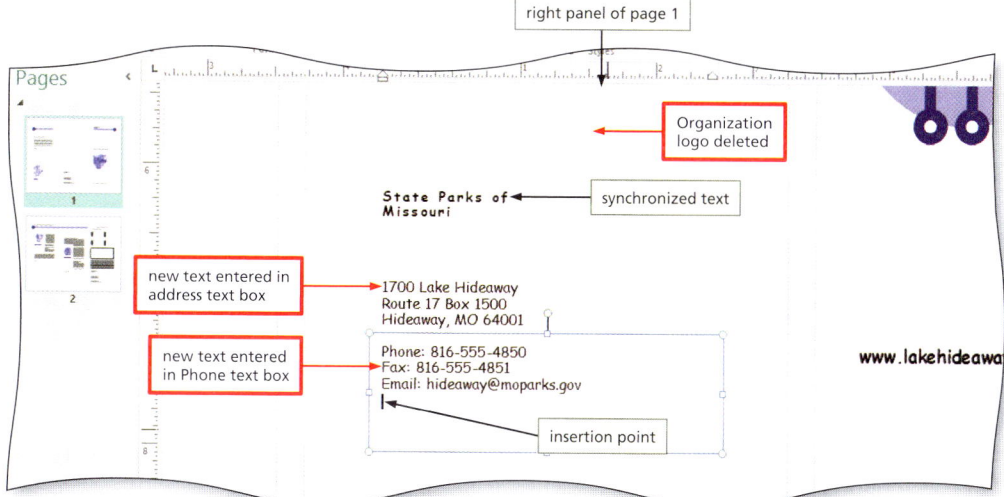

right panel of page 1

Organization logo deleted

State Parks of Missouri — synchronized text

new text entered in address text box
1700 Lake Hideaway
Route 17 Box 1500
Hideaway, MO 64001

new text entered in Phone text box
Phone: 816-555-4850
Fax: 816-555-4851
Email: hideaway@moparks.gov

insertion point

www.lakehideawa

Figure 2–8

BTW
Smart Tags
The AutoCorrect Options button and the Paste Options button are smart tags. Recall from Module 1 that a smart tag appears when Publisher has options to show you, such as the Information button that appears as an uppercase I.

Copying, Cutting, and Pasting

In each of the Office 2016 applications, you can store or copy text and objects for later use. The **Office Clipboard** is a temporary storage area that holds up to 24 items (text or graphics) copied from any Office program. The Office Clipboard is different from the **Windows Clipboard** associated with the operating system, which can contain only one item at a time.

Copying is the process of placing items on the Office Clipboard; the item also remains in the publication. **Cutting**, by contrast, removes the item from the publication before placing it on the clipboard. The copy and cut functions transfer text or objects to the Windows Clipboard as well as to the Office Clipboard. Cutting is different from deleting. Deleted items are not placed on either clipboard. **Pasting** is the process of copying an item from either clipboard into the publication at the location of the insertion point or selection.

Table 2–2 describes various methods to copy, cut, paste, and delete selected text.

BTW
Stylus
If you are using your finger on a touch screen and are having difficulty completing the steps in this module, consider using a stylus. Many people find it easier to be precise with a stylus rather than with a finger. In addition, with a stylus you see the pointer. If you still are having trouble completing the steps with a stylus, try using a mouse.

Table 2–2 Copy, Cut, Paste, and Delete				
Method	**Copy**	**Cut**	**Paste**	**Delete**
shortcut menu	Right-click to display the shortcut menu and then click Copy	Right-click to display the shortcut menu and then click Cut	Right-click to display the shortcut menu and then click Paste	Right-click to display the shortcut menu and then click Delete Text
ribbon	Click the Copy button (Home tab | Clipboard group)	Click the Cut button (Home tab | Clipboard group)	Click the Paste button (Home tab | Clipboard group)	Not available
keyboard	Press CTRL+C	Press CTRL+X	Press CTRL+V	Press the DELETE key or BACKSPACE key

BTW
Touch Galleries
If you are using a mouse or stylus, galleries, such as the Font Color gallery, display their choices in small, colored squares. If you are displaying the gallery via touch gestures, Windows 10 senses the touch gesture and displays the gallery with much larger, colored squares, making it easier to tap the one you want.

In Publisher, you can copy, cut, paste, and delete objects as well as text. If you are copying text, it is advisable to select from the beginning letter of the text and include any ending spaces, tabs, punctuation, or paragraph marks. That way, when you cut or paste, the text will be spaced properly. If you are copying, cutting, pasting, and deleting objects, the object must be selected. Publisher normally pastes objects from either clipboard into the center of the displayed page layout if no object is selected.

The next step in editing the brochure is to include the website address at the bottom of the center panel. One way to enter this information in the brochure is to type it. Recall, however, that you already typed this information on the right panel. Thus, a timesaving alternative would be to copy and paste the text.

To Copy and Paste

In the brochure, you want to copy the website address from one panel to the other. *Why? Copying and pasting reduces errors that might result from retyping information.* The following steps copy and paste the website address.

- Scroll until the lower portion of both the right and middle panels are visible.

- Click the website address text box to select it.

- Drag through the text to be copied (the website address in this case).

- Click the Copy button (Home tab | Clipboard group) to copy the selected item in the publication to the Office Clipboard (Figure 2–9).

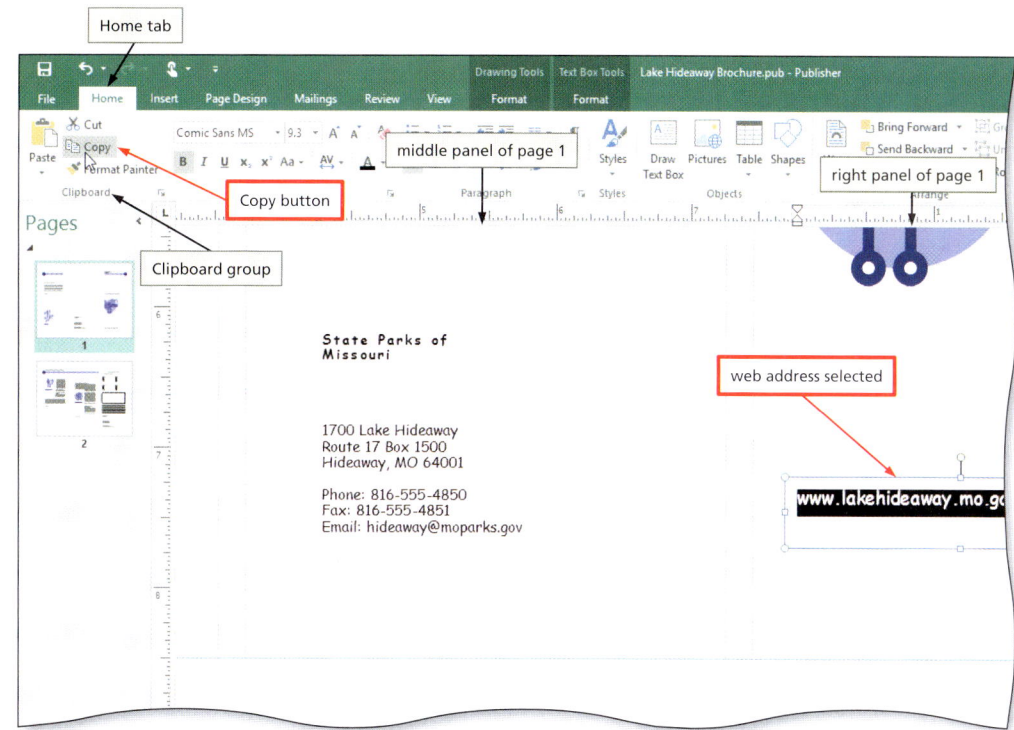

Figure 2–9

- Click the phone number text box at the bottom of the center panel and position the insertion point on the blank line underneath the email address.

- Click the Paste button (Home tab | Clipboard group) to paste the copied item into the text box. Do not press any other keys (Figure 2–10).

Q&A Should I select the text before pasting?
No. If you are not replacing text, you position the insertion point at the desired location and then paste.

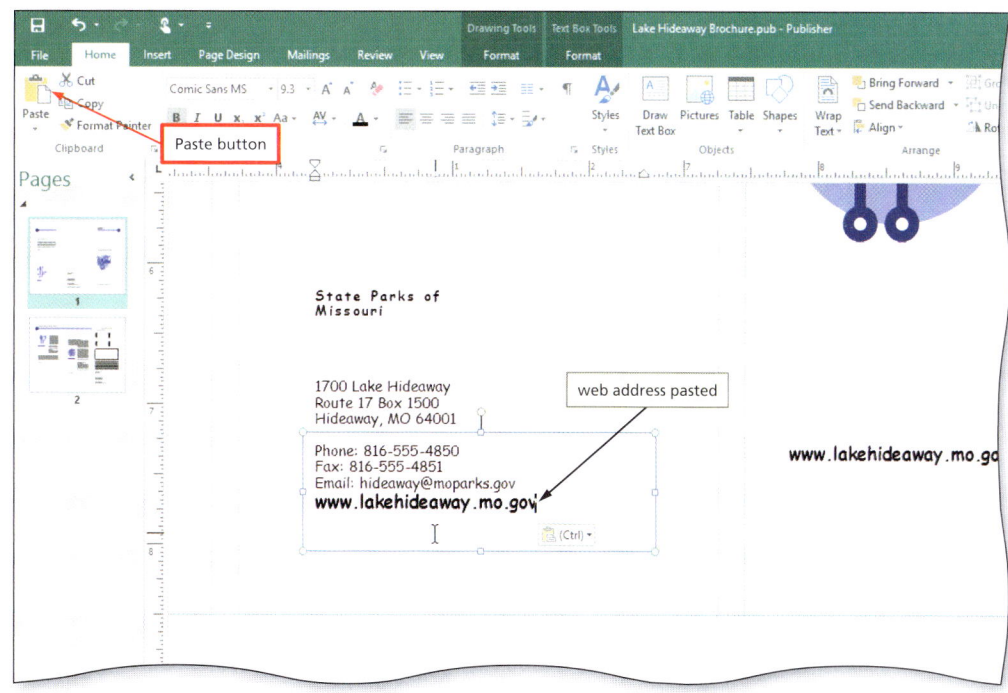

Figure 2–10

Other Ways

1. Right-click selected item, click Copy on shortcut menu, right-click where item is to be pasted, click desired Paste button on shortcut menu

2. Select item, press CTRL+C, position insertion point at paste location, press CTRL+V

Paste Options Button

After you paste, Publisher may display the Paste Options button. Clicking the **Paste Options** button displays the Paste Options menu, which contains buttons representing formatting choices. They also appear when you click the Paste arrow (Home tab | Clipboard group). Table 2–3 describes some of the Paste options. Depending on the contents of the clipboard, you may see different buttons with advanced options for pasting, especially when cutting and pasting graphics.

Table 2–3 Paste Options		
Button	**Option**	**Result**
	Paste	Pastes the copied content *as is* without any formatting changes
	Keep Source Formatting	Keeps the formatting of the text you copied
	Merge Formatting	Changes the formatting so that it matches the text around it
	Keep Text Only	Pastes the copied text as plain unformatted text and removes any styles or hyperlinks

To Select a Paste Option

1 CUSTOMIZE BROCHURE | **2 EDIT TEXT & OBJECTS** | 3 SWAP PICTURES | 4 CREATE PICTURE STYLES & SHAPES
5 USE STYLISTIC SETS | 6 SEARCH ONLINE PICTURES | 7 INSERT CAPTIONS | 8 CHECK PUBLICATION | 9 PACK

The following steps select the 'Keep Text Only' paste option. *Why? The website address should match the font style in the center panel.*

- Click the Paste Options button that appears below the pasted information to display the Paste Options menu (Figure 2–11).

 **Experiment**

- Point to each of the Paste Options buttons to see their ScreenTips.

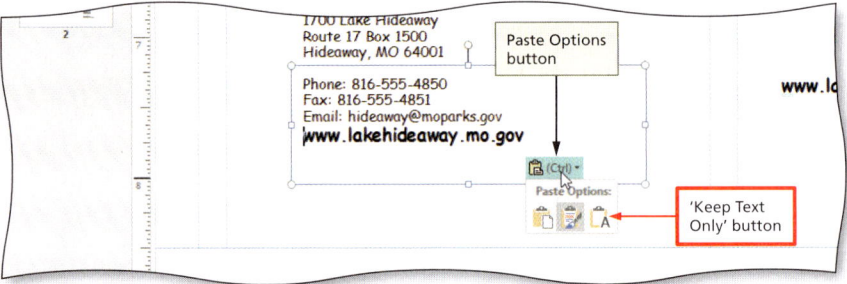

Figure 2–11

- Click the 'Keep Text Only' button to paste without the original bold formatting (Figure 2–12).

Q&A
Can I change my mind and choose a different paste option?
Yes, if you change it before typing anything else. Otherwise, you would have to delete and paste again.

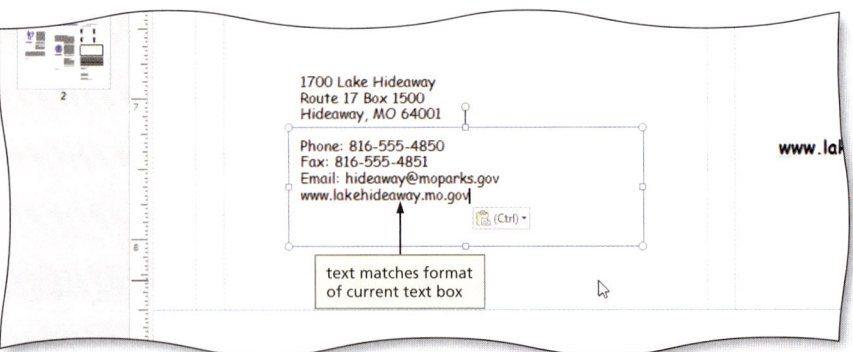

Figure 2–12

Other Ways

1. Press CTRL key, click Paste Options button	2. Click Paste arrow (Home tab | Clipboard group), click Paste Options button	3. Click Paste Options button on shortcut menu

Typing Paragraphs of Text

When you type paragraphs of text, you will use Publisher's wordwrap feature. **Wordwrap** allows you to type words in a text box continually without pressing the ENTER key at the end of each line. When the insertion point reaches the right margin of a text box, Publisher automatically positions the insertion point at the beginning of the next line. As you type, if a word extends beyond the right margin, Publisher automatically positions that word on the next line or hyphenates the word and moves the insertion point.

How do you decide on a brochure's content?

Gather all the information, such as stories, graphics, logos, colors, shapes, style information, and watermarks. Save copies or versions along the way. If you have to create objects from scratch, have someone else evaluate your work and give you constructive feedback. If you are using forms in your brochure, verify the manner in which the viewer will return the form. Check and double-check all prices, addresses, and phone numbers.

Publisher creates a new paragraph, or **hard return,** each time you press the ENTER key. Thus, as you type text in a text box, do not press the ENTER key when the insertion point reaches the right margin. Instead, press the ENTER key only in these circumstances:

- To insert blank lines in a text box
- To begin a new paragraph
- To terminate a short line of text and advance to the next line
- To respond to questions or prompts in Publisher dialog boxes, panes, and other on-screen objects

To view where in a publication you pressed the ENTER key or SPACEBAR key, you may find it helpful to display formatting marks. A **formatting mark**, sometimes called a **nonprinting character**, is a special character that Publisher displays on the screen, but one that is not visible on a printed publication. For example, the paragraph mark (¶) is a formatting mark that indicates where you pressed the ENTER key. A raised dot (·) appears where you pressed the spacebar. An end of field marker (¤) is displayed to indicate the end of text in a text box. Other formatting marks are discussed as they appear on the screen.

BTW

Moving Text
If you want to use your mouse to move text from one location to another, you can select the text and then drag it to the new location. Publisher will display a small rectangle attached to the pointer as you position the pointer in the new location. Moving text or objects also can be accomplished by cutting and then pasting.

To Edit Heading Text in the Left Panel

The left panel will appear as the inside fold when the brochure is first opened. It contains text boxes for a heading and summary text. The following steps edit the heading text.

① Scroll to the top of the left panel.

② In the left panel, click to select the Back Panel Heading placeholder text. Type `Camping & Hiking` to replace the text (Figure 2–13).

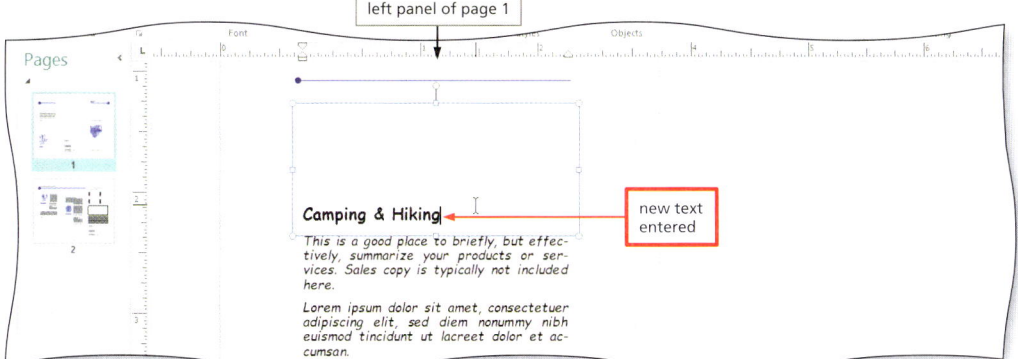

Figure 2–13

To Display Formatting Marks

The following step displays formatting marks, if they do not show already on the screen. *Why? The formatting marks help you see where you pressed the* ENTER *key and the* SPACEBAR *key, among other actions.*

- If it is not selected already, click the Special Characters button (Home tab | Paragraph group) to display formatting marks (Figure 2–14).

Q&A What if I do not want formatting marks to show on the screen?
If you feel the formatting marks clutter the screen, you can hide them by clicking the Special Characters button again. The figures presented in the rest of this module show the formatting marks.

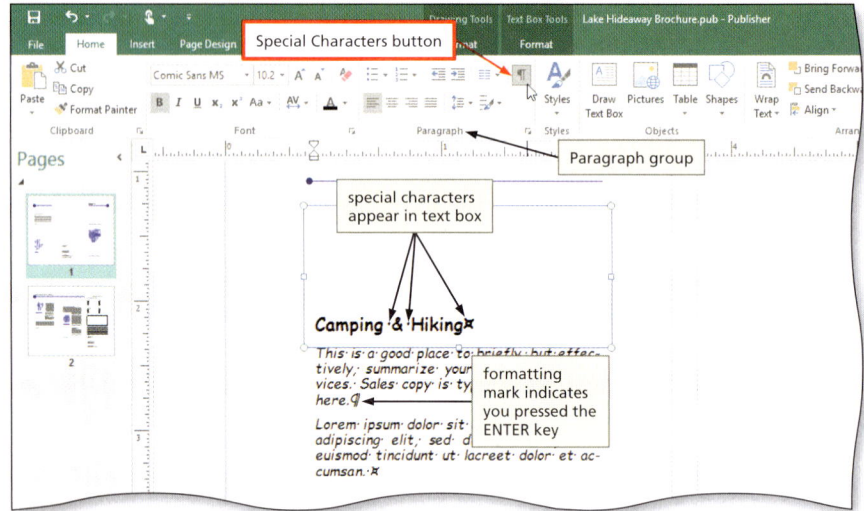

Figure 2–14

Other Ways

1. Press CTRL+SHIFT+Y

To Wordwrap Text as You Type

The next step in creating the brochure is to type the text in the left panel. The following steps wordwrap the text in the text box. *Why? Using wordwrap ensures consistent margins.*

- Click to select the placeholder text in the text box below the heading.
- Type Our campground, surrounded by beautiful woods, provides a great setting for relaxing and enjoying nature. All of our campsites have picnic tables and campfire rings, with a nice assortment of tent sites, water/electric sites, and full hookups. and notice that Publisher wraps the text when you get close to the right edge of the text box.
- Press the ENTER key to finish the first paragraph.
- Type With 21 miles of hiking trails, there is a path to fit everyone: from wheelchair-accessible paths to Level 4 trails. to finish the text (Figure 2–15).

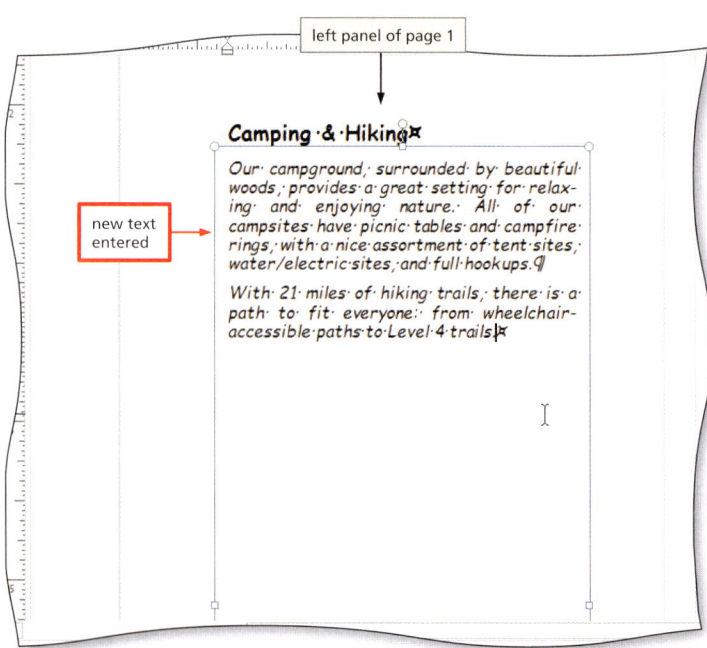

Figure 2–15

Swapping Pictures

In Publisher 2016, you can use the scratch area to manipulate and swap pictures. Recall that the **scratch area** is the gray area that appears outside the publication page. It is used as a temporary holding area; if you are not sure where you want to move an item, you can drag it to the scratch area. When inserting a single picture, you can drag it to the scratch area. When you insert multiple pictures at one time, Publisher arranges the thumbnails or puts them in a column in the scratch area, instead of on top of one another on your page. Unlike the clipboard, the scratch area is saved with the publication. The pictures in the scratch area will still be there the next time you open the publication. The scratch area does not print and contains the same items, regardless of which page of the publication is displayed.

Recall that many templates include picture placeholders, each with a picture icon. After the placeholder is replaced with a picture, the icon changes to a **swap icon**. Pictures in the scratch area also have swap icons. You can drag the swap icon to swap pictures with one another, or you can right-click the swap icon to display a shortcut menu with more options.

BTW

Organizing Files and Folders

You should organize and store files in folders so that you easily can find the files later. For example, if you are taking an introductory computer class called CIS 101, a good practice would be to save all Publisher files in a Publisher folder in a CIS 101 folder. For a discussion of folders and detailed examples of creating folders, refer to the Office and Windows module at the beginning of this book.

To Insert Multiple Pictures from a Storage Device

1 CUSTOMIZE BROCHURE | 2 EDIT TEXT & OBJECTS | 3 SWAP PICTURES | 4 CREATE PICTURE STYLES & SHAPES
5 USE STYLISTIC SETS | 6 SEARCH ONLINE PICTURES | 7 INSERT CAPTIONS | 8 CHECK PUBLICATION | 9 PACK

The following steps insert multiple pictures from a storage device. *Why? Selecting and placing multiple pictures in the scratch area allows you to see what different pictures might look like in the publication.* To complete these steps, you will need to use the photos located in the Data Files. Please contact your instructor for information about accessing the Data Files.

- On the status bar, click the 'Show Whole Page' button to display the entire page.
- Click Insert on the ribbon to display the Insert tab.
- Click the Pictures button (Insert tab | Illustrations group) to display the Insert Picture dialog box.
- Navigate to the Data Files and the Module 02 folder.
- One at a time, CTRL+click the files, Campers, Lake, and Map to select the three pictures (Figure 2–16).

Q&A Why do I have to use the CTRL key?
CTRL+clicking allows you to select multiple items, rather than selecting them one at a time.

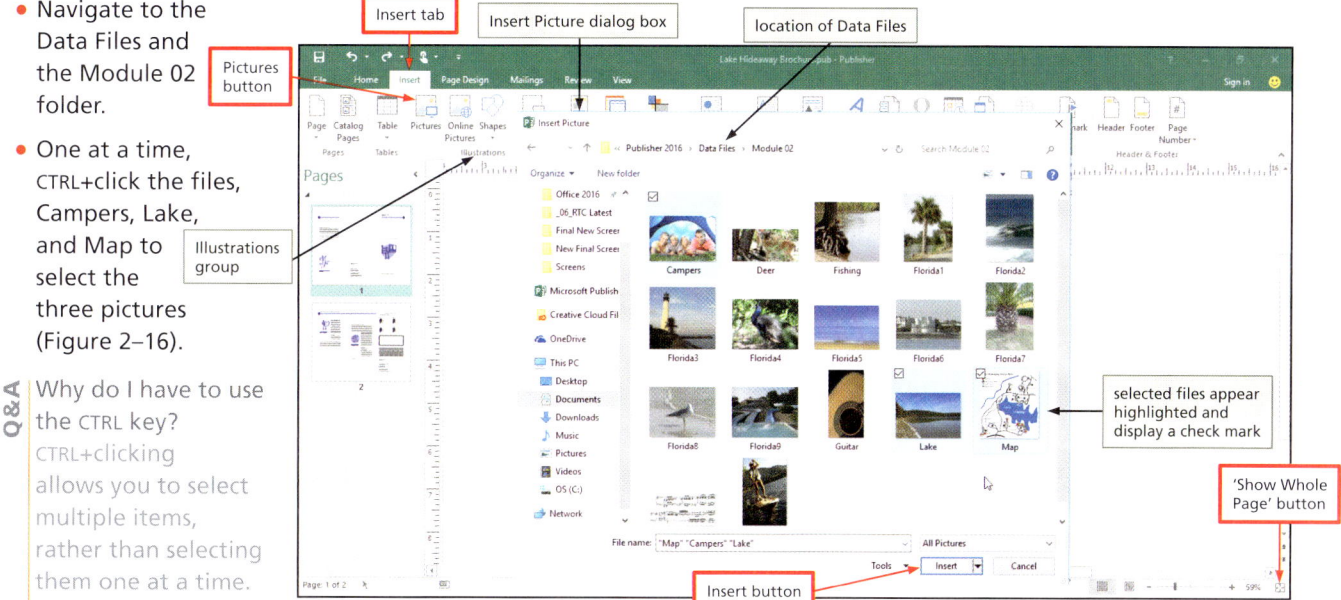

Figure 2–16

My file list looks different. Did I do something wrong?
No. Your window probably is set for a different view. Right-click the window, click View, and then select a different view.

2

- Click the Insert button (Insert Picture dialog box) to place the pictures in the scratch area (Figure 2–17).

Courtesy of Maryland Department of Natural Resource

Q&A

My picture displays in the middle of the publication rather than in the scratch area. What did I do wrong?

If you choose just one picture, it is displayed in the middle of the publication. Multiple selections appear in the scratch area. You can drag your picture to the scratch area, if necessary.

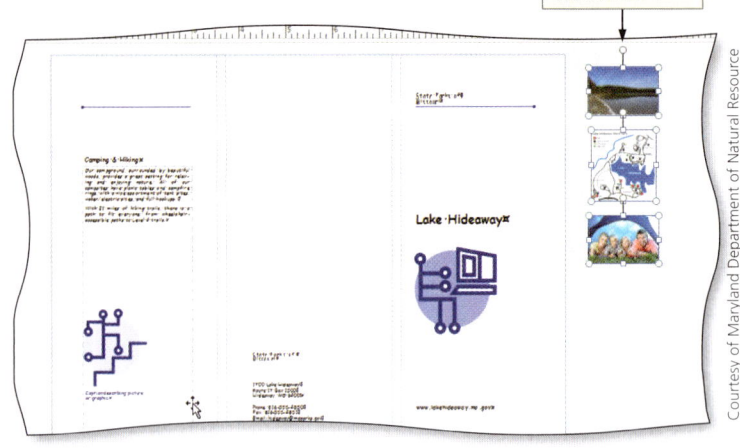

Figure 2–17

To Swap Pictures

1 CUSTOMIZE BROCHURE | 2 EDIT TEXT & OBJECTS | 3 SWAP PICTURES | 4 CREATE PICTURE STYLES & SHAPES
5 USE STYLISTIC SETS | 6 SEARCH ONLINE PICTURES | 7 INSERT CAPTIONS | 8 CHECK PUBLICATION | 9 PACK

When you decide to swap one picture for another, you drag the new picture toward the old picture. When Publisher displays a pink boundary, release the mouse button (or lift your finger away from the screen if you are using touch gestures). It is a good idea to swap pictures that have the same orientation. *Why? Pictures with the same orientation as the template fit the area better and are not scaled disproportionately.* **Portrait** pictures are taller than they are wide; **landscape** pictures are wider than they are tall. The following steps swap the pictures from the scratch area with the template graphics in the brochure.

1

- Click the scratch area away from the pictures to deselect them.

- In the scratch area, click the photo you wish to use in the brochure (in this case the picture of the campers) to display the swap icon (Figure 2–18).

Q&A

The swap icon disappeared. Did I do something wrong?

You may have moved the pointer away from the picture. Move the pointer back over the top of the selected picture to display the swap icon.

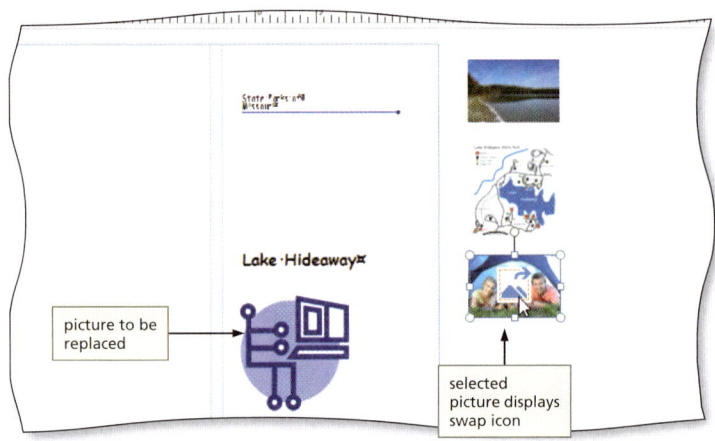

Figure 2–18

2

- From the scratch area, drag the swap icon of the photo you wish to swap to a location over a current graphic on the page. (In this case, drag the picture of the campers to a location over the graphic in the right panel.) Do not release the mouse button (Figure 2–19).

©iStock.com/monkeybusinessimages

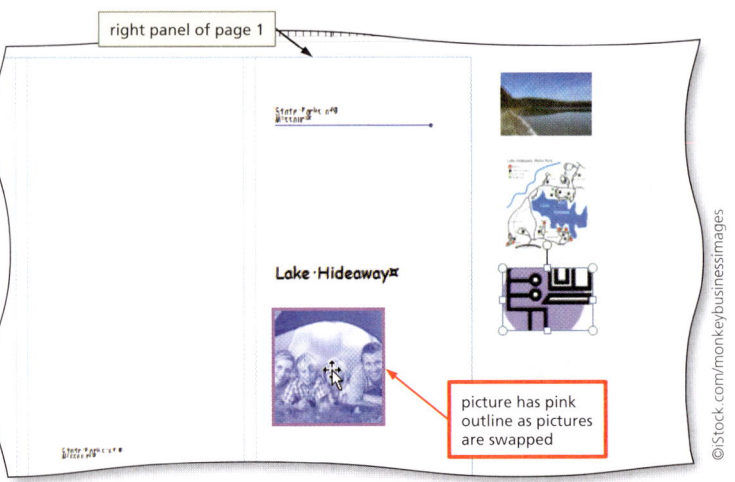

Figure 2–19

3

- When the pink boundary is displayed, release the mouse button to swap the pictures (Figure 2–20).

Q&A My picture is no longer in full color. Did I do something wrong?
No. Publisher applies the color scheme to swapped pictures. You will change that later in the module.

Figure 2–20

4

- Repeat Steps 1 through 3 to swap the map with the picture on the left panel (Figure 2–21).

Q&A Should I edit the caption?
No, you will edit the caption later in the module.

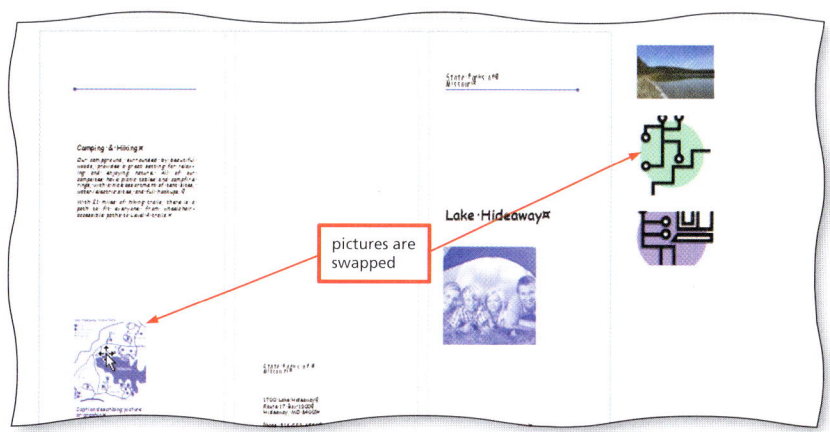

Figure 2–21

Other Ways

1. Select two pictures, click Swap button (Picture Tools Format tab | Swap group)

To Use a Picture as a Background

1 CUSTOMIZE BROCHURE | 2 EDIT TEXT & OBJECTS | 3 SWAP PICTURES | 4 CREATE PICTURE STYLES & SHAPES
5 USE STYLISTIC SETS | 6 SEARCH ONLINE PICTURES | 7 INSERT CAPTIONS | 8 CHECK PUBLICATION | 9 PACK

Many brochures use pictures in the background. *Why? A picture adds interest and removes the stark white color around objects in the brochure.* In this brochure, you will apply a picture to the background, using a picture from the scratch area and the shortcut menu. The following steps apply a picture to the background of page 1 of the brochure.

1

- Right-click the picture you wish to use as a background (in this case, the lake picture) to display the shortcut menu.

- Point to 'Apply to Background' on the shortcut menu to display the Apply to Background submenu (Figure 2–22).

Q&A Will the picture also be placed on page 2?
No, not unless you go to page 2 and apply it there. Each page of a publication has a unique background area.

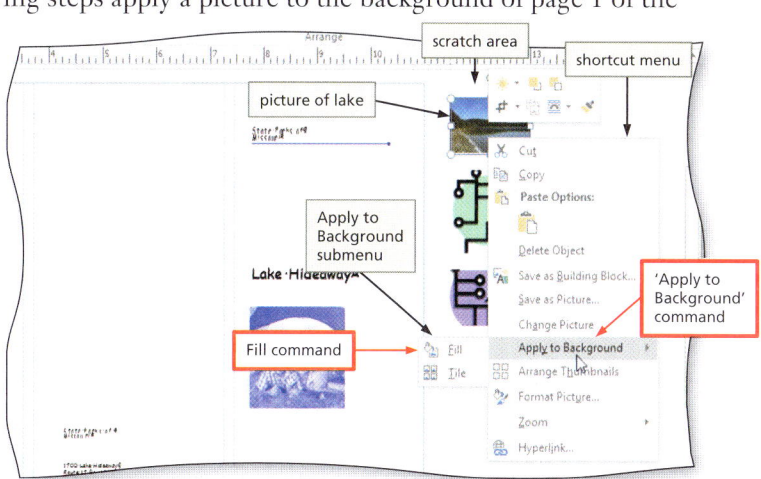

Figure 2–22

2

- Click Fill on the Apply to Background submenu to place the picture in the background of the page (Figure 2–23).

- Press CTRL+Z to remove the picture from the background. Right-click the lake picture again, click 'Apply to Background', and then click Tile to view the difference between Fill and Tile. When you are finished, perform Steps 1 and 2 again.

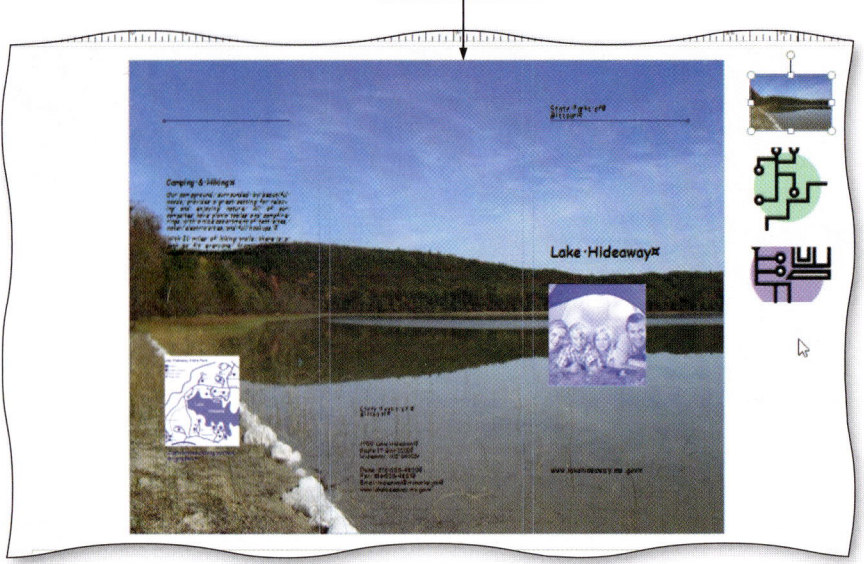

lake picture appears as background

Figure 2–23

Other Ways

1. Click Background button (Page Design tab | Page Background group), click More Backgrounds in Background gallery, click 'Picture or texture fill', click File, navigate to picture, double-click picture, click OK button (Format Background dialog box)

BTW

The Ribbon and Screen Resolution
Publisher may change how the groups and buttons within the groups appear on the ribbon, depending on the computer or mobile device's screen resolution. Thus, your ribbon may look different from the ones in this book if you are using a screen resolution other than 1366 × 768.

Resetting Pictures and Picture Styles

If Publisher applies a color scheme to your graphic, or if the picture does not fit correctly in the picture placeholder, you can use the **Reset command** to revert the picture to its original coloring and better fit it in the placeholder. Publisher also provides **picture styles** that allow you easily to change the basic rectangle format to a more visually appealing style and designer look. The Picture Style gallery has more than 20 picture styles that include a variety of shapes, borders, and scallops. The Picture Tools Format tab on the ribbon contains other adjustments, such as adding a border and picture formatting options that you will learn about in a later module.

To Reset Pictures

1 CUSTOMIZE BROCHURE | 2 EDIT TEXT & OBJECTS | 3 SWAP PICTURES | 4 CREATE PICTURE STYLES & SHAPES
5 USE STYLISTIC SETS | 6 SEARCH ONLINE PICTURES | 7 INSERT CAPTIONS | 8 CHECK PUBLICATION | 9 PACK

The following steps reset both pictures on page 1 of the brochure to remove the color scheme changes.

1

- Select the picture you wish to reset (in this case the picture of the campers on the right panel).

- Click the Reset Picture button (Picture Tools Format tab | Adjust group) to reset the picture (Figure 2–24).

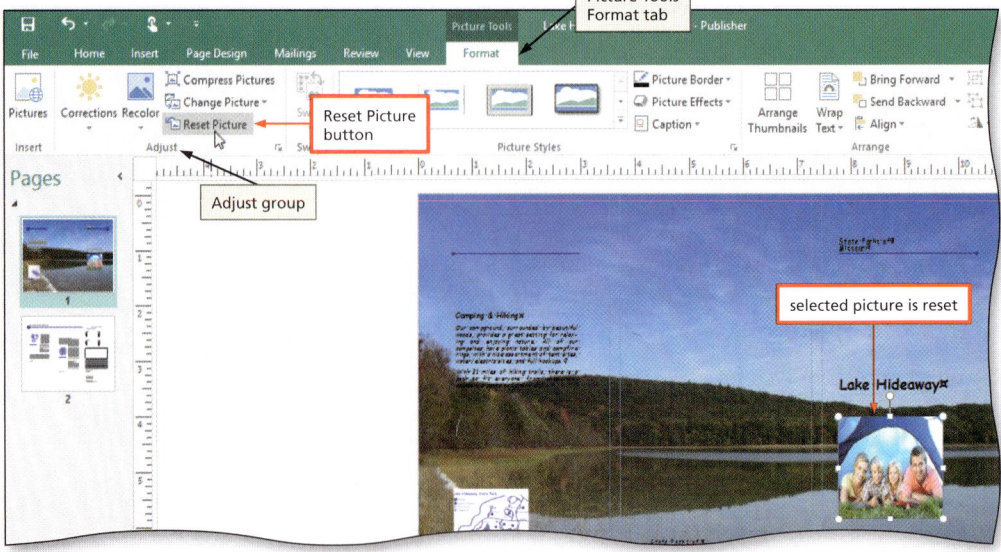

Picture Tools Format tab

Reset Picture button

Adjust group

selected picture is reset

Figure 2–24

- Select the map graphic in the left panel. Click the Reset Picture button (Picture Tools Format tab | Adjust group) to reset the picture (Figure 2–25).

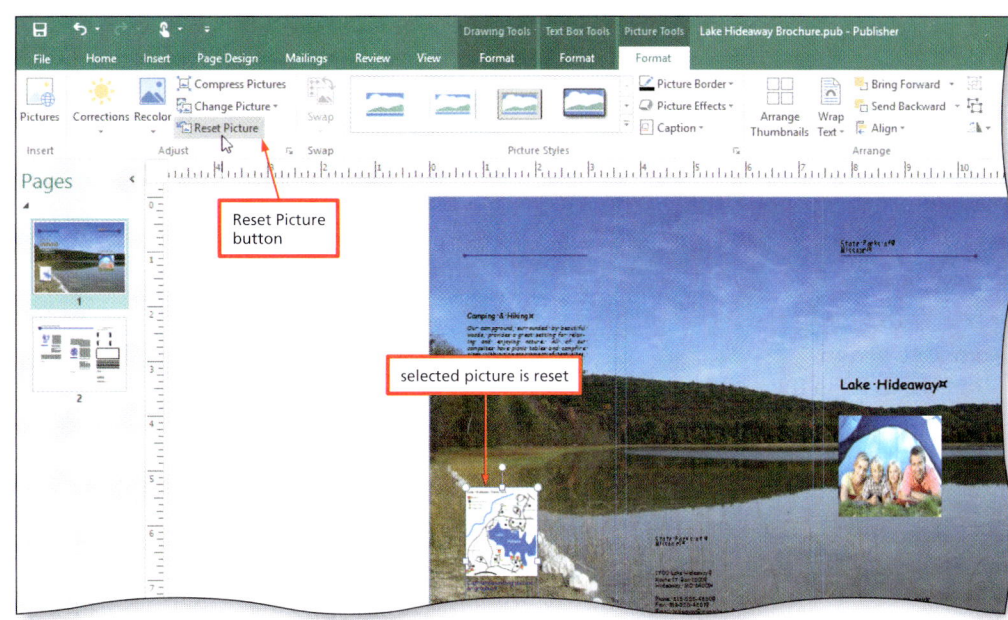

Figure 2–25

To Resize a Picture

The following step resizes the graphic in the right panel of page 1.

Select the picture of the campers in the right panel. Drag the lower-right handle until the picture is approximately 2 inches by 1.33 inches (shown in Figure 2–26).

To Apply a Picture Style

1 CUSTOMIZE BROCHURE | 2 EDIT TEXT & OBJECTS | 3 SWAP PICTURES | 4 CREATE PICTURE STYLES & SHAPES
5 USE STYLISTIC SETS | 6 SEARCH ONLINE PICTURES | 7 INSERT CAPTIONS | 8 CHECK PUBLICATION | 9 PACK

The picture on the front of the brochure will use a picture style slanting up and right. *Why? Researchers say that an upward slant adds energy to a publication and directs the reader's eye toward the inside of the brochure, with a 3-D look.* The following steps apply a picture style to the picture on the front of the brochure.

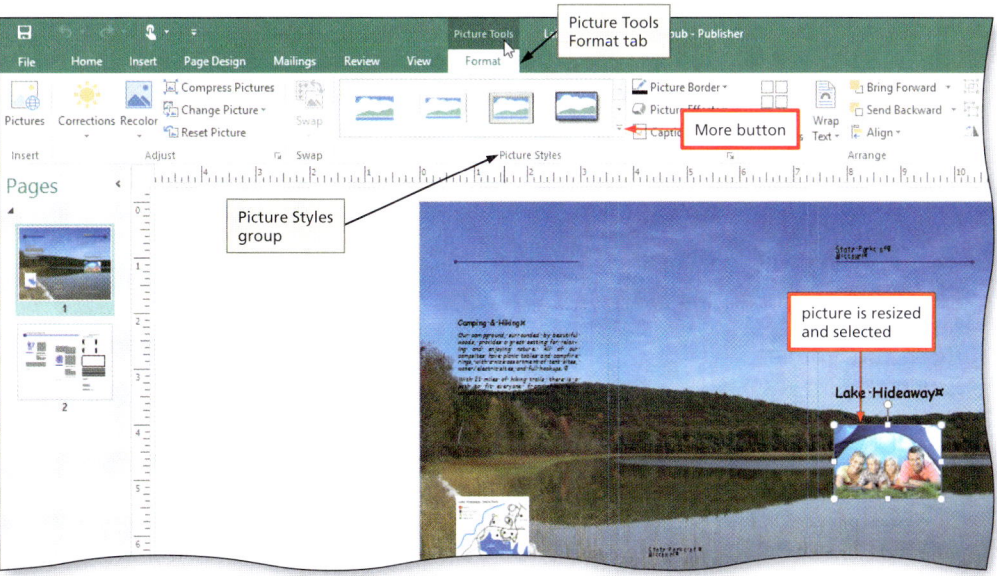

- If necessary, select the desired picture (in this case the picture of the campers in the right panel).

- On the ribbon, click Picture Tools Format to display the Picture Tools Format tab (Figure 2–26).

Figure 2–26

- Click the More button (Picture Tools Format tab | Picture Styles group) to display the Picture Styles gallery (Figure 2–27).

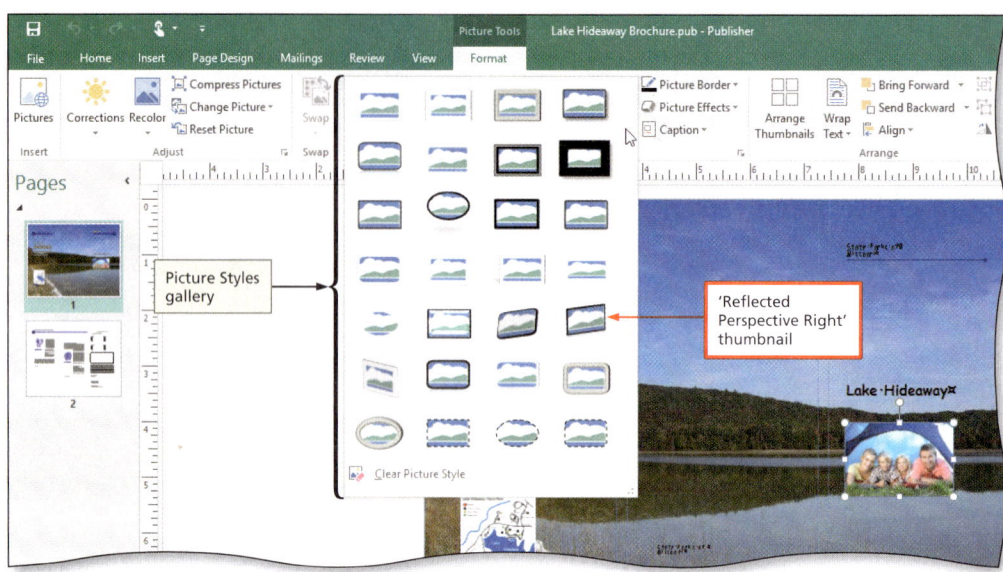

Experiment

- Point to various picture styles in the Picture Styles gallery and watch the format of the picture change in the publication window.

Figure 2–27

- Click the 'Reflected Perspective Right' thumbnail in the Picture Styles gallery to apply the selected style to the picture (Figure 2–28).

Figure 2–28

To Change the Border Color and Weight

1 CUSTOMIZE BROCHURE | 2 EDIT TEXT & OBJECTS | 3 SWAP PICTURES | 4 CREATE PICTURE STYLES & SHAPES

5 USE STYLISTIC SETS | 6 SEARCH ONLINE PICTURES | 7 INSERT CAPTIONS | 8 CHECK PUBLICATION | 9 PACK

The following steps change the border color of the picture and the weight, or size, of the border. *Why? A lighter, stronger border will make the picture stand out from the background.*

- Select the picture of the campers, if necessary.

- Click the Picture Border button (Picture Tools Format tab | Picture Styles group) to display the Picture Border gallery (Figure 2–29).

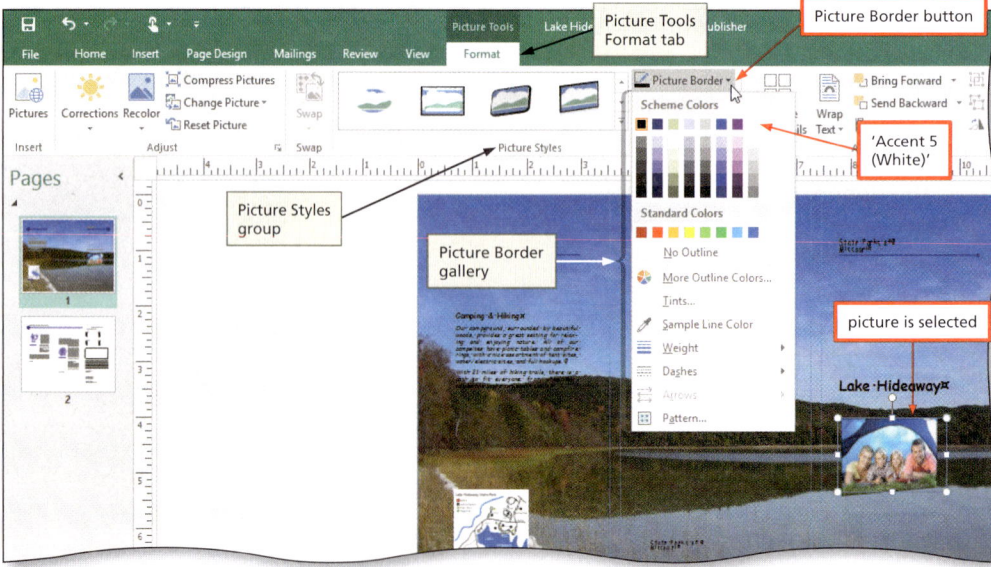

Figure 2–29

- Click 'Accent 5 (White)' in the Scheme Colors area to change the border.
- Click the Picture Border button (Picture Tools Format tab | Picture Styles group) again, to display the Picture Border gallery.
- Point to the Weight command to display the Weight submenu (Figure 2–30).

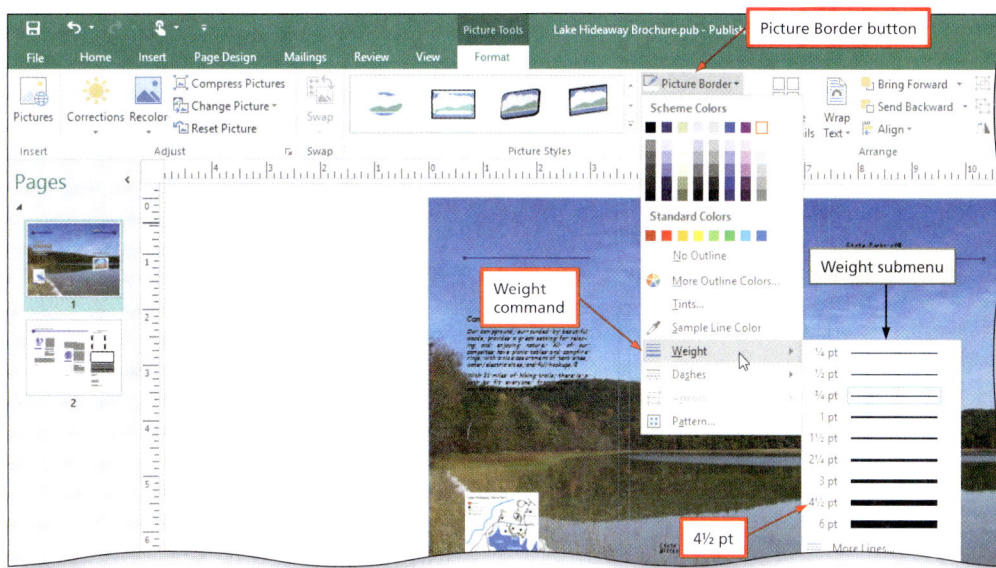

Figure 2–30

- Click 4½ pt on the Weight menu to change the weight of the border (Figure 2–31).

Figure 2–31

Other Ways
1. To change border color, right-click shape, click Format Picture on shortcut menu, click Colors and Lines tab (Format Picture dialog box), in Line area click Color button, click desired color	2. To change border weight, right-click shape, click Format Picture on shortcut menu, click Colors and Lines tab (Format Picture dialog box), in Line area click width up or down button

To Change the Font Color

1 CUSTOMIZE BROCHURE | 2 EDIT TEXT & OBJECTS | 3 SWAP PICTURES | 4 CREATE PICTURE STYLES & SHAPES
5 USE STYLISTIC SETS | 6 SEARCH ONLINE PICTURES | 7 INSERT CAPTIONS | 8 CHECK PUBLICATION | 9 PACK

The following steps change the font color to white in several text boxes. *Why? White lettering will be easier to read with the dark picture background.*

- Select the text in the title, Lake Hideaway.
- Click the Font Color arrow (Home tab | Font Group) to display the Font Color gallery (Figure 2–32).

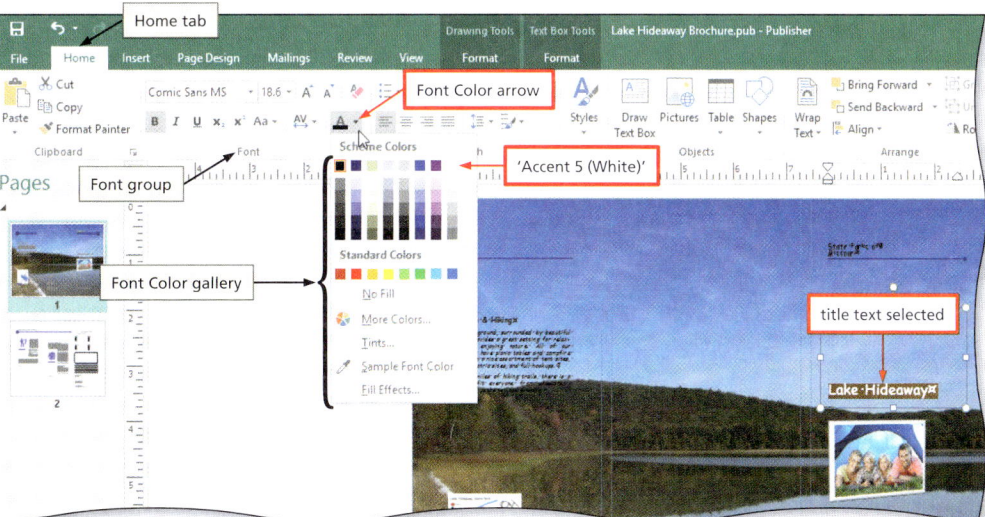

Figure 2–32

• Click 'Accent 5 (White)' in the Font Color gallery to change the font color to white.

• Deselect the text to view the white text (Figure 2–33).

Figure 2–33

• Repeat Steps 1 and 2 to change the font color for all of the other text boxes on page 1, with the exception of the text box in the upper portion of the right panel (Figure 2–34).

Q&A Is there a way to change all of the font color faster?

It would be difficult to change text color globally; however, you can use CTRL+A to select all of the text in a text box, which may be faster than dragging through it. And, once you have the font color chosen, the Font Color button retains the color so you can just click it for subsequent color changes without having to display the gallery.

Could I use the format painter to copy the formatting?

No, not for white only. The format painter would also copy the font and font size to the other locations.

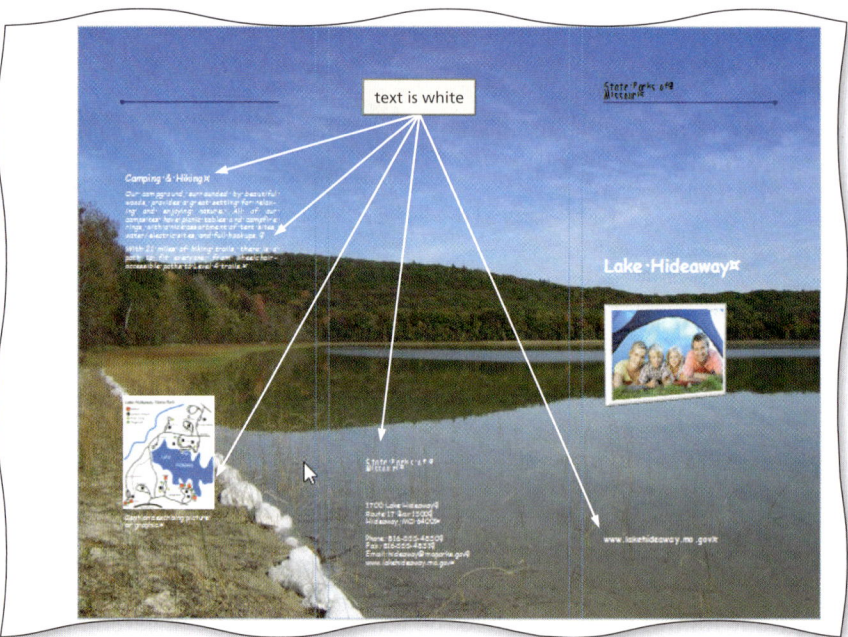

Figure 2–34

Other Ways

1. Click Font Color arrow on mini toolbar, click desired color

2. Click Font Color arrow (Text Box Tools Format tab | Font Group), click desired color

3. Right-click selected text, point to Change Text on shortcut menu, click Font on Change Text submenu, click Font color arrow (Font dialog box), click desired color, click OK button

To AutoFit Headings

The following step uses the Best Fit option to autofit the headings on page 1.

1 One a time, right-click the text in each heading text box and the text in the URL text box, and then click Best Fit on the shortcut menu (Figure 2–35).

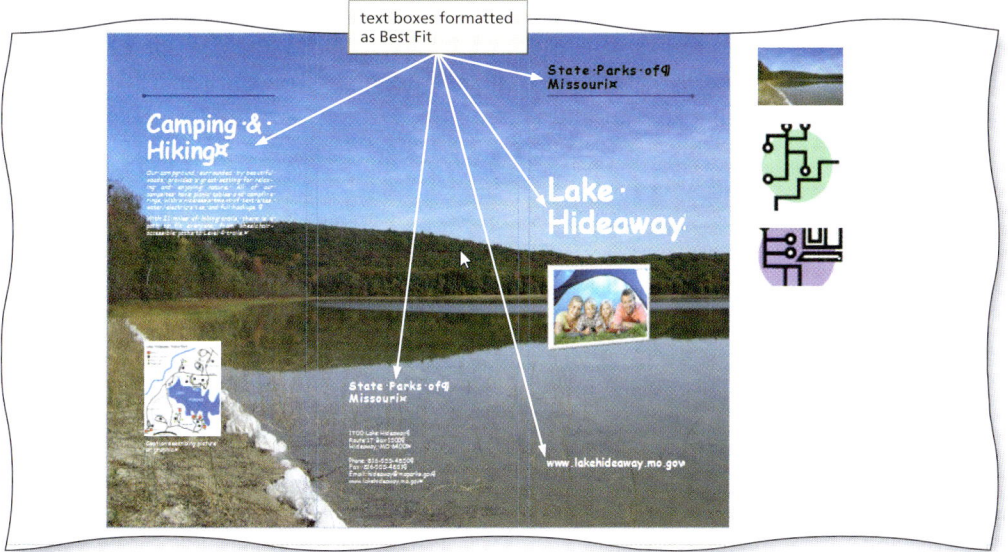

Figure 2–35

To Increase the Font Size of the Story

The following steps use the 'Increase Font Size' button to make the text bigger on page 1.

1 Select the story text in the left panel.

2 Click the 'Increase Font Size' button (Home tab | Font group) several times until the text is enlarged to 12 pt (Figure 2–36).

3 Deselect the text.

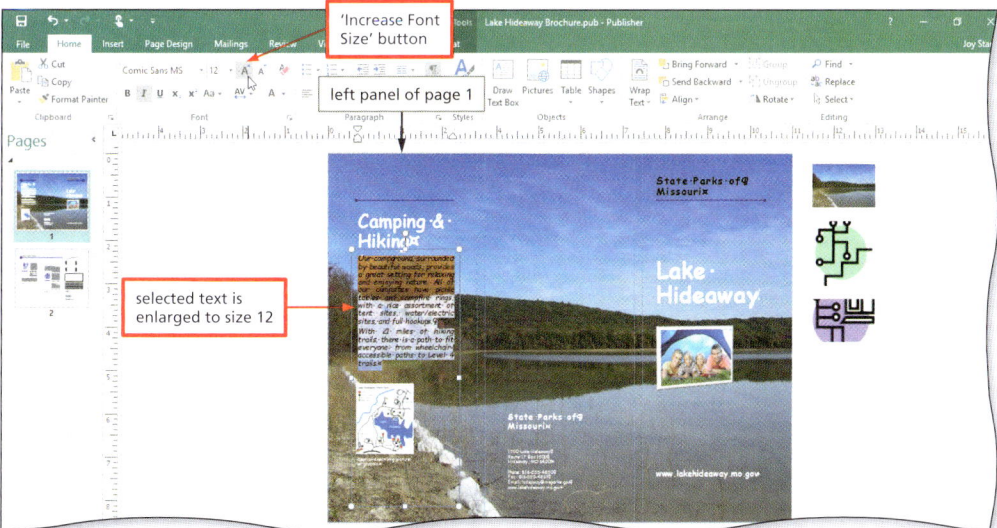

Figure 2–36

BTW
Superscripts and Subscripts
Two special font effects are superscript and subscript. A superscript is a character that appears slightly higher than other text on a line, such as that used in footnotes (reference[1]). A subscript is text that is slightly lower than other text on a line, such as that used in scientific formulas (H_2O).

Shapes

Publisher has more than 150 shapes that you can use to create logos, graphics, banners, illustrations, and other ornamental objects. You can apply fill effects, shadows, reflections, glows, pictures, and other special effects to shapes. When you click the Shapes button (Insert tab | Illustrations group), Publisher populates a Recently Used Shapes area that appears at the top of the Shapes gallery. You can choose your desired shape from that area or from the regular categories. You will learn about more advanced shape effects in a later module.

To Insert a Shape

1 CUSTOMIZE BROCHURE | 2 EDIT TEXT & OBJECTS | 3 SWAP PICTURES | 4 CREATE PICTURE STYLES & SHAPES
5 USE STYLISTIC SETS | 6 SEARCH ONLINE PICTURES | 7 INSERT CAPTIONS | 8 CHECK PUBLICATION | 9 PACK

The following steps insert a rectangle shape across the top of the publication. ***Why?*** *The rectangle will serve as a kind of banner for the brochure.*

1

- Make sure no text or objects are selected and then display the Insert tab.
- Click the Shapes button (Insert tab | Illustrations group) to display the Shapes gallery (Figure 2–37).

Q&A Why is my gallery different?
Publisher displays the most recently used shapes at the top of the gallery. The recently used shapes on your computer may differ.

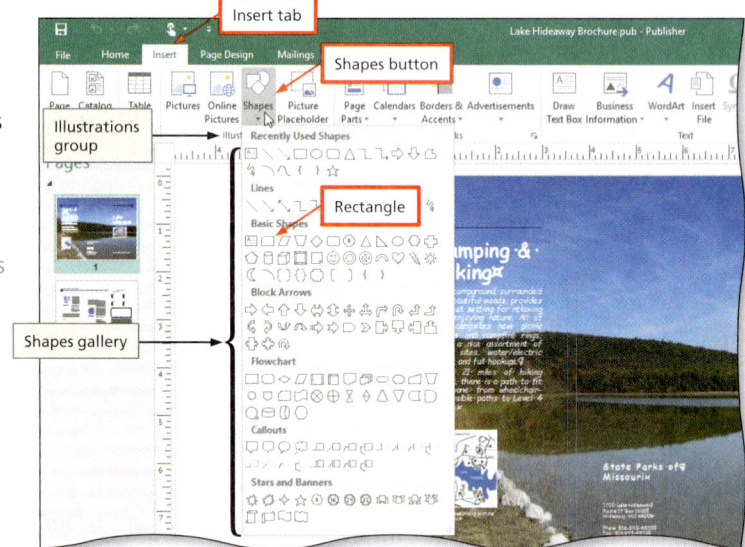

Figure 2–37

2

- Click the desired shape button (in this case, Rectangle) in the Basic Shapes category to select it.
- Move the pointer into the workspace. Beginning in the upper left corner of the page layout, drag a shape across the top of page 1, approximately 1⅛ inches high (Figure 2–38).

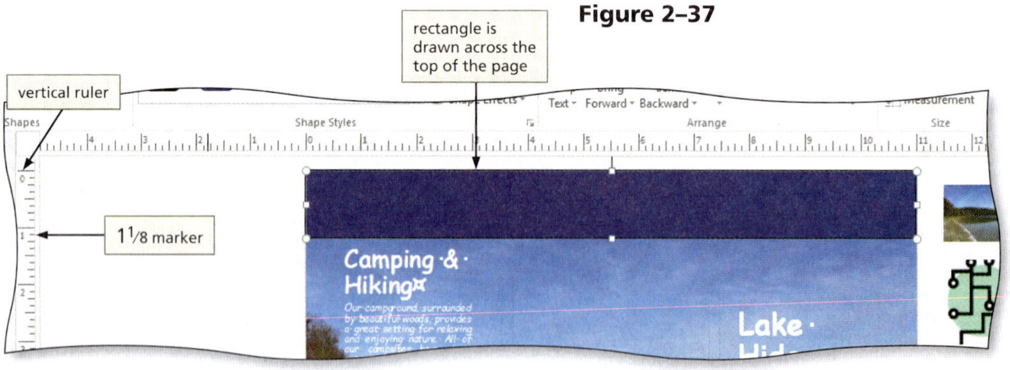

Figure 2–38

Q&A How can I tell how high the shape is?
Use the vertical ruler to estimate 1⅛ inches.

Why did the rectangle fill with blue?
Blue is the default shape color assigned by the color scheme. You will change it in the next steps.

Other Ways

1. Click More button (Drawing Tools Format tab | Insert Shapes group), click desired shape button in gallery, draw shape

To Recolor a Shape

In the following steps, you will change the fill color of the shape and its outline to white. *Why?* Publisher uses the color scheme when creating shapes. This color scheme uses a dark blue fill and a black outline.

1

• With the shape still selected, click the Shape Fill arrow (Drawing Tools Format tab | Shape Styles group) to display the Shape Fill gallery (Figure 2–39).

Q&A Why did the Drawing Tools Format tab appear? When a shape is selected, Publisher automatically displays the Drawing Tools Format tab.

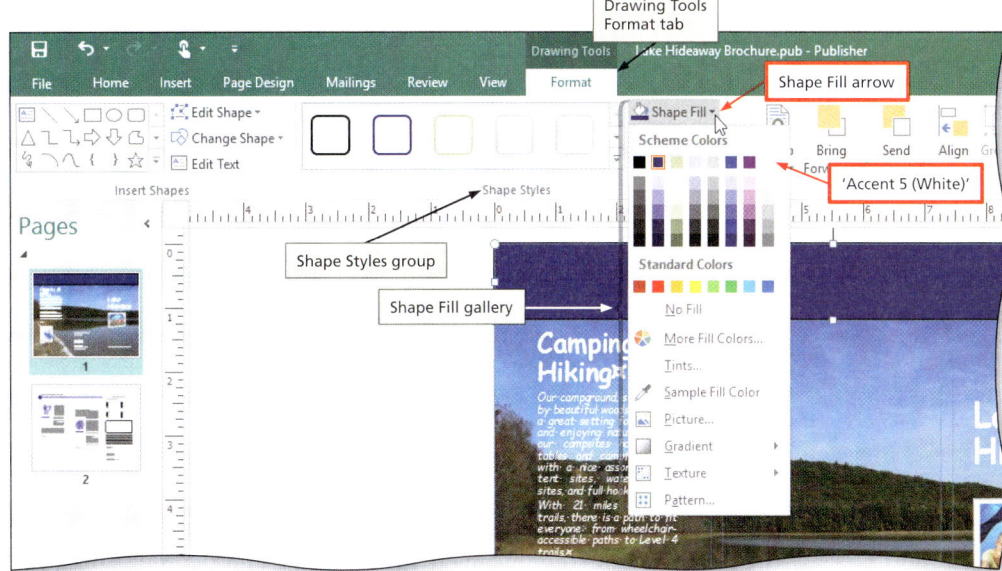

Figure 2–39

2

• Click 'Accent 5 (White)' in the Scheme Colors area in the gallery to change the shape color.

• With the shape still selected, click the Shape Outline arrow (Drawing Tools Format tab | Shape Styles group) to display the Shape Outline gallery (Figure 2–40).

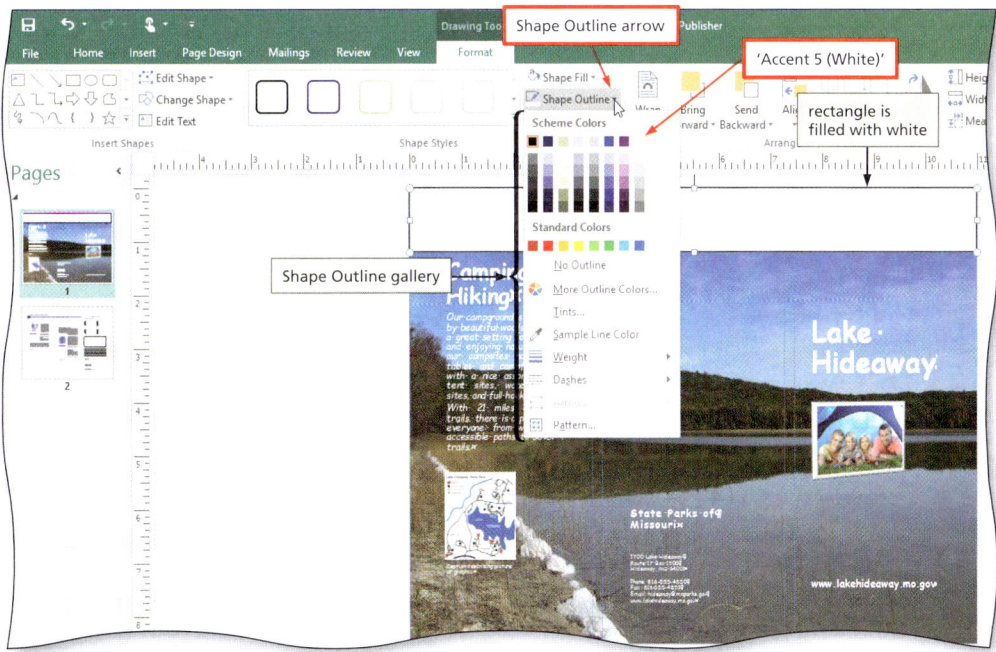

Figure 2–40

3

- Click White in the color gallery to change the outline color (Figure 2–41).

Did the outline border change?
Yes. The only outline you may see is the selection border.

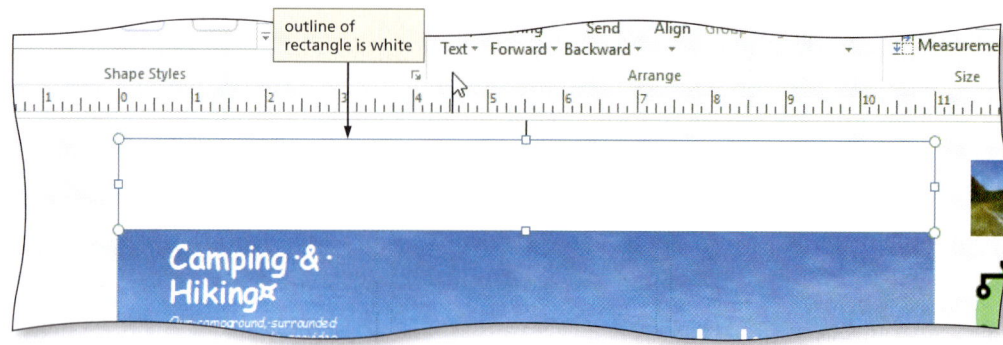

Figure 2–41

Other Ways

1. To change fill color, click Shape Fill arrow on mini toolbar, click desired color

2. To change fill color, right-click shape, click Format AutoShape on shortcut menu, click Color button in Fill area, click desired color

3. To change border color, click Shape outline arrow on mini toolbar, click desired color

4. To change border color, right-click shape, click Format AutoShape on shortcut menu, click Color arrow in Line area, click desired color

To Send a Shape Backward

1 CUSTOMIZE BROCHURE | 2 EDIT TEXT & OBJECTS | 3 SWAP PICTURES | **4 CREATE PICTURE STYLES & SHAPES**
5 USE STYLISTIC SETS | 6 SEARCH ONLINE PICTURES | 7 INSERT CAPTIONS | 8 CHECK PUBLICATION | 9 PACK

In Publisher, **layering**, or **ordering**, means to make purposeful decisions on how objects appear in front of one another. For example, when you are using a template, any new object you insert appears in front of template objects automatically. When objects are layered, the most forward object will eclipse the objects below it. Building a publication in layers from the back to the front ensures that you will be aware of any objects that might obstruct one another and that your choices provide interesting backgrounds. You can reorder most objects, including shapes, tables, text boxes, pictures, and clip art.

The following steps move the rectangle behind the text and decorative lines. *Why? The recently inserted shape is obstructing the view of the objects below it.* You also will save the file again in the last step.

1

- With the shape still selected, click the Send Backward button (Drawing Tools Format tab | Arrange group) three times (Figure 2–42).

Should I click the upper part of the button or the arrow below it?
Click the upper part, which is the button itself.

Why should I click it three times?
Publisher reorders objects one at a time. In this case, there are two lines and a text box that need to come forward.

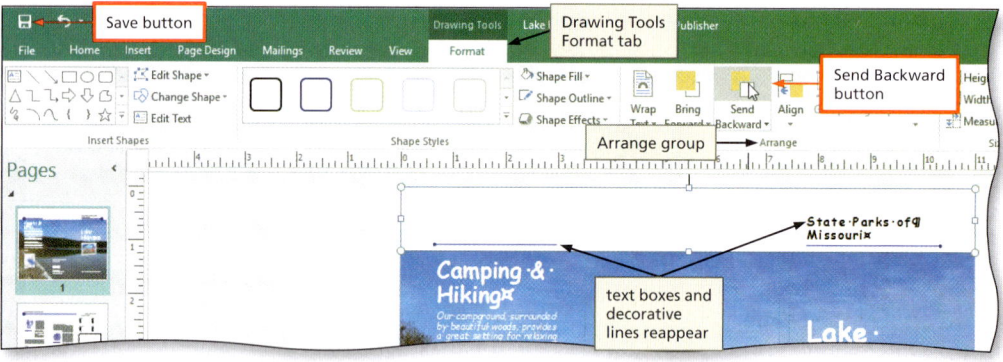

Figure 2–42

2

- Click the Save button on the Quick Access Toolbar to overwrite the previously saved file.

Break Point: If you wish to take a break, this is a good place to do so. Exit Publisher. To resume at a later time, run Publisher, open the file called Lake Hideaway Brochure, and continue following the steps from this location forward.

Editing the Inside Panels of a Brochure

As you edit the inside panels of the brochure, you will change text, edit the form text boxes, and change the pictures and captions. Headings introduce information about the topic and describe specific products or services. Secondary headings and the stories below them organize topics to make it easier for readers to understand the information.

To Switch to Page 2

1 CUSTOMIZE BROCHURE | 2 EDIT TEXT & OBJECTS | 3 SWAP PICTURES | 4 CREATE PICTURE STYLES & SHAPES
5 USE STYLISTIC SETS | 6 SEARCH ONLINE PICTURES | 7 INSERT CAPTIONS | 8 CHECK PUBLICATION | 9 PACK

The following step uses the Page Navigation pane to move to page 2. *Why? The Page Navigation pane is the only way to move among pages by clicking; however, you can press the* F5 *key and enter the new page number.*

1

• Click the Page 2 icon in the Page Navigation pane to display page 2.

• If necessary, zoom to Whole Page view (Figure 2–43).

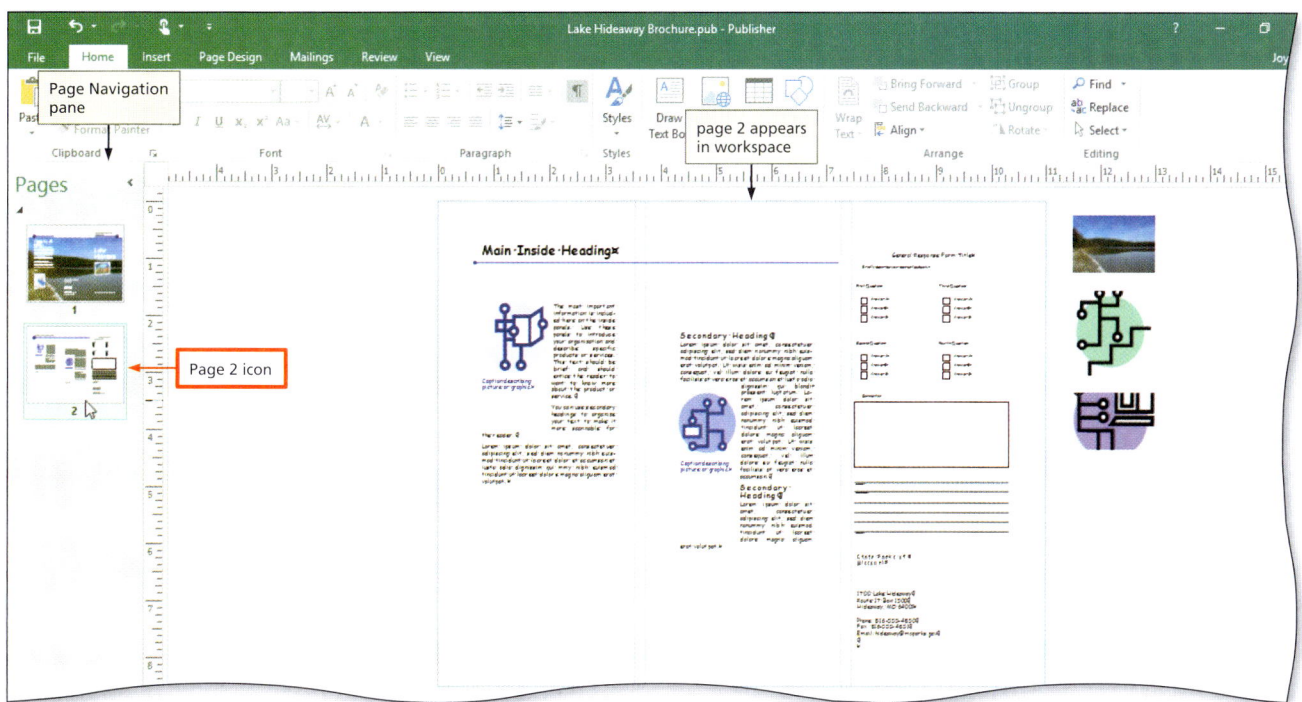

Figure 2–43

Other Ways

1. Press F5, enter page number, click OK button

To Insert and Format a Shape

The following steps insert a blue rectangle at the bottom of page 2 to provide continuity between the pages.

1 Display the Insert tab.

2 Click the Shapes button (Insert tab | Illustrations group) to display the Shapes gallery.

③ Click the desired shape button (in this case, the Rectangle) in the Basic Shapes category to select it.

④ Move the pointer into the workspace and then drag a shape across the bottom of page 2, approximately ¾ inches high.

⑤ If the Phone text box does not display the website, right-click the text box and then click Best Fit on the shortcut menu (Figure 2–44).

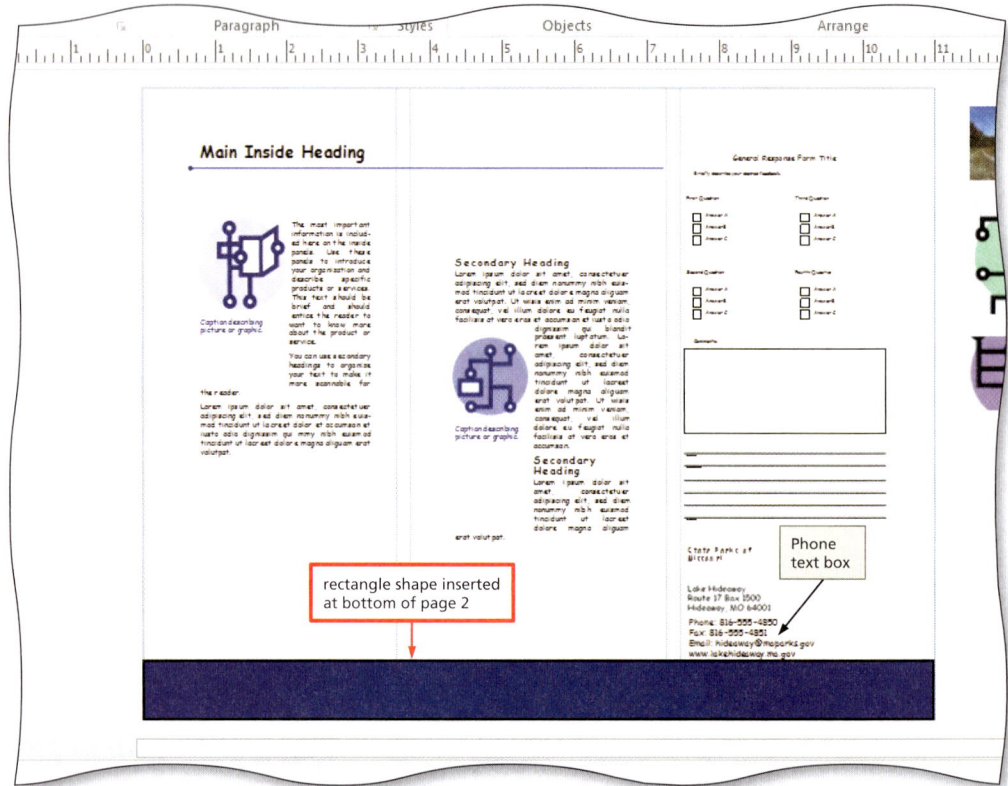

Figure 2–44

To Edit the Left Panel on Page 2

The following steps edit the text on the left panel of page 2. As you edit the text, zoom and scroll as necessary to view the text.

① In the left panel of page 2, click the placeholder text in the 'Main Inside Heading' text box to select it.

② Type `Park Attractions` to complete the page heading.

③ Click the placeholder text for the story in the left panel.

④ To create the story heading, press CTRL+B to bold the text. Type `Water` and then press the ENTER key. Press CTRL+B to turn off bold and press the ENTER key again.

⑤ Type `Our beautiful lake offers excellent canoeing, kayaking, and stand-up paddleboarding. Learn about the fascinating history of Lake Hideaway with a guided kayak tour. Paddle the lake and enjoy the Ozark scenery.` and then press the ENTER key to create the first paragraph.

6 Type `Our cozy, clean beach is a great place to swim and play. Bring your sunscreen, beach chair, picnic, and board! Or, you can rent canoes, kayaks, and paddleboards at the park office.` to complete the story (Figure 2–45).

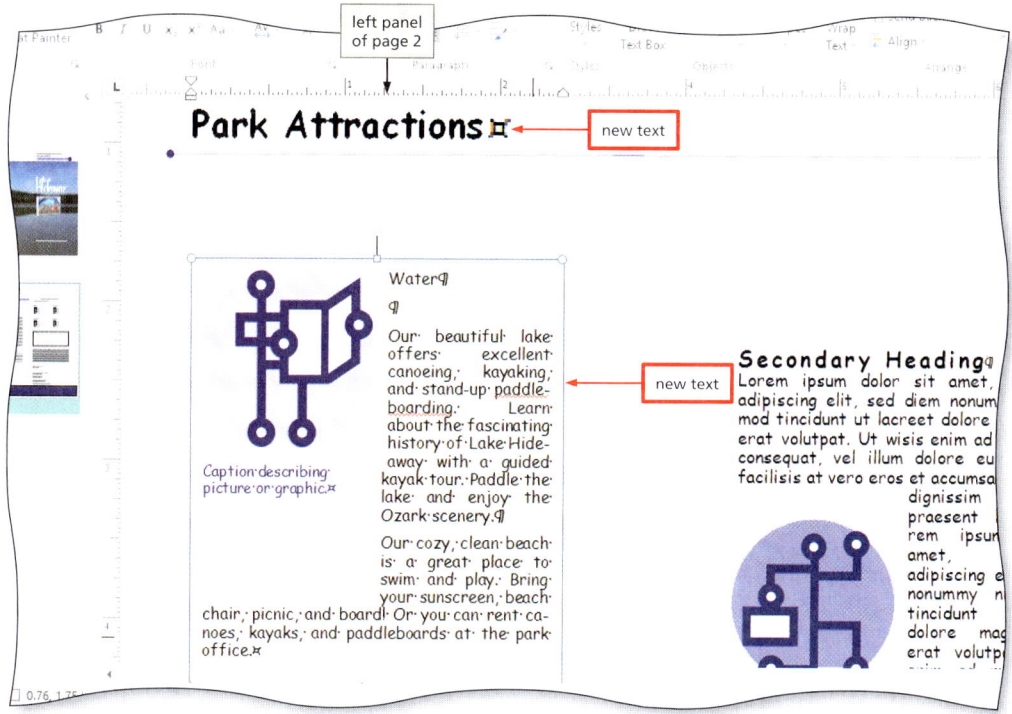

Figure 2–45

To Edit the Middle Panel on Page 2

The following steps edit the text in the middle panel of page 2. As you edit the text, zoom and scroll as necessary to view the text. Later in the module, you will format the text.

1 In the middle panel of page 2, click the first Secondary Heading placeholder text in the middle panel to select it.

2 Type `Wildlife` to complete the text.

3 Click the story below the heading to select the placeholder text.

4 Type `Our state park offers an outstanding setting for viewing, photographing, and studying creatures in their natural habitats. The opportunities range from observing deer, foxes, coyotes, and beavers in the deeper woods, to bird-watching our 120 different species.` and then press the ENTER key to create the first paragraph.

5 Type `Small animals, such as rabbits, raccoons, and squirrels, abound near our trails and campsites. Take a dusk drive around the park to see our beautiful animal families. No hunting is allowed in the park.` to complete the story.

6 Click the second Secondary Heading placeholder text on the middle panel to select it.

7 Type `Fishing` to complete the text.

8 Click the story below the heading to select the placeholder text.

⑨ Type `Lake Hideaway offers great fishing whether from a shore, boat, or dock. Fishing season begins on the last Saturday in April and ends on November 15th every year. Anglers commonly catch crappie, walleye, catfish, and bass. The lake also offers good fishing for a number of other species including gar, paddlefish, sunfish, and common carp.` to complete the story (Figure 2–46).

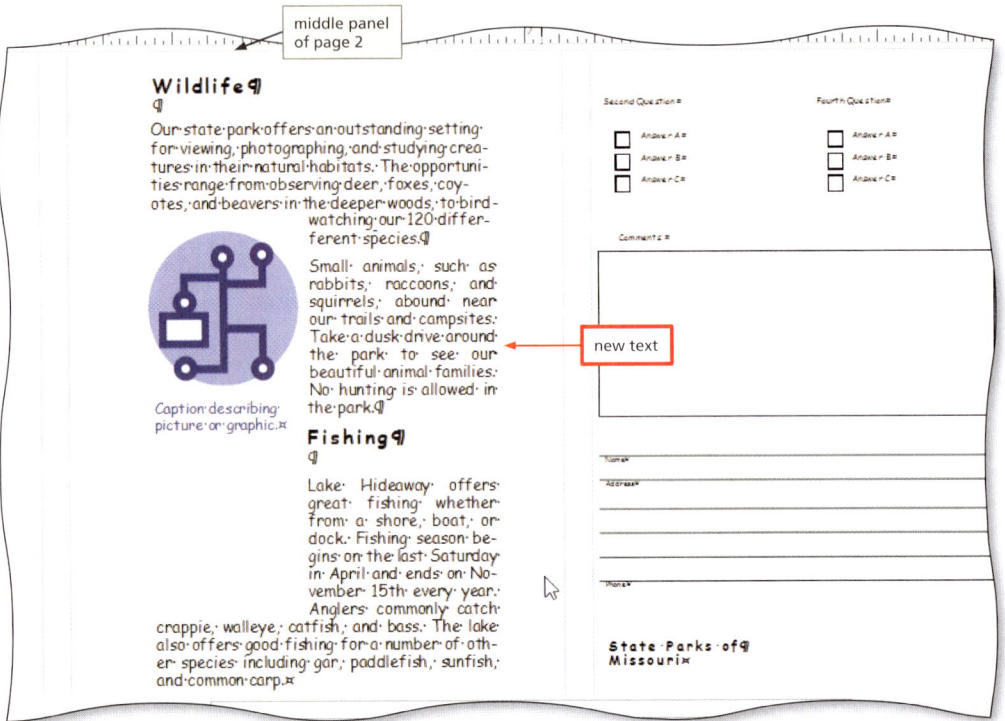

Figure 2–46

To Edit the Form

Publisher forms consist of text boxes, graphic boxes, and lines position in an attractive and usable format. The check boxes consist of a graphic and a text box grouped together. A **grouped object** consists of more than one object linked together for logical reasons, such as the parts of a masthead or a picture with its caption. Grouped objects are moved, edited, and formatted together as one. When necessary, grouped objects can be formatted individually by clicking a specific object after selecting the group. They can be ungrouped if you want to move or resize them independently. Alternately, individual objects can be grouped if you want to keep them together.

The following steps edit form text boxes and the grouped check boxes in the right panel of page 2.

① On the right panel of page 2, click the text in the General Response Form Title text box to select the placeholder text.

② Click the Zoom In button on the status bar to zoom to approximately 230%.

③ Type `For more information...` to complete the text.

④ Click the instruction text box below the heading to select the placeholder text.

⑤ Type `Fill out the following form and send it to the address listed below.` to finish entering the text.

⑥ If necessary, scroll down to display the check box area.

⑦ Click the First Question heading to select the placeholder text.

⑧ Type `Camping & Hiking` to change the heading and then click outside the text box to deselect it.

⑨ Repeat the process to replace each of the other three headings shown in Figure 2–47.

⑩ Click the text, Answer A, below the Camping & Hiking heading, in order to select only the placeholder text, not the check box. Do not double-click.

⑪ Type `Reservations` to change the placeholder text.

⑫ Repeat the process to edit all of the other check boxes in the form as shown in Figure 2–47.

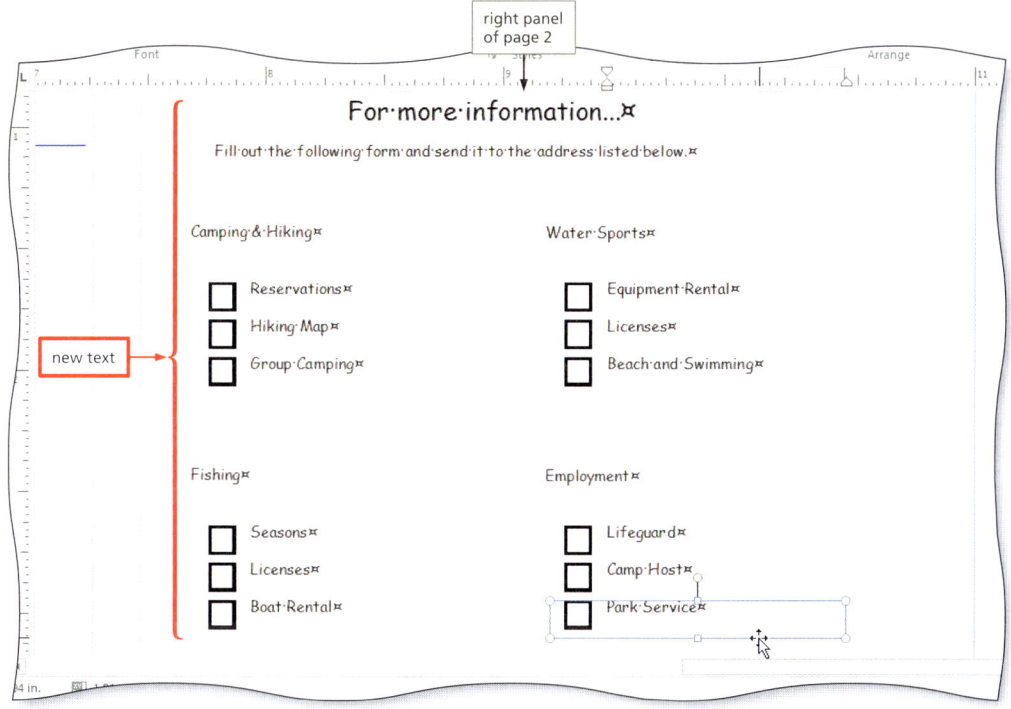

Figure 2–47

Stylistic Sets

Publisher includes a special kind of font feature called a stylistic set. A **stylistic set** is an organized set of alternate letters and glyphs, allowing you to change what a font looks like. A **glyph** is a special stroke that appears in text that is not part of the normal font set. Diacritical marks, such as the umlaut (ä) or cedilla (ç), use glyphs.

Besides its regular display, almost every font has three common stylistic sets: bold, italic, and the combination of bold and italic. The letters are displayed in the same font but use a heavier or slanted glyph. Another example with which you may be familiar is a font family that has both serif and sans serif stylistic sets. A **serif** is

BTW
Serif Fonts
Serif fonts are considered Oldstyle when they display a slanted serif. Fonts are considered Modern when they use horizontal serifs.

BTW
Swashes
A swash is an exaggerated serif or glyph that typically runs into the space above or below the next letter. Some swashes can cause an unattractive appearance when used with adjacent descending letters such as g, j, or y; however, when used correctly, a swash produces a flowing, linear appearance that adds interest to the font.

small line, flourish, or embellishment that crosses the strokes of letters in some fonts. A **sans serif**, meaning without flourish, set has no extra embellishment at the end of characters. Other stylistic sets include alternates for characters such as e, j, g, or y. The extra characters with accompanying glyphs have to be a part of the font set when it is installed. On a typical Publisher installation, only a few font families contain complete stylistic sets. Some fonts, such as Gabriola, allow you to choose a **stylistic alternate** set, which creates a random pattern from among the various stylistic sets available for the current font.

Typography refers to specialized effects and fonts, including stylistic sets, drop caps, number styles, and glyphs. Ligatures, stylistic sets, swashes, and stylistic alternates, as well as some alphabetic characters that are not part of the English language, also are created with glyphs. You will learn more about typography in future modules.

To Format with a Stylistic Set

1 CUSTOMIZE BROCHURE | 2 EDIT TEXT & OBJECTS | 3 SWAP PICTURES | 4 CREATE PICTURE STYLES & SHAPES
5 USE STYLISTIC SETS | 6 SEARCH ONLINE PICTURES | 7 INSERT CAPTIONS | 8 CHECK PUBLICATION | 9 PACK

The following steps choose a stylistic set for the heading. *Why? Stylistic sets add interest and flair to headings.*

1

- Select the text, For more information..., at the top of the right panel of page 2.
- Click Text Box Tools Format on the ribbon to display the Text Box Tools Format tab.
- With the text selected, click the Stylistic Sets button (Text Box Tools Format tab | Typography group) to display the Stylistic Sets gallery (Figure 2–48).

Experiment

- Point to each stylistic set and watch the live preview in the text box.

Q&A
Do all fonts have fancy stylistic sets?
No, usually only **OpenType** or scalable fonts contain stylistic sets other than bold and italic.

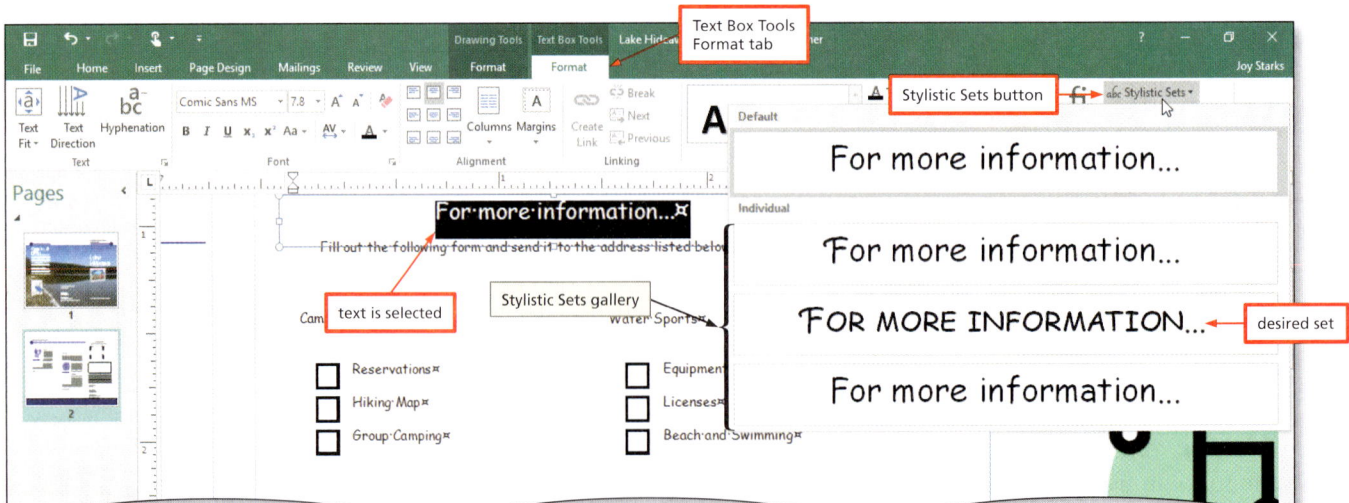

Figure 2–48

- Click the desired set (in this case, the second one from the bottom) to apply the stylistic set to the selected text (Figure 2–49).

Are any fancier stylistic sets available?
Yes. The Gabriola font has some fancier stylistic sets with large glyphs, but those will not fit in with the style of the brochure.

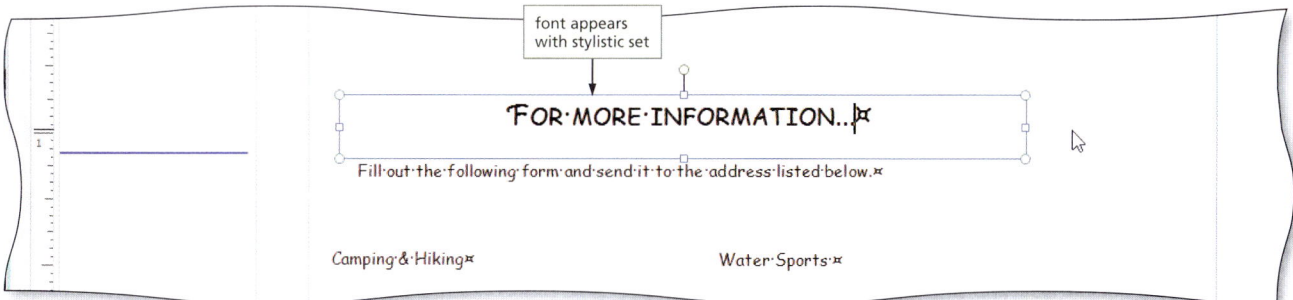

Figure 2–49

- Scroll to the left panel on page 2 and Select the text, `Park Attractions` at the top of the right panel.

- With the text selected, click the Stylistic Sets button (Text Box Tools Format tab | Typography group) to display the Stylistic Sets gallery.

- Click the desired set (in this case, the second one from the bottom) to apply the stylistic set to the selected text (Figure 2–50).

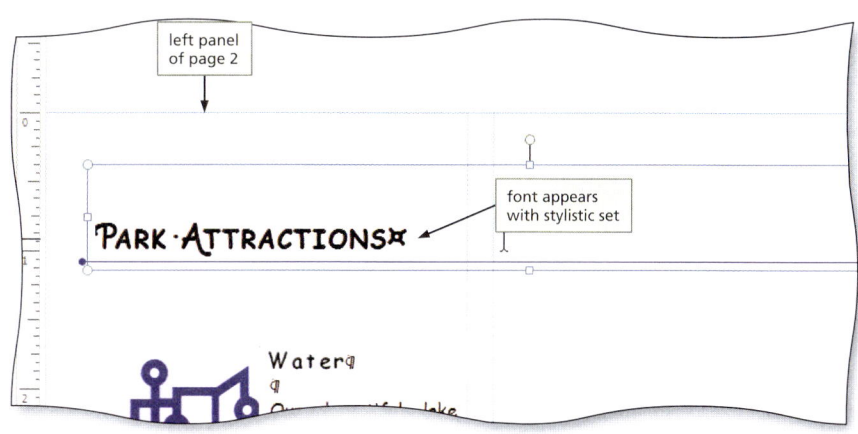

Figure 2–50

Online Pictures

Sometimes you may want to locate images or clip art from the web, also called **online pictures**. Publisher 2016 uses a Bing Image Search to help you locate images licensed under Creative Commons. The resulting images may or may not be royalty and copyright free. You must read the specific license for any image you plan to use, even for educational purposes.

To Search for Online Pictures

1 CUSTOMIZE BROCHURE | 2 EDIT TEXT & OBJECTS | 3 SWAP PICTURES | 4 CREATE PICTURE STYLES & SHAPES
5 USE STYLISTIC SETS | **6 SEARCH ONLINE PICTURES** | 7 INSERT CAPTIONS | 8 CHECK PUBLICATION | 9 PACK

The following steps use the Bing Image Search to locate pictures of a paddleboard and a deer. If you cannot find the specific image, you may use another appropriate image. Make sure you review the license to ensure you can comply. The size of your pictures may vary. If you want to use the exact image shown in the figures, you may retrieve the image from the Data Files.

- Zoom to display the entire page. Deselect any objects or pictures.

- Display the Insert tab and then click the Online Pictures button (Insert tab | Illustrations group) to display the Insert Pictures dialog box.

- Type **paddleboard** in the Bing Image Search text box to enter the search term. Press the ENTER key to display pictures related to paddleboards.

- Click a picture of a paddleboard similar to the one shown in Figure 2–51.

Q&A My pictures are different. Did I do something wrong?
No. The results of your search will be different from that shown in the figure.

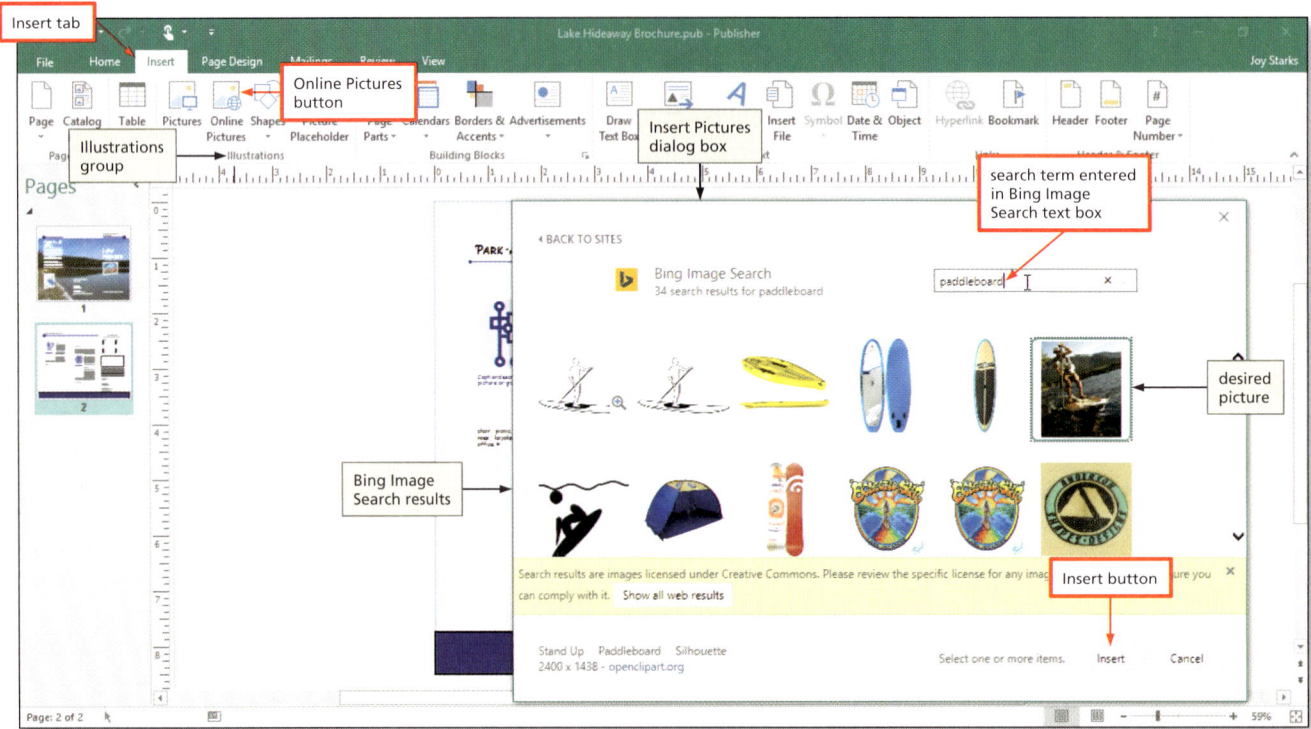

Figure 2–51

2

- Click the Insert button (Insert Pictures dialog box) to place the selected picture in the publication.

- Drag the picture to the scratch area (Figure 2–52).

Q&A I would like to use the exact picture. What should I do?
If you cannot find the exact picture with your Bing search and want to use it, you may insert the picture from the Data Files using the Pictures button (Insert tab | Illustrations group). Please contact your instructor for information about accessing the Data Files.

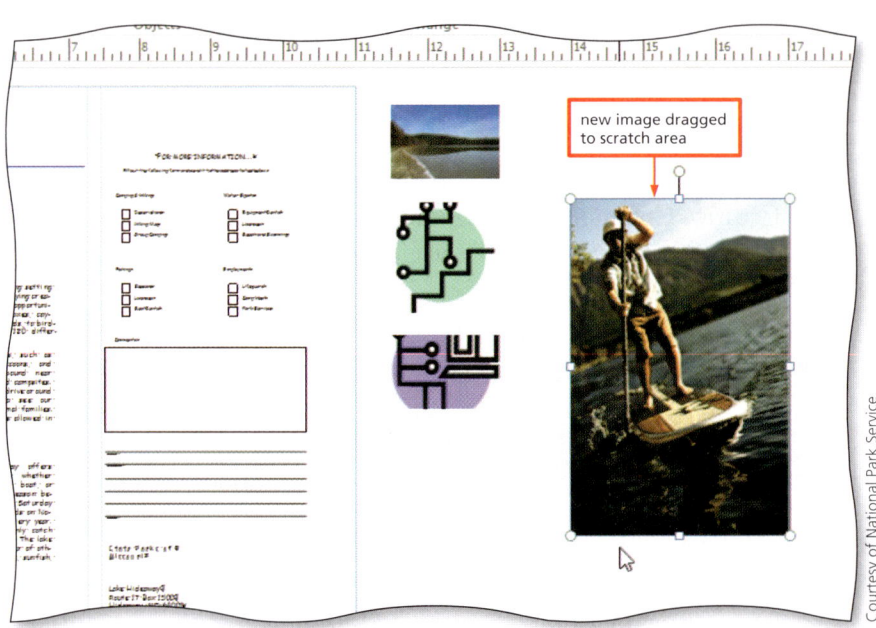

Courtesy of National Park Service

Figure 2–52

3

• Repeat Steps 1 and 2 to insert a picture of a deer and a picture of someone fishing. Scroll and zoom as necessary to view all of the pictures in the scratch area (Figure 2–53).

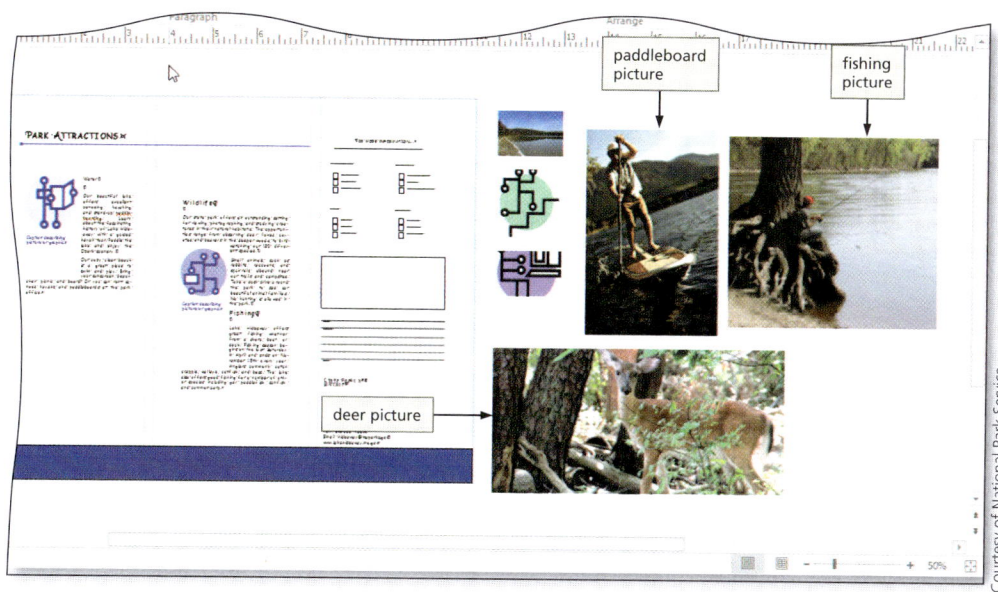

paddleboard picture

fishing picture

deer picture

Figure 2–53

Other Ways

1. Click Insert Pictures button (Picture Tools Format tab | Insert group), enter search term (Insert Pictures dialog box), press ENTER key

2. Right-click picture, point Change Picture on shortcut menu, click Change Picture on Change Picture submenu, enter search term (Insert Pictures dialog box), press ENTER key

---

To Select Multiple Objects by Dragging

1 CUSTOMIZE BROCHURE | 2 EDIT TEXT & OBJECTS | 3 SWAP PICTURES | 4 CREATE PICTURE STYLES & SHAPES
5 USE STYLISTIC SETS | **6 SEARCH ONLINE PICTURES** | **7 INSERT CAPTIONS** | **8 CHECK PUBLICATION** | **9 PACK**

The following steps select all of the pictures in the scratch area. *Why? They must be selected in order to arrange them in the next series of steps.*

1

• In the scratch area, drag, starting above and to the left of the first thumbnail, moving down and to the right, to include all of the pictures. Do not release the mouse button (or, if you are using touch, do not lift your finger) (Figure 2–54).

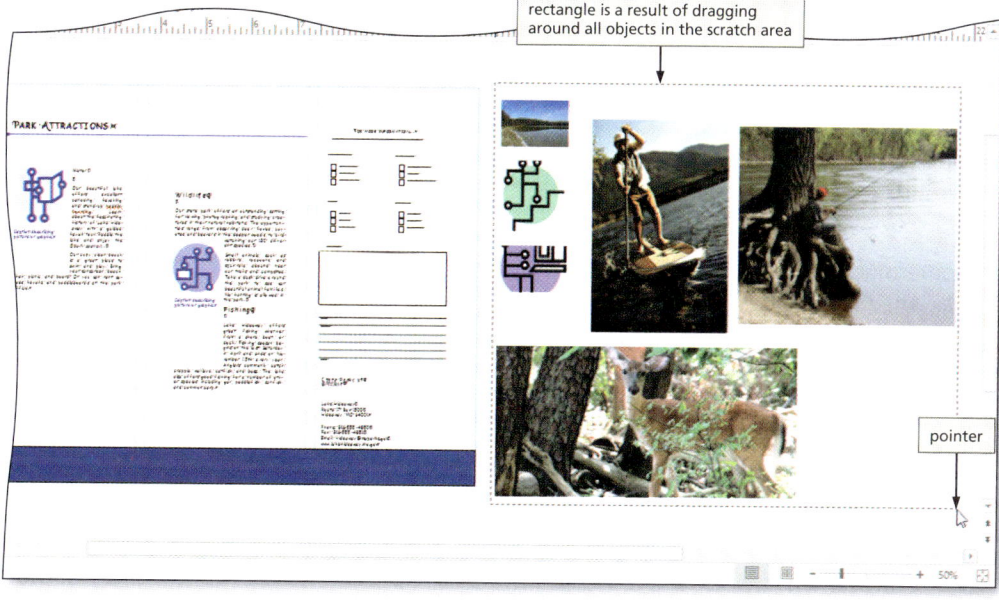

rectangle is a result of dragging around all objects in the scratch area

pointer

Figure 2–54

2

- Release the mouse button to select all of the pictures (Figure 2–55).

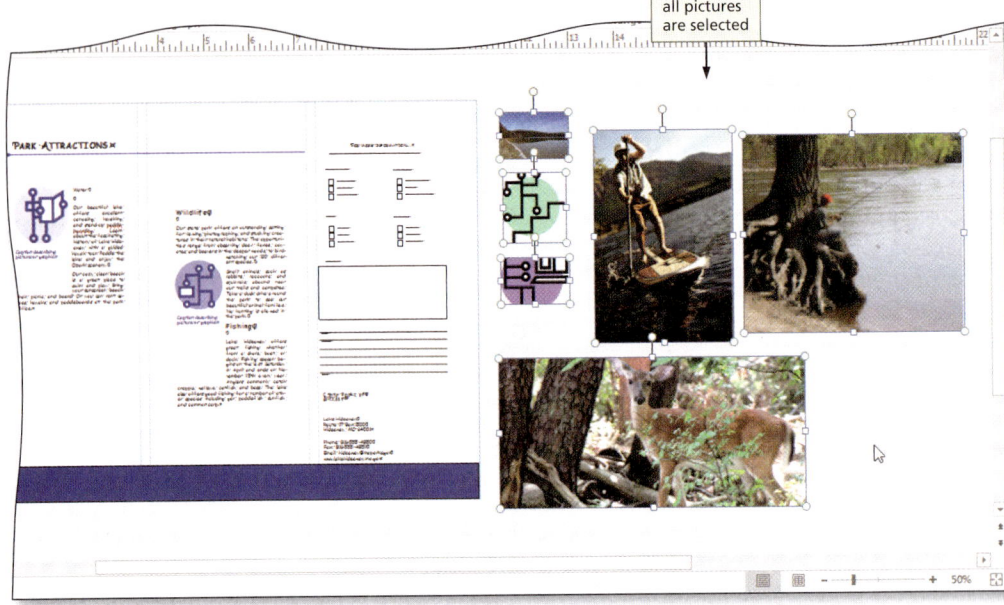

all pictures are selected

Figure 2–55

Other Ways

1. CTRL+click each object in the scratch area

To Arrange Thumbnails

1 CUSTOMIZE BROCHURE | 2 EDIT TEXT & OBJECTS | 3 SWAP PICTURES | 4 CREATE PICTURE STYLES & SHAPES
5 USE STYLISTIC SETS | 6 SEARCH ONLINE PICTURES | 7 INSERT CAPTIONS | 8 CHECK PUBLICATION | 9 PACK

When you **arrange thumbnails** in the scratch area, all of the pictures are reduced to thumbnail size and are aligned in rows and columns. *Why? A **thumbnail** is a reduced-size version of a larger graphic image used to help recognize and organize pictures, and to save space.* The following step arranges thumbnails.

1

- With the pictures selected, display the Picture Tools Format tab.

- Click the Arrange Thumbnails button (Picture Tools Format tab | Arrange group) to arrange the thumbnails (Figure 2–56).

Q&A

My tab disappeared. Did I do something wrong?
No. The Picture Tools Format tab displays only when a picture is selected. Arranging the thumbnails may have deselected the pictures.

My thumbnails are in a different order. Did I do something wrong?
No. Your thumbnails will differ.

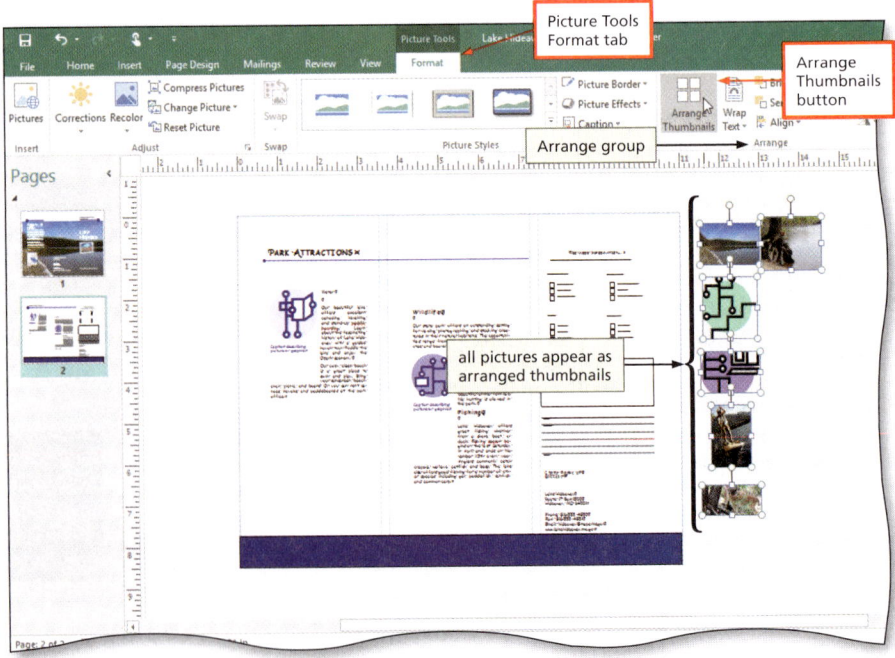

Picture Tools Format tab

Arrange Thumbnails button

Arrange group

all pictures appear as arranged thumbnails

Figure 2–56

Other Ways

1. Select pictures in scratch area, right-click any picture, click Arrange Thumbnails on shortcut menu

To Swap, Place, and Reset Pictures

The following steps change the pictures on page 2. Later in the module, you will resize them and edit the captions.

1 Zoom to Whole Page view, if necessary.

2 In the scratch area, click the photo you wish to use in the left panel of the brochure (in this case, the picture of the paddleboard) to display the swap icon.

3 From the scratch area, drag the swap icon of the photo to a location over the graphic in the left panel. When you see a pink boundary, drop the picture.

4 Click the paddleboard picture again to select only the picture, not the caption. Click the Reset Picture button (Picture Tools Format tab | Adjust group) to remove the color scheme.

5 Repeat Steps 2 through 4 to swap and reset the deer picture in the middle panel.

6 Drag the fishing picture from the scratch area to the bottom of the left panel, right-aligned with the text above it (Figure 2–57).

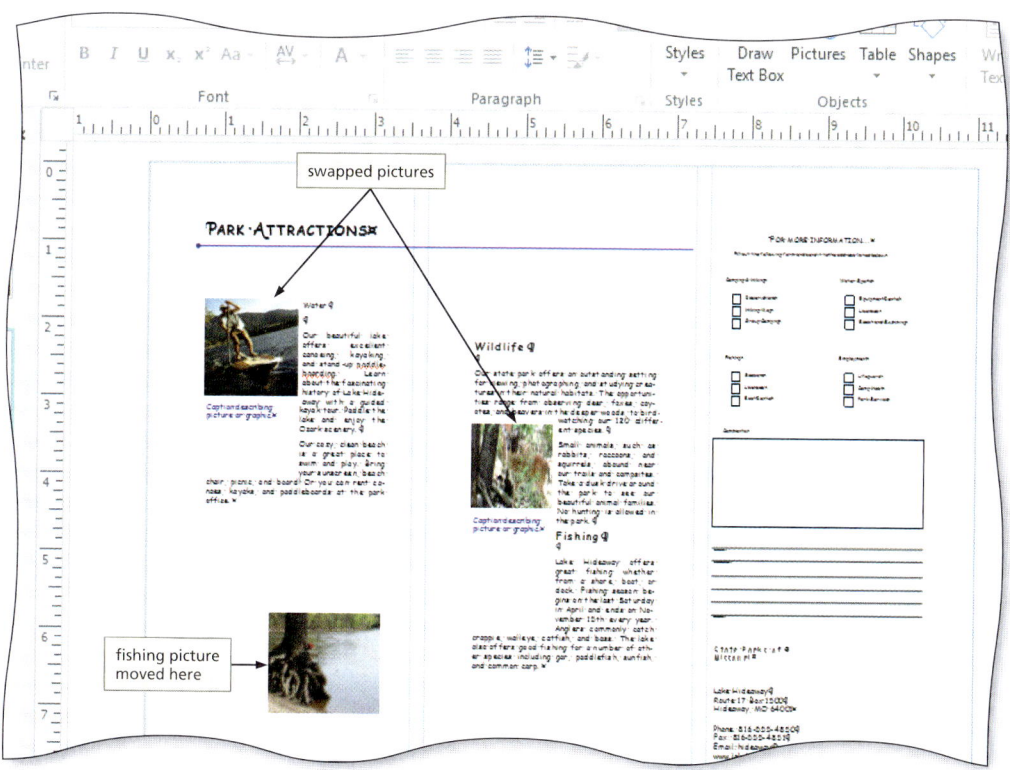

Figure 2–57

BTW

OpenType Fonts
Stylistic sets are more common in OpenType fonts. An **OpenType** font is a cross-platform, scalable font format with a wider range of characters than TrueType or PostScript fonts. If your printer can support them, OpenType fonts display a small computer icon or an uppercase O next to the font name when you click the Font arrow (Text Box Tools Format tab | Font group).

Captions

A **caption** is explanatory or identification text or a title that accompanies a graphic, figure, or photo. A caption can be as simple as a figure number, as you see in the figures of this book, or a caption can identify people, places, objects, or actions occurring in the graphic. When using Publisher templates, some captions already exist near a graphic. In those cases, the caption is a text box grouped with a graphic. If a graphic or photo does not have a caption, you can add one using the Caption gallery.

To Edit Captions

The following steps edit the text in the captions on page 2. *Why? A caption explains the graphic to the reader.*

- Scroll to the desired caption (in this case, the left panel of page 2).

- Click the caption text below the photo to select it, and then type `Enjoy` and then press the ENTER key. Type `paddleboarding` and then press the ENTER key. Type `on the lake!` to replace the text. If Publisher capitalizes the first letter on lines 2 and 3, use the AutoCorrect Options button as you did earlier in the module.

- If necessary, drag the right handle of the picture and caption grouping to the left until the picture is better proportioned (Figure 2–58).

Q&A

Can you delete a caption?

Yes, but be sure to delete the text box as well as the text. If the caption is part of a group, click once to select the group, then point to the border of the text box and click to select it. Finally, press the DELETE key to delete the caption text box.

Should I fix the red wavy line below the word, paddleboarding?

No. You check spelling later in the module.

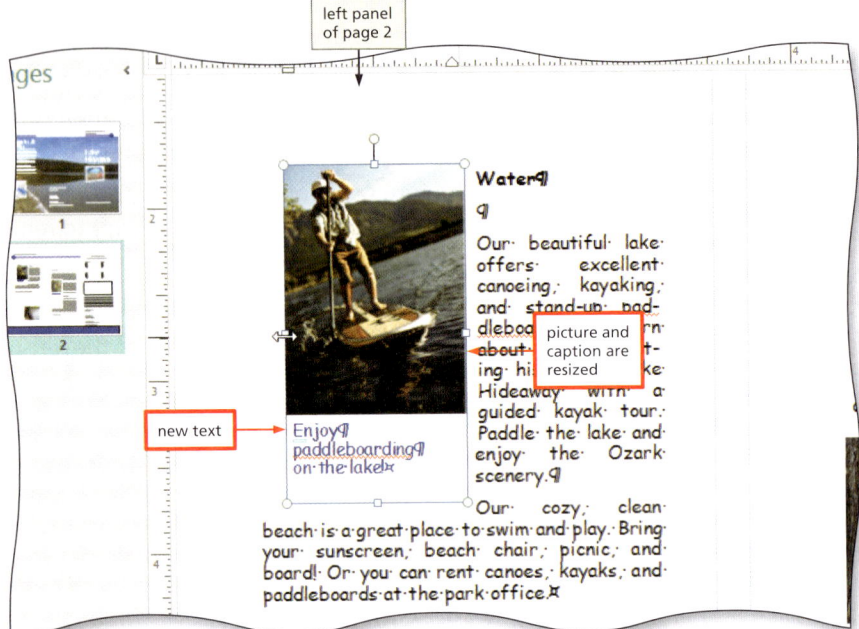

Figure 2–58

- Scroll to the caption on the middle panel of page 2 and then click the caption text below the photo to select it.

- Type `We guarantee deer` and then press the ENTER key. Type `sightings!` to complete the caption (Figure 2–59).

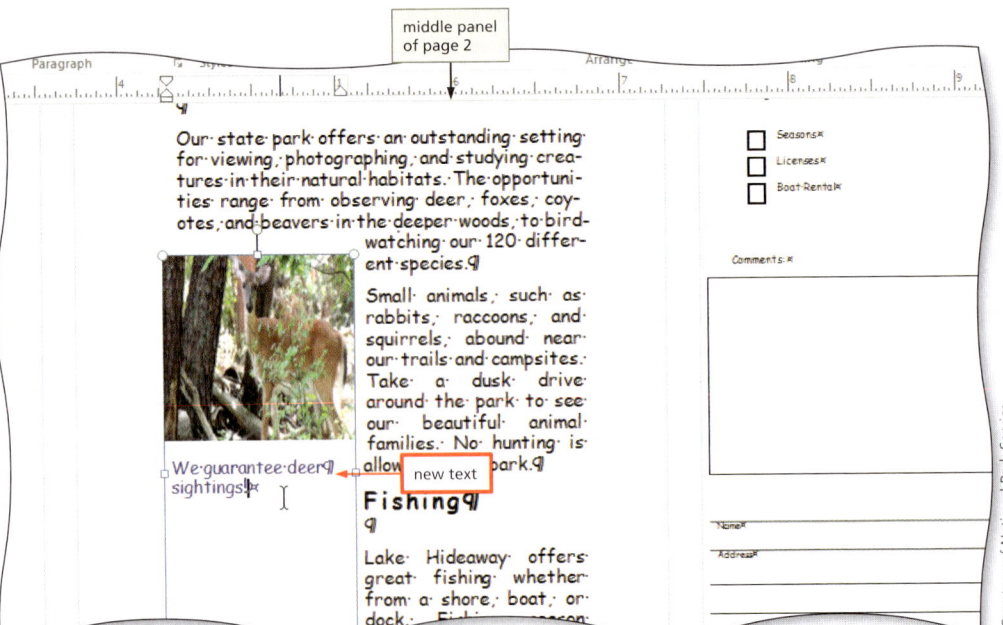

Figure 2–59

To Ungroup

The picture and caption are grouped or linked together in order to make moving them easier. The following steps ungroup the caption. **Why?** *Ungrouped, the caption text box can be resized.*

1
- With the picture/caption group selected, display the Home tab, if necessary.
- Click the Ungroup button (Home tab | Arrange group) to ungroup (Figure 2–60).

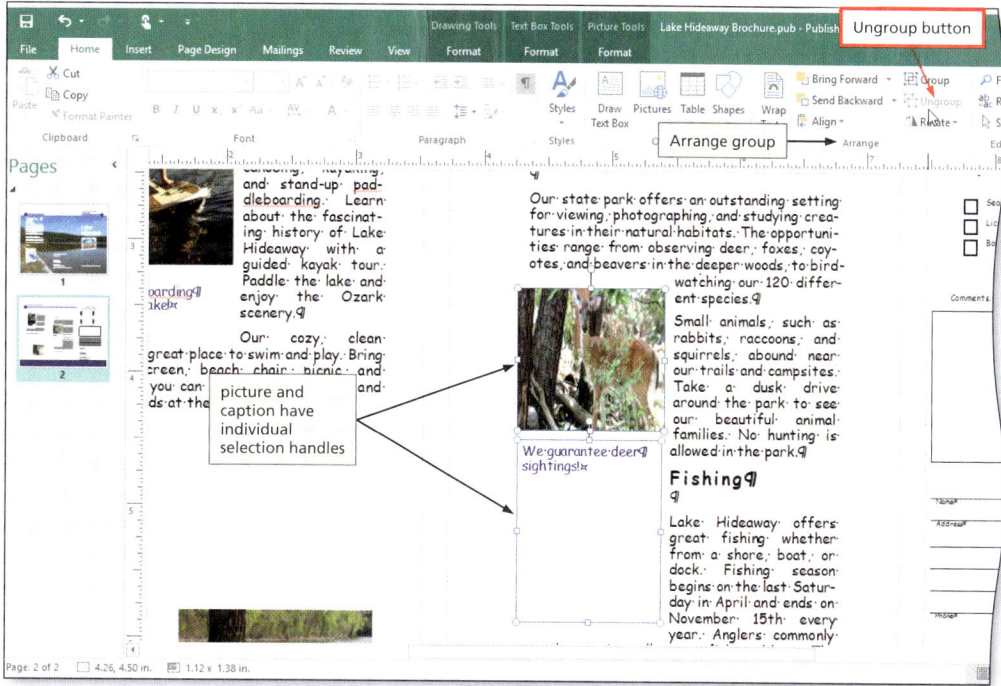

Figure 2–60

2
- Deselect and then select only the caption text box. Resize the text box by dragging the lower-center handle upward as shown in Figure 2–61.

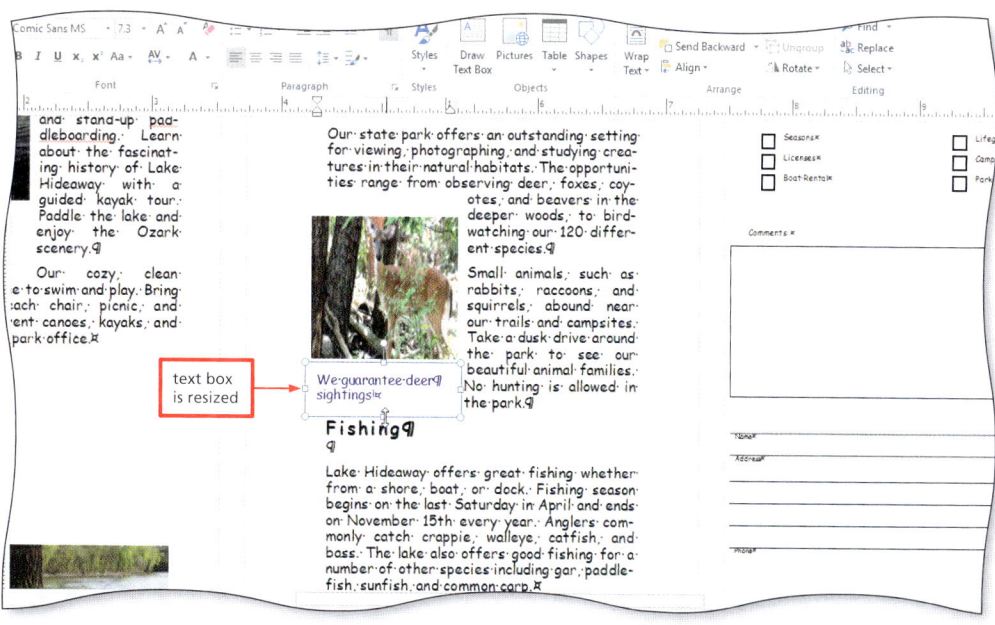

Figure 2–61

To Adjust Font Sizes on Page 2

The following steps adjust font sizes in several text boxes on page 2 to make the text larger and more legible.

1 Right-click the heading text, Park Attractions, and then click Best Fit on the shortcut menu.

2 Select the text in the left column (not the caption). Click the Increase Font size button (Home tab | Font group) until the text size is 10.

3 Select the text in the middle column (not the caption). Click the Increase Font size button (Home tab | Font group) until the text size is 10.

4 Select the middle column text box (not the picture or caption). Drag the upper-center sizing handle upward until the title aligns with the title in the left column, and so that all of the text is displayed at the bottom of the middle panel (Figure 2–62).

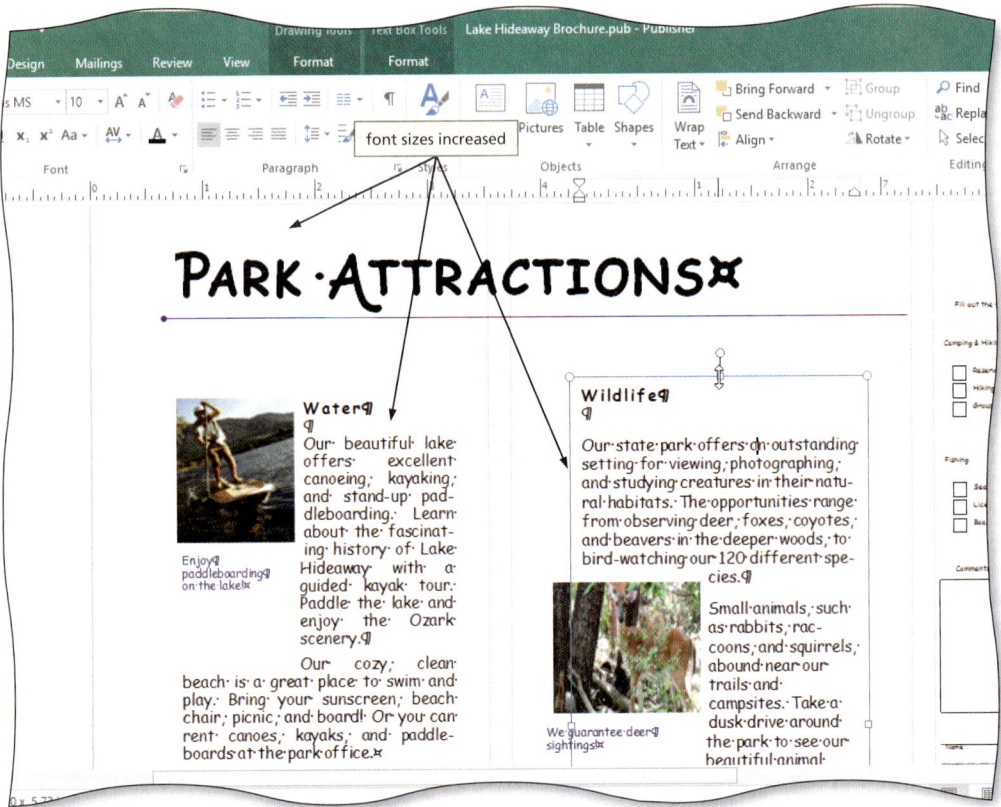

Figure 2–62

To Use the Caption Gallery

1 CUSTOMIZE BROCHURE | 2 EDIT TEXT & OBJECTS | 3 SWAP PICTURES | 4 CREATE PICTURE STYLES & SHAPES
5 USE STYLISTIC SETS | 6 SEARCH ONLINE PICTURES | 7 INSERT CAPTIONS | 8 CHECK PUBLICATION | 9 PACK

The following steps add a decorative caption to an existing photo using the Caption gallery. *Why? A decorative caption adds interest and color.*

1

- Click the fishing picture to select it and zoom to 150%.
- Click Picture Tools Format on the ribbon to display the Picture Tools Format tab.

- Click the Caption button (Picture Tools Format tab | Picture Styles group) to display its gallery and then scroll to the bottom of the gallery (Figure 2–63).

🔍 **Experiment**

- Point to each caption style in the gallery to see its effect on the publication.

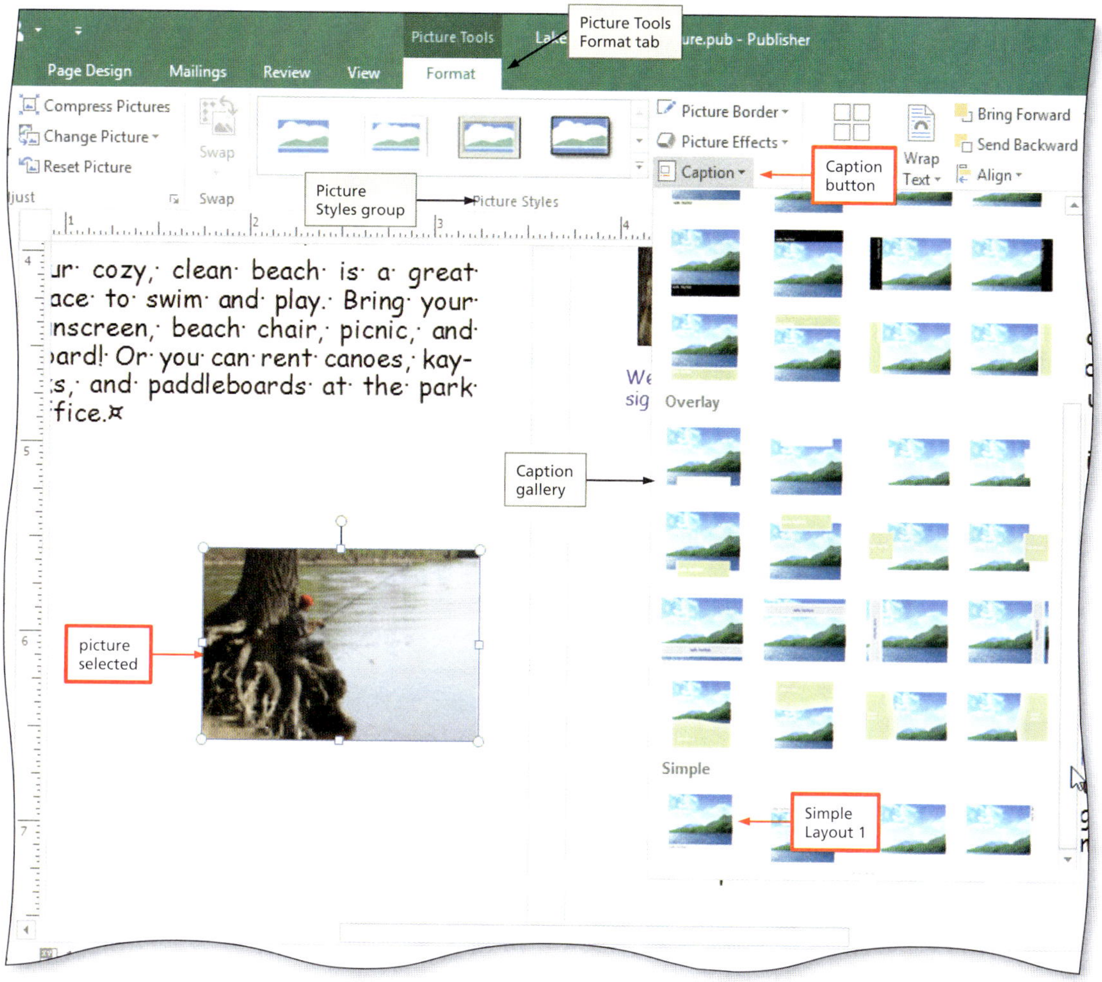

Figure 2–63

2

- Click the Simple Layout 1 thumbnail to apply the caption style to the picture.

- Select the caption text and then type `Relax while fishing!` to enter the caption.

- Select the caption text again, click the Font Color arrow (Home tab | Font group), and then click 'Accent 1 (Dark Blue)' in the Font Color gallery to match the color of the other captions. If necessary, change the font to Comic Sans MS.

- Click outside the text to remove the selection (Figure 2–64).

Figure 2–64

3

- Click the Page 1 icon in the Page Navigation pane to return to page 1.

- Click the map and then click the Caption button (Picture Tools Format tab | Picture Styles group) to display its gallery.

Q&A My Caption button is dimmed. What should I do?
Click the Ungroup button (Home tab | Arrange group). Select the textbox and delete it. Select the picture. The Caption button should be enabled at that point.

- Click the 'Tint Layout 1' thumbnail in the Formatted section in the Picture Styles gallery to apply the caption style to the picture.

- Select the caption and then type `Just off Route 17` to replace the caption text below the map (Figure 2–65).

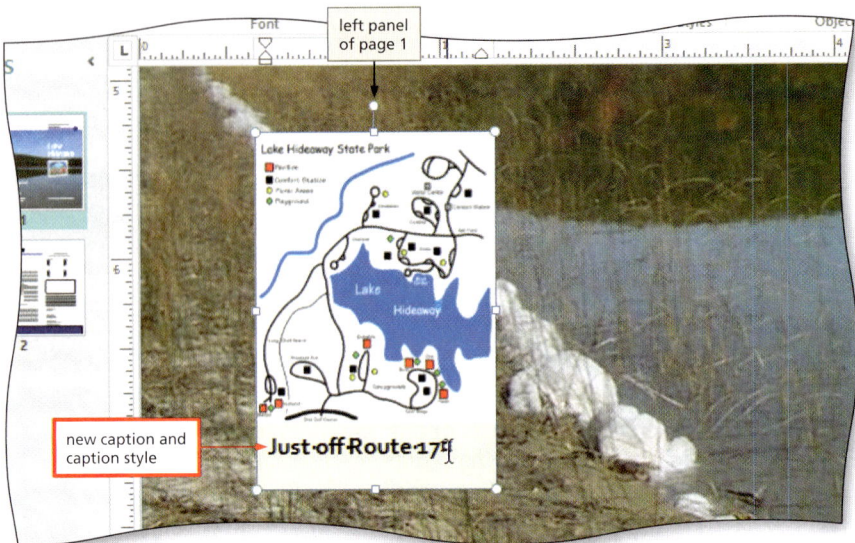

Figure 2–65

Checking the Publication

Recall that you checked a publication for spelling errors as you typed in Module 1. A wavy, red line indicated a word that was not in Publisher's dictionary. You then used the shortcut menu to choose the correct word. Additionally, Publisher can check the entire publication once you have finished editing it. The process of checking your entire publication for spelling errors moves from text box to text box and offers suggestions for words it does not find in its dictionary. Publisher does not look for grammatical errors.

CONSIDER THIS

What is the best way to eliminate errors in the brochure?

If possible, proofread the brochure with a fresh set of eyes, that is, at least one to two days after completing the first draft. Insert repeated elements and special objects, such as watermarks and logos, which need to be placed around, or behind, other objects. Look at text wrapping on every graphic. Ask someone else to proofread the brochure and give you suggestions for improvements. Revise it as necessary and then use the spelling and design checking features of the software.

A second kind of publication check is called the Design Checker. The **Design Checker** finds potential design problems in the publication, such as objects hidden behind other objects, text that does not fit in its text box, or a picture that is scaled disproportionately. As with the spelling check, you can choose to correct or ignore each design problem.

To Check the Spelling of the Entire Publication

The following steps check the entire brochure for spelling errors. *Why? You should check the spelling on every publication after you finish editing it.*

1
- Click Review on the ribbon to display the Review tab.
- Click the Spelling button (Review tab | Proofing group) to begin the spelling check in the current location, which in this case is inside the caption text box (Figure 2–66).

Q&A Can I check spelling of just a section of a publication?
Yes, select the text before starting the spelling check.

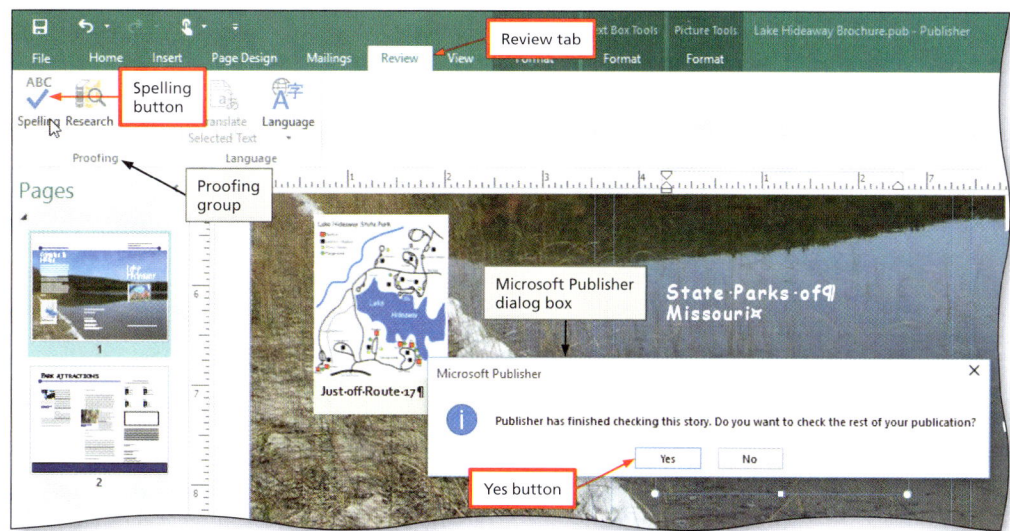

Figure 2–66

2
- When Publisher finishes checking the caption text box, click the Yes button (Microsoft Publisher dialog box) to tell Publisher to check the rest of the publication. If your publication displays a different error, accept or ignore it as necessary (Figure 2–67).

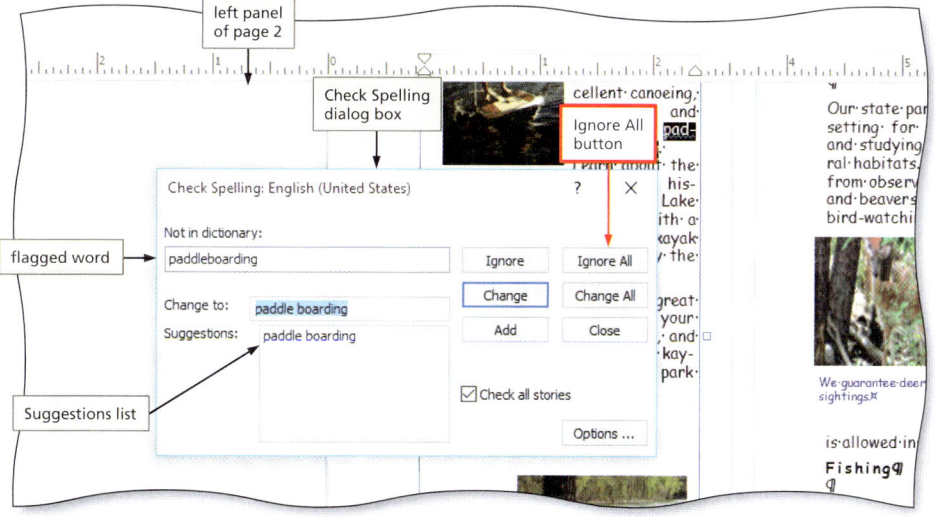

Figure 2–67

3
- Click the Ignore All button (Check Spelling dialog box) to ignore the flagged word each time it occurs (in this case, paddleboarding).
- If Publisher flags any other words, choose the correct spelling in the Suggestions list, click the Change button, and then continue the spelling check until the next error is identified or the end of the publication is reached.
- When the Microsoft Publisher dialog box is displayed indicating the spelling check is complete, click the OK button to close the dialog box.

Other Ways
1. Right-click flagged word, click Spelling on shortcut menu   2. Press F7

To Run the Design Checker

The following steps run the Design Checker. *Why? The Design Checker troubleshoots and identifies potential design problems in the publication.*

- Click File on the ribbon to open the Backstage view and, by default, select the Info tab (Figure 2–68).

Q&A Will the Design Checker fix the problems automatically?
In some cases, you will have the option of choosing an automatic fix for the issue; in other cases, you will have to fix the problem manually.

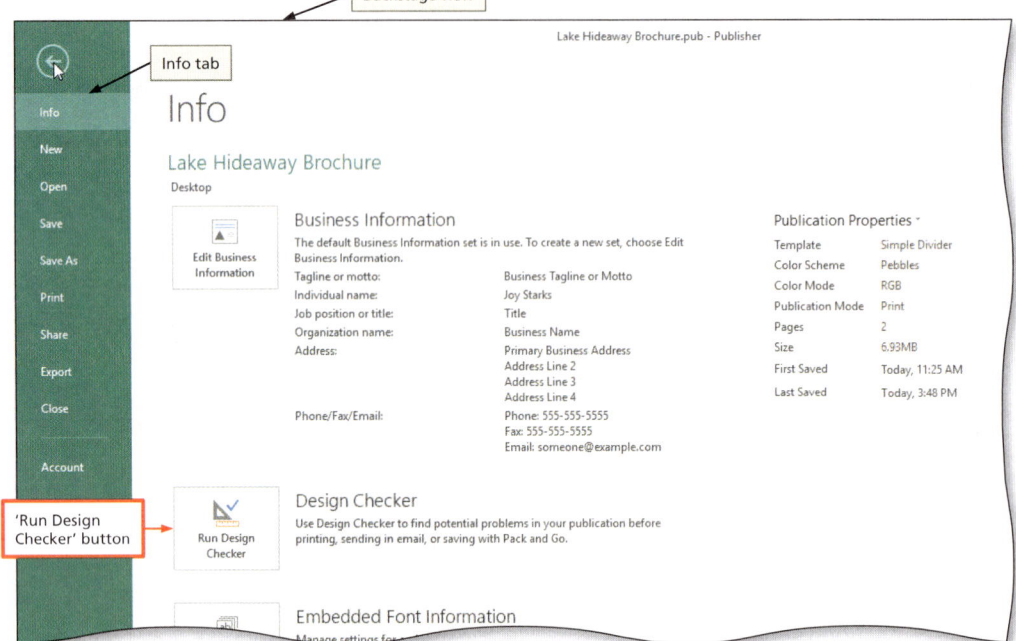

Figure 2–68

- Click the 'Run Design Checker' button in the Info gallery to display the Design Checker task pane (Figure 2–69).

Q&A What are the links at the bottom of the Design Checker task pane?
You can click the link, Design Checker Options, to specify the order in which the Design Checker checks the pages of your publication or to specify which kinds of design issues to include. The second link offers tips from the Publisher Help system about running the Design Checker.

What are the listed design problems?
A small amount of space appears between the margin of the page and the closest object to the margin. This is intentional and was part of the template, but the Design Checker notes the problem for your information only. Publication objects may be close to the printable area margin. This also is just a warning. The brochure will print correctly.

3

- Fix any issues not related to space or low resolution images. Click the 'Close Design Checker' button in the Design Checker task pane to close the Design Checker and return to the publication.
- Click the Save button on the Quick Access Toolbar to overwrite the previously saved file.

Q&A How do I fix a picture that is not scaled proportionally?
In the Design Checker task pane, point to the error, and then click the button that appears to the right of the error. On the resulting menu, click 'Fix Rescale Picture'.

Figure 2–69

Break Point: If you wish to take a break, this is a good place to do so. Exit Publisher. To resume at a later time, run Publisher, open the file called Lake Hideaway Brochure, and continue following the steps from this location forward.

Previewing and Printing

When you work with multi-page publications, it is a good idea to preview each page before printing. Additionally, if you decide to print on special paper, or print on both sides of the paper, you must adjust certain settings on the Print tab in the Backstage view.

To Preview Multiple Pages and Print

1 CUSTOMIZE BROCHURE | 2 EDIT TEXT & OBJECTS | 3 SWAP PICTURES | 4 CREATE PICTURE STYLES & SHAPES
5 USE STYLISTIC SETS | 6 SEARCH ONLINE PICTURES | 7 INSERT CAPTIONS | **8 CHECK PUBLICATION** | **9 PACK**

Previewing both pages in the publications is the first step in getting it ready for outside printing as you examine what the printed copy will look like from your desktop. The following steps preview and then print the brochure on both sides. *Why? Printing on both sides gives you the opportunity to check your panels and folds and to view the brochure as your readers will view it.* If your printer does not have the capability to print double-sided, follow your printer's specifications to print one side of the brochure, turn it over, and then print the reverse side.

- If necessary, display page 1.
- Click File on the ribbon to open the Backstage view.
- Click the Print tab in the Backstage view to display the Print gallery.
- Click the 'View Multiple Sheets' button to display the Multiple Sheets gallery (Figure 2–70).

◄ | What are the rulers in the Print gallery?
Q&A | Publisher displays rulers at the top and left of the print preview to help you verify the size of the printed page. You can turn off the ruler display by clicking the Ruler button.

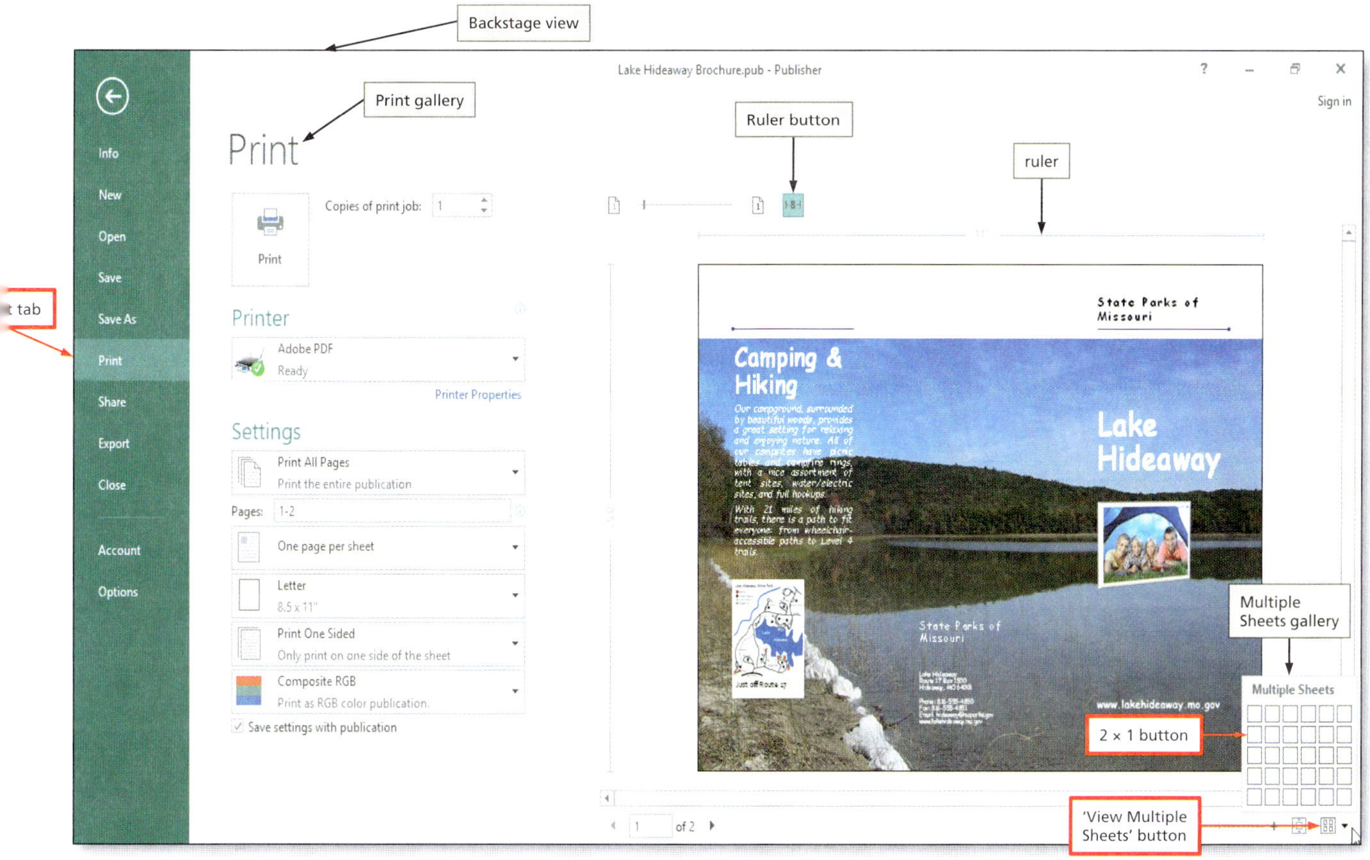

Figure 2–70

- Click the '2 × 1' button to display the pages above one another.
- Click the 'Print One Sided' button to display the list of options (Figure 2–71).

Q&A

If the brochure has only two pages, why do all of those preview grids exist?

Publisher allows for more pages in every kind of publication, should you decide to add them. If you click a button in the grid for more than two pages — either horizontally or vertically — the size of the preview is reduced.

Is that the best way to preview the brochure?

Viewing two full pages with intensive graphics and text may give you a good overview of the publication; however, do not substitute the preview for checking the publication for errors by reading the content carefully and running the spelling and design checking tools.

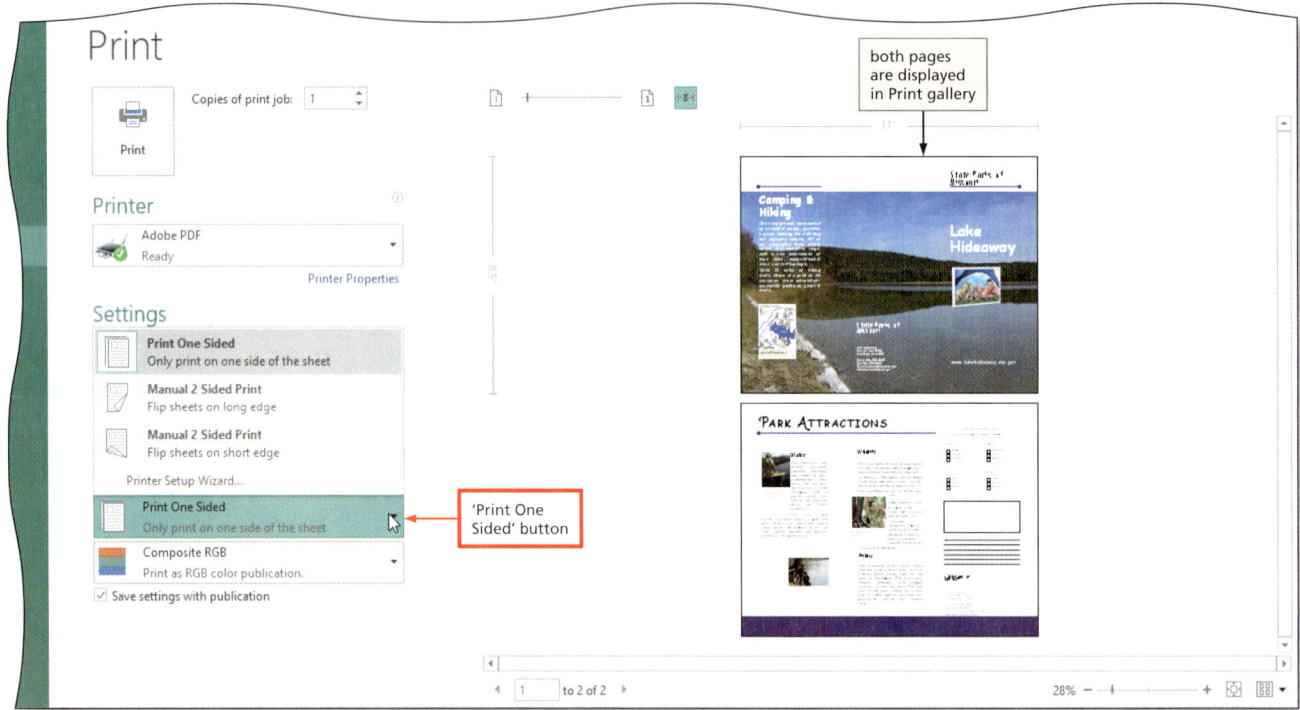

Figure 2–71

- If your list displays a 'Print On Both Sides (Flip sheets on long edge)' command, click it to select automatic printing of both sides.
- If your list displays a 'Manual 2 Sided Print (Flip sheets on long edge)' command, click it to select manual printing.
- Click the Print button to print the brochure. When the printer stops, retrieve the printed publication.

Other Ways

1. Press CTRL+P, choose settings, click Print button (Print gallery)

BTW

View Multiple Sheets Grid

In multipage publications, you can use the View Multiple Sheets grid to choose how the pages display in the print preview. For example, choosing 5 × 2 in the grid will cause Publisher to display five pages vertically (high) and two pages across (wide) for a total display of 10 pages.

Printing Considerations

When they need mass quantities of publications, businesses generally **outsource**, or submit their publications to an outside printer, for duplicating. You must make special considerations when preparing a publication for outside printing.

How do you make wise, professional printing choices?
Make a firm decision that quality matters, and consult with several commercial printers ahead of time. Get prices, color modes, copies, paper, and folding options in writing before you finish your brochure. Brochures are more effective on heavier paper, with strong colors and a glossy feel. Together with the commercial printer, select a paper that is going to last. Check to make sure the commercial printer can accept Microsoft Publisher 2016 files.

If you start a publication from scratch, it is best to **set up** the publication for the type of printing you want before you place objects on the page. Otherwise, you may be forced to make design changes at the last minute. You also may set up an existing publication for a printing service. In order to provide you with experience in setting up a publication for outside printing, this project guides you through the preparation steps — even if you are submitting this publication only to your instructor.

Printing options, such as whether to use a copy shop or commercial printer, have advantages and limitations. You may have to make some trade-offs before deciding on the best printing option. Table 2–4 shows some of the questions you can ask yourself about printing.

BTW

Printer Memory
Some printers do not have enough memory to print a wide variety of images and colors. In these cases, the printer prints up to a certain point on a page and then stops — resulting in only the top portion of the publication printing. Check with your instructor to see if your printer has enough memory to work with colors.

Table 2–4 Choosing a Printing Option			
Consideration	**Questions to Ask**	**Desktop Option**	**Professional Options**
Color	Is the quality of photos and color a high priority?	Low to medium quality	High quality
Convenience	Do I want the easy way?	Very convenient and familiar	Time needed to explore different methods, unfamiliarity
Cost	How much do I want to pay?	Printer supplies and personal time	High-resolution color/high quality is expensive; the more you print, the less expensive the per-copy price
Quality	How formal is the purpose of my publication?	Local event; narrow, personal audience	Business, marketing, professional services
Quantity	How many copies do I need?	1 to 10 copies	10 to 500 copies: use a copy shop; 500+ copies: use a commercial printer
Turnaround	How soon do I need it?	Immediate	Rush outside printing is probably an extra cost

Paper Considerations

Professional brochures are printed on a high grade of paper to enhance the graphics and provide a longer lasting document. Grades of paper are based on weight. Desktop printers commonly use **20-lb. bond paper**, which means they use a lightweight paper intended for writing and printing. A commercial printer might use 60-lb. glossy or linen paper.

The finishing options and their costs are important considerations that may take additional time to explore. **Glossy paper** is a coated paper, produced using a heat process with clay and titanium. **Linen paper**, with its mild texture or grain, can support high-quality graphics without the shine and slick feel of glossy paper. Users sometimes choose a special stock of paper, such as cover stock, card stock, or text stock. This textbook is printed on 45-lb. blade-coated paper. **Blade-coated paper** is coated and then skimmed and smoothed to create the pages you see here.

BTW

Distributing a Document
Instead of printing and distributing a hard copy of a document, you can distribute the document electronically. Options include sending the document via email; posting it on cloud storage (such as OneDrive) and sharing the file with others; posting it on a social networking site, blog, or other website; and sharing a link associated with an online location of the document. You also can create and share a PDF or XPS image of the document.

These paper and finishing options may seem burdensome, but they are becoming conveniently available to desktop publishers. Local office supply stores have shelf after shelf of various types of computer paper specifically designed for laser and ink-jet printers. Some of the paper you can purchase has been prescored for specific folding.

Color Considerations

When printing colors, Publisher uses a color scheme called RGB. **RGB** stands for the three colors — red, green, and blue — used to print the combined colors of your publication. RGB provides the best color matching for graphics and photos. Desktop printers may convert the RGB specifications to CMYK, which stands for cyan, magenta, yellow, and key (black). Professional printers, on the other hand, can print your publication using color scheme processes, or **libraries**. These processes include black and white, spot color, and process color.

In **black-and-white printing**, the printer uses only one color of ink (usually black, but you can choose a different color if you want). You can add accent colors to your publication by using different shades of gray or by printing on colored paper. Your publication can have the same range of subtleties as a black-and-white photo.

A **spot color** is used to accent a black-and-white publication. Newspapers, for example, may print their masthead in a bright, eye-catching color on page 1 but print the rest of the publication in black and white. **Spot-color printing** uses semitransparent, premixed inks typically chosen from standard color-matching guides, such as Pantone. Choosing colors from a **color-matching library** helps ensure high-quality results, because printing professionals who license the libraries agree to maintain the specifications, control, and quality.

In a spot-color publication, each spot color is **separated** on its own plate and printed on an offset printing press. The use of spot colors has become more creative in the last few years. Printing services use spot colors of metallic or florescent inks, as well as screen tints, to provide color variations without increasing the number of color separations and cost. If your publication includes a logo with one or two colors, or if you want to use color to emphasize line art or text, then consider using spot-color printing.

Process-color printing, or four-color printing, means your publication can include color photos and any color or combination of colors, using a print shop's CMYK process-color library.

Process-color printing is the most expensive proposition; black-and-white printing is the cheapest. Using color increases the cost and time it takes to process the publication. When using either the spot-color or the process-color method, the printer first must output the publication to film on an **image setter**, which recreates the publication on film or photographic paper. The film then is used to create color **printing plates**. Each printing plate transfers one of the colors in the publication onto paper in an offset process. Publisher can print a preview of these individual sheets showing how the colors will separate before you take your publication to the printer.

A newer printing technology called **digital printing** uses toner instead of ink to reproduce a full range of colors. Digital printing does not require separate printing plates. Digital printing usually is cheaper than offset printing without sacrificing any quality.

Special Paper

Printing the brochure on a high grade of paper results in a professional look. A heavier stock paper helps the brochure to stand up better in display racks, although any paper will suffice. **Brochure paper** is a special paper with creases that create a professional-looking fold and with a paper finish that works well with color and graphics.

To Print on Special Paper

If you have special paper, you would perform the following steps to choose that special paper before printing. See your instructor for assistance in choosing the correct option associated with your printer.

1. Open the Backstage view and then click the Print tab.
2. Click the Printer Properties link below the Printer Status box to display your printer's Properties dialog box.
3. Find the paper or quality setting and then choose the paper.
4. Click the OK button in the Printer Properties dialog box to return to the Backstage view.

Packing the Publication for the Printing Service

The publication file can be packed for the printing service in two ways. The first way is to give the printing service the Publisher file in Publisher format using the Pack and Go Wizard. The second way is to save the file in a format called Encapsulated PostScript. Both of these methods are discussed in the following sections. Alternately, some printing services will take a Publisher document in its native format (.pub) without any packing; although, in that case, the printing service may not have the exact fonts and will substitute.

BTW
PostScript Files
If you decide to submit a PostScript dump, or file, to an outside printer or service bureau, include a copy of the original document as well — for backup purposes. Many shops slowly are changing over from Macintosh-based to cross-platform based operations. If an error occurs, the printer technician can correct the error from the original document without requiring you to make another trip to the print shop.

To Use the Pack and Go Wizard

1 CUSTOMIZE BROCHURE | 2 EDIT TEXT & OBJECTS | 3 SWAP PICTURES | 4 CREATE PICTURE STYLES & SHAPES
5 USE STYLISTIC SETS | 6 SEARCH ONLINE PICTURES | 7 INSERT CAPTIONS | 8 CHECK PUBLICATION | 9 PACK

The **Pack and Go Wizard** guides you through the steps to collect and pack all the files the printing service needs and then compresses the files. *Why? Publisher checks for and embeds the TrueType fonts used in the publication, in case the printing service does not have those fonts available.* The following steps use the Pack and Go Wizard to ready the publication for submission to a commercial printing service. These steps create a compressed, or zipped, folder on your storage device.

- Click File on the ribbon to open the Backstage view.
- Click the Export tab in the Backstage view to display the Export gallery.
- In the Pack and Go area, click the 'Save for a Commercial Printer' tab.
- Click the 'Pack and Go Wizard' button to begin the Pack and Go Wizard.
- If necessary, use the Browse button in the Pack and Go Wizard dialog box to navigate to and select your storage location (Figure 2–72).

Q&A Should I save my file first?
You do not have to save it again; however, if you plan to store the publication on a storage device other than the one on which you previously saved the brochure, save it again on the new medium before beginning the process.

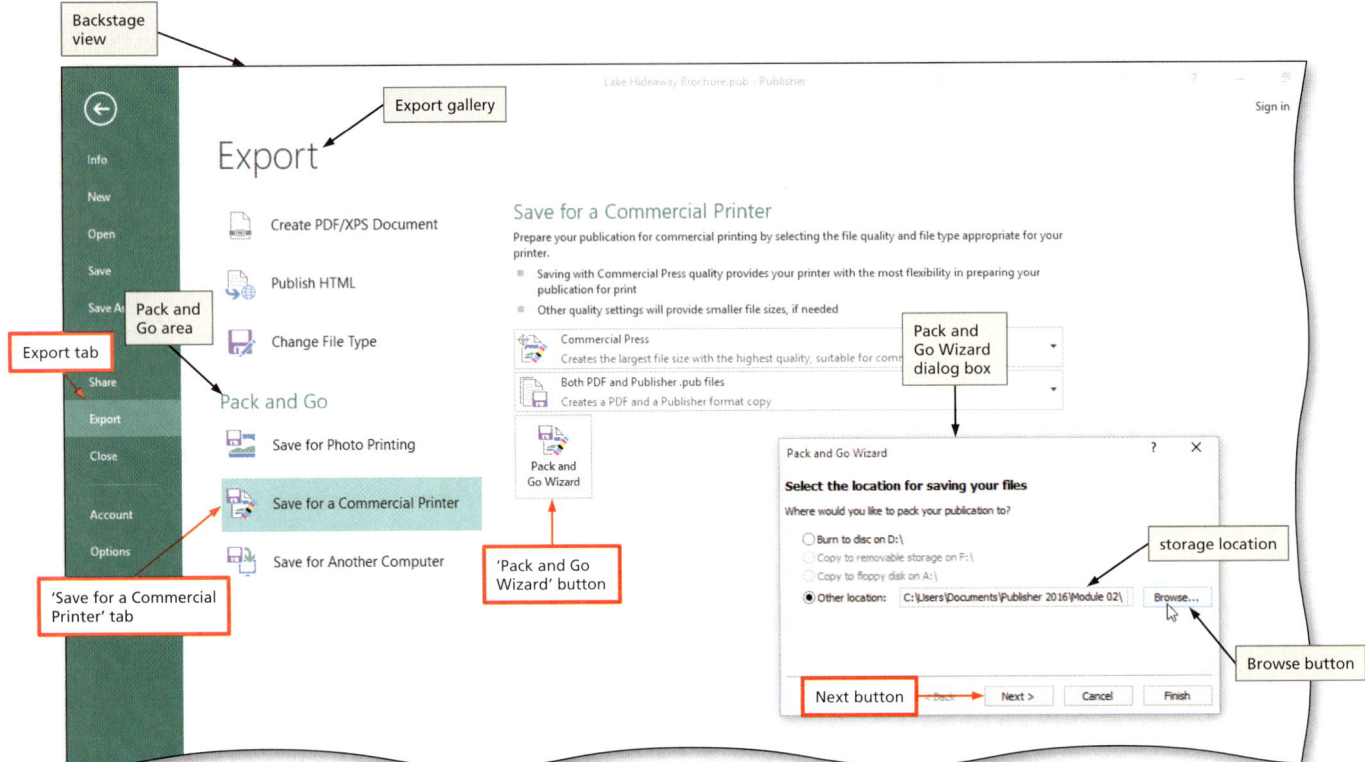

Figure 2–72

2

- When Publisher displays the next Pack and Go Wizard dialog box, if necessary, click the Next button to save the compressed file.

- When the final Pack and Go Wizard dialog box is displayed, remove the check mark in the 'Print a composite proof' check box (Figure 2–73).

Q&A What if I make a change to the publication after running the Pack and Go Wizard?
The file is saved in a compressed format on your storage location, with the same file name as your Publisher file. If you make changes to the publication after packing the files, be sure to run the Pack and Go Wizard again so that the changes are part of the packed publication.

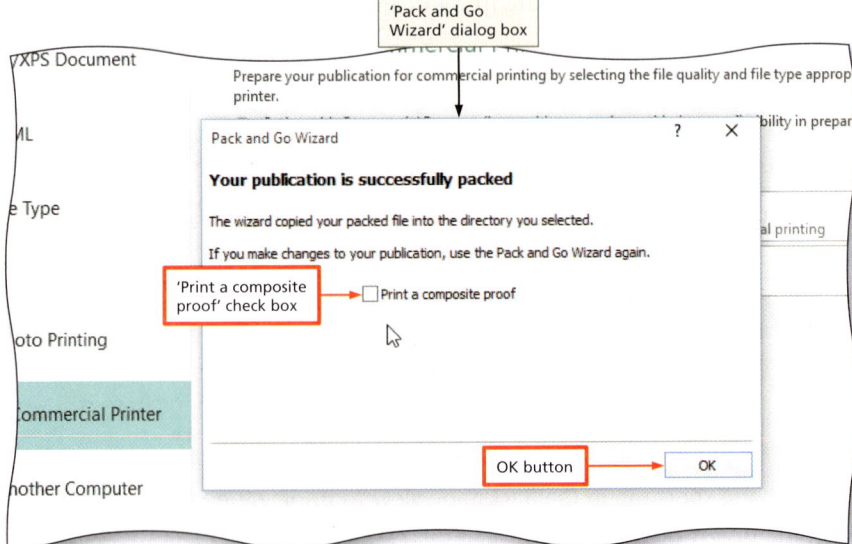

Figure 2–73

- Click the OK button to close the Pack and Go Wizard dialog box.
- Exit Publisher. If a Microsoft Publisher dialog box appears, click the Don't Save button to exit Publisher.
- Sign out of your Microsoft Account if necessary.

Summary

In this module, you have learned how to choose make choices about brochures and brochure templates as you edited headings and other text boxes. You copied and pasted using special paste options, and you displayed formatting marks as the text wrapped in paragraphs. Then, you swapped pictures and reset them. After applying a picture style, you changed the border and fill color of the picture and an added shape. On the inside page of the brochure, you used a stylistic set for the headings. Then, you inserted pictures using an online search. You edited all captions and used the caption gallery. Finally, you checked the spelling and the design of the publication before packing it for a printing service.

BTW

Automatic Saving
Publisher can save your publication at regular intervals for you. In the Backstage view, click the Options tab and then click Save (Publisher Options dialog box). Select the 'Save AutoRecover information every 10 minutes' check box. In the minutes box, specify how often you want Publisher to save files. Do not use AutoRecover as a substitute for regularly saving your work.

CONSIDER THIS

What decisions will you need to make when creating your next publication?
Use these guidelines as you complete the assignments in this module and create your own publications outside of this class.

1. Decide on the purpose, shelf life, and layout.
    a) Select a template that matches your need.
    b) Choose font and color schemes determined by the brochure's purpose and audience.
2. Create the brochure.
    a) Replace all placeholder and default text.
    b) Copy and paste text when possible to prevent the introduction of new errors.
    c) Edit forms.
    d) Use appropriate pictures with captions.
    e) Swap pictures when possible so that they will fit in the space.
3. Identify how to format various objects in the brochure.
    a) Copy formats for consistency.
    b) Use stylistic sets to enhance the brochure.
4. Proofread and check the publication.
    a) Read the brochure.
    b) Ask another person to read it.
    c) Use the spelling check feature.
    d) Use the Design Checker.
5. Plan for printing and packing.
    a) Choose correct printing options.
    b) Consult with a commercial printing service.
    c) Use the Pack and Go Wizard.

Apply Your Knowledge

Reinforce the skills and apply the concepts you learned in this module.

Swapping Graphics

Note: To complete this assignment, you will be required to use the Data Files. Please contact your instructor for information about accessing the Data Files.

Instructions: Run Publisher and open the file called Apply 2–1 Picture Collage from the Data Files. The document contains pictures from your recent Florida vacation. You produce the collage shown in Figure 2–74.

Perform the following tasks:

1. Click the Pictures button (Insert tab | Illustrations group). Navigate to the Data Files and the Module 02 folder. CTRL+click each of the Florida pictures to select them. Click the Insert button to insert the multiple pictures into the publication, and if necessary, move them to the scratch area.

Figure 2–74

2. With the pictures still selected, click the Arrange Thumbnails button (Picture Tools Format tab | Arrange Group).
3. One at a time, swap the pictures for the empty picture placeholders. Arrange the pictures on the page layout as desired.
4. If requested by your instructor, replace one of the pictures with a picture of you.
5. Choose one picture for the background. To apply it, right-click its swap icon, point to 'Apply to Background' on the shortcut menu, and then click Fill on the Apply to Background submenu.
6. Save the collage on your storage device with the file name, Apply 2–1 Picture Collage Complete.
7. Submit the revised document in the format specified by your instructor.
8. ✳ Do you think a caption on each picture would make the publication look cluttered? Why or why not?

Extend Your Knowledge

Extend the skills you learned in this module and experiment with new skills. You may need to use Help to complete the assignment.

Creating a Brochure from Scratch

Note: To complete this assignment, you will be required to use the Data Files. Please contact your instructor for information about accessing the Data Files.

Instructions: Run Publisher. You are to start from scratch and create the brochure shown in Figure 2–75. You will insert images you obtain online, change the color and font scheme, create panel guides, and add other formatting to the brochure.

Perform the following tasks:

1. Click BUILT-IN, and then click Brochures. Scroll to the Blank Sizes area, and then click the Letter (Landscape) thumbnail.

2. Choose the Maroon color scheme and the Office 1 font scheme. Click the CREATE button to create the publication.

3. When the publication is displayed, maximize the window, if necessary. If necessary, click the Special Characters button (Home tab | Paragraph group) to display special characters.

4. Use Help to read about creating guides and then perform the following tasks:

   a. To create panel guides, drag from the vertical ruler into the publication to create a nonprinting guide, stopping at 3⅝" as measured on the horizontal ruler. Drag another guide from the vertical ruler into the publication, stopping at 7⅜".

   b. In the Page Navigation pane, right-click the page 1 icon, and then click 'Insert Duplicate Page' on the shortcut menu. You will leave page 2 blank for future content.

   c. If necessary, click the Page 1 icon in the Page Navigation pane to return to page 1 in the brochure.

   d. Save the publication on your storage device with the file name, Extend 2–1 Team Training Brochure.

5. Click the Online Pictures button (Insert tab | Illustrations group). Use Bing Image Search to insert a picture of the earth or a globe similar to the one shown in Figure 2–75. Be sure you review the specific copyright license of any pictures you use from the web. Drag the picture to the scratch area and then click the Arrange Thumbnails button (Picture Tools Format tab | Arrange group) to reduce the size of the thumbnail.

6. Repeat Step 5 to insert three photos of state map outlines — you may have to enter the search term of a specific state, such as Kentucky state outline. Review the specific copyright license of any pictures you use from the web.

7. To create the right panel, which serves as the front of the brochure, do the following:

   a. Drag the earth to the right panel. Position it approximately in the center, vertically; and resize it so that it almost fills the panel horizontally. Click the More button (Picture Tools Format | Pictures Styles), and choose an appropriate picture style, such as the Drop Shadow Rectangle. Deselect the picture.

   b. Click the 'Draw Text Box' button (Home tab | Objects group). Drag to create a text box at the top of the right panel, approximately 1½" tall. Stay within the margin and guides. Type `Early Response Team Training` to enter the text. Right-click the text, and then click Best Fit on the shortcut menu.

   c. Click the 'Draw Text Box' button (Home tab | Objects group). Drag to create another text box in the lower portion of the right panel. Type `A collaborative effort to provide a caring presence in the aftermath of disaster` to enter the text in the text box. Right-click the text, and then click Best Fit on the shortcut menu.

Figure 2–75

Continued >

Extend Your Knowledge *continued*

8. To create the left panel:

   a. Create another text box in upper part of the left panel. Type **Our Mission** in the text box Use the 'Increase Font Size' button to make the font size approximately 36.

   b. Create a larger text box below the Our Mission text box, approximately 4½" high. Click inside the text box, and change the font size to 16. Type the following paragraphs letting Publisher wrap the text:

   Early Response Team Training (ERTT) fills an important need in the early days after a disaster. It is important to note that ERTs are trained primarily to respond within their own communities.

   Each class is 8 hours long. Topics include safety, response situations, equipment, team building, and the safe sanctuaries policy.

   You must be at least 18 years old to receive this certification.

   c. Create a text box at the bottom of the panel, still within the margins and guides of the left panel. Type **www.ertt.org** to enter the web address. When Publisher capitalizes the first letter, use the AutoCorrect Options button to remove the capitalization. Autofit the text.

   d. If requested by your instructor, change the web address to your webpage or Facebook page.

9. Use Help to read about the Align and Distribute commands related to objects.

10. To create the middle panel of page 1:

   a. Create another text box in upper part of the center panel. Type **Serving:**. Use the 'Increase Font Size' button (Home tab | Font group) to make the font size approximately 36.

   b. One at a time, drag the state outline graphics from the scratch area to the middle panel. Place them in the approximate locations shown in Figure 2–75.

   c. Select one of the state outline graphics. Click the Caption button (Picture Tools Format tab | Picture Styles group) and choose a caption style, such as Reversed Layout 1. Type the name of the state in the resulting caption text box. Repeat the process for the other two state outline graphics.

   d. Drag around all three graphics and captions in the middle panel. Click the Align Objects button (Drawing Tools Format tab | Arrange group) and then click Distribute Vertically on the Align Objects menu.

11. Click the Background button (Page Design tab | Page Background group) and then click 'Accent 2 Horizontal Gradient' in the Background gallery.

12. Click the Shapes button (Insert tab | Illustrations group) and then click the Rectangle shape in the Shapes gallery. Drag a rectangle across the top of page 1. With the rectangle selected, click the Shape Outline arrow and then click 'Accent 5 (White)' in the Shape Outline gallery. Click the Shape Fill arrow (Drawing Tools Format tab | Shapes Styles group) and then click 'Accent 5 (White)' in the Shape Fill gallery. Click the Send Backward button (Drawing Tools Format tab | Arrange group) three times to move the rectangle behind the text boxes.

13. Check the brochure for spelling errors and design errors and fix them as necessary. Save the file again.

14. Use the Pack and Go Wizard as described in the module, to pack the publication.

15. Preview the publication using the Print gallery. If possible, print the publication on special brochure paper

16. ✳ When would you use a template instead of creating a brochure from scratch? Would formatting the font before you type be easier than selecting text and formatting it afterward?

Expand Your World

Create a solution that uses cloud and web technologies by learning and investigating on your own from general guidance.

Creating a Webpage with a Brochure Link

Instructions: If you do not have a OneDrive account, create one. For a detailed example of the procedure, refer to the Office and Windows module. Run Publisher and open one of your brochures. Save the brochure on OneDrive. You would like to create a webpage with a link to download one of your brochures stored on the cloud, because many company websites include a link to download a print copy of various brochures.

Perform the following tasks:

1. Run the Notepad app or other text editor app on your computer. Enter the code from Figure 2–76, leaving the ninth line blank, as shown.

2. If requested to do so by your instructor, change the words, My Web Page, to your name in line five.

3. Save the file on your storage device, using MyWebPage.html as the file name. Do not close the text editor window.

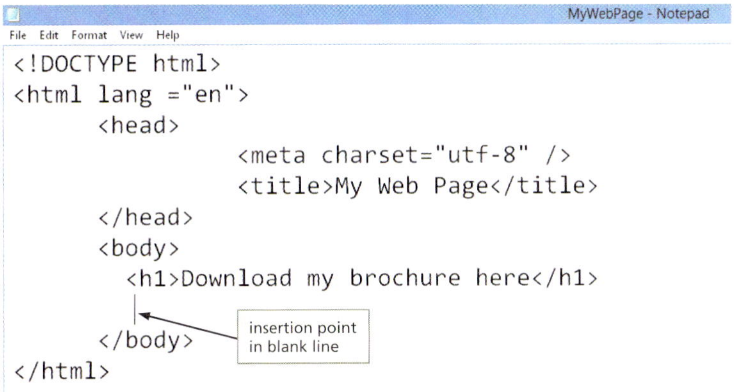

```
MyWebPage - Notepad
File  Edit  Format  View  Help
<!DOCTYPE html>
<html lang ="en">
        <head>
                    <meta charset="utf-8" />
                    <title>My Web Page</title>
        </head>
        <body>
          <h1>Download my brochure here</h1>

        </body>
</html>
```

insertion point in blank line

Figure 2–76

4. Run a browser and navigate to your OneDrive account.

5. Right-click the stored brochure file to display the shortcut menu, and then click Embed. When prompted, click the Generate button (Embed dialog box). When OneDrive displays the HTML code, press CTRL+C to copy the highlighted code.

6. Go back to the text editor window and position the insertion point on line nine. Press CTRL+V to paste the code into the file. If necessary, click Format on the menu bar and then click Word Wrap to enable the feature. Save the HTML file again and then close the window.

7. To view your webpage, open a File Explorer window and then navigate to the location of your saved HTML file. Double-click the MyWebPage.html file. If the browser asks permission to run the ActiveX content, click the 'Allow blocked content' button.

8. Submit the assignment in the format specified by your instructor.

9. ✺ Does your school provide a brochure about its program? Can you download the brochure from the school's website? Do you think it still is good to have a hard copy? Why?

In the Labs

Design, create, modify, and/or use a publication following the guidelines, concepts, and skills presented in this module. Labs 1 and 2, which increase in difficulty, require you to create solutions based on what you learned in the module; Lab 3 requires you to apply your creative thinking and problem-solving skills to design and implement a solution.

Lab 1: **Creating a Bi-Fold DVD Insert**

Note: To complete this assignment, you will be required to use the Data Files. Please contact your instructor for information about accessing the Data Files.

Continued >

In the Labs *continued*

Problem: A friend of yours has produced a DVD of original music. She would like you to design the insert that will be packaged with the DVD. You decide to look through Publisher's templates for an appropriate file to use as a starting point. You create the CD/DVD label shown in Figure 2–77.

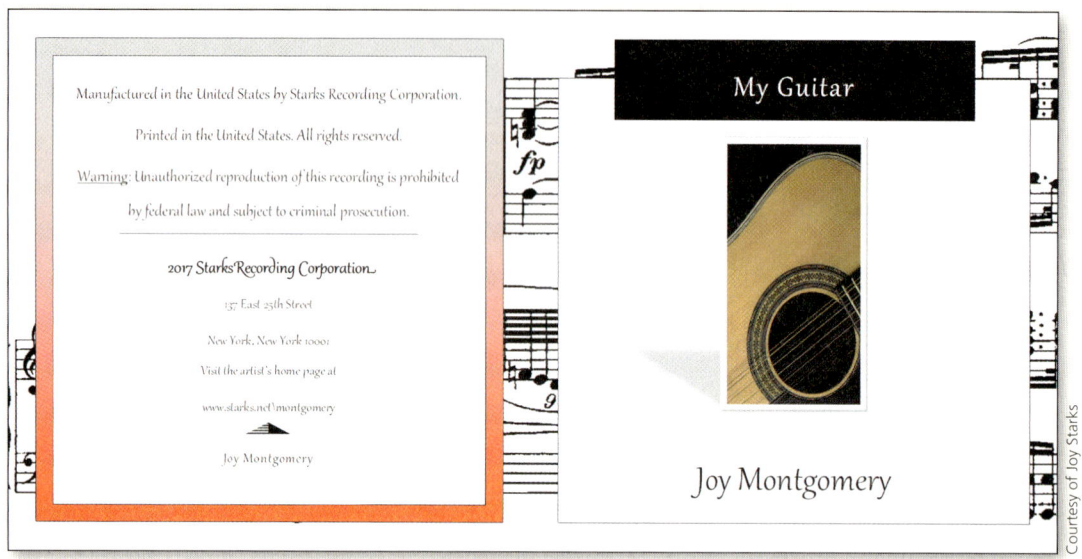

Figure 2–77

Perform the following tasks:

1. Run Publisher. Click BUILT-IN and then scroll as necessary to click the Labels thumbnail. Click the All Media folder.

2. In the CD/DVD Labels area, click CD/DVD Booklet thumbnail.

3. In the Customization area, choose the Parrot color scheme and the Calligraphy font scheme.

4. Click the CREATE button.

5. Use the Pictures button (Insert tab | Illustrations group) to insert the picture of the music from the Data Files. Move the picture to the scratch area. Right-click the picture, point to 'Apply to Background' on the shortcut menu, and then click Fill on the Apply to Background menu to place the picture in the background of the page.

6. Perform the following steps to edit objects in the right panel:

   a. Click the CD Title and then type **My Guitar** to complete the name of the DVD. Right-click the text and then click Best Fit on the shortcut menu. Click the Performer's Name text and then type **Joy Montgomery** to enter the performer. Right-click the text and then click Best Fit on the shortcut menu. Select the text and then press CTRL+C to copy it to the Clipboard.

   b. If requested by your instructor, replace Joy Montgomery with your name.

   c. Right-click the graphic, point to Change Picture on the shortcut menu, and then click Change Picture on the Change Picture menu to display the Insert Pictures dialog box. Navigate to the Data Files and then double-click the file named Guitar. Click the Reset Picture button (Picture Tools Format tab | Adjust group) to reset the picture.

   d. With the picture selected, click the More button (Picture Tools Format tab | Picture Styles group) and then click 'Perspective Shadow, White' in the Picture Style gallery.

   e. With the picture still selected, click the Picture Border button (Picture Tools Format tab | Picture Styles group), point to the Weight command, and then click 3 to change the weight of the border.

7. Perform the following steps to edit objects in the left panel:

   a. Click the text in the first text box and then type the following text, pressing the ENTER key and the end of each sentence.

   ```
   Manufactured in the United States by Starks
   Recording Corporation.
   Printed in the United States. All rights reserved.
   Warning: Unauthorized reproduction of this
   recording is prohibited by federal law and subject
   to criminal prosecution.
   ```

   b. Select the text in the Business Name text box. Type `2017 Starks Recording Corporation` to complete the text. Right-click the text and then click Best Fit on the shortcut menu. Select the text. Click the Stylistic Sets button (Text Box Tools Format tab | Typography group) and then choose the last stylistic set in the gallery.

   c. Select the text in the Address text box. Type `137 East 25th Street` and then press the ENTER key. Type `New York, New York 10001` to complete the text. Right-click the text and then click Best Fit on the shortcut menu.

   d. Select the text in the Phone text box. Type `Visit the artist's home page at` and then press the ENTER key. Type `www.starks.net\montgomery` to complete the text. Right-click the text and then click Best Fit on the shortcut menu.

   e. Click the text, Organization. Press CTRL+V to paste the text from the clipboard. Click the Paste Options button and then click the 'Keep Text Only' button.

8. Check the publication for spelling and design errors, and fix them as necessary. Save the file with the name, Lab 2–1 DVD Label.

9. Use the Pack and Go Wizard as described in the module to pack the publication.

10. Submit the file in the format specified by your instructor.

11. ✳ For extra credit, right-click Page 1 in the Page Navigation pane, and insert a new page. Insert pictures of your favorite artist. Create a text box with a list of songs. How did you decide on picture and text box placement?

Lab 2: Editing an Order Form with Stylistic Sets

Note: To complete this assignment, you will be required to use the Data Files. Please contact your instructor for information about accessing the Data Files.

Problem: The Biology Club is selling poinsettias and wreaths for the Christmas season. The members started creating a form, but they would like you to make it more appealing. You create the form shown in Figure 2–78.

Perform the following tasks:

1. Run Publisher and open the file called Lab 2–2 Order Form from the Data Files.

2. Click the heading. Type `Biology Club Order Form` to replace the text. Change the font to Gabriola. Change the font size to 22. Change the font color to red. Resize the text box as necessary to display all of the text.

3. If requested by your instructor, change the name of the club to an organization with which you have an affiliation.

Continued >

In the Labs *continued*

4. With the heading text still selected, click the Stylistic Sets button (Text Box Tools Format tab | Typography group). Select a fancy stylistic set. Resize the text box as necessary to display all of the glyphs.

5. Select the text in the Item # text box. Change the font to Gabriola and the font size to 11. double-click the Format Painter button (Home tab | Clipboard group) to copy the formatting.

6. One at a time, select each of the other text boxes on the form to apply the formatting. It is okay if the alignment changes. If necessary, resize any text boxes that are too small to accommodate the font change. When formatting is complete, click the Format Painter button again to turn off the format painter.

7. Select the picture. Click the Caption button (Picture Tools Format tab | Picture Styles group) to display the Caption gallery. Choose the Offset – Layout 3 caption style. Edit the caption to say: We deliver on campus!

Figure 2–78

8. Check the brochure for spelling errors and design errors, and fix them as necessary. Save the order form on your storage device with the file name, Lab 2–2 Order Form Complete.

9. Submit the file as directed by your instructor.

10. ✷ How might you have created this order form from scratch? Does Publisher have the individual components that you could add? Would that have been easier than trying to customize a built-in form?

Lab 3: Consider This: Your Turn

Creating a Youth Baseball League Brochure

Problem: Your brother has asked you to help him create a brochure announcing the sign-up dates for the youth baseball league that he coaches.

Perform the following tasks:

Part 1:   Pick an appropriate color and font scheme for the brochure, and include a sign-up form. Type **Preseason Sign-Up** as the brochure title. Type **Youth Baseball League** to replace the Business Name text. Type your address and phone number in the appropriate text boxes. Delete the logo. Replace all graphics with sports-related clip art. Edit the captions to match. Edit the sign-up form with appropriate events, such as T-Ball, Coach Pitched, and Little League. Include times and prices. The league commissioner will send you content for the stories at a later date.

Part 2:   ✷ On a separate piece of paper, make a table similar to Table 2–1 in this module, listing the type of exposure, information, audience, and purpose of the communication. Turn in the table with your printout.

3 Designing a Newsletter

Objectives

You will have mastered the material in this module when you can:

- Describe the advantages of using the newsletter medium and identify the steps in its design process
- Edit a newsletter template
- Set page options
- Edit a masthead
- Import text files
- Navigate pages
- Continue a story across pages and insert continued notices

- Customize the ribbon
- Use Publisher's Edit Story in Microsoft Word feature
- Insert and edit marginal elements
- Revise a newsletter
- Apply decorative drop caps
- Drag and drop text
- Check hyphenation in stories
- Create a template with property changes

Introduction

Desktop publishing is becoming an increasingly popular way for businesses of all sizes to produce their printed publications. The desktop aspects of design and production make it easy and inexpensive to produce high-quality publications in a short time. **Desktop publishing** (DTP) encompasses performing all publishing tasks from a desk, including the planning, designing, writing, and layout, as well as printing, collating, and distributing. With a personal computer and a software program, such as Publisher, you can create a professional publication from your computer without the cost and time of using a professional printing service.

Project — Shelter Newsletter

Newsletters are a popular way for offices, businesses, schools, and other organizations to distribute information to their clientele. A **newsletter** usually is a double-sided multipage publication with newspaper features, such as columns and a masthead, and the added eye appeal of sidebars, pictures, and other graphics.

Newsletters have several advantages over other publication media. Typically, they are cheaper to produce than brochures. Brochures, designed to be in circulation longer as a type of advertising, are published in greater quantities and on more expensive paper than newsletters, making brochures more costly. Newsletters also differ from brochures in that newsletters commonly have a shorter shelf life, making newsletters a perfect forum for information with dates. Newsletters are narrower and more focused in scope than newspapers; their eye appeal is more distinctive. Many companies distribute newsletters to interested audiences; however, newsletters also are becoming an integral part of many marketing plans to widen audiences, because they offer a legitimate medium by which to communicate services, successes, and issues.

The project in this module uses a Publisher newsletter template to produce the Shelter Days newsletter shown in Figure 3 – 1. This monthly publication informs readers about the Brisbane County Animal Shelter. The shelter's four-page newsletter contains a masthead, headings, stories, sidebars, pullquotes, a calendar, and graphics.

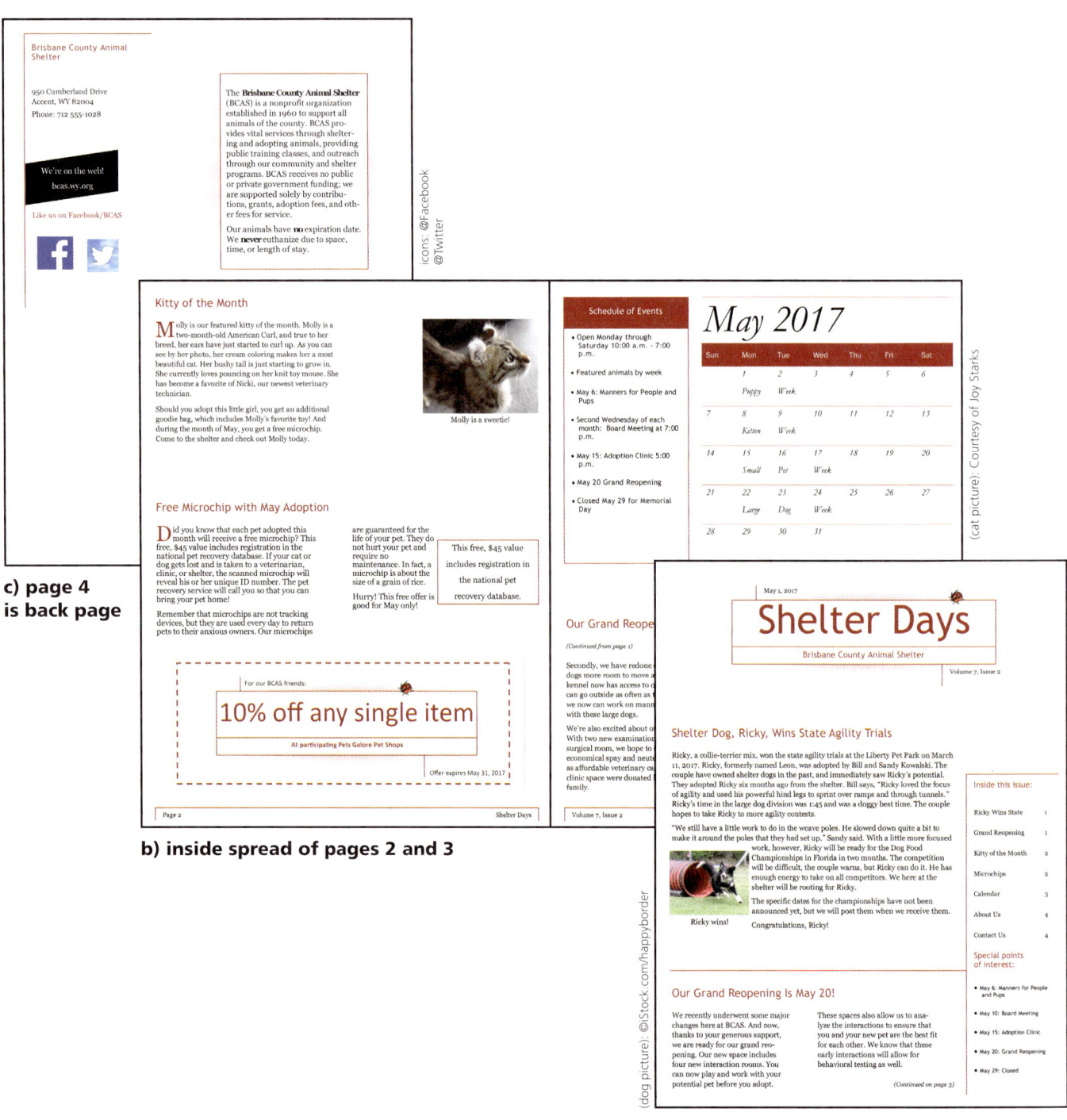

c) page 4 is back page

b) inside spread of pages 2 and 3

a) page 1

Figure 3–1

The following roadmap identifies general activities you will perform as you progress through this module:

1. Select a newsletter template and EDIT PUBLICATION OPTIONS.
2. IMPORT text from files and CONNECT STORIES across pages.
3. USE CONTINUED NOTICES.
4. CUSTOMIZE the RIBBON.
5. EDIT USING Microsoft WORD when necessary.
6. INSERT MARGINAL ELEMENTS.
7. APPLY DROP CAPS and HYPHENATE.
8. CREATE a TEMPLATE and change properties.

How do you decide on the purpose and audience of a newsletter?

Designing an effective newsletter involves a great deal of planning in order to deliver a message in the clearest, most attractive, and most effective way possible. Spend time brainstorming ideas for the newsletter with other members of the organization. Ask yourself why you want to create a newsletter in the first place and what message you want to convey. Remember that newsletters both communicate and educate. Identify the scope of the newsletter and whether you want the topic to be general in nature or more specific — perhaps about only one aspect of the organization. Use the phrase, "I want to tell <audience> about <topic> because <purpose>." Decide on one purpose, and adjust your plans to match that purpose.

As you decide on your audience, ask yourself these questions:

• Who will be reading the stories?

• What are the demographics of this population? That is, what are their characteristics, such as gender, age, educational background, and heritage?

• Why do you want those people to read your newsletter?

Decide if the audience is composed of local, interested clientele, patrons, employees, prospective customers, or family members. Keep in mind the age of your readers and their backgrounds, including both present and future readers.

CONSIDER THIS

Benefits and Advantages of Newsletters

Table 3–1 lists some benefits and advantages of using the newsletter medium.

Table 3–1 Benefits and Advantages of Using a Newsletter	
Purpose	**Benefits and Advantages**
Exposure	An easily distributed publication via office mail, by bulk mail, or electronically A pass-along publication for other interested parties A coffee-table reading item in reception areas
Education	An opportunity to inform in a nonrestrictive environment A directed education forum for clientele Increased, focused feedback that is unavailable in most advertising
Contacts	A form of legitimized contact A source of free information to build credibility An easier way to expand a contact database than other marketing tools
Communication	An effective medium to highlight the inner workings of a company A way to create a discussion forum A method to disseminate more information than a brochure
Cost	An easily designed medium using desktop publishing software An inexpensive method of mass production A reusable design using a newsletter template

For an introduction to Windows and instructions about how to perform basic Windows tasks, read the Office and Windows module at the beginning of this book, where you can learn how to resize windows, change screen resolution, create folders, move and rename files, use Windows Help, and much more.

Publisher's newsletter templates include stories, graphics, sidebars, and other elements typical of newsletters using a rich collection of intuitive design, layout, typography, and graphic tools. Because Publisher takes care of many of the design issues, using a template to begin a newsletter gives you the advantage of proven layouts with fewer chances of publication errors.

Newsletter Design Choices

Publisher's many design-planning features include more than 100 different newsletter templates from which you may choose, each with its own set of design, color, font, and layout schemes. Each newsletter template produces four pages of stories, graphics, page numbers, and other objects in the same way. The difference is the location and style of the shapes and graphics, as well as the specific kind of decorations unique to each publication set. A **publication set** is a predefined group of shapes, designed in patterns to create a template style. A publication set is consistant across publication types; for example, the Bars newsletter template has the same shapes and style of objects as does the Bars brochure template. A publication set helps in branding a company across publication types.

Another choice you have when making decisions about newsletter design is how the pages will be organized and ultimately printed. A **one-page spread** displays and prints the pages individually in portrait mode — the printed pages would need to be stapled or bound in some way. A **two-page spread** displays the first and last pages individually, but displays the middle pages as two facing pages similar to a book format. If you have special newsletter paper, such as 11×17, the pages print landscape, so you can fold the newsletter. Other print sizes are available as built-in templates, listed within the Blank Pages section. In the workspace, a two-page spread makes it easier to see how the pages will look when open. Stories and figures spanning a two-page spread rarely need notices about continuation. In a two-page spread, the page on the left is called a **verso page**. The page on the right is called a **recto page**.

To Choose a Newsletter Template and Options

The following steps choose a newsletter template and change its options.

1 Run Publisher and then click BUILT-IN to display the built-in templates.

2 Scroll as necessary and then click the Newsletters thumbnail to display the Newsletter templates.

3 Scroll to the section labeled, More Installed Templates, and then click the Nature thumbnail to choose the template.

4 Click the Color scheme button in the template information pane. Scroll as necessary and then click Orange to choose the color scheme.

5 Click the Font scheme button, scroll as necessary, and then click Urban to choose the font scheme.

6 Do not click the Business information button because it is not used in this publication.

7 Click the Page size button in the Options area and then, if necessary, click 'Two-page spread' to choose how the template will display.

8 If necessary, click to remove the check mark in the 'Include customer address' check box (Figure 3–2).

9 Click the CREATE button to create the publication based on the template settings.

For an introduction to Office and instructions about how to perform basic tasks in Office apps, read the Office and Windows module at the beginning of this book, where you can learn how to run an application, use the ribbon, save a file, open a file, print a file, exit an application, use Help, and much more.

BTW
Touch Screen Differences
The Office and Windows interfaces may vary if you are using a touch screen. For this reason, you might notice that the function or appearance of your touch screen differs slightly from this module's presentation.

Built-In Templates

Home › Newsletters

Nature

thumbnail preview

Nature template thumbnail

Kid Stuff   Layers   Level   Linear Accent   Marble   Marquee

Mobile   Nature   Network   Pinwheels   Pixel   Profile

Note: To help you locate screen elements that are referenced in the step instructions, such as buttons and commands, this book places a red outline around the callouts that point to these screen elements.

Punctuation   Quadrant   Radial   Refined   Rhythm

Color scheme button

Font scheme button

Page size button

CREATE button

Customize
Color scheme:
Orange

Font scheme:
Urban
Trebuchet
Georgia

Business information:
Create new...

Options
Page size:
Two-page spread

☐ Include customer address

CREATE

Figure 3–2

To Set Publisher Display Settings

As discussed in Module 2, it is helpful to display formatting marks, which indicate where in the publication you pressed the ENTER key, the SPACEBAR key, and other keys. The following steps display formatting marks and open the Page Navigation pane to display all of the pages of the newsletter.

1 If the Special Characters button (Home tab | Paragraph group) is not selected already, click it to display formatting marks on the screen.

2 If the Page Navigation pane is not displayed, click the Page Number button on the status bar to open the Page Navigation pane. If the Page Navigation pane is minimized, click the 'Expand Page Navigation Pane' button to maximize it.

CONSIDER THIS

How do you decide about options for the layout and printing?

Choosing a layout and printing option before you even write the stories is a daunting, yet extremely important, task. The kind of printing process and paper you will be using will affect the cost and, therefore, the length of the newsletter. Depending on what you can afford to produce and distribute, the layout may need more or fewer stories, graphics, columns, and sidebars. Base your decisions on content that will be repeated in future newsletters.

Make informed decisions about the kind of alignment you plan to use. Choose the paper size and determine how columns, a masthead, and graphics will affect your layout. Decide what kinds of features in the newsletter should be close to each other. A consistent look and feel with simple, eye-catching graphics normally is the best choice for the publication set. Plan to include one graphic with each story. Because newsletters usually are mass-produced, collated, and stapled, you should make a plan for printing and decide if you are going to publish it in-house or externally. Choose a paper that is going to last until the next newsletter.

To Set Page Options

Publisher newsletters can display one, two, or three columns of story text, or mix the format. *Why? Changing the number of columns in a story or mixing the format adds visual interest.* Inside pages also can display calendars and forms. The following steps select page options for the various pages in the newsletter.

1

- With page 1 of the newsletter displayed in the workspace, click Page Design on the ribbon to display the Page Design tab.

- Click the Options button (Page Design tab | Template group) to display the Page Content dialog box.

- Click the Columns button to display its list (Figure 3–3).

Q&A Does the column choice affect the objects down the right side of the newsletter page? No, the number of columns that you choose will be displayed in the stories only, and the choice affects only the current page.

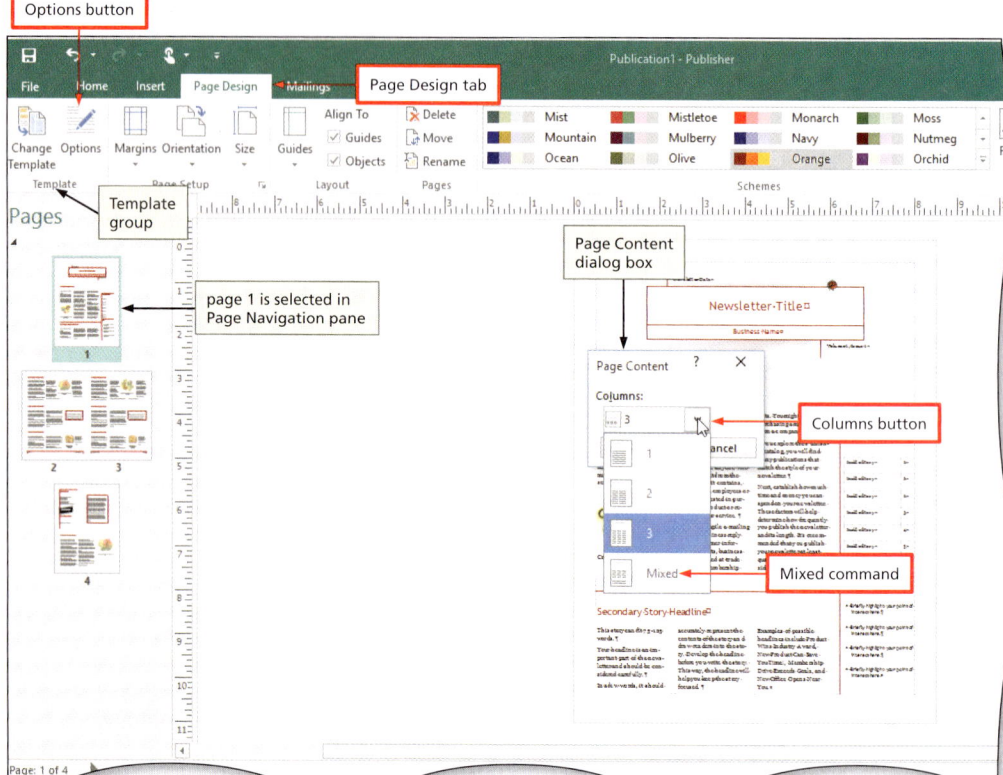

Figure 3–3

2

- Click Mixed in the Columns list to choose a mixed number of columns for the stories on page 1.

- Click the OK button (Page Content dialog box) to change the options for the page (Figure 3–4).

Q&A Is one choice better than another one? No, it is a personal or customer preference. Longer stories may need to be continued at different places, depending upon how many columns of text you have. The more columns you have, the more white space is created on the page.

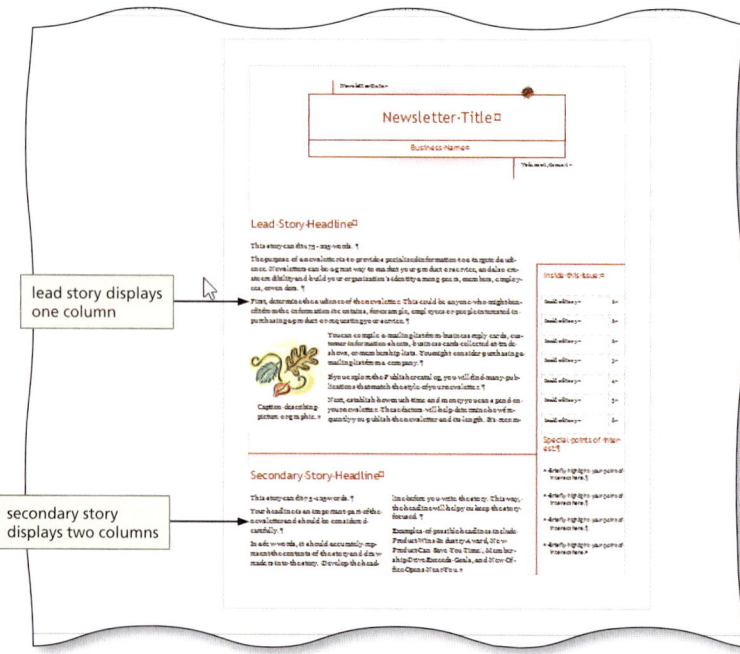

Figure 3–4

3

- In the Page Navigation pane, click the 'Page 2 and Page 3' icon to display the pages in the workspace.

- Click the Options button (Page Design tab | Template group) to display the Page Content dialog box.

- Click the 'Select a page to modify' button to display its list (Figure 3–5).

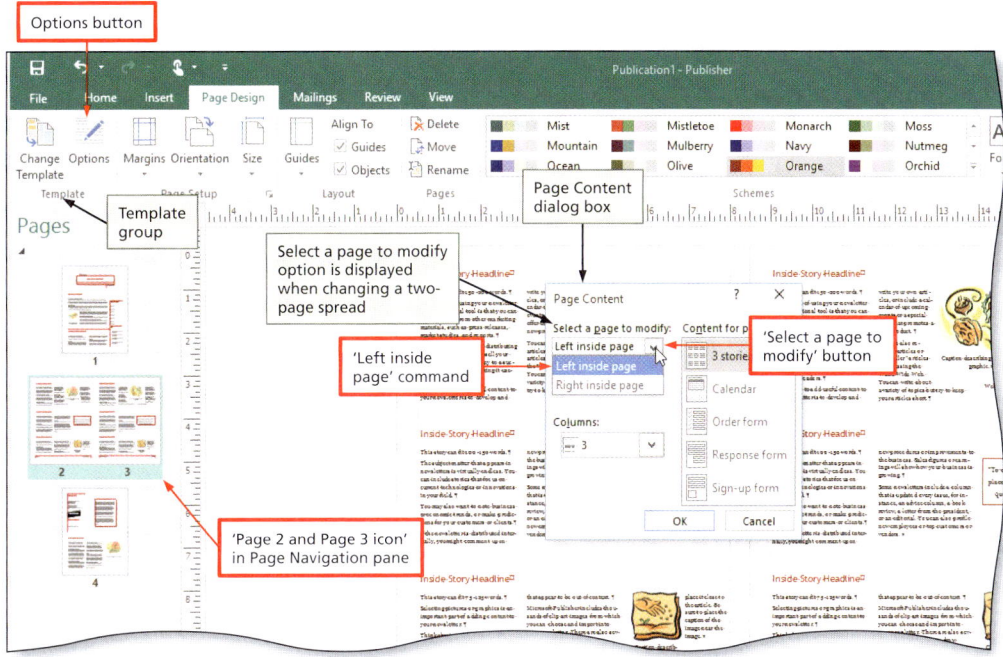

Figure 3–5

4

- Click 'Left inside page' to choose the verso page, if necessary.

- Click the Columns button to display its list (Figure 3–6).

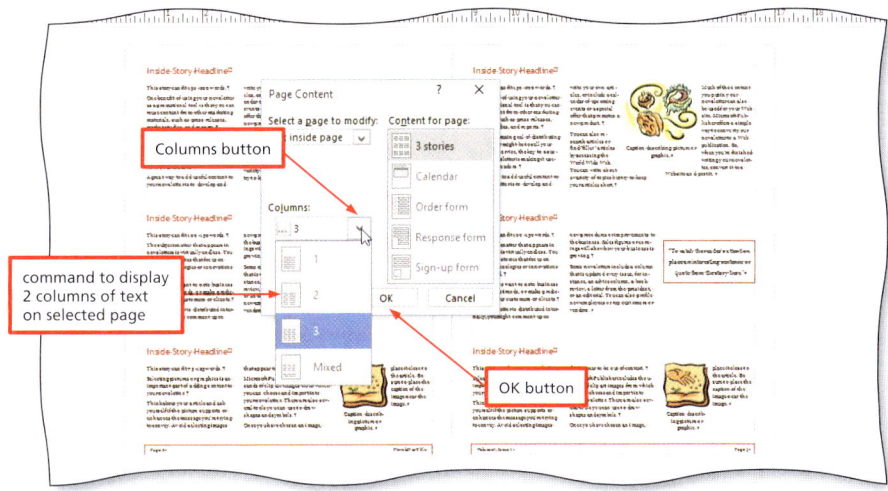

Figure 3–6

5

- Click 2 in the Columns list to choose a two-column format for the stories on page 2.

- Click the OK button (Page Content dialog box) to close the dialog box (Figure 3–7).

Q&A Can I move pages around in my newsletter?

Yes, you can right-click in the Page Navigation pane and then choose Move on the shortcut menu. Publisher will display a dialog box, allowing you to specify which page to move and the new location.

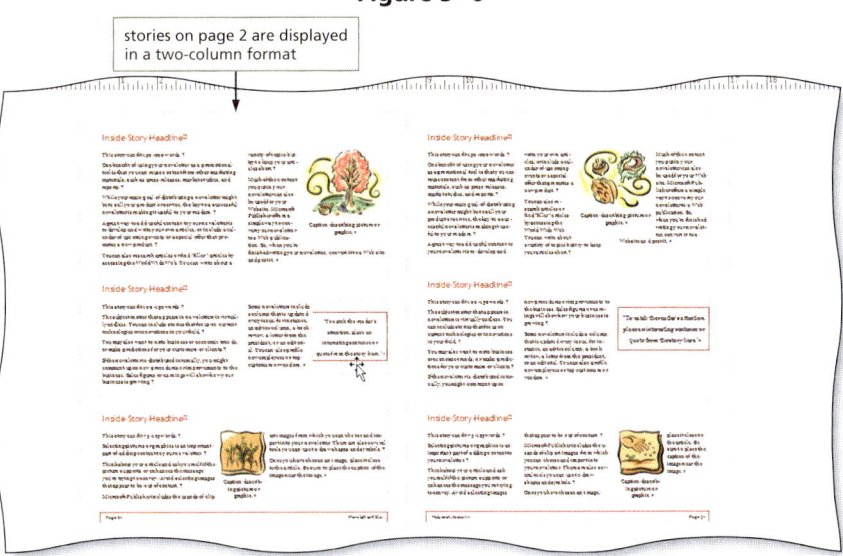

Figure 3–7

6

- Click the Options button (Page Design tab | Template group) to display the Page Content dialog box again.

- Click the 'Select a page to modify' button and then click 'Right inside page' to choose the recto page.

- Click the Columns button and then click 2 in the Columns list to choose 2 columns.

- In the Content for page area, click Calendar to insert a calendar on the recto page (Figure 3–8).

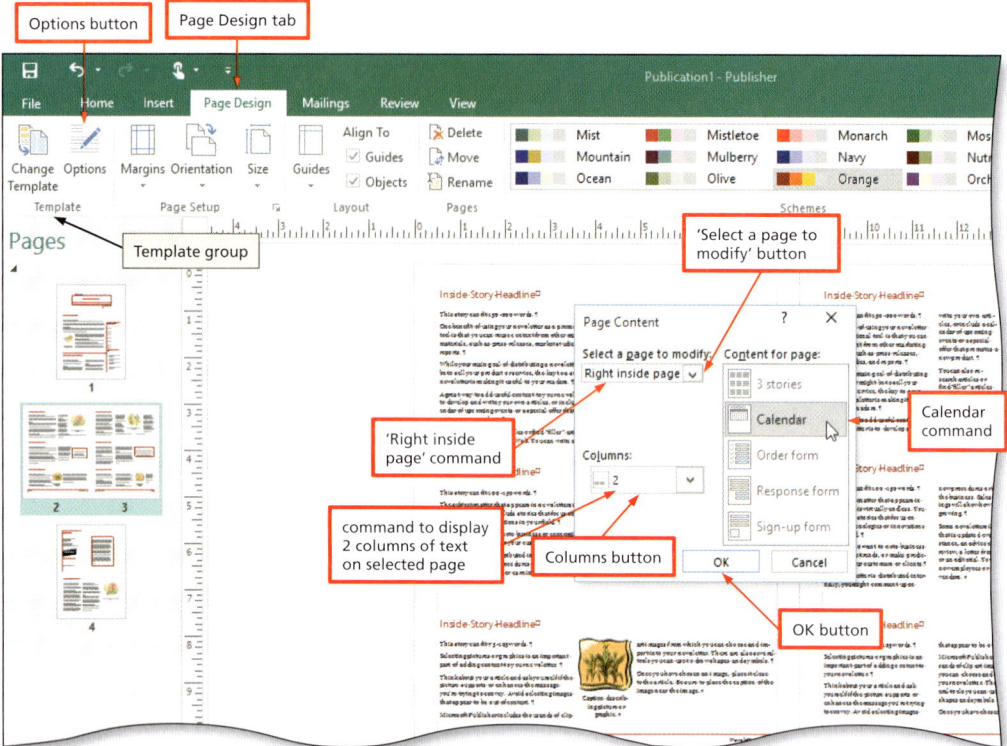

Figure 3–8

7

- Click the OK button (Page Content dialog box) to close the dialog box.

- Click the Save button on the Quick Access Toolbar. Browse to the storage location. Save the file with the file name, Shelter Newsletter (Figure 3–9).

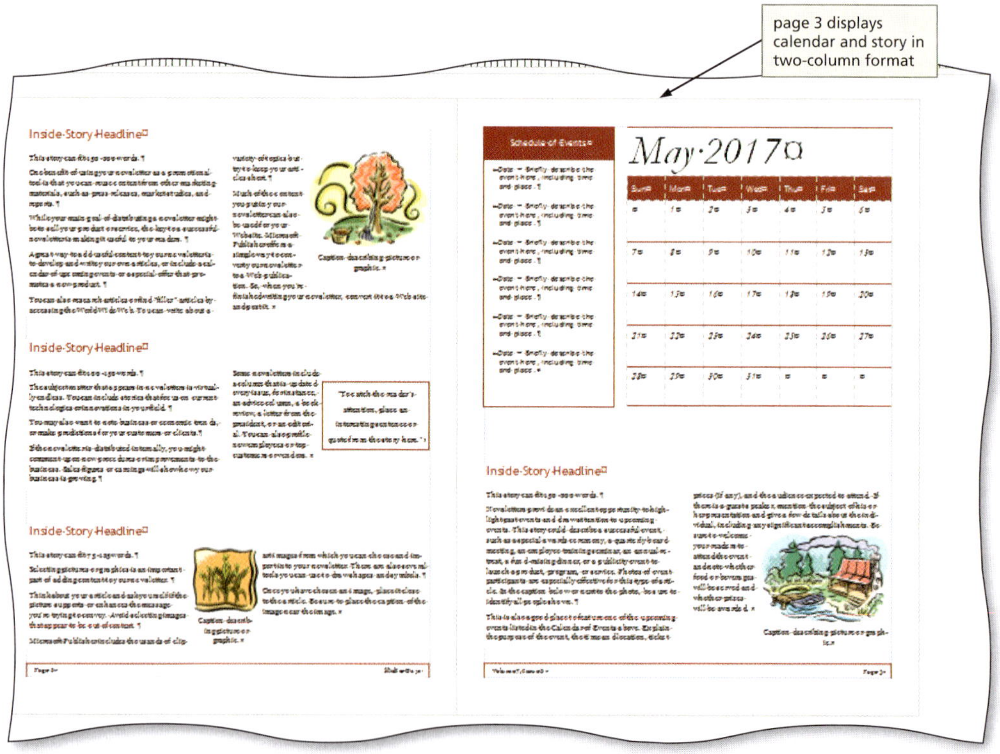

Q&A

My calendar is different. Did I do something wrong?
No. The calendar option uses the current month on your system. Any month is acceptable for this project.
You will learn how to change calendar dates in a later module.

Should I change the options for the back page?
No. You will edit those objects individually later in the module.

Figure 3–9

Changing the Number of Pages in a Newsletter

Not all newsletters are four pages long. Some will have more or fewer pages. The following sections describe how to delete pages from or add pages to a newsletter template.

TO DELETE PAGES FROM A NEWSLETTER

If you were designing a newsletter with only two pages, it would be best to delete pages 2 and 3 because page 4 already is formatted to be a back page in most templates. Pages 2 and 3 have inside page numbers and graphics. If you wanted to delete pages 2 and 3, you would perform the following steps.

1. Right-click the 'Page 2 and Page 3' icon in the Page Navigation pane to display the shortcut menu.
2. Click Delete on the shortcut menu to delete pages 2 and 3. When Publisher displays the Delete Page dialog box for confirmation, click Both pages and then click the OK button (Delete Page dialog box).

TO ADD PAGES TO A NEWSLETTER

If you wanted to add extra pages to a newsletter, you would perform the following steps.

1. Right-click the 'Page 2 and Page 3' icon in the Page Navigation pane to display the shortcut menu.
2. Click Insert Page on the shortcut menu to insert a new page. Follow the directions in the Insert Newsletter Pages dialog box to insert either a left-hand page, a right-hand page, or both, and then click the OK button (Insert Newsletter Pages dialog box).

Editing the Masthead

Most newsletters contain a masthead similar to those used in newspapers. A **masthead** is a box or section printed in each issue that lists information, such as the name, publisher, location, volume, and date. The Publisher-designed masthead, included in the Nature newsletter publication set, contains several text boxes and colors that create an attractive, eye-catching graphic to complement the set.

BTW

Zooming

Recall that the F9 key toggles between the current page view and 100% magnification or actual size. **Toggle** means the same key will alternate views, or turn a feature on and off. Editing text is easier if you view the text at 100% magnification or higher.

To Edit the Masthead

1 EDIT PUBLICATION OPTIONS | 2 IMPORT & CONNECT STORIES | 3 USE CONTINUED NOTICES | 4 CUSTOMIZE RIBBON
5 EDIT USING WORD | 6 INSERT MARGINAL ELEMENTS | 7 APPLY DROP CAPS & HYPHENATE | 8 CREATE TEMPLATE

The following steps edit text in the masthead, including the volume and issue number. *Why? Publications typically use volume numbers to indicate the number of years the publication has been in existence. The issue number indicates its sequence. Volume numbers and issue numbers do not necessarily correlate to the calendar year and months. Schools, for example, sometimes start in the fall with Volume 1, Issue 1.*

1

- Click the Page 1 icon in the Page Navigation pane to change the display to page 1.
- Click the text, Newsletter Title, to select it and then zoom to 150%.
- Type `Shelter Days` to replace the text. Right-click the text and then click Best Fit on the shortcut menu (Figure 3–10).

Q&A Why does my font look different?
Publisher replaces the selected text with the font from the publication set. Your font may differ from the one shown.

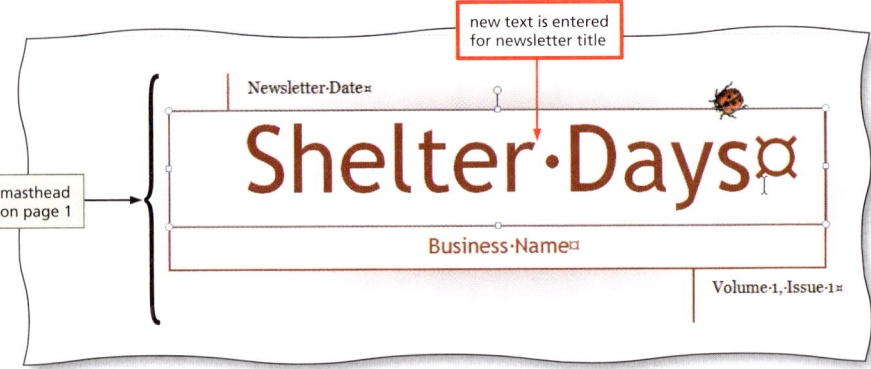

Figure 3–10

2

- Click the default text in the Business Name text box and then press CTRL+A to select all of the text.
- Type `Brisbane County Animal Shelter` to replace the text (Figure 3–11).

Figure 3–11

3

- Click the placeholder text in the Newsletter Date text box to select it.
- Type `May 1, 2017` to replace the text.
- Click the placeholder text in the Volume 1, Issue 1 text box to select it.
- Type `Volume 7, Issue 2` to replace the text (Figure 3–12).

Figure 3–12

BTW

Text in Overflow
The overflow area is an invisible storage location within a publication that holds extra text. You can move text out of overflow and back into a publication by one of several means: flowing text into a new text box, autofitting text, enlarging the text box, changing the text size, changing the margins within the text box, or deleting some of the text in the text box.

Newsletter Text

Newsletter content may come to you, as the desktop publisher, in various ways. Authors may submit their stories in email or as attachments. Others may post a Microsoft Word document or a graphic on the company's common storage location. Still other authors may handwrite their stories or record them on a recording device. In those cases, you will have to type the story yourself.

How do you gather topics and research stories?

Gather credible, relevant information in the form of stories, pictures, dates, figures, tables, and discussion threads. Plan far enough ahead so that you have time to take pictures or gather graphics for each story — even if you end up not using them. Stay organized; keep folders of information and store pictures and stories together. If you have to write a story from scratch, gather your data, do your research, and have an informed reader go over your content.

The same principles of audience, purpose, and topic apply to individual stories, just as they do for the newsletter as a whole. Evaluate your sources for authority, timeliness, and accuracy. Be especially wary of information obtained from the web. Any person, company, or organization can publish a webpage on the Internet. Ask yourself these questions about the source:

- Authority: Does a reputable institution or group support the source? Is the information presented without bias? Are the author's credentials listed and verifiable?

- Timeliness: Is the information up to date? Are the dates of sources listed? What is the last date that the information was revised or updated?

- Accuracy: Is the information free of errors? Is it verifiable? Are the sources clearly identified?

Identify the sources for your text and graphics. Notify all writers of important dates, and allow time for gathering the data. Make a list for each story: include the author's name, the approximate length of the story, the electronic format, and associated graphics. Ask the author for suggestions for headlines. Consult with colleagues about other graphics, features, sidebars, and the masthead.

Acknowledge all sources of information; do not plagiarize. Not only is plagiarism unethical, it also is considered an academic crime that can have severe consequences, such as failing a course or being expelled from school.

When you summarize, paraphrase (rewrite information in your own words), present facts, give statistics, quote exact words, or show a map, chart, or other graphical image, you must acknowledge the source. Information that commonly is known or accessible to the audience constitutes **common knowledge** and does not need to be acknowledged. If, however, you question whether certain information is common knowledge, you should document it — just to be safe.

Publisher allows users to import text and graphics from many sources, from a variety of different programs, and in many different file formats. Publisher uses the term, **importing**, to describe inserting text or objects from any other source into the Publisher workspace. Publisher uses the term, **story**, when referring to text that is contained within a single text box or a chain of linked text boxes. Each newsletter template provides **linked text boxes**, or text boxes whose text flows from one to another. In the templates, two or three text boxes may be linked automatically; however, if a story is too long to fit in the linked text boxes, Publisher will offer to link even more text boxes for easy reading.

Replacing Placeholder Text Using an Imported File

Publisher suggests that 175 to 225 words will fit in the space allocated for the lead story. The story is displayed in a two-column text box format that connects, or links, the running text from one text box to the next. Publisher links text boxes according to your settings, and it displays arrow buttons to navigate to the next and previous text boxes.

This edition of Shelter Days contains several stories, some of which have been typed previously and stored using Microsoft Word, as they might be in a business setting. The stories, located in the Data Files, are ready to be used in the newsletter. Please contact your instructor for information about accessing the Data Files. The final story you will type yourself. Each story will include a **headline**, which is a short phrase printed at the top of a story, usually in a bigger font than the story. A headline summarizes the story that follows it.

BTW

The Ribbon and Screen Resolution
Publisher may change how the groups and buttons within the groups appear on the ribbon, depending on the computer's screen resolution. Thus, your ribbon may look different from the ones in this book if you are using a screen resolution other than 1366 × 768.

BTW

Publisher Help
At any time while using Publisher, you can find answers to questions and display information about various topics through Publisher Help. Used properly, this form of assistance can increase your productivity and reduce your frustrations by minimizing the time you spend learning how to use Publisher. For instruction about Publisher Help and exercises that will help you gain confidence in using it, read the Office and Windows module at the beginning of this book.

To Edit the Lead Story Headline

The following steps edit the Lead Story Headline placeholder text.

1 Click the placeholder text, Lead Story Headline, on page 1 to select it.

2 Type `Shelter Dog, Ricky, Wins State Agility Trials` to replace the text (Figure 3–13).

Figure 3–13

To Import a Text File

1 EDIT **PUBLICATION** OPTIONS | 2 **IMPORT & CONNECT STORIES** | 3 USE CONTINUED NOTICES | 4 CUSTOMIZE RIBBON
5 EDIT USING WORD | 6 INSERT MARGINAL ELEMENTS | 7 APPLY DROP CAPS & HYPHENATE | 8 CREATE TEMPLATE

The following steps import a text file to replace the Publisher-supplied placeholder text for the lead story. *Why?* *Importing the story prevents typographical errors created by retyping the text.* To complete these steps, you will be required to use the Data Files. Please contact your instructor for information about accessing the Data Files.

- Scroll down to display the story below the headline. Zoom to approximately 120%.

- Click the placeholder text in the story to select it (Figure 3–14).

🔍 **Experiment**

- Read the placeholder text in order to learn about design suggestions related to newsletter publications.

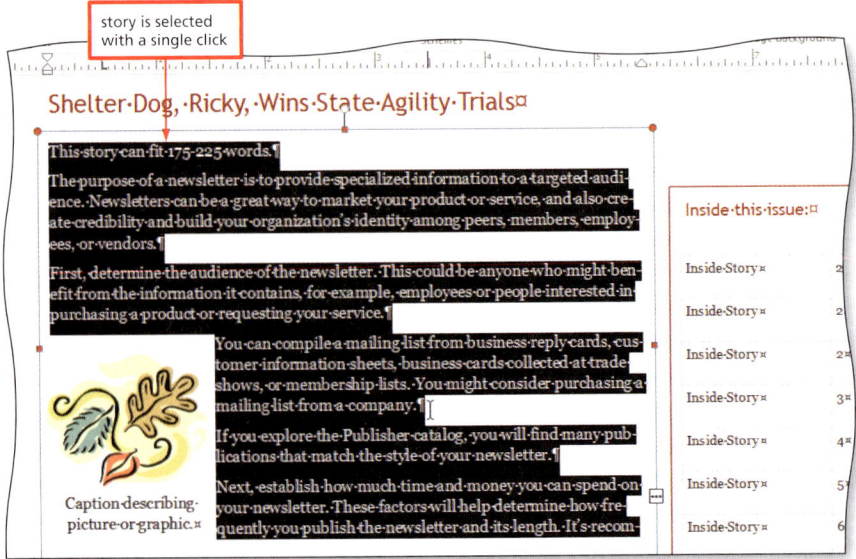

Figure 3–14

2

- Display the Insert tab.

- Click the Insert File button (Insert tab | Text group) to display the Insert Text dialog box.

- Navigate to the location of the file to be opened (in this case, the Module 03 folder in the Publisher Data Files) (Figure 3–15).

Q&A

What kinds of text files can Publisher import?

Publisher can import files from most popular applications. If you click the 'All Text Formats' button (Insert Text dialog box), you can see a list of specific file types.

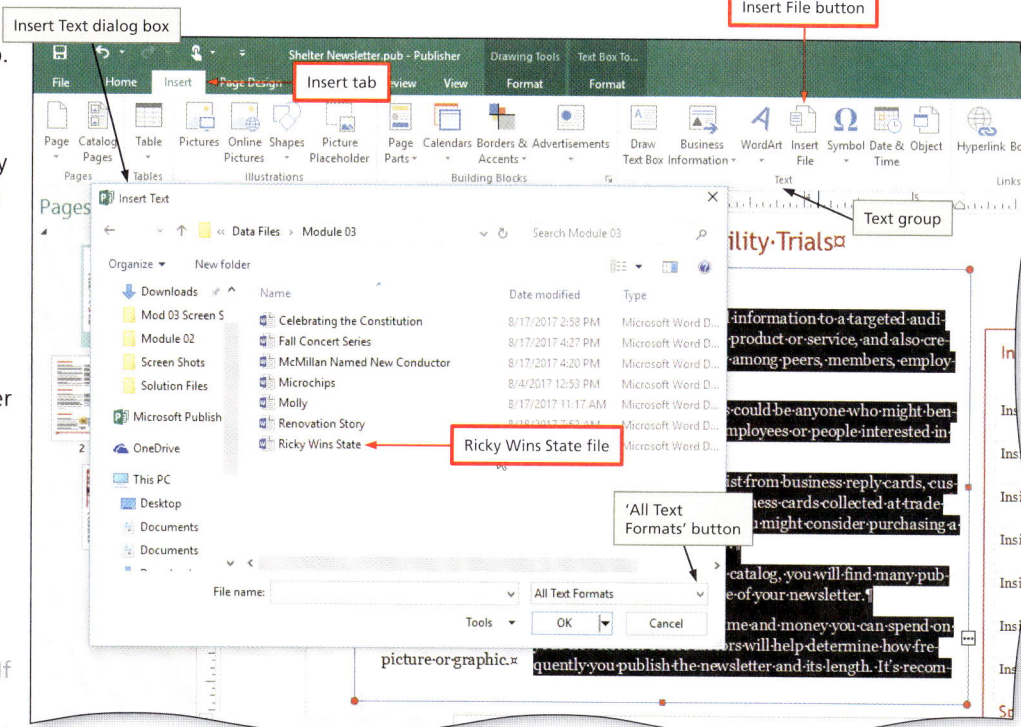

Figure 3–15

3

- Double-click the Ricky Wins State file to insert the text into the newsletter (Figure 3–16).

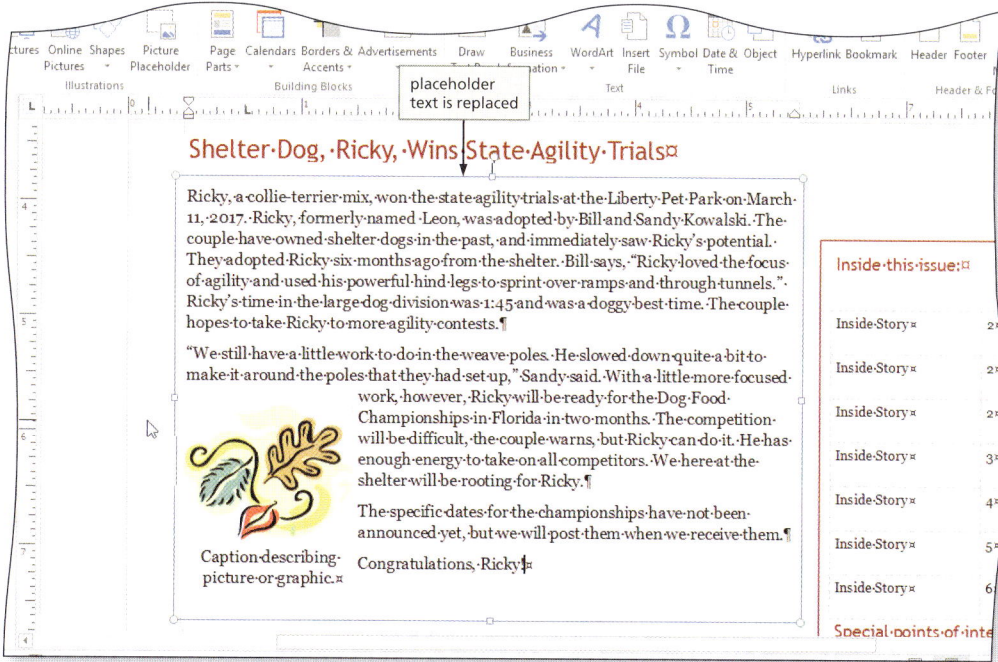

Figure 3–16

Other Ways

1. Right-click story, point to Change Text on shortcut menu, click Text File on Change Text submenu, click file name, click OK button (Insert Text dialog box)

To Edit the Secondary Story Headline

The following steps edit the Secondary Story Headline placeholder text.

1 Scroll down on page 1 and then click the placeholder text, 'Secondary Story Headline', to select it.

2 Type `Our Grand Reopening Is May 20!` to replace the text (Figure 3–17).

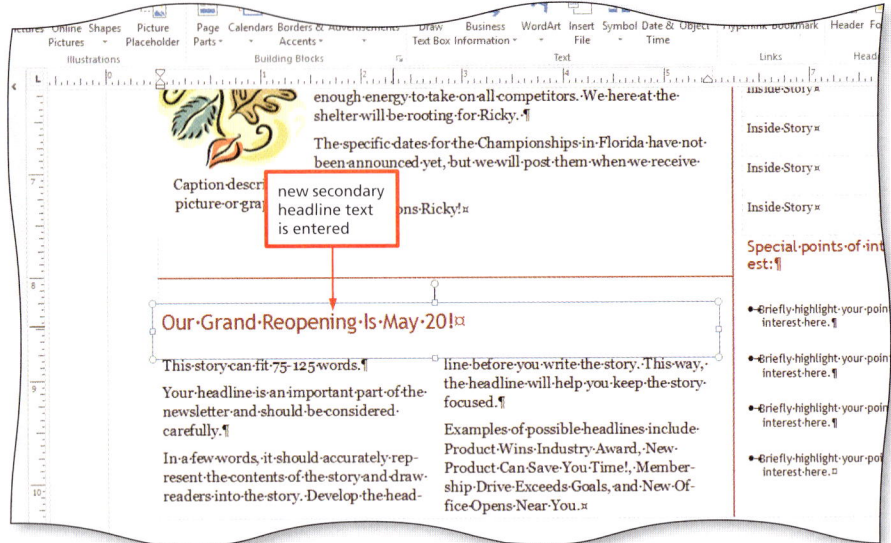

Figure 3–17

To Continue a Story across Pages

1 EDIT PUBLICATION OPTIONS | 2 IMPORT & CONNECT STORIES | 3 USE CONTINUED NOTICES | 4 CUSTOMIZE RIBBON
5 EDIT USING WORD | 6 INSERT MARGINAL ELEMENTS | 7 APPLY DROP CAPS & HYPHENATE | 8 CREATE TEMPLATE

As you import text, if a story contains more text than will fit in the default text box, Publisher displays a message to warn you. **Why?** *You then have the option to allow Publisher to connect, or* **autoflow**, *the text to another available text box or to flow the text yourself, manually.* The following steps import a story and continue it from page 1 to page 2 using Publisher dialog boxes. To complete these steps, you will be required to use the Data Files. Please contact your instructor for information about accessing the Data Files.

1
- Click the secondary story placeholder text on page 1 to select it.
- Click the Insert File button (Insert tab | Text group) to display the Insert Text dialog box.
- If necessary, navigate to the location of the Data Files and then double-click the file named, Renovation Story, to insert the text file (Figure 3–18).

Q&A
Why did Publisher display a dialog box and move to page 2?
The story was too large to fit in the space provided on page 1. Publisher moved to the first available text box with default or placeholder story text.

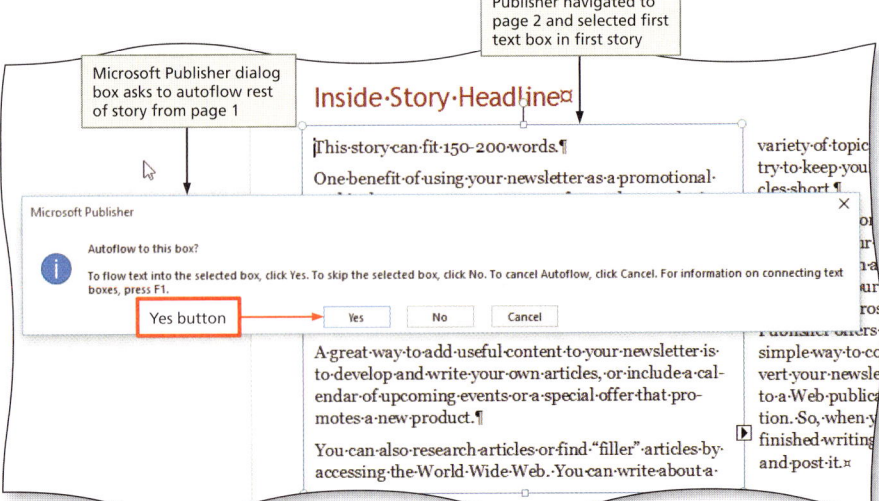

Figure 3–18

2

- In the Microsoft Publisher dialog box, click the Yes button to autoflow the story to the selected text box (Figure 3–19).

Q&A What do the three Autoflow buttons do?

If you click the Yes button, as you did here, Publisher will insert the rest of the text in the currently selected text box. If you click the No button, Publisher will move to the next story text box and ask again. If you click the Cancel button, you will have to flow the text manually.

What if I have no more spare text boxes in which to flow the text?

Publisher will ask if you want new text boxes created. If you answer yes, Publisher automatically will create a new page with new text boxes.

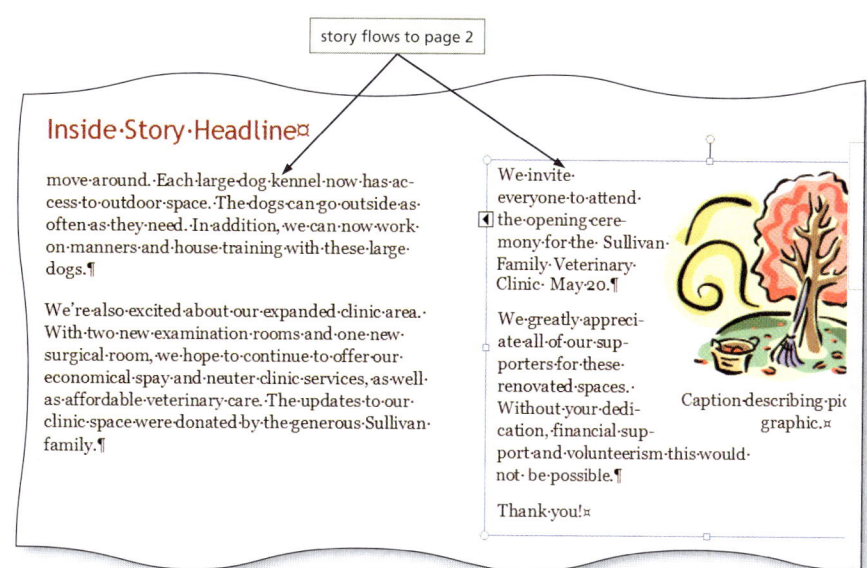

Figure 3–19

To Follow a Story across Pages

1 EDIT PUBLICATION OPTIONS | **2 IMPORT & CONNECT STORIES** | 3 USE CONTINUED NOTICES | 4 CUSTOMIZE RIBBON
5 EDIT USING WORD | 6 INSERT MARGINAL ELEMENTS | 7 APPLY DROP CAPS & HYPHENATE | 8 CREATE TEMPLATE

Publisher provides a way to move quickly back and forth through a continued story. *Why? While reading and editing the story, you may forget where the rest of the story is located or want to jump to its location quickly.* The following steps use the Next and Previous buttons to follow the story from text box to text box, across pages.

1

- Click the Page 1 icon in the Page Navigation pane and navigate to the Our Grand Reopening Is May 20! story at the bottom of the page.

- Click the second text box in the story to display the Previous and Next buttons (Figure 3–20).

Q&A Do all text boxes have Previous and Next buttons?

No. Only text boxes that contain a linked story display the buttons.

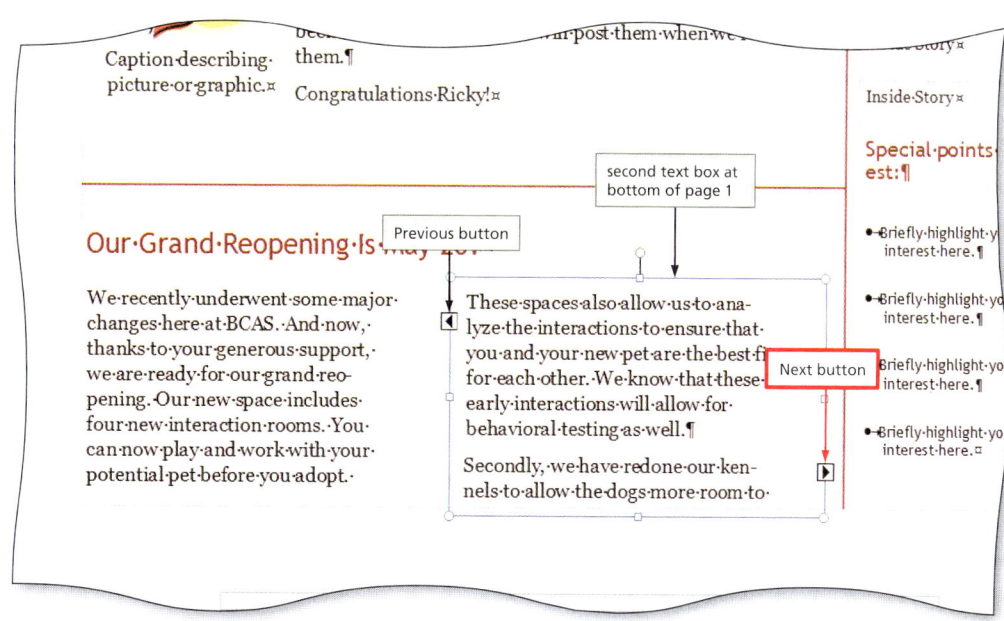

Figure 3–20

2

- Click the Next button to move to the rest of the story — the first text box at the top of page 2 (Figure 3–21).

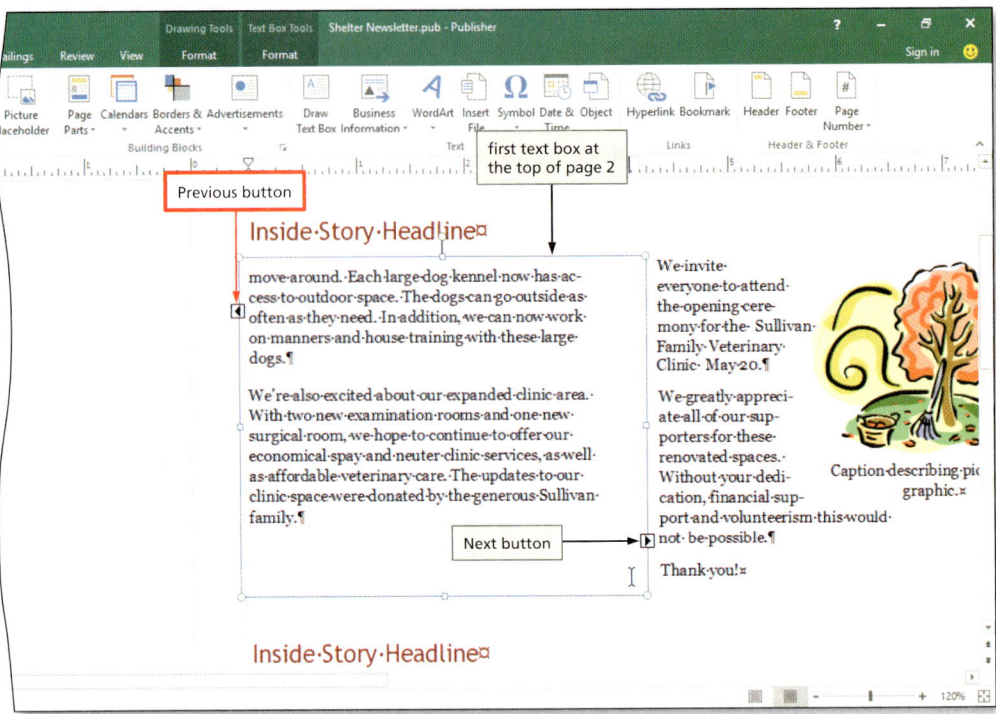

Figure 3–21

3

- Click the Previous button to move back to the first part of the story — the second text box at the bottom of page 1 (Figure 3–22).

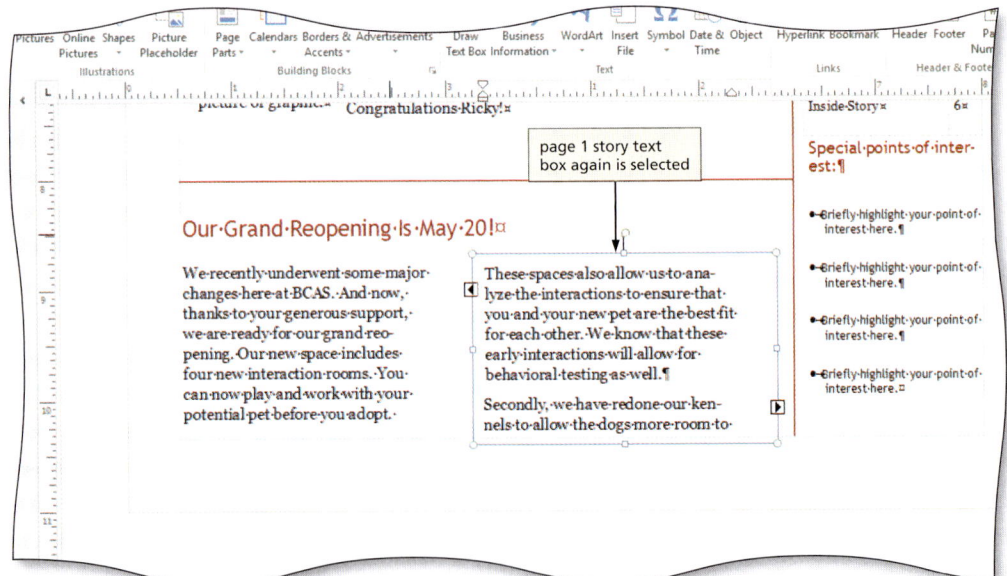

Figure 3–22

Other Ways

1. Select text box, click Previous or Next button (Text Box Tools Format tab | Linking group)

1 EDIT PUBLICATION OPTIONS | 2 IMPORT & CONNECT STORIES | 3 USE CONTINUED NOTICES | 4 CUSTOMIZE RIBBON
5 EDIT USING WORD | 6 INSERT MARGINAL ELEMENTS | 7 APPLY DROP CAPS & HYPHENATE | 8 CREATE TEMPLATE

To Break a Text Box Link

Sometimes, you might change your mind about where to continue a story. In that case, you have two choices. You can undo the previous insertion and autoflow again, or you can break the connection and create a manual one. When you break a connection, the extra text that cannot fit in the text box is placed in **overflow**. *Why? Unlike the Clipboard, the overflow area is maintained when you save the publication, allowing you to access it at any time.* The following step breaks the connection between the story at the bottom of page 1 and its continuation at the top of page 2.

1

- If necessary, navigate to page 1 and the story at the bottom of the page and then click the second column in the story to select the text box.

- Display the Text Box Tools Format tab.

- Click the Break button (Text Box Tools Format tab | Linking group) to break the connection to the rest of the story (Figure 3–23).

Q&A Where is the rest of the story now?
Publisher places it in a special overflow area as indicated by the 'Text in Overflow' button in Figure 3–23. The text box on page 2 becomes blank.

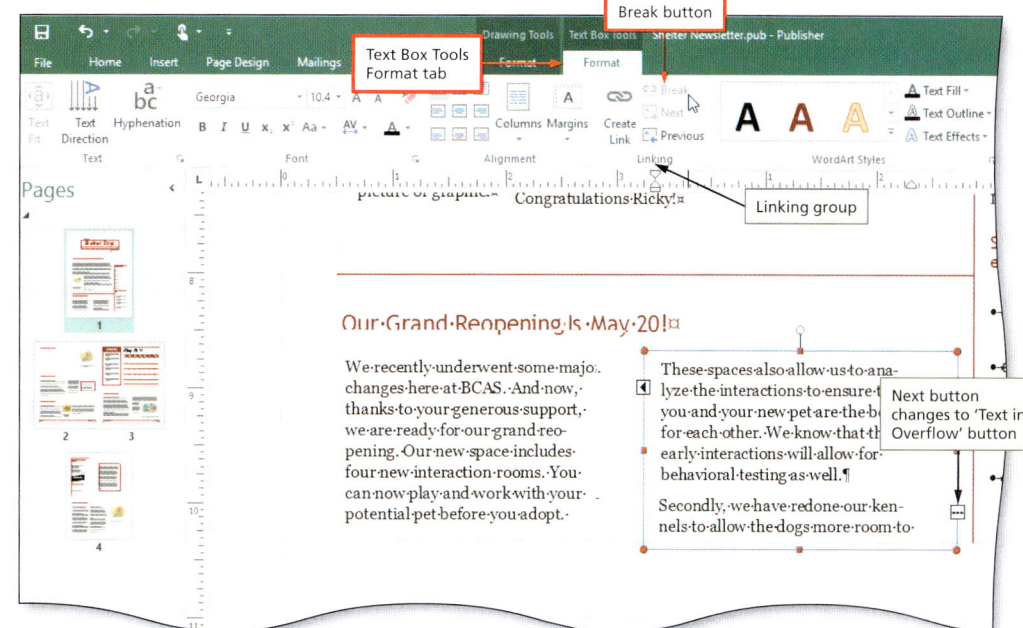

Figure 3–23

To Manually Continue the Story across Pages

1 EDIT PUBLICATION OPTIONS | 2 IMPORT & CONNECT STORIES | 3 USE CONTINUED NOTICES | 4 CUSTOMIZE RIBBON
5 EDIT USING WORD | 6 INSERT MARGINAL ELEMENTS | 7 APPLY DROP CAPS & HYPHENATE | 8 CREATE TEMPLATE

The following steps manually move the text from the overflow area to another text box. *Why? You cannot see the text while it is in overflow.*

1

- If necessary, select the text box that displays the 'Text in Overflow' button.

- Click the 'Text in Overflow' button to display the pitcher-shaped pointer (Figure 3–24).

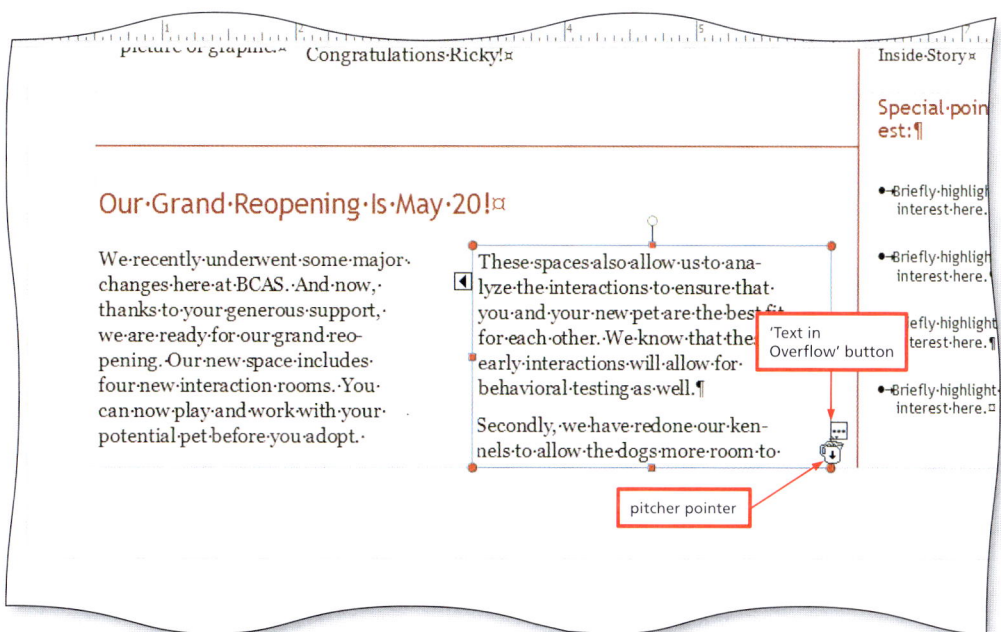

Figure 3–24

2

- Click the 'Page 2 and Page 3' icon in the Page Navigation pane to display the pages.

- Scroll as necessary to display the story at the bottom of page 3.

- With the pitcher-shaped pointer, click the placeholder text in the story to continue the Our Grand Reopening Is May 20! text (Figure 3–25).

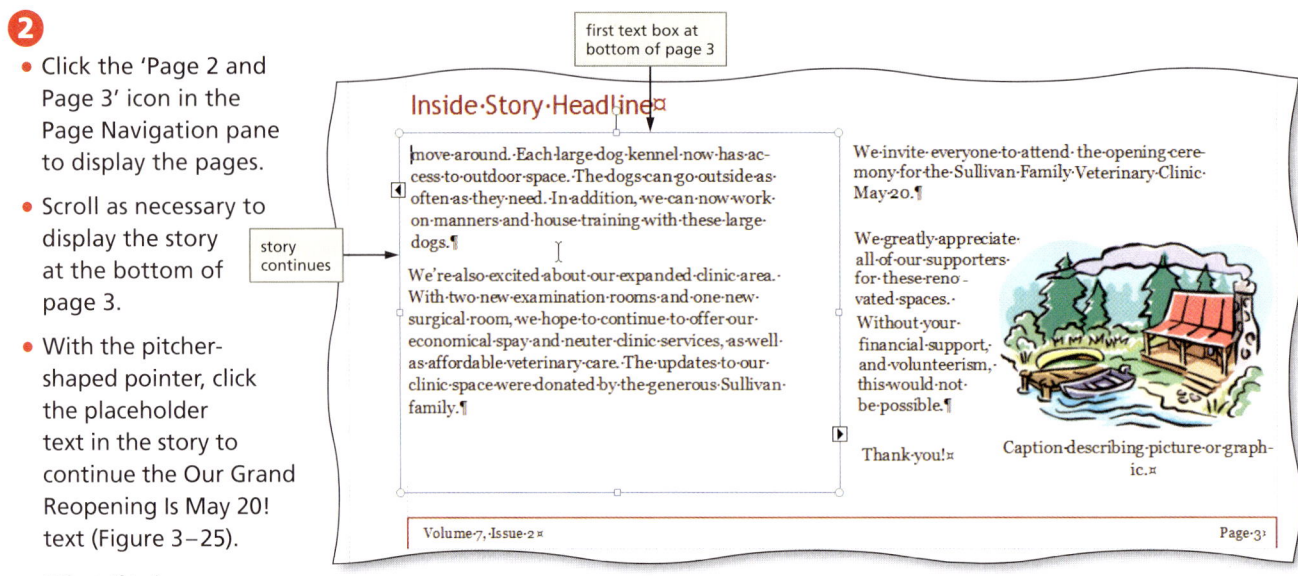

Figure 3–25

Q&A What if I change my mind and want to continue to a different text box?

You can click the Undo button on the Quick Access Toolbar, or you can click the last column of the story on page 1 and then click the Break button (Text Box Tools Format tab | Linking Group). You then can click the 'Text in Overflow' button again.

Other Ways

1. Select unlinked text box, click Create Link button (Text Box Tools Format tab | Linking group), click new text box

To Format with Continued Notices

1 EDIT PUBLICATION OPTIONS | 2 IMPORT & CONNECT STORIES | 3 USE CONTINUED NOTICES | 4 CUSTOMIZE RIBBON
5 EDIT USING WORD | 6 INSERT MARGINAL ELEMENTS | 7 APPLY DROP CAPS & HYPHENATE | 8 CREATE TEMPLATE

In print publications for stories that flow from one page to another, it is good practice to add **continued notices**, or **jump lines**, to guide readers through the story. *Why? A continued notice helps readers find the rest of the story easily.* The following steps format the last text box on page 1 with a continued on notice. Then, on page 3, the first text box in the rest of the story is formatted with a continued from notice.

1

- Click the Page 1 icon in the Page Navigation pane and then navigate to the bottom of the page.

- Right-click the second column of text in the lead story to display the shortcut menu (Figure 3–26).

Q&A Will Publisher ask me what page number to use?

No. The placement of the notices and the page numbering are automatic.

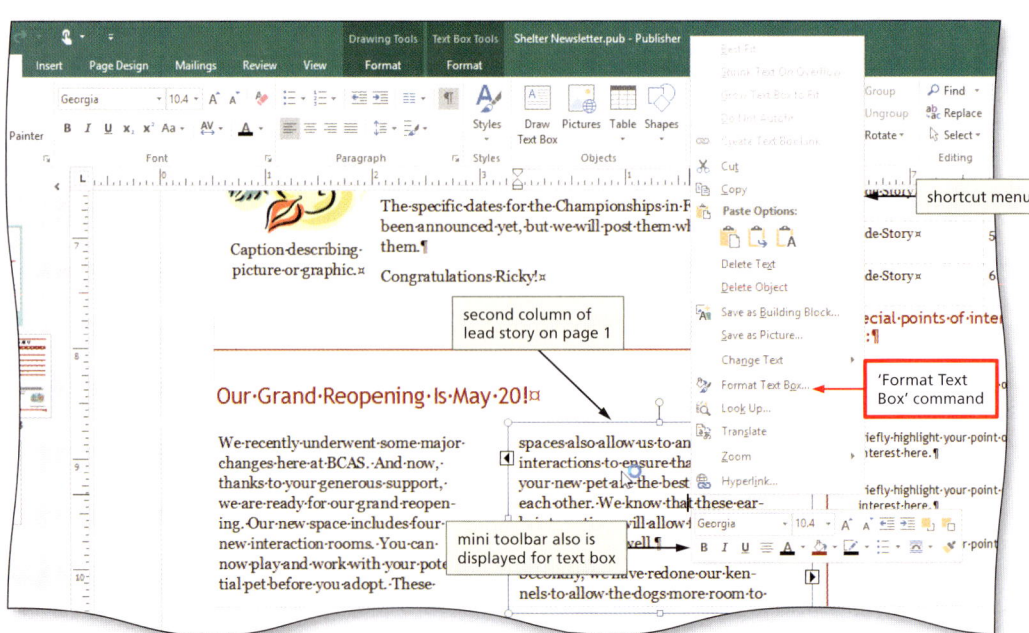

Figure 3–26

2

- Click 'Format Text Box' on the shortcut menu to display the Format Text Box dialog box.

- Click the Text Box tab to display its settings.

- Click to display a check mark in the 'Include "Continued on page…"' check box (Figure 3–27).

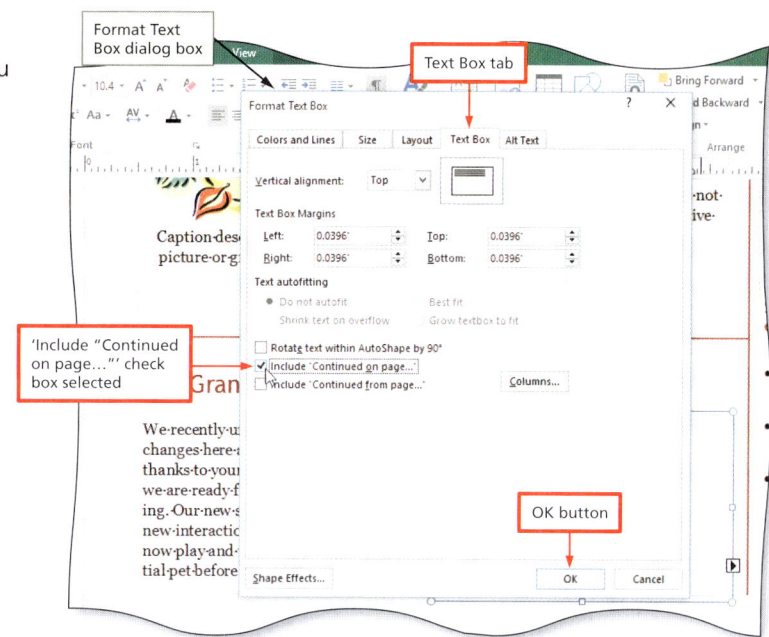

Figure 3–27

3

- Click the OK button (Format Text Box dialog box) to insert the continued on notice (Figure 3–28).

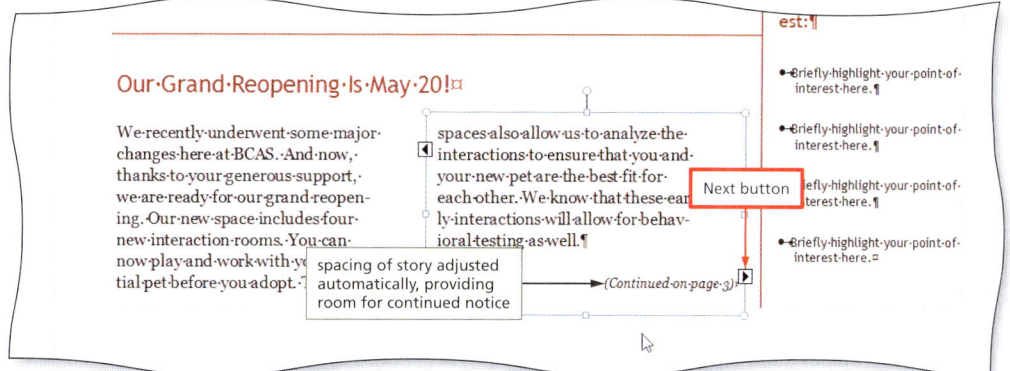

Figure 3–28

4

- Click the Next button to move to the rest of the story on page 3.

- Right-click the text in the first text box to display the shortcut menu and then click 'Format Text Box' on the shortcut menu to display the Format Text Box dialog box.

- If necessary, click the Text Box tab (Format Text Box dialog box) to display its settings.

- Click to display a check mark in the 'Include "Continued from page…"' check box (Figure 3–29).

Q&A What do I do if my dialog box is covering up the text box?

The setting changes will take place when you click the OK button. If you want to see both the dialog box and the text box, you can drag the title bar of the dialog box to a better location.

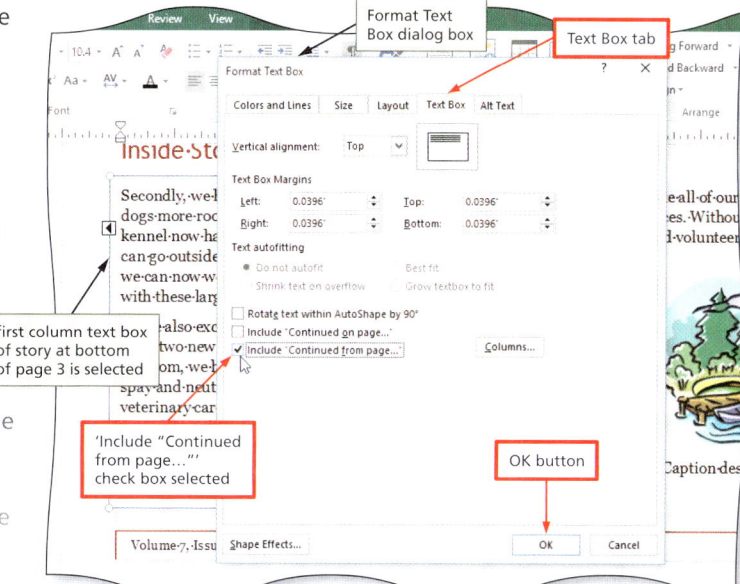

Figure 3–29

5
- Click the OK button (Format Text Box dialog box) to insert the continued from notice (Figure 3–30).

🔍 **Experiment**

- Use the Next and Previous buttons to move between the linked text boxes on pages 1 and 3. Examine the continued notices with the supplied page numbers.

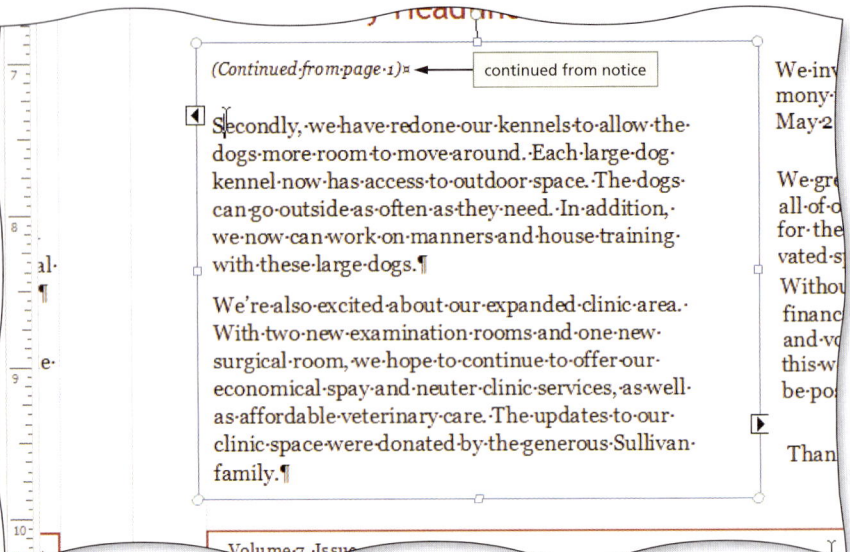

Figure 3–30

Other Ways

1. Select text box, click Format Text Box Dialog Box Launcher (Text Box Tools Format tab | Text group), click Text Box tab (Format Text Box dialog box), click 'Include "Continued on page…"' or 'Include "Continued from page…"', click OK button

To Edit the Headlines for the Continued Story

The following step edits the inside headline for the continued story.

1 Click the Inside Story Headline placeholder text to select it and then type `Our Grand Reopening Is May 20!` to replace the text (Figure 3–31).

Figure 3–31

To Edit Page 2

The following steps edit the headline and import the text for two stories on page 2, and delete the third story to make room for later content. To complete these steps, you will be required to use the Data Files. Please contact your instructor for information about accessing the Data Files.

1 Scroll to display the top portion of page 2 and then click the Inside Story Headline placeholder text above the first story to select it. Recall that the first story text box is blank because of the autoflow change.

2 Type `Kitty of the Month` to replace the selected headline.

3 Click inside the empty story text box to position the insertion point.

4 Click the Insert File button (Insert tab | Text group) to display the Insert Text dialog box.

5 If necessary, navigate to the Data Files and then double-click the file named, Molly, to insert the text file.

6 Repeat steps 1 through 5 for the second story on page 2. Use the text, Free Microchip with May Adoption, as the headline. Insert the text file named Microchips for the story.

7 Zoom to approximately 80% to display both stories and headlines (Figure 3–32).

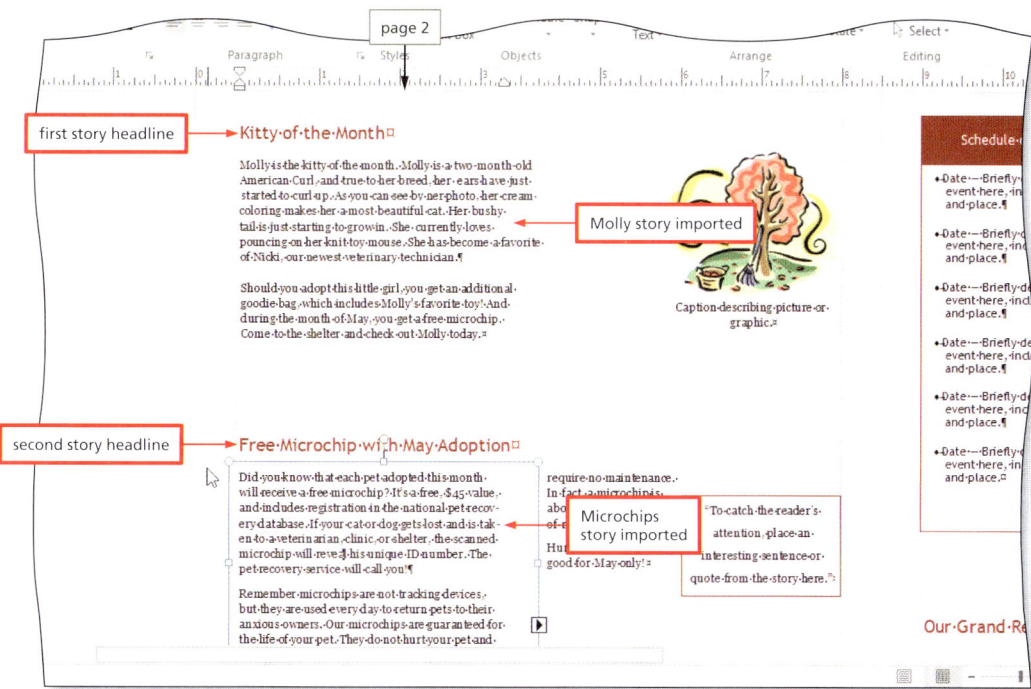

Figure 3–32

To Delete Objects on Page 2 and Page 4

The following steps remove the headline, story, and graphic on page 2. You will fill that area later in the module. The steps also remove the headline, story, and graphic at the bottom of page 4. The organization plans to fold the newsletter and mail it, so the bottom of page 4 will be reserved for mailing labels and postage.

1 Navigate to the bottom of page 2.

2 Drag to select the template headline, story, graphic, and caption.

3 Press the DELETE key to delete the selected objects.

4 Navigate to the top of page 2. Click between the graphic and story to select the second text box of the story, which is empty. Press the DELETE key.

5 Navigate to the bottom of page 4. Drag to select the template headline, story, graphic, and caption (Figure 3–33).

6 Press the DELETE key to delete the selected items.

7 Click the Save button on the Quick Access Toolbar to save the file again with the same file name, and in the same location.

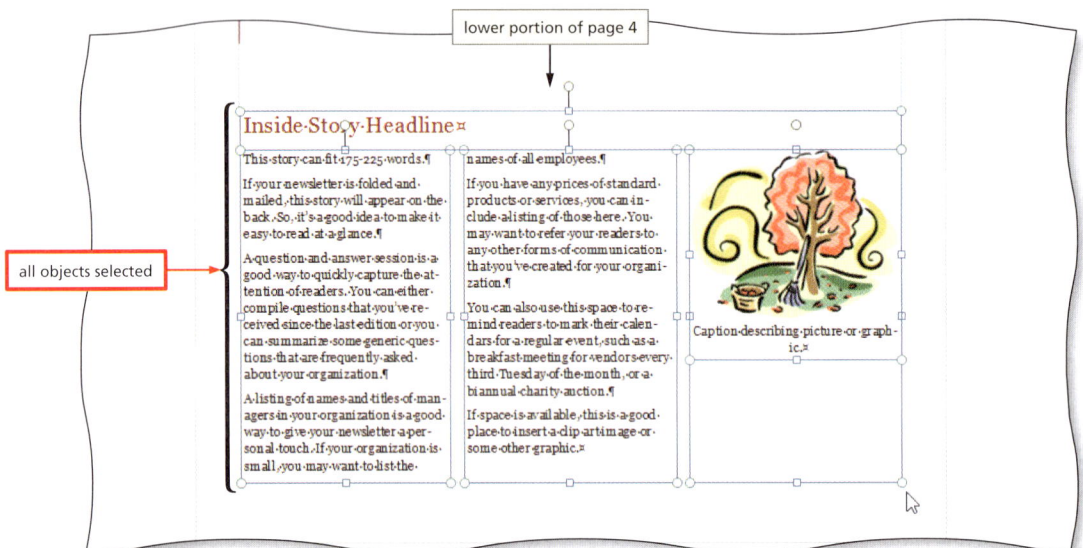

Figure 3–33

> **Break Point:** If you wish to take a break, this is a good place to do so. Exit Publisher. To resume at a later time, run Publisher, open the file called Shelter Newsletter, and continue following the steps from this location forward.

Customizing the Ribbon

It is easy to **customize**, or personalize, the ribbon the way that you want it. You can

- Create custom groups and custom tabs to contain frequently used commands
- Rearrange or rename buttons, groups, and tabs to fit your work style
- Rename or remove buttons and boxes from an existing tab and group
- Add new buttons to a custom group

When you add new buttons to the ribbon, you may choose from a list that includes commands that you may use elsewhere in Publisher such as those on shortcut menus, commands from the Backstage view, or other commands that are not on the ribbon. Or, you can create a new button that executes a command or set of commands that you record. You will create such a button later in this book. In this module, you will create a custom group on the Review tab and add a command that is not currently on the ribbon. The command will appear as a button in the new custom group.

You can customize the ribbon in all of the Microsoft Office applications, but the customizations are application-specific. The changes you make to the Publisher ribbon will not change the ribbon in any other Microsoft Office application. When you no longer need the customization, it can be removed individually, or the entire ribbon can be reset to its default settings, removing all customizations.

To Customize the Publisher Ribbon

1 EDIT PUBLICATION OPTIONS │ 2 IMPORT & CONNECT STORIES │ 3 USE CONTINUED NOTICES │ 4 CUSTOMIZE RIBBON

5 EDIT USING WORD │ 6 INSERT MARGINAL ELEMENTS │ 7 APPLY DROP CAPS & HYPHENATE │ 8 CREATE TEMPLATE

The following steps add the Edit Story in Microsoft Word button to a new group on the Review tab on the ribbon. *Why? The Review tab has empty space to hold custom groups. The other tabs are full. Adding a custom group to one of the other tabs would compress the existing groups, which might make it more difficult to locate buttons and boxes.*

1
- Click File on the ribbon to open the Backstage view and then click Options to display the Publisher Options dialog box.
- Click the Customize Ribbon tab in the left pane (Publisher Options dialog box) to display the options for customizing the ribbon.
- Click the 'Choose commands from' button to view the list of commands (Figure 3–34).

Q&A
Why are some commands not in the ribbon?
Publisher is a powerful program with many commands. Including all of the available commands on the ribbon would be overwhelming to many users. Publisher includes the more frequently used or popular commands in its default set.

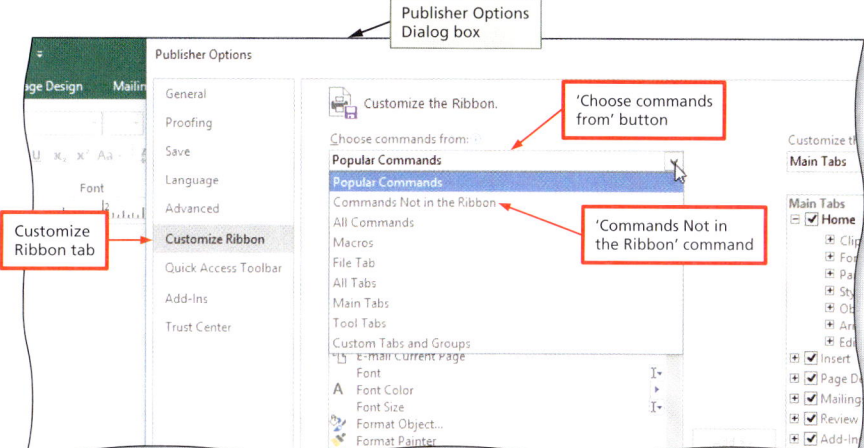

Figure 3–34

2
- Click 'Commands Not in the Ribbon' to display the list.
- Click the command you want to add (in this case, the 'Edit Story in Microsoft Word' command).
- Click Review in the list of Main Tabs to select the destination tab and then click the New Group button to create a custom group.
- Click the Add button to add the chosen command to the new group (Figure 3–35).

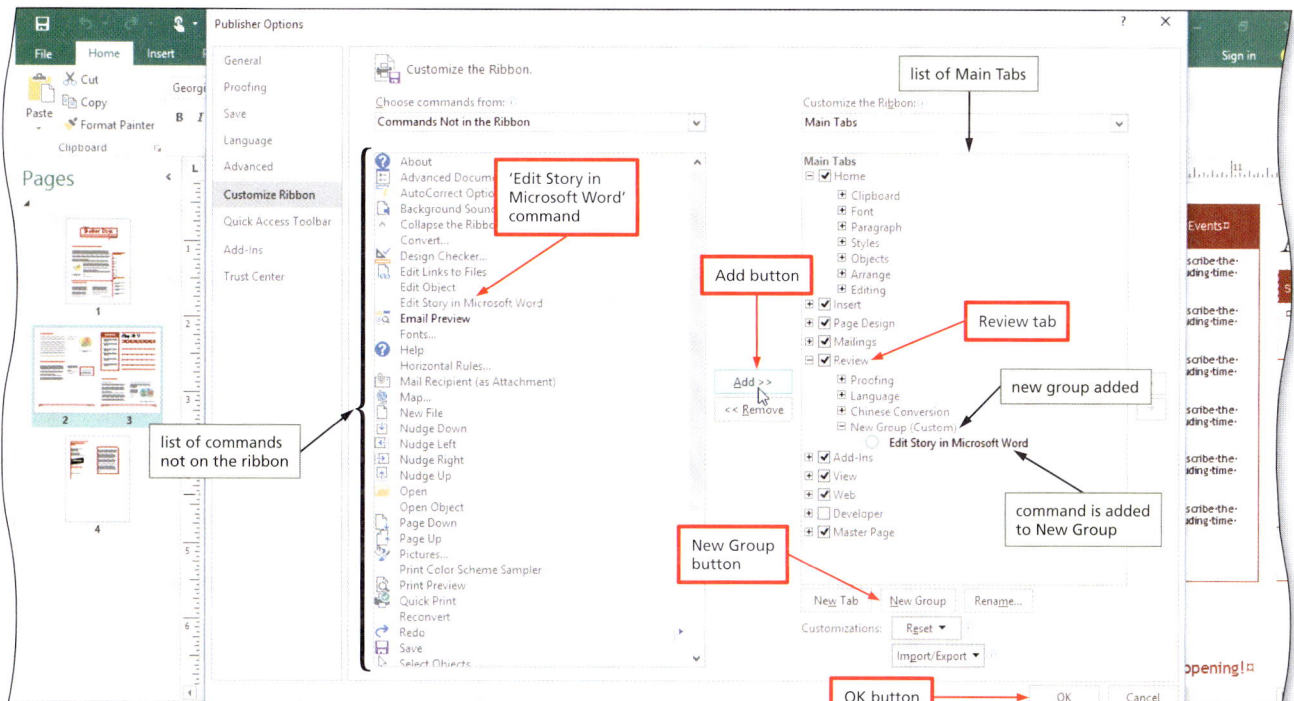

Figure 3–35

Q&A Can I add more than one command to the ribbon?
Yes, but you have to add them one at a time.

Do I have to add commands to a new group?
Yes. Commands can be added only to custom groups. The default tabs and groups cannot be changed.

3
- Click the OK button (Publisher Options dialog box) to close the dialog box and to create the custom group.

- Click Review on the ribbon to display the Review tab and its new group and button (Figure 3–36).

Q&A Can I rename the custom group?
Yes, you can rename any group or command by clicking the Rename button in the Publisher Options dialog box. As you rename, you can choose a custom icon for the command.

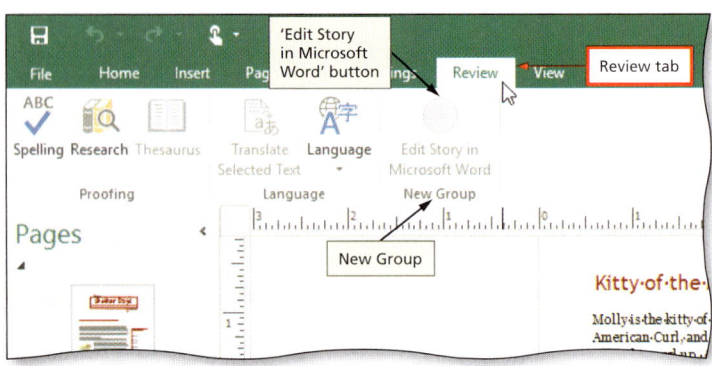

Figure 3–36

Other Ways

1. Right-click ribbon, click 'Customize the Ribbon' on shortcut menu, choose or create groups, add commands, click OK button (Publisher Options dialog box)

BTW
Whole Page View
The 'Show Whole Page' button on the right side of the Publisher status bar displays the entire page. Page editing techniques, such as moving graphics, inserting new objects, and aligning objects, are performed more easily in Show Whole Page view. You also may choose different magnifications and views by clicking the Zoom arrow (View tab | Zoom group).

Editing Stories in Microsoft Word

You have seen that you can edit text directly in Microsoft Publisher or import text from a previously stored file. A third way to edit text is to use Microsoft Word as your editor. Publisher provides an easy link between the two applications.

If you need to edit only a few words, it is faster to continue using Publisher. If you need to edit a longer story or one that is not available on your storage device, it sometimes is easier to edit the story in Word. Many users are accustomed to working in Word and want to take advantage of available Word features, such as grammar checking and revision tracking. It may be easier to drag and drop paragraphs in a Word window than to perform the same task in a Publisher window, especially when it involves moving across pages in a larger Publisher publication. Editing your stories in Word allows you to manipulate the text using the full capabilities of a word processing program.

While you are editing a story in Word, you cannot edit the corresponding text box in Publisher; Publisher displays a gray box instead of the text. When you close Word, control returns to Publisher and the text appears.

Occasionally, if you have many applications running, such as virus protection and other memory-taxing programs, Publisher may warn you that you are low on computer memory. In that case, exit the other applications and try editing the story in Word again.

To Edit a Story Using Microsoft Word

1 EDIT PUBLICATION OPTIONS | 2 IMPORT & CONNECT STORIES | 3 USE CONTINUED NOTICES | 4 CUSTOMIZE RIBBON
5 EDIT USING WORD | 6 INSERT MARGINAL ELEMENTS | 7 APPLY DROP CAPS & HYPHENATE | 8 CREATE TEMPLATE

The following steps use Microsoft Word in conjunction with Publisher to create the text on the back page of the newsletter. ***Why?*** *Some people find it easier to edit stories using Microsoft Word.* Microsoft Word version 6.0 or later must be installed on your computer for this procedure to work.

1

- If necessary, navigate to page 4 and then scroll to display the story text box in the upper portion of page 4.

- Click the placeholder text in the story to select it.

- If necessary, display the Review tab (Figure 3–37).

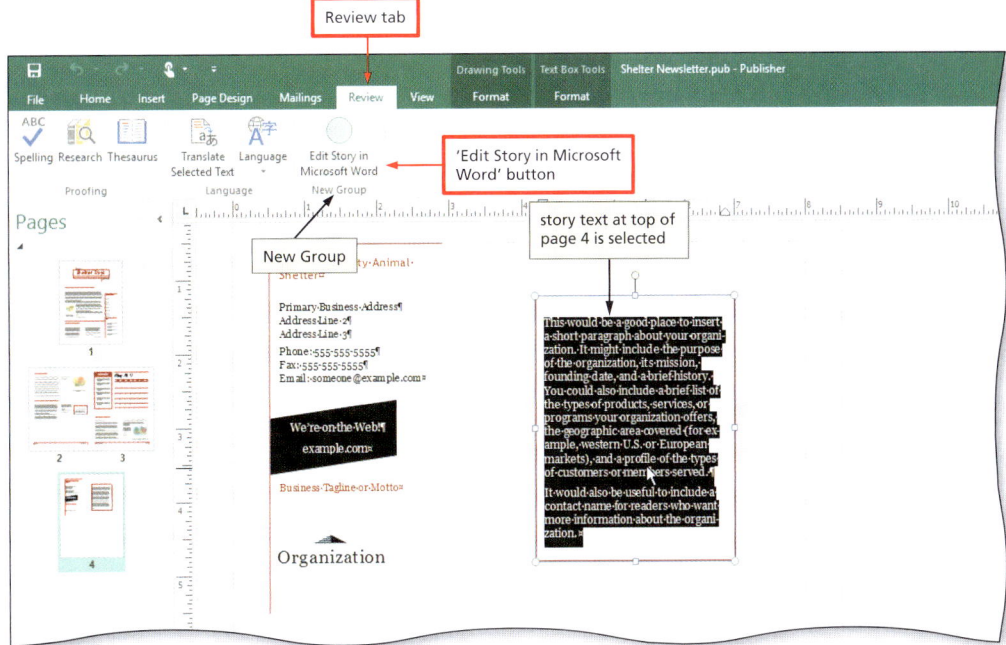

Figure 3–37

2

- Click the 'Edit Story in Microsoft Word' button (Review tab | New Group) to run the Word program.

- Press CTRL+A to select all of the text, and then type The Brisbane County Animal Shelter (BCAS) is a nonprofit organization established in 1960 to support all animals of the county. BCAS provides vital services through sheltering and adopting animals, providing public training classes, and outreach through our community and shelter programs. BCAS receives no public or private government funding; we are supported solely by contributions, grants, adoption fees, and other fees for service. to replace the placeholder text. Press the ENTER key to finish the first paragraph (Figure 3–38).

Q&A

Why are my formatting marks not showing in Microsoft Word?
It is possible that someone has turned off formatting marks. Click the 'Show/Hide ¶' button (Word Home tab | Paragraph Group) to turn them on and off.

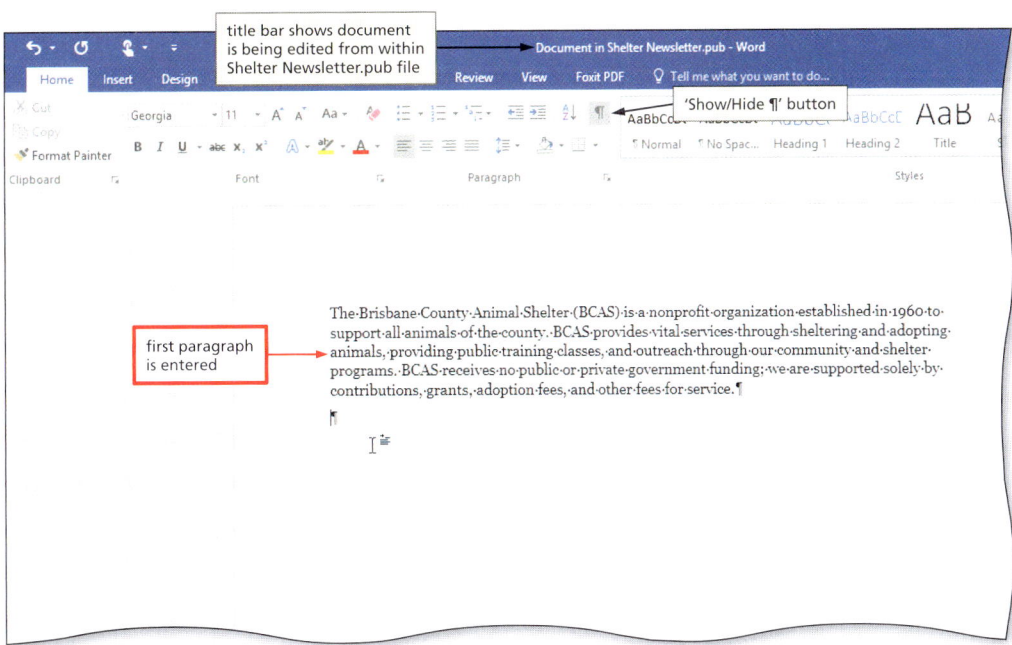

Figure 3–38

- Type `Our animals have no expiration date. We never euthanize due to space, time, or length of stay.` to finish the text (Figure 3–39).

Q&A Why are my fonts different?
Usually, the Word text displays the same formatting as the previous text in Publisher. Your display may differ depending on available fonts.

The·Brisbane·County·Animal·Shelter·(BCAS)·is·a·nonprofit·organization·established·in·1960·to· support·all·animals·of·the·county.·BCAS·provides·vital·services·through·sheltering·and·adopting· animals,·providing·public·training·classes,·and·outreach·through·our·community·and·shelter· programs.·BCAS·receives·no·public·or·private·government·funding;·we·are·supported·solely·by· contributions,·grants,·adoption·fees,·and·other·fees·for·service.¶

Our·animals·have·no·expiration·date.·We·never·euthanize·due·to·space,·time,·or·length·of·stay.¶

second paragraph is entered

Figure 3–39

To Format while Editing in Microsoft Word

1 EDIT PUBLICATION OPTIONS | 2 IMPORT & CONNECT STORIES | 3 USE CONTINUED NOTICES | 4 CUSTOMIZE RIBBON
5 EDIT USING WORD | 6 INSERT MARGINAL ELEMENTS | 7 APPLY DROP CAPS & HYPHENATE | 8 CREATE TEMPLATE

The following step uses the CTRL key to select multiple sections of nonadjacent text and format them in Microsoft Word. **Why?** *You cannot select nonadjacent text in Publisher.*

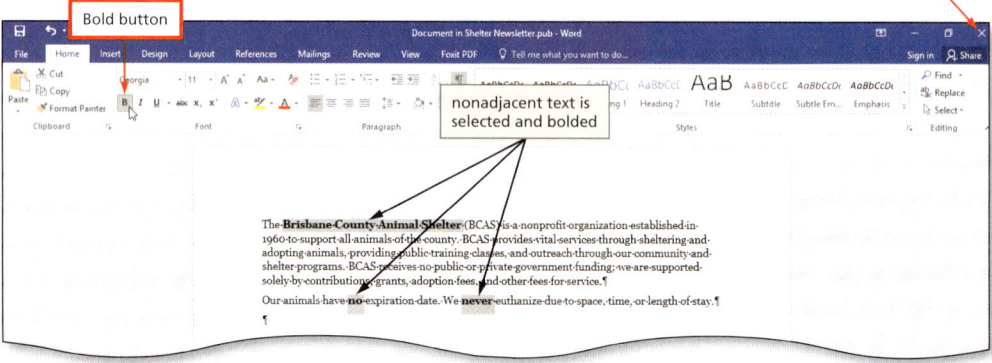

- Drag to select the words, Brisbane County Animal Shelter, in the first paragraph.

- One at a time, CTRL+drag to select the words, no and never, in the second paragraph.

- Click the Bold button (Home tab | Font group) on the Word ribbon to bold the selected text (Figure 3–40).

Bold button

Close button

nonadjacent text is selected and bolded

Figure 3–40

To Exit Word and Return to Publisher

1 EDIT PUBLICATION OPTIONS | 2 IMPORT & CONNECT STORIES | 3 USE CONTINUED NOTICES | 4 CUSTOMIZE RIBBON
5 EDIT USING WORD | 6 INSERT MARGINAL ELEMENTS | 7 APPLY DROP CAPS & HYPHENATE | 8 CREATE TEMPLATE

The following step exits Word and returns to Publisher. **Why?** *You must exit Word in order to edit the text box in Publisher.*

- Click the Close button on the title bar of the Document in Shelter Newsletter.pub - Word window to exit Word (Figure 3–41).

Q&A Why do I see only gray lines instead of the text?
Running Microsoft Word from within Microsoft Publisher is a drain on your system's memory and on the refresh rate of your screen. Try navigating to page 1 and then back to page 4 to refresh the screen.

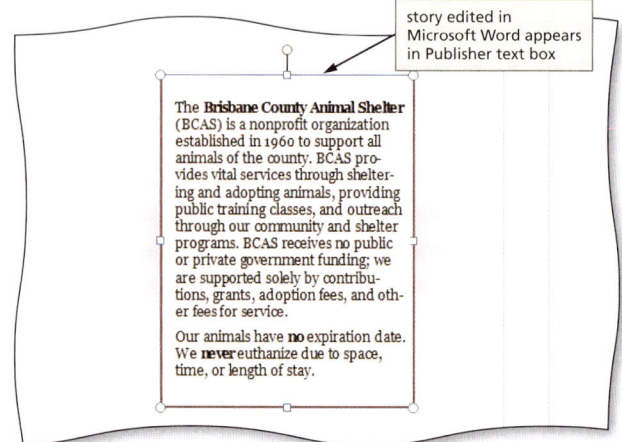

story edited in Microsoft Word appears in Publisher text box

The **Brisbane County Animal Shelter** (BCAS) is a nonprofit organization established in 1960 to support all animals of the county. BCAS provides vital services through sheltering and adopting animals, providing public training classes, and outreach through our community and shelter programs. BCAS receives no public or private government funding; we are supported solely by contributions, grants, adoption fees, and other fees for service.

Our animals have **no** expiration date. We **never** euthanize due to space, time, or length of stay.

Figure 3–41

To Edit Other Objects on Page 4

Table 3–2 lists text and deletions for the other objects on page 4.

Table 3–2	Text for Page 4
Location	**Text**
Organization logo	<delete>
Business Name	Brisbane County Animal Shelter
Primary Business Address	950 Cumberland Drive Accent, WY 82004
Phone, Fax, Email text box	Phone: 712 555-1028
Business Tagline or Motto	Like us on Facebook/BCAS
Attention getter	We're on the web! bcas.wy.org

The following steps delete the logo and edit other text boxes on page 4. As you edit the text boxes, zoom and scroll as necessary.

1 In the left portion of page 4, select the Organization logo and delete it.

2 If necessary, select the default Business Name text and replace it with the text from Table 3–2.

3 Click the default text in the Primary Business Address text box. Press CTRL+A to select all of the text. Enter the text from Table 3–2.

4 Select the default text in the Phone, Fax, Email text box and then enter the text from Table 3–2.

5 Select the Business Tagline or Motto placeholder text and then enter the text from Table 3–2. If necessary, right-click the text and then click Best Fit on the shortcut menu.

6 Select the text in the attention getter. Right-click to display the shortcut menu and then, if Best Fit does not display a check mark, click Best Fit on the shortcut menu. Enter the text from Table 3–2. As you enter the web address, if Publisher changes the first letter to an uppercase B, point to the letter, click the AutoCorrect Options button, and then click 'Undo Automatic Capitalization' (Figure 3–42).

7 Click the Save button on the Quick Access Toolbar to save the file again with the same file name and in the same location.

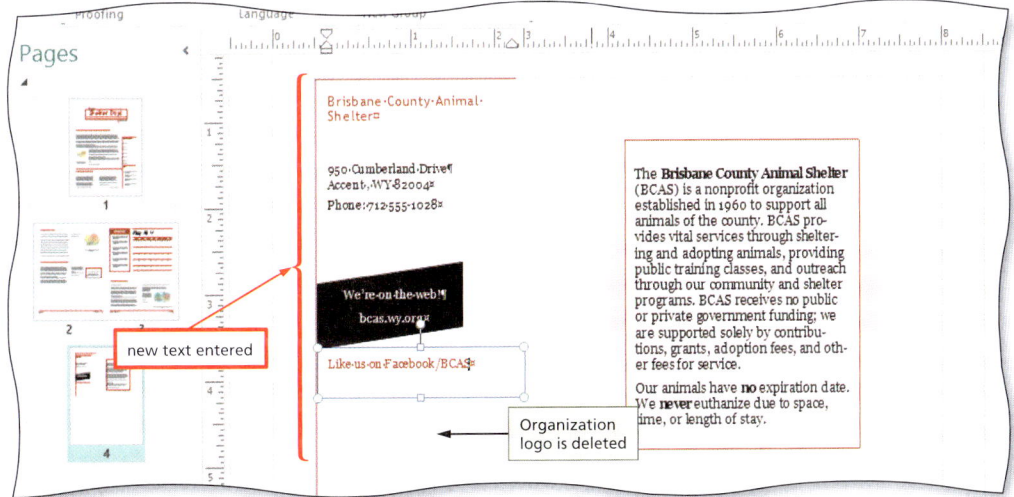

Figure 3–42

BTW
Bullets and Soft Returns
If you are editing a bulleted list, a soft return will not repeat the bullet. This is ideal for short phrases and lists within a single bullet.

Marginal Elements

Publisher newsletter templates include marginal elements and layout features to make the newsletter more attractive and to add interest to the page. A **sidebar**, or breakout, is a small piece of text, set off with a box or graphic, and placed beside a story. It contains text that is not vital for understanding the main text but usually adds interest or additional information. Tables of contents, art boxes, and bulleted points of interest are examples of sidebars. A newsletter **table of contents**, or margin table, usually is a narrow, short list that is used to refer readers to specific pages or to present listed or numeric items in the margin area. A **pull quote**, or **pullout**, is an excerpt from the main story used to highlight the concepts within the story or to attract readers. Pull quotes, like sidebars, can be set off with a box or graphic. Graphics, shapes, and borders also are used sometimes as marginal elements.

To Edit Sidebars

1 EDIT PUBLICATION OPTIONS | 2 IMPORT & CONNECT STORIES | 3 USE CONTINUED NOTICES | 4 CUSTOMIZE RIBBON
5 EDIT USING WORD | **6 INSERT MARGINAL ELEMENTS** | **7 APPLY DROP CAPS & HYPHENATE** | **8 CREATE TEMPLATE**

The newsletter template used in this module includes two sidebars on page 1. The first one is a table of contents. The second is a bulleted list about special points of interest. *Why?* *Some newsletters use a sidebar table as an index to locate stories in longer newsletters; sidebars also are used to break up a page with lots of text and attract readers to inside pages. Other newsletters use sidebar tables to display numerical data and lists.* Table 3–3 lists the text for the sidebars that you will edit in the following steps.

Table 3–3 Text for Sidebars		
Inside this issue:	Ricky Wins State	1
	Grand Reopening	1
	Kitty of the Month	2
	Microchips	2
	Calendar	3
	About Us	4
	Contact Us	4
Special points of interest:	May 6: Manners for People and Pups	
	May 10: Board Meeting	
	May 15: Adoption Clinic	
	May 20: Grand Reopening	
	May 20: Closed	

1
- Navigate to page 1.
- Locate the Inside this issue sidebar and then click Inside Story in the first row to select it. Zoom as necessary (Figure 3–43).

Q&A What are the dotted gray lines in the table?
Publisher displays dotted gray lines to indicate the size of each cell in the table. A **cell** is the text box located where a table column and table row intersect. The lines do not print.

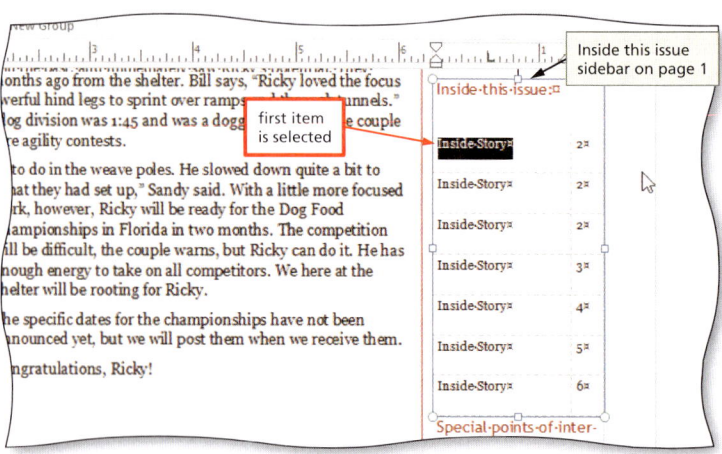

Figure 3–43

- Type `Ricky Wins State` to replace the text and then press the TAB key. Complete the table with the data from Table 3–3. Use the TAB key to move from cell to cell.

- Scroll down to the second sidebar, Special points of interest, and then click the bulleted list to select it.

- Type the list as shown in Table 3–3, pressing the ENTER key at the end of each line (Figure 3–44).

Could I click the next cell instead of using the TAB key?
You could click the cell, but you then would need to select the page number and type to replace it. Pressing the TAB key both advances to and selects the data in the next cell.

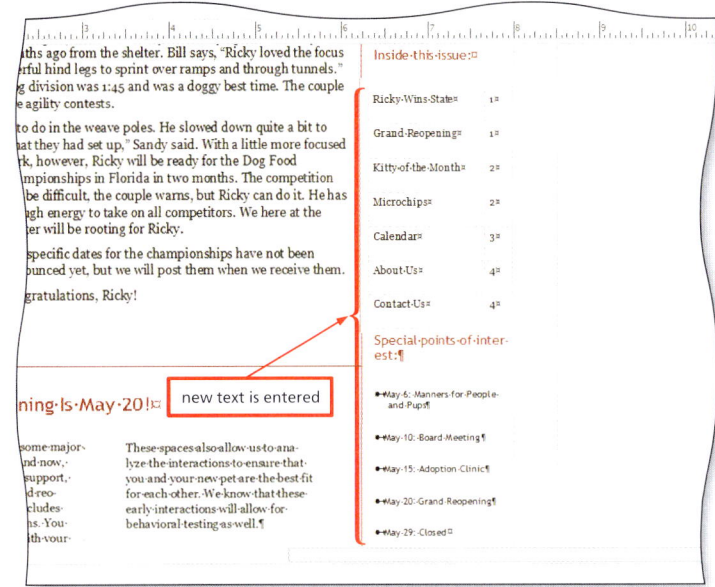

Figure 3–44

To Use a Soft Return

The following steps edit the title of the Special points of interest sidebar, so that it appears on two lines, without the hyphen. **Why?** *A title or heading looks better without hyphens. A title also looks better when the line lengths are balanced or more equal in length.*

Recall that a hard return is created when you press the ENTER key. A hard return also creates a new paragraph with appropriate paragraph spacing. For example, a typical setting might be that lines are single-spaced as they wrap, but paragraphs are double-spaced — meaning Publisher creates a blank line between paragraphs. If you do not want paragraph spacing but you do want a new line, you can use a **soft return** or **manual line break**. To create a soft return you press the SHIFT+ENTER keys.

- Navigate to the Special points of interest title.
- Click the title to select it and then type `Special points` to create the first line.
- Press SHIFT+ENTER to create a soft return (Figure 3–45).

What is the symbol that appeared at the end of the line?
Publisher displays the curved arrow or manual line break symbol when you press SHIFT+ENTER, so that you can see the keystroke and differentiate it from a paragraph mark or hard return. The symbol does not print.

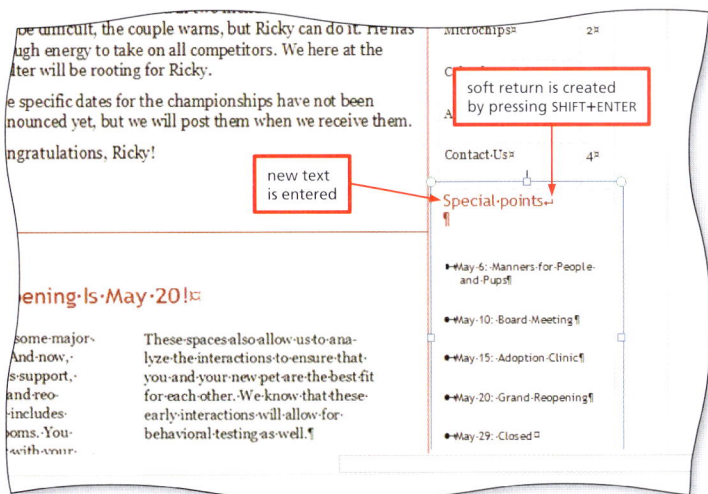

Figure 3–45

2

- Type of interest to complete the heading (Figure 3–46).

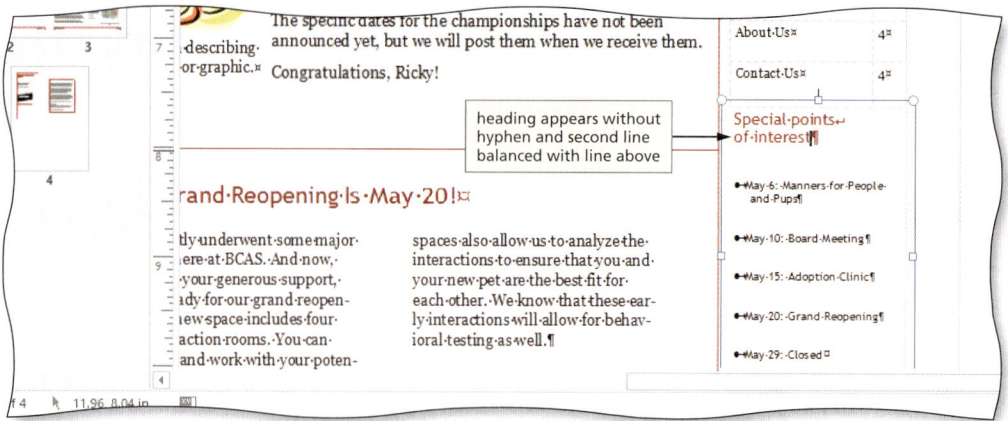

Figure 3–46

To Edit a Pull Quote

1 EDIT PUBLICATION OPTIONS | 2 IMPORT & CONNECT STORIES | 3 USE CONTINUED NOTICES | 4 CUSTOMIZE RIBBON
5 EDIT USING WORD | 6 INSERT MARGINAL ELEMENTS | **7 APPLY DROP CAPS & HYPHENATE** | 8 CREATE TEMPLATE

People often make reading decisions based on the size of the story. Using a pull quote brings a small portion of the text to their attention. ***Why?*** *Pull quotes invite the reader to read the story; they also are useful for breaking the monotony of long columns of text and for adding visual interest.* The following steps insert a pull quote using function keys to copy and paste the quote from the story.

1

- Navigate to the second story, Free Microchip with May Adoption, on page 2.

- Drag to select the text in the second sentence.

- Press CTRL+C to copy the sentence to the Clipboard (Figure 3–47).

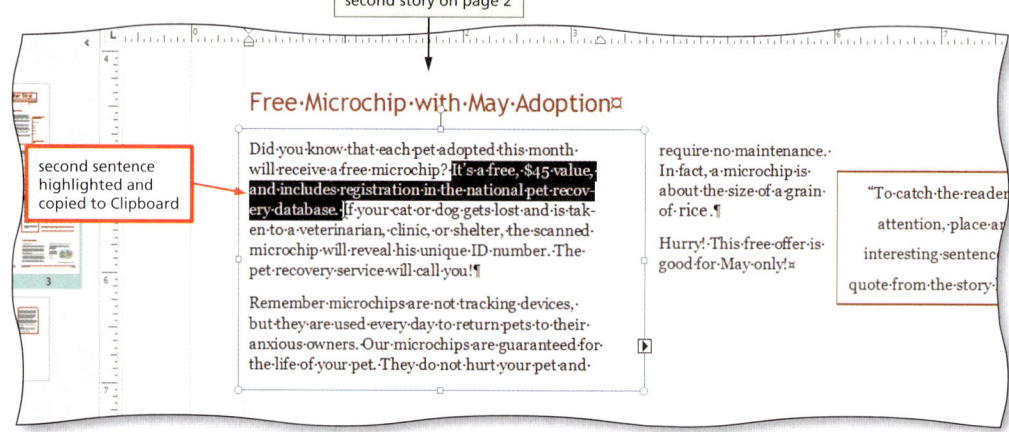

Figure 3–47

Q&A How should I choose the text for the pull quote?

Layout specialists say pull quotes should summarize the intended message in one or two sentences.

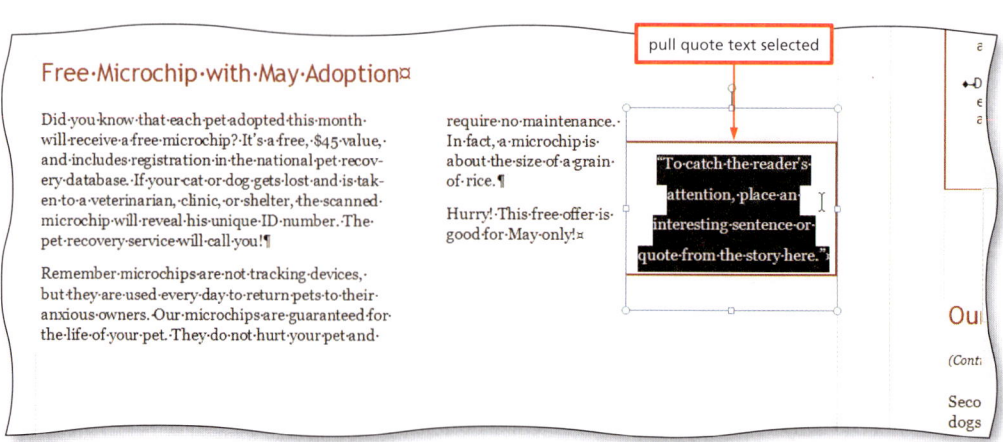

2

- Click to select the pull quote placeholder text to the right of the story (Figure 3–48).

Figure 3–48

❸

- Press CTRL+V to paste the sentence from the Clipboard.

- Click the Paste Options button and then click the 'Keep Text Only' button to accept the destination formatting (Figure 3–49).

Q&A How would I insert a pull quote if one did not exist?

Click the Page Parts button (Insert tab | Building Blocks group) to display the Page Parts gallery. Choose a pull quote in the Pull Quotes area. When the pull quote appears in the publication, move it to the desired location and then edit the text.

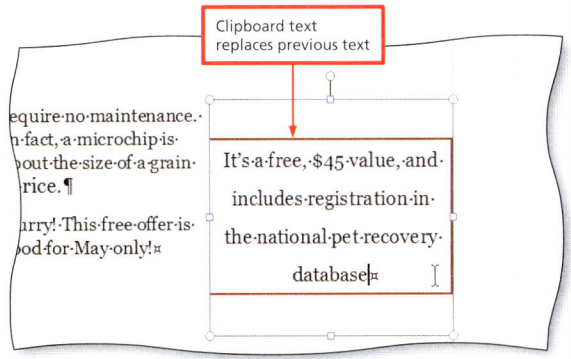

Figure 3–49

To Edit the Calendar

The following steps edit the calendar on page 3. On the left side of the calendar is a bulleted list similar to that on page 1. On the right side is a table of dates. Each date is a text box that you can edit. You will learn more about tables in a later module.

❶ Navigate to the top of page 3 and zoom to approximately 110%.

❷ Click the Schedule of Events bulleted list. Type the following list, pressing the ENTER key at the end of every line except the last:

```
Open Monday through Saturday 10:00 a.m. - 7:00 p.m.

Featured animals by week

May 6: Manners for People and Pups

Second Wednesday of each month: Board Meeting at 7:00 p.m.

May 15: Adoption Clinic 5:00 p.m.

May 20: Grand Reopening

Closed May 29 for Memorial Day
```

❸ Click to the right of the number on the first Monday of the calendar. Press the ENTER key and then type   `Puppy`   as the notation. Do not press the ENTER key after typing the word.

❹ Using Figure 3–50 as a guide, enter the other calendar date notations in a similar manner (Figure 3–50).

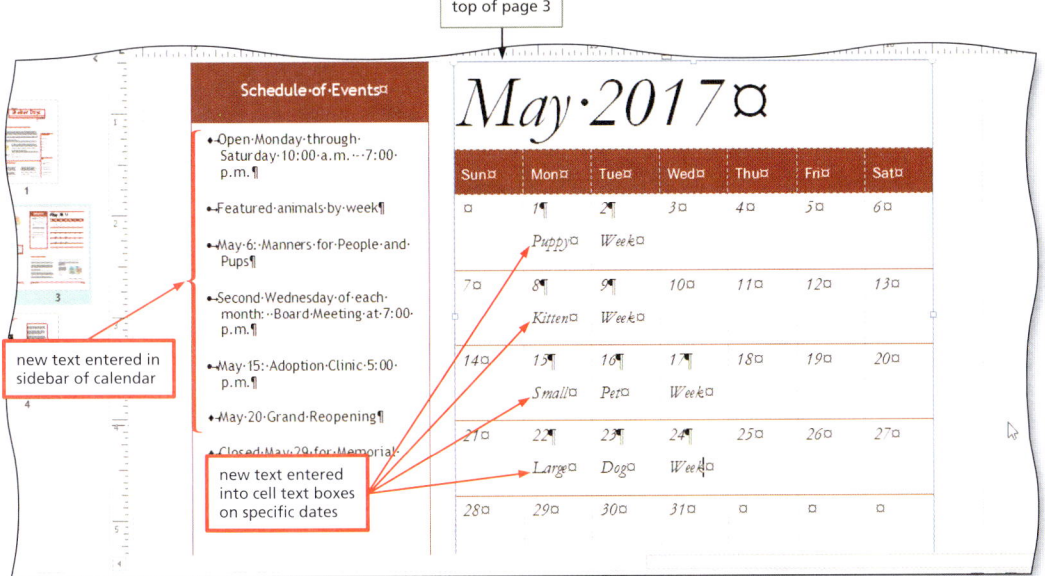

Figure 3–50

Using Graphics in a Newsletter

Marginal elements and stories in newsletters often contain graphics and pictures. Most graphic designers employ a simple technique for deciding how many graphics are too many: They hold the publication at arm's length and glance at it. Then, closing their eyes, they count the number of things they remember. Remembering more than five graphics indicates too many; fewer than two indicates too few. Without question, graphics can make or break a publication. The world has come to expect them. Used correctly, graphics enhance the text, attract the eye, and brighten the look of the publication. If you use graphics from the web, make sure you review the copyright licenses to ensure you can comply with copyright restrictions.

CONSIDER THIS

How do you decide on the best layout?

As you insert graphics and arrange stories, follow any guidelines from the authors or from the company for which you are creating the newsletter. Together, determine the best layout for visual appeal and reliable dissemination of content. Make any required changes. Print a copy and mark the places where sidebars and pull quotes would make sense. Verify that all photos have captions.

In newsletters, you should use photos as true-to-life representations for stories about employees, services, and products. Drawings, on the other hand, can explain, instruct, entertain, or represent images for which you have no picture. The careful use of graphics can add flair and distinction to your publication.

To Replace a Graphic Using the Shortcut Menu

1 EDIT PUBLICATION OPTIONS | 2 IMPORT & CONNECT STORIES | 3 USE CONTINUED NOTICES | 4 CUSTOMIZE RIBBON

5 EDIT USING WORD | **6 INSERT MARGINAL ELEMENTS** | 7 APPLY DROP CAPS & HYPHENATE | 8 CREATE TEMPLATE

The following steps replace a graphic using the shortcut menu. *Why? Using the shortcut menu is a quick way to change a picture without having to navigate the ribbon.* To complete these steps, you will be required to use the Data Files. Please contact your instructor for information about accessing the Data Files.

1

- Navigate to page 1.

- Click the graphic and caption in the lead story and then click the graphic again to select only the graphic.

- Press the F9 key to zoom the object to 100%.

- Right-click the graphic to display the shortcut menu and then point to Change Picture on the shortcut menu to display the Change Picture submenu (Figure 3–51).

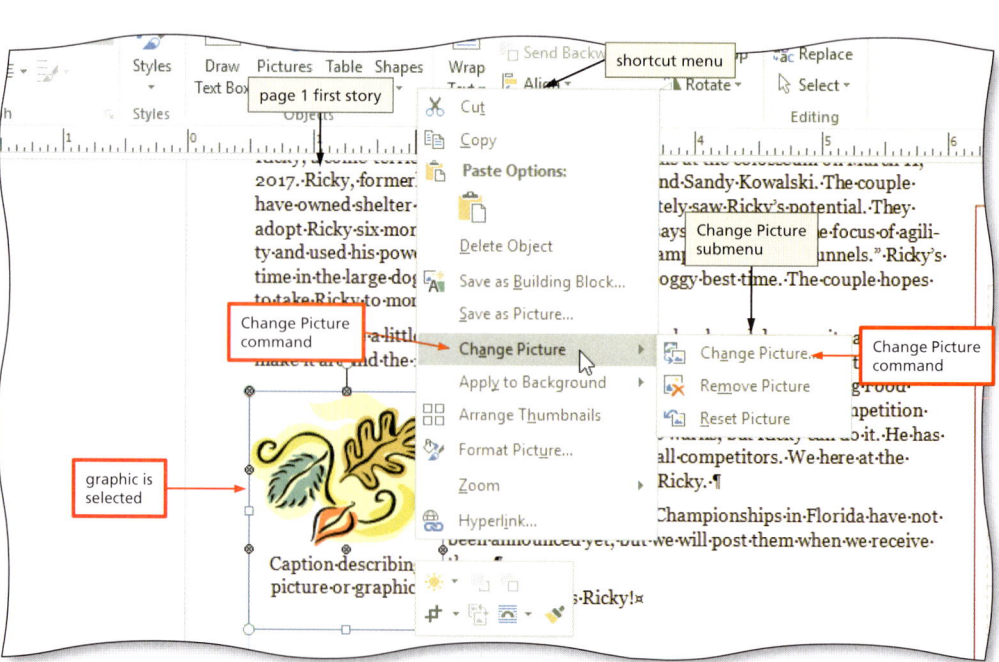

Figure 3–51

2

- Click Change Picture on the Change Picture submenu to display the Insert Pictures dialog box (Figure 3–52).

Q&A What do the other choices on the Change Picture submenu do?
The Remove Picture command deletes the picture but retains the picture placeholder. The Reset Picture command removes any previous cropping or resizing.

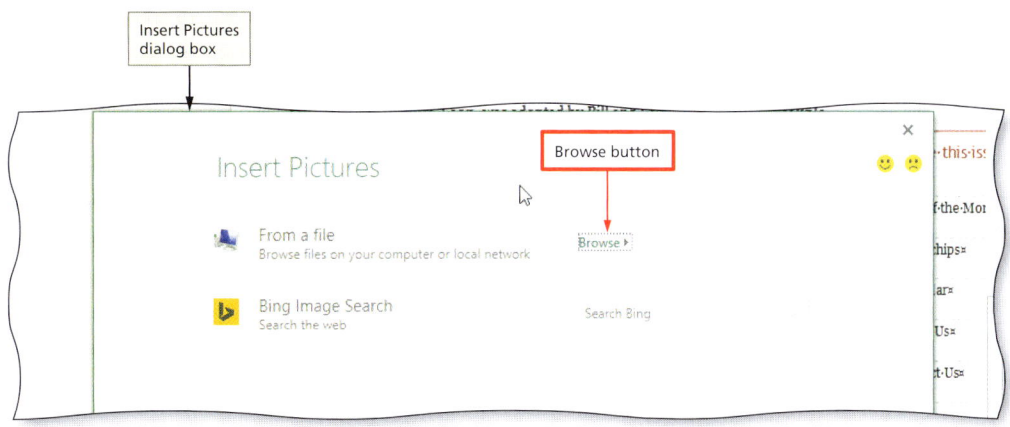

Insert Pictures dialog box

Browse button

Insert Pictures

From a file
Browse files on your computer or local network   Browse ▸

Bing Image Search
Search the web   Search Bing

Figure 3–52

3

- Click the Browse button (Insert Pictures dialog box) in the From a file area to display the Insert Picture dialog box.

- Navigate to the location of the Data Files and double-click the file named Ricky to replace the picture.

- Select the placeholder text in the caption and then type `Ricky wins!` to replace the caption (Figure 3–53).

Q&A What if I choose a larger or smaller picture?
Because you are replacing the graphic, rather than inserting a picture, Publisher resizes the picture to fit the space. The picture automatically is scaled in proportion.

Ricky picture inserted

new caption text

Figure 3–53

To Replace the Graphic and Caption on Page 2

The following steps use the Bing Image Search to locate a picture of a kitten. If you cannot find the specific image, you may use another appropriate image. Make sure you review the license to ensure you can comply with copyright laws. The size of your pictures may vary. If you want to use the exact image shown in the figures, you may retrieve the image from the Data Files. Please contact your instructor for information about accessing the Data Files.

1 Navigate to the top of page 2.

2 Select only the graphic beside the first story. Right-click the graphic, point to Change Picture on the shortcut menu, and then click Change Picture on the Change Picture submenu to display the Insert Pictures dialog box.

3 Type `kitten` in the Bing Image Search box and then press the ENTER key to begin the search.

4 Scroll as necessary in the Bing Image Search dialog box and then double-click a picture similar to the one in Figure 3–54 to replace the graphic.

5 Replace the caption by typing, `Molly is a sweetie!` as the caption text (Figure 3–54).

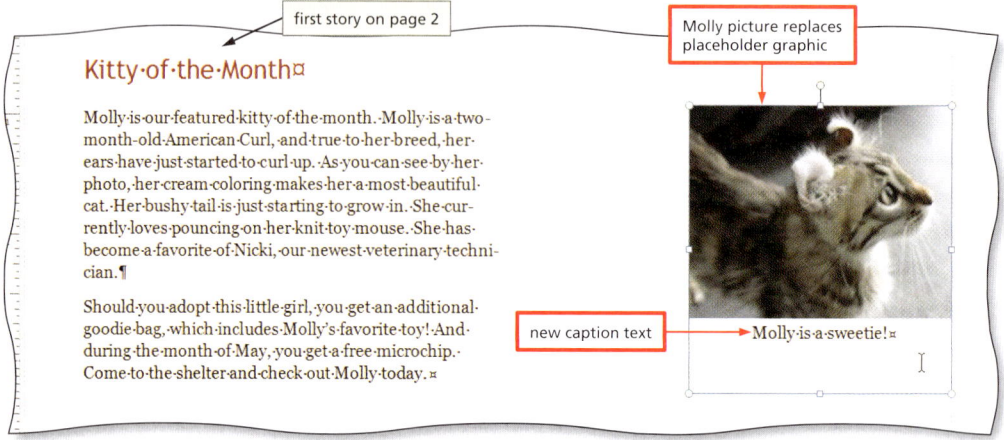

Figure 3–54

To Replace the Graphic and Caption on Page 3

The following steps use the Bing Image Search to locate a picture of an animal shelter. If you cannot find the specific image, you may use another appropriate image. Make sure you review the license to ensure you can comply with its restrictions. The size of your pictures may vary. If you want to use the exact image shown in the figures, you may retrieve the image from the Data Files. Please contact your instructor for information about accessing the Data Files.

1 Navigate to the bottom of page 3.

2 Right click the existing graphic and use the shortcut menu to replace the graphic. Use a Bing Image Search for the term, animal shelter. Use a graphic similar to the one in Figure 3–55.

3 Replace the caption by typing, `Brisbane County Animal Shelter` as the caption text.

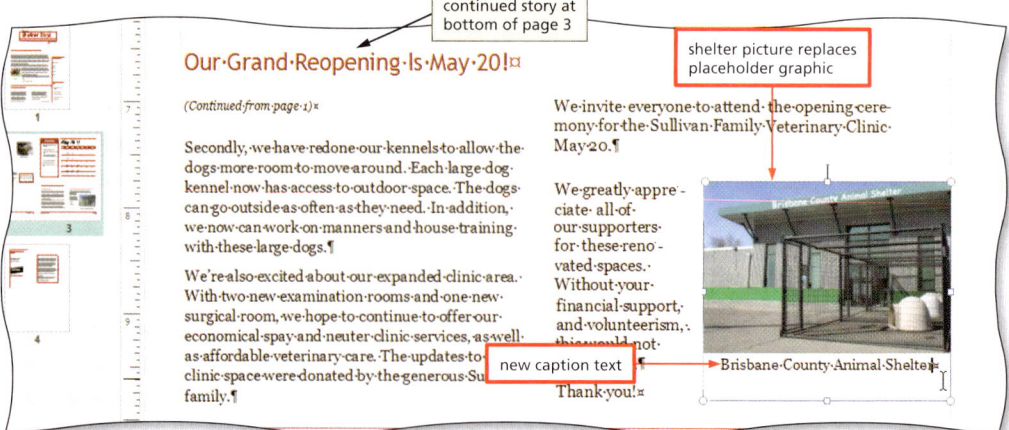

Figure 3–55

To Insert a Graphic on Page 2

The following steps insert a graphic on page 2 from the Data Files. Please contact your instructor for information about accessing the Data Files.

1 Navigate to the bottom of page 2.

2 Display the Insert tab.

3 Click the Pictures button (Insert tab | Illustrations group) to display the Insert Picture dialog box.

4 Navigate to the Data Files and then insert the Coupon graphic.

5 In the publication, drag the graphic to the empty space at the bottom of page 2.

6 Click outside the graphic to deselect it (Figure 3–56).

Figure 3–56

To Insert Graphics on Page 4

The following steps insert graphics on page 4 from the Data Files. Please contact your instructor for information about accessing the Data Files.

1 Navigate to page 4. One at a time, insert the Facebook graphic and the Twitter graphic. Resize if necessary and then move the graphics to a location below the Facebook notation in the middle of the page (Figure 3–57).

2 Click the Save button on the Quick Access Toolbar to save the file again, with the same file name and in the same location.

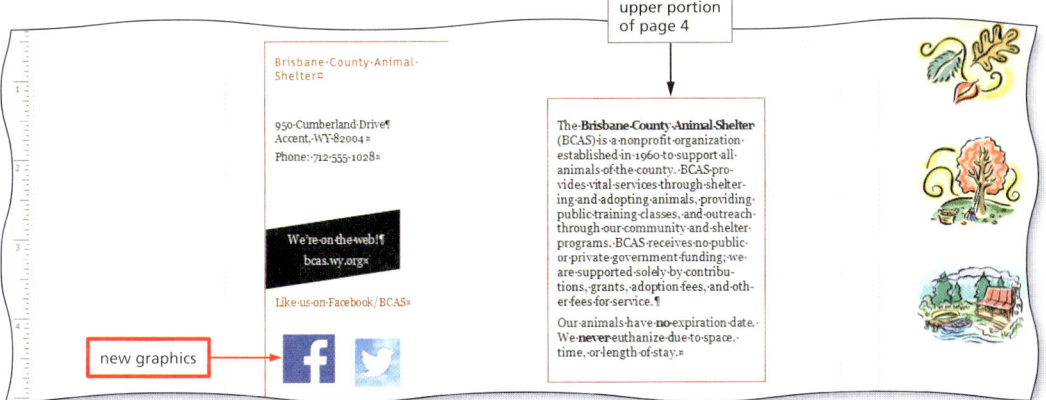

Figure 3–57

Break Point: If you wish to take a break, this is a good place to do so. Exit Publisher. To resume at a later time, run Publisher, open the file called Shelter Newsletter, and continue following the steps from this location forward.

BTW
Conserving Ink and Toner
If you want to conserve ink or toner, you can instruct Publisher to print draft quality documents by tapping or clicking File on the ribbon to open the Backstage view and then tapping or clicking the Print tab in the Backstage view to display the Print gallery. Click the Printer Properties link and then, depending on your printer, click the Print Quality button and choose Draft in the list. Close the Printer Properties dialog box and then click the Print button as usual.

Revising a Newsletter

As discussed in Module 1, once you complete a publication, you may find it necessary to make changes to it. Before submitting a newsletter to a customer or printing service, you should proofread it. While **proofreading**, you look for grammatical errors and spelling errors. You want to be sure the layout, graphics, and stories make sense. If you find errors, you must correct, make changes to, or edit the newsletter. Other readers, perhaps customers or editors, may want to proofread your publication and make changes, such as moving text or adding embellishments, such as a drop cap. You also should check how Publisher has hyphenated your stories.

CONSIDER THIS

How should you proofread and revise a newsletter?
As you proofread the newsletter, look for ways to improve it. Check all grammar, spelling, and punctuation. Be sure the text is logical and transitions are smooth. Where necessary, add text, delete text, reword text, and move text to different locations. Ask yourself these questions:

• Does the title suggest the topic?

• Does the first line of the story entice the reader to continue?

• Is the purpose of the newsletter clear?

• Are all sources acknowledged?

The final phase of the design process is a synthesis involving proofreading, editing, and publishing. Publisher offers several methods to check for errors in your newsletter. None of these methods is a replacement for careful reading and proofreading.

To Create a Drop Cap

1 EDIT PUBLICATION OPTIONS | 2 IMPORT & CONNECT STORIES | 3 USE CONTINUED NOTICES | 4 CUSTOMIZE RIBBON
5 EDIT USING WORD | 6 INSERT MARGINAL ELEMENTS | 7 APPLY DROP CAPS & HYPHENATE | 8 CREATE TEMPLATE

A dropped capital letter, or **drop cap**, is a decorative, large initial capital letter extending down below the other letters in the line. If the text wraps to more than one line, the paragraph typically wraps around the dropped capital letter. The following steps create a dropped capital letter M to begin the word, Molly, in the story on page 2. **Why?** *A drop cap will set off the paragraph and draw the reader's eye toward the beginning of the story.*

1

• Navigate to page 2 and then click to the left of the letter, M, at the beginning of the story about Molly to position the insertion point. Zoom to approximately 120%.

• Display the Text Box Tools Format tab.

• Click the Drop Cap button (Text Box Tools Format tab | Typography group) to display the Drop Cap gallery (Figure 3–58).

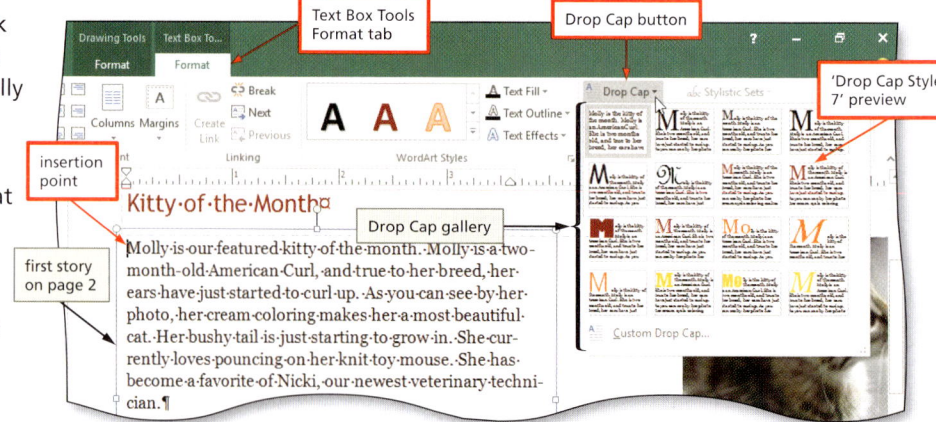

Figure 3–58

Experiment

• Point to each of the available drop caps in the Drop Cap gallery to preview the different styles.

2

• Click the 'Drop Cap Style 7' preview to select it (Figure 3–59).

Q&A Will this drop cap look inconsistent with the other fonts on the page?
The font is still Georgia, which will match the rest of the paragraph's characters.

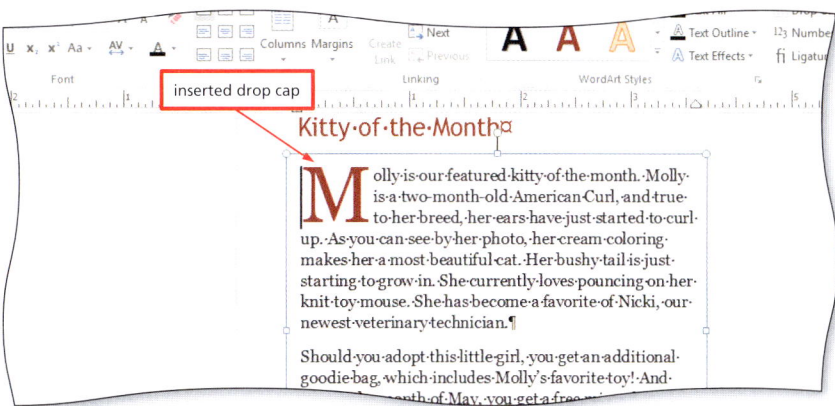

Figure 3–59

To Customize a Drop Cap

1 EDIT PUBLICATION OPTIONS | 2 IMPORT & CONNECT STORIES | 3 USE CONTINUED NOTICES | 4 CUSTOMIZE RIBBON
5 EDIT USING WORD | 6 INSERT MARGINAL ELEMENTS | **7 APPLY DROP CAPS & HYPHENATE** | **8 CREATE TEMPLATE**

The Drop Cap dialog box allows you to customize the drop cap. You can format the number of lines in the drop cap or even change it to an **up cap**, in which the larger letter extends up above the rest of the text. You also can change the font, font style, and color of the text.

Once created, the customized style is added to the Drop Cap gallery for the current publication. ***Why?*** *Publisher makes it available to use in other portions of the publication, if desired.* The following steps change the drop cap size to two lines.

1

• With the insertion point still positioned before the desired letter (in this case, the M of Molly), click the Drop Cap button (Text Box Tools Format tab | Typography group) again to display the Drop Cap gallery (Figure 3–60).

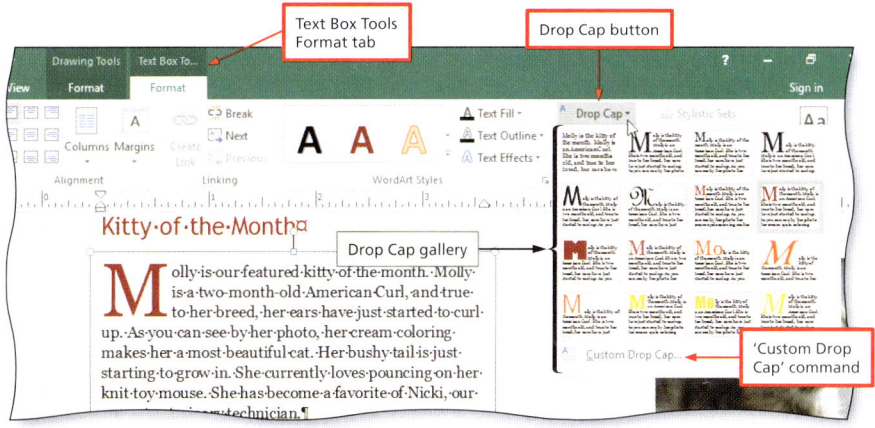

Figure 3–60

2

• Click 'Custom Drop Cap' at the bottom of the gallery to display the Drop Cap dialog box.

• Click the 'Size of letters' down arrow until the height of the drop cap is 2 lines high (Figure 3–61).

Experiment

• Change other settings in the Drop Cap dialog box and watch the contents of the Preview area change. When you are finished experimenting, return all options to the settings in Figure 3–61.

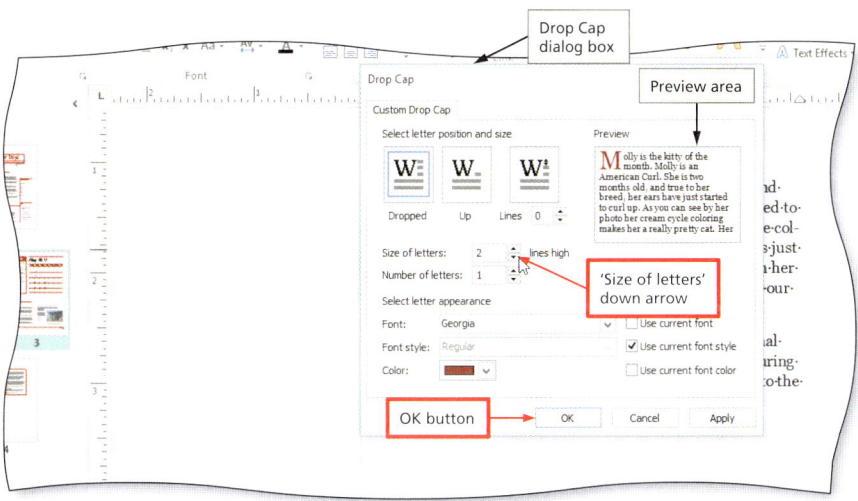

Figure 3–61

3

- Click the OK button (Drop Cap dialog box) to apply the formatting (Figure 3–62).

Q&A

Is a drop cap limited to a single letter?

No, you can format up to 15 contiguous letters and spaces as drop caps at the beginning of each paragraph.

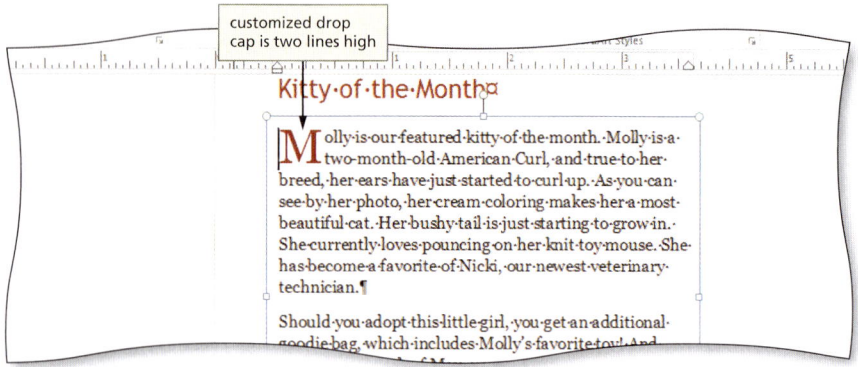

customized drop cap is two lines high

Kitty·of·the·Month¤

M olly·is·our·featured·kitty-of-the-month.·Molly·is·a-two-month-old·American·Curl,·and·true·to·her-breed,·her·ears·have·just·started·to·curl·up.·As·you·can-see·by·her·photo,·her·cream·coloring·makes·her·a·most-beautiful·cat.·Her·bushy·tail·is·just·starting·to·grow·in.·She·currently·loves·pouncing·on·her·knit·toy·mouse.·She-has·become·a·favorite·of·Nicki,·our·newest·veterinary-technician.¶

Should·you·adopt·this·little·girl,·you·get·an·additional-goodie·bag,·which·includes·Molly's·favorite·toy! And

Figure 3–62

To Reuse a Customized Drop Cap

1 EDIT PUBLICATION OPTIONS | 2 IMPORT & CONNECT STORIES | 3 USE CONTINUED NOTICES | 4 CUSTOMIZE RIBBON
5 EDIT USING WORD | 6 INSERT MARGINAL ELEMENTS | 7 APPLY DROP CAPS & HYPHENATE | 8 CREATE TEMPLATE

Anytime you use a special feature in a multipage publication, it is a good idea to use it more than once when possible. *Why? That way, your feature does not look like an afterthought or a mistake, but like a conscious design decision.* The following steps use the customized drop cap again for a second story.

1

- Navigate to the second story on page 2.

- Position the insertion point before the letter, D, in the word, Did, at the beginning of the story.

- Click the Drop Cap button (Text Box Tools Format tab | Typography group) to display the Drop Cap gallery (Figure 3–63).

2

- Click 'Custom Drop Cap Number 1' in the gallery to apply the recently created drop cap.

Figure 3–63

Moving Text

If you decide to move text, such as words, characters, sentences, or paragraphs, you first select the text to be moved and then use drag-and-drop editing or the cut-and-paste technique to move the selected text. With **drag-and-drop editing**, you drag the selected item to the new location and then insert, or drop, it there. Moving text in this manner does not transfer data to the Office Clipboard or the Windows Clipboard, nor does it cause Publisher to display the Paste Options button. Any format changes to the text must be made manually.

When moving text between pages, use the cut-and-paste method. When moving text a long distance or between apps, use the Office Clipboard task pane to cut and paste. When moving text a short distance, the drag-and-drop technique is more efficient; thus, the following steps demonstrate drag-and-drop editing.

To Drag and Drop Text

1 EDIT PUBLICATION OPTIONS | 2 IMPORT & CONNECT STORIES | 3 USE CONTINUED NOTICES | 4 CUSTOMIZE RIBBON
5 EDIT USING WORD | 6 INSERT MARGINAL ELEMENTS | **7 APPLY DROP CAPS & HYPHENATE** | **8 CREATE TEMPLATE**

The editor of the newsletter has decided that two paragraphs on page 3 should be inverted. ***Why?*** *The editor feels that the story will read better with the change.* The following steps move paragraphs by dragging and dropping.

- Navigate to the continued story at the bottom of page 3.

- Triple-click to select the next to the last paragraph (Figure 3–64).

Q&A Could I drag to select the paragraph?
Yes; however, it is more efficient to triple-click, which automatically selects the entire paragraph and the paragraph mark at the end.

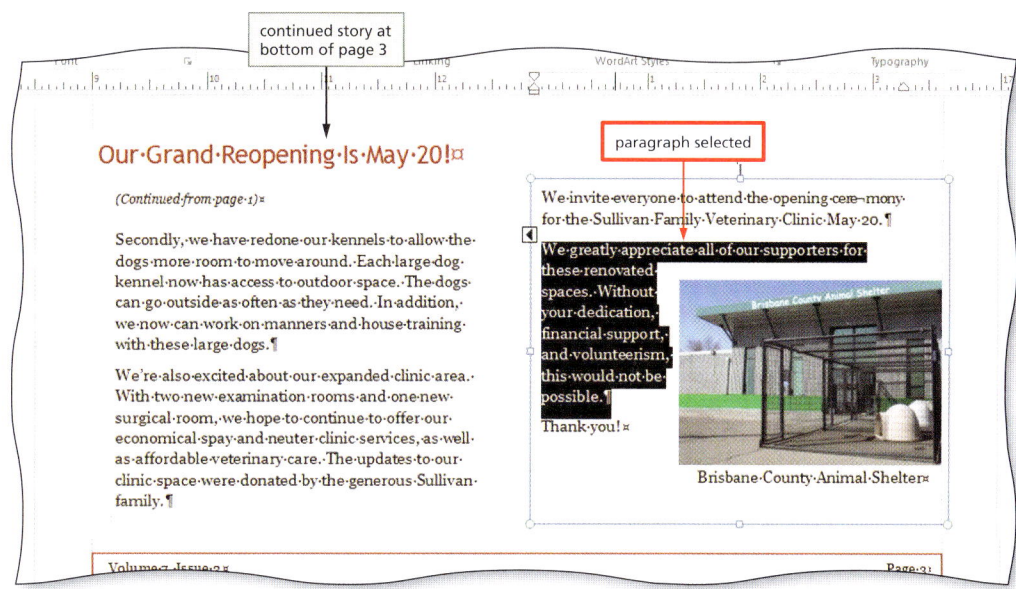

Figure 3–64

- Drag the selection to the beginning of the previous paragraph. Do not release the mouse button (Figure 3–65).

Q&A I am not able to drag the selection. What did I do wrong?
It may be that someone has turned off drag-and-drop editing. Click File on the ribbon to open the Backstage view. Click the Options tab and then click Advanced in the Publisher Options dialog box. Make sure a check mark appears in the 'Allow text to be dragged and dropped' check box.

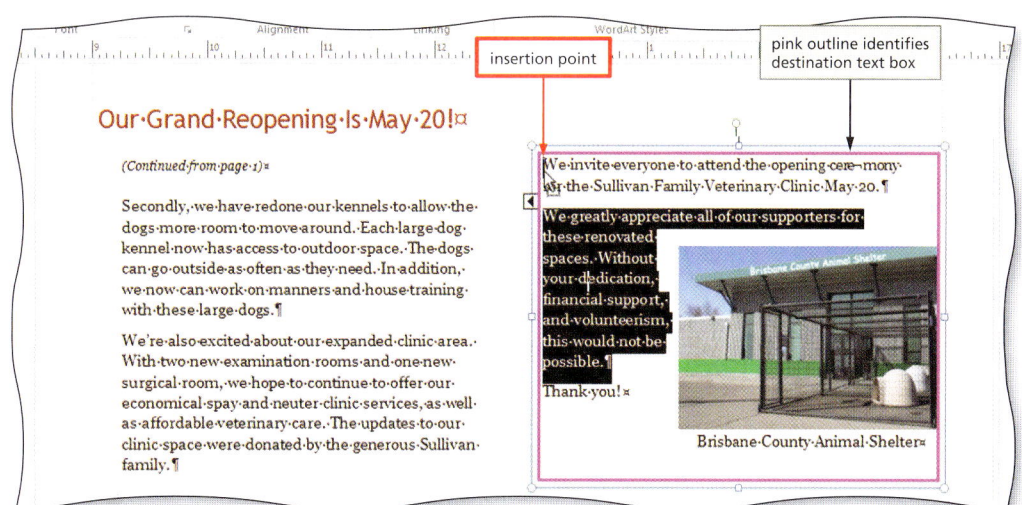

Figure 3–65

3

- Release the mouse button (or, if you are using a touch screen, lift your finger) to move the selected text to the location of the pointer.

- Click outside the selection to deselect (Figure 3–66).

Q&A

What if I accidentally drag text to the wrong location?

Click the Undo button on the Quick Access Toolbar or press CTRL+Z and try again.

Can I use drag-and-drop editing to move any selected item?

Yes, you can select words, sentences, phrases, and graphics and then use drag-and-drop editing to move them.

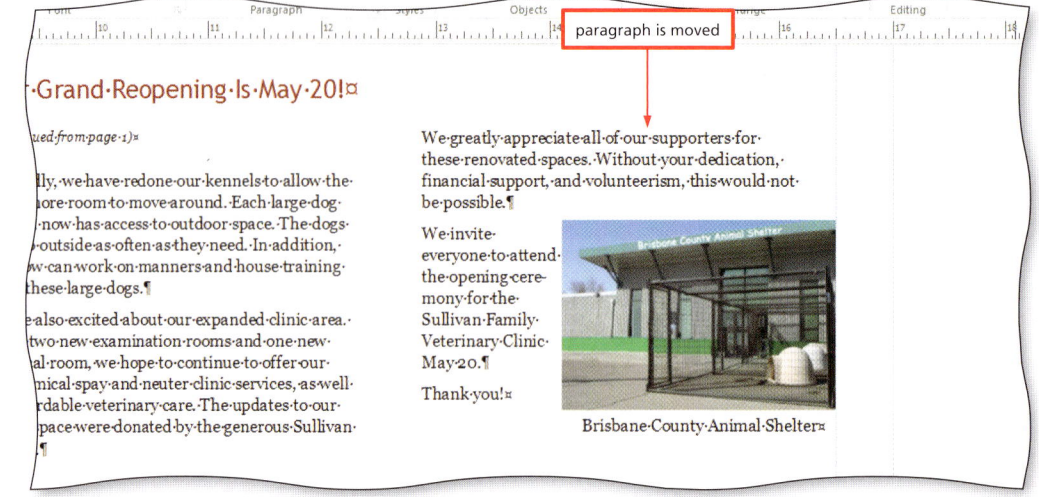

Figure 3–66

To Check the Spelling and Design

The following steps check the entire publication for spelling errors and then run the Design Checker.

1 Press the F7 key to begin the spelling check in the current location, which in this case is inside the caption text box.

2 If Publisher flags any words, choose the correct spelling in the Suggestions list, click the Change button (Check Spelling dialog box), and then continue the spelling check until the next error is identified or the end of the text box is reached.

3 Click the Yes button (Microsoft Publisher dialog box) to tell Publisher to check the rest of the publication. If the publication displays a different error, correct or ignore it as necessary.

4 Click the OK button (Microsoft Publisher dialog box) to close the dialog box.

5 Click File on the ribbon to open the Backstage view and, by default, select the Info tab.

6 Click the 'Run Design Checker' button in the Info gallery to display the Design Checker task pane.

7 If your publication has problems other than objects near the margin, point to the error in the Select an item to fix list (Design Checker task pane). When an arrow appears on the right side of the error, click the arrow and then click 'Go to this Item' on the menu. Fix or ignore the flagged item as necessary.

8 Click the Close button on the Design Checker task pane to close the Design Checker and return to the publication.

Hyphenation

Hyphenation refers to splitting a word that otherwise would extend beyond the right margin. Because Publisher bases hyphenation only on words in its dictionary, it is a good idea to review the hyphenation. Publisher's hyphenation feature allows you to hyphenate the text automatically or manually, insert optional or **nonbreaking hyphens**, and set the maximum amount of space allowed between a word and the right margin without hyphenating the word. When you use **automatic hyphenation**, Publisher automatically inserts hyphens where they are needed. When you use **manual hyphenation**, Publisher searches for the text to hyphenate and asks you whether you want to insert the hyphens in the text. Some rules for hyphenation include:

- Hyphenate only at standard syllable breaks.
- Do not change the hyphen location of words that already are hyphenated.
- Avoid hyphenating words in the first or last line of a paragraph.
- Avoid hyphenations that leave only two letters at the beginning or end of a line.
- Avoid hyphenating two lines in a row.
- Avoid hyphenating a line across text boxes or pages.
- Avoid hyphenating proper nouns.

BTW

Choosing a Different Hyphenation Location

When using the Hyphenation dialog box, Publisher shows all the possible hyphenation locations at appropriate syllable breaks (shown in Figure 3–68). The current choice is highlighted in blue. You can choose to hyphenate at one of the other places in the word by clicking the hyphen and then clicking the Yes button.

To Check Hyphenation

1 EDIT PUBLICATION OPTIONS | 2 IMPORT & CONNECT STORIES | 3 USE CONTINUED NOTICES | 4 CUSTOMIZE RIBBON
5 EDIT USING WORD | 6 INSERT MARGINAL ELEMENTS | 7 APPLY DROP CAPS & HYPHENATE | 8 CREATE TEMPLATE

The following steps hyphenate the stories. *Why? Hyphenating allows you to make decisions about where the hyphens will be placed.* You will choose to hyphenate manually, which means you can specify where the hyphen should occur, or if it should occur, rather than have Publisher hyphenate the story automatically.

1

- Navigate to page 1 and click the lead story.

- Display the Text Box Tools Format tab.

- Click the Hyphenation button (Text Box Tools Format tab | Text group) to display the Hyphenation dialog box (Figure 3–67).

Q&A What is the hyphenation zone? The **hyphenation zone** is the maximum amount of space Publisher allows between a word and the right margin without hyphenating the word. To reduce the number of hyphens, increase the hyphenation zone. To reduce the ragged edge of the right margin, decrease the hyphenation zone.

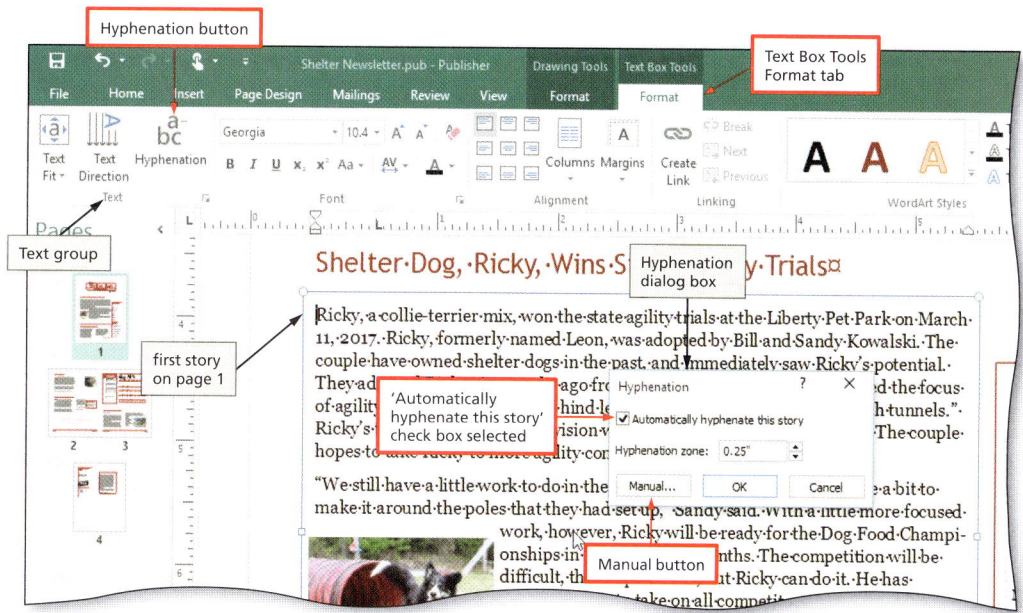

Figure 3–67

2

- Click to remove the check mark in the 'Automatically hyphenate this story' check box (Hyphenation dialog box shown in Figure 3-67).

- Click the Manual button (Hyphenation dialog box) to hyphenate the story manually and to display the Hyphenate dialog box, which displays the first hyphenation choice (Figure 3-68).

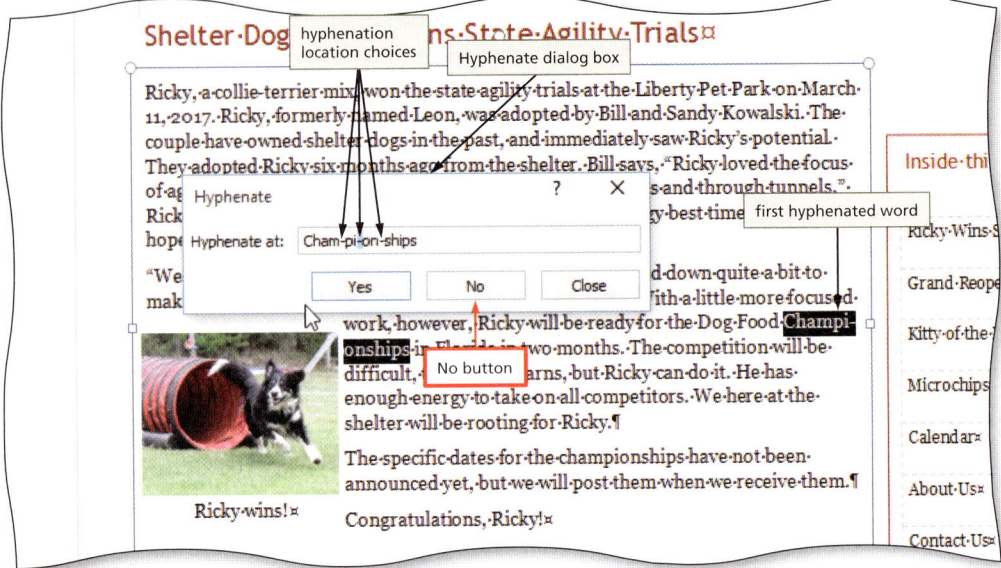

Figure 3-68

Q&A Why is the text already hyphenated?
The default value is automatic hyphenation. Publisher hyphenates after the standard syllables.

3

- Click the No button (Hyphenate dialog box) because this word, Championship, is a proper noun.

- If Publisher stops at the word, announced, click the No button because this word is on the first line of the third paragraph and it results in two-character hyphenation. When no other hyphenation choices exist in the current story, Publisher will display a dialog box as shown in Figure 3-69.

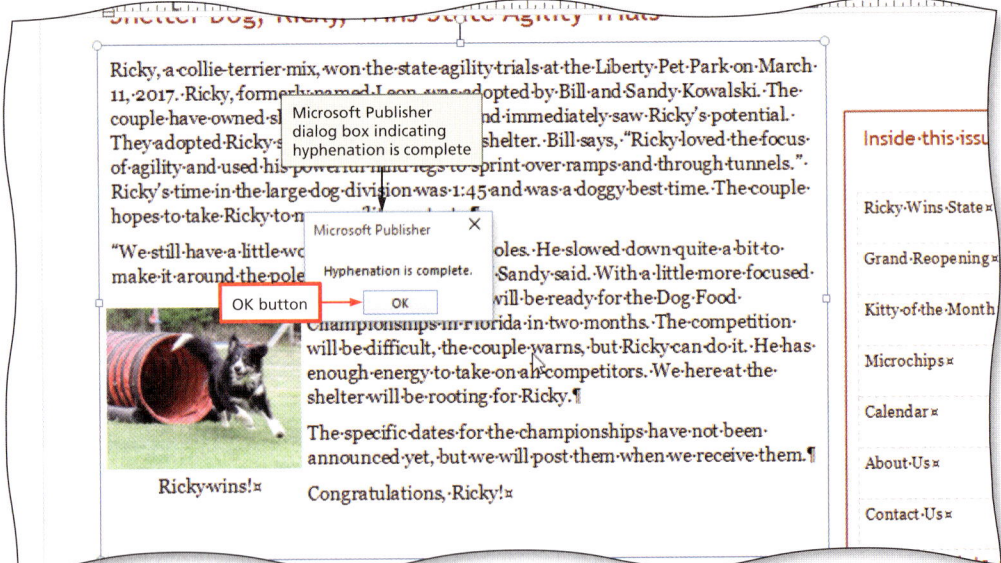

Figure 3-69

Q&A My hyphenation stopped on a different word. What should I do?
Because of fonts and resolution, your system may stop at a different word. Use the rules discussed in this module to evaluate your word and choose the correct hyphenation.

4

- Click the OK button when the hyphenation for the story is complete.

- One at a time, repeat Steps 1 through 3 for the other stories and sidebars in the publication, adjusting the hyphens as necessary.

- Continue to click the Yes or No button (Hyphenation dialog box) using the hyphenation rules listed previously.

Q&A What sort of hyphenation issues might I find?

You may have to choose to hyphenate at a different location by clicking the hyphen in the Hyphenate dialog box. You may find the hyphenation correct, in which case you will click the Yes button. Or, you may decide not to hyphenate because it would create two hyphens in a row.

5

• When you are finished hyphenating all of the stories, click the Save button on the Quick Access Toolbar to overwrite the previously saved file.

Other Ways

1. Press CTRL+SHIFT+H, choose settings, click OK button (Hyphenation dialog box), make hyphenation choices, click OK button (Microsoft Publisher dialog box)

To Print the Newsletter

1 EDIT PUBLICATION OPTIONS | 2 IMPORT & CONNECT STORIES | 3 USE CONTINUED NOTICES | 4 CUSTOMIZE RIBBON
5 EDIT USING WORD | 6 INSERT MARGINAL ELEMENTS | **7 APPLY DROP CAPS & HYPHENATE** | **8 CREATE TEMPLATE**

While it often is cheaper in business situations to outsource newsletter printing, you may want to print a copy on a desktop printer. ***Why?*** *Printing will allow you to proofread more easily and also assess the look and feel of the newsletter.*

If you have access to a printer that can accept **tabloid** size, 17 × 11.5 inch paper, you can print double-sided and then fold the paper to create the newsletter. If you want to print double-sided on 8.5 × 11 inch paper, the newsletter will print on the back and front of two pages that you then can staple. The following steps make choices about printing the newsletter.

1

• Click File on the ribbon to open the Backstage view and then click the Print tab to display the Print gallery.

• In the Settings area, click the 'One page per sheet' button to display its list (Figure 3–70).

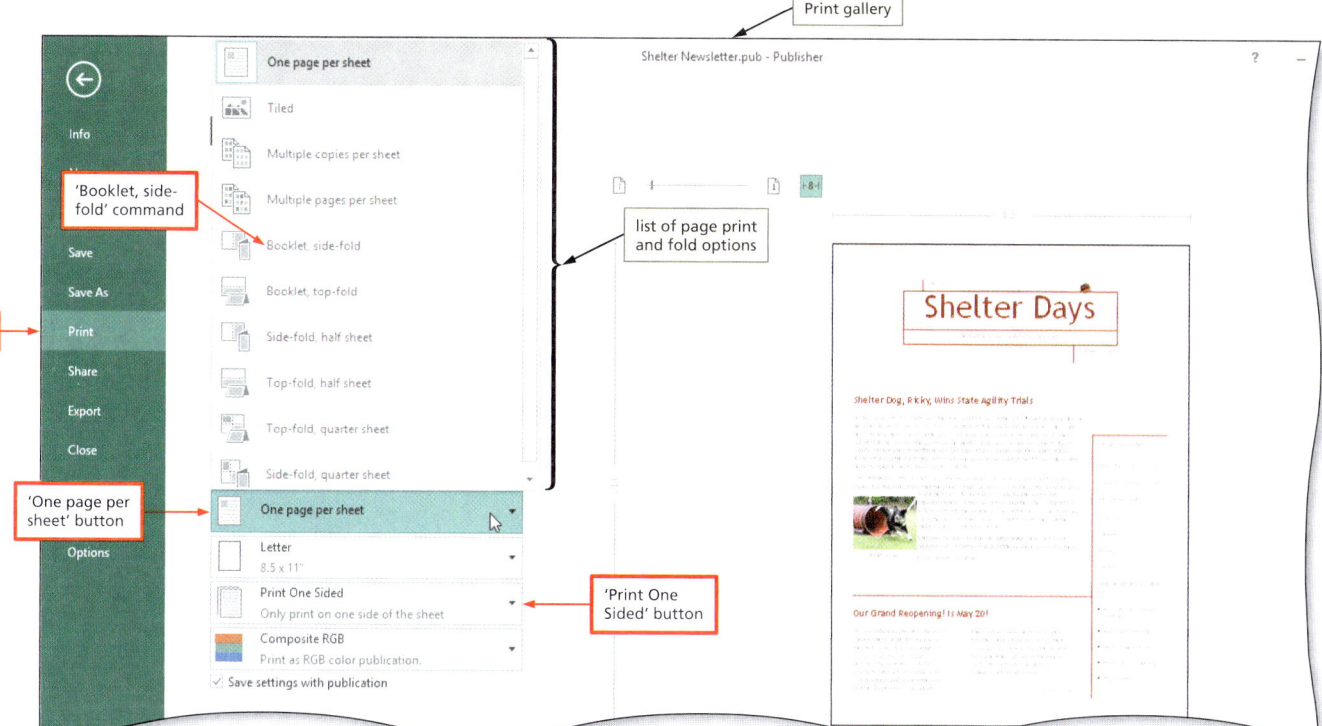

Figure 3–70

2

- Click 'Booklet, side-fold' to specify how the newsletter will print.
- Click the 'Print One Sided' button and then click the appropriate manual or duplex print setting (Figure 3–71).

🔍 **Experiment**

- Click the Back button on the status bar to see the inside two-page spread. If necessary, click the 'Fit to Sheet' button on the Print gallery task bar.

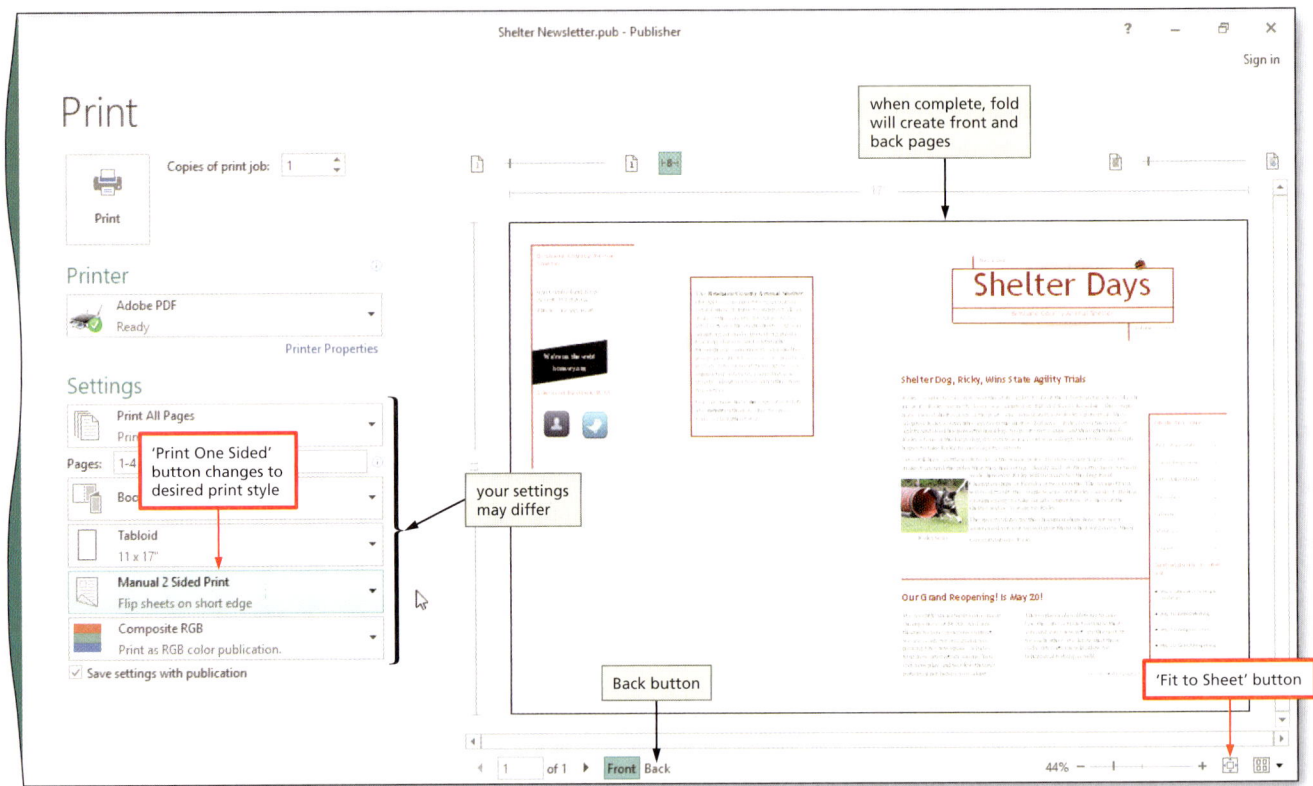

Figure 3–71

 3

- If the printer is capable of handling oversized paper and you have access to 17 × 11.5 inch paper, load the paper into the printer and then click the Print button in the Print gallery.
- If you cannot do oversize printing, click the Backstage view Back button to return to the publication workspace.

Creating a Template

Newsletters typically retain their masthead, color scheme, font scheme, and other graphics from issue to issue. In a first issue, you must make design choices and implement them to make sure the newsletter is displayed correctly, and reviewing that takes time. You will not have to do all of that for subsequent issues. Once the decisions have been made and the publication has been distributed, you can reuse the same publication as a template. Additionally, Publisher allows you to add it to the templates on your computer.

Saving the Template and Setting File Properties

Recall that in the Office and Windows module at the beginning of this book, you set file properties using properties in the Backstage view (Info tab); however, two specific properties can be set at the time you save a publication or template. The author and tag properties can be entered in any of the Save As dialog boxes, which can save you several steps. A **tag** is a custom property that helps you find and organize files.

Where should a company store its templates?

On a business computer, for an organization that routinely uses templates, templates should be saved in the default location. Publisher stores templates within the program data in a folder named, Custom Office Templates. Templates stored in the default location are displayed in the catalog when you click the My Templates button. Templates, however, can be stored in several places: on a personal computer, on a web server, or on a common drive for use by multiple employees or students.

To Create a Template with Property Changes

1 EDIT PUBLICATION OPTIONS | 2 IMPORT & CONNECT STORIES | 3 USE CONTINUED NOTICES | 4 CUSTOMIZE RIBBON | 5 EDIT USING WORD | 6 INSERT MARGINAL ELEMENTS | 7 APPLY DROP CAPS & HYPHENATE | **8 CREATE TEMPLATE**

The following steps create a template with property changes and save it on a personal storage device. *Why? It is not recommended to save templates on lab computers or computers belonging to other people, because you may not want others to use your templates due to privacy issues.*

- Click File on the ribbon to open the Backstage view.
- Click the Export tab, and then click the 'Change File Type' tab to display the Save Publication gallery.
- Click Template in the Publisher File Types area to save the file as a Publisher template (Figure 3–72).

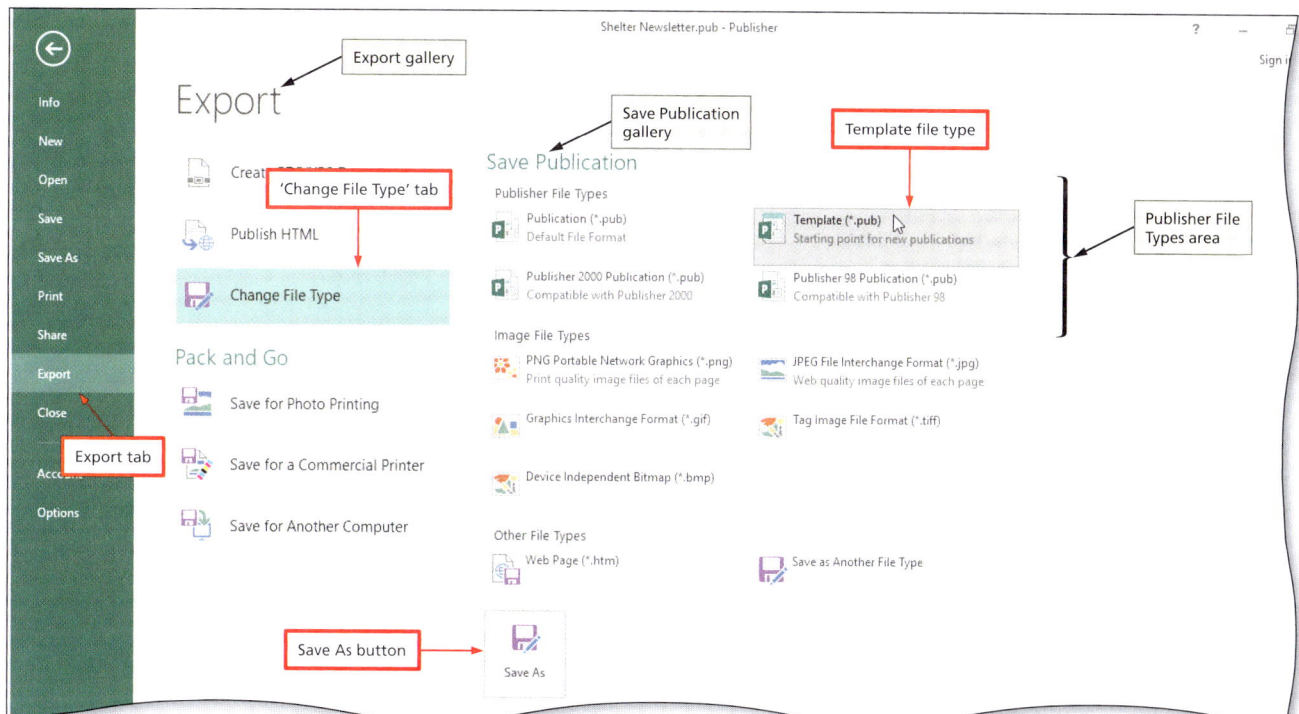

Figure 3–72

2

- Click the Save As button to display the Save as Template dialog box.

- Type `Newsletter Template` to change the name of the publication. Do not press the ENTER key.

- Navigate to your preferred storage location.

  If requested by your instructor, double-click the Authors text box in the lower portion of the dialog box and then type your name to replace the text.

- Click the Tags text box and then type `monthly newsletter` to add the tag words (Figure 3–73). The current text in the Tags text box will disappear as you start to type.

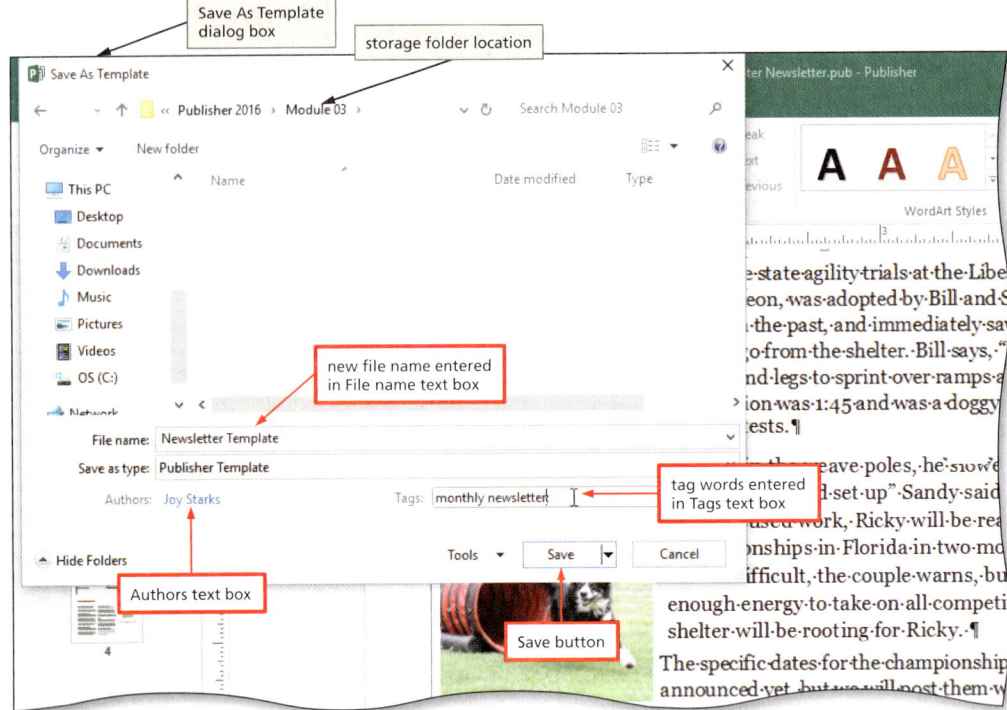

Figure 3–73

Q&A Can I make the newsletter template read-only so that users will have to save updates with a different file name?
Yes. After saving and exiting Publisher, open the File Explorer window. Right-click the file name, click Properties on the shortcut menu, and then place a check mark in the Read-only attribute (Publication Properties dialog box | General tab).

3

- Click the Save button (Save As dialog box) to save the template.

Other Ways

1. In Backstage view, click Save As, choose location (Save As dialog box), enter name of newsletter, click 'Save as type' button, click Publisher Template, click Save button

To Remove All Ribbon Customization and Exit Publisher

When working in a lab environment, it is advisable to remove the ribbon customization. The following steps remove all ribbon customization.

1 Click File on the ribbon to open the Backstage view and then click Options to display the Publisher Options dialog box.

2 Click Customize Ribbon in the left pane (Publisher Options dialog box) to display the options for customizing the ribbon.

3 Click the Reset button (Publisher Options dialog box) and then click 'Reset all customizations' in the list.

4 Click the Yes button (Microsoft Office dialog box).

5 Click the OK button (Publisher Options dialog box) to close the dialog box.

6 To exit Publisher, click the Close button on the right side of the title bar.

7 If a Microsoft Publisher dialog box is displayed, click the Don't Save button so that any changes you have made are not saved.

Summary

In this module, you learned how to select template options for a newsletter, such as the number of columns and special content. After editing the masthead components, you imported stories from external files and created original stories using the Edit Story in Microsoft Word command. As stories flowed across pages, you inserted continued notices. You edited sidebars, pull quotes, and the calendar. In revising the newsletter, you applied decorative drop caps, used drag-and-drop editing techniques, hyphenated the stories, checked the spelling, and ran the Design Checker. Finally, you saved the newsletter both as a Publisher file and as a Publisher template that the company can edit each month.

What decisions will you need to make when creating your next newsletter?

Use these guidelines as you complete the assignments in this module and create your own publications outside of this class.

1. Decide on the layout.

    a) Select a template and options that matches your need.

    b) Set columns and options for each page purpose and audience.

2. Edit the masthead.

3. Gather the text content.

    a) Import stories when possible.

    b) Edit stories in Microsoft Word when necessary.

    c) Flow long stories to other text boxes.

    d) Format continued stories with continued notices.

4. Create and edit marginal elements.

5. Insert other elements, such as advertisements.

6. Edit graphics and captions.

7. Revise as necessary.

    a) Proofread and check the publication.

    b) Run a hyphenation check.

8. Create a template for future use.

CONSIDER THIS

Apply Your Knowledge

Reinforce the skills and apply the concepts you learned in this module.

Creating a Newsletter

Note: To complete this assignment, you will be required to use the Data Files. Please contact your instructor for information about accessing the Data Files.

Instructions: A fifth-grade teacher would like you to create a newsletter for her class and parents. They have provided some stories and will give you others at a later time. You produce the first page of the newsletter shown in Figure 3–74.

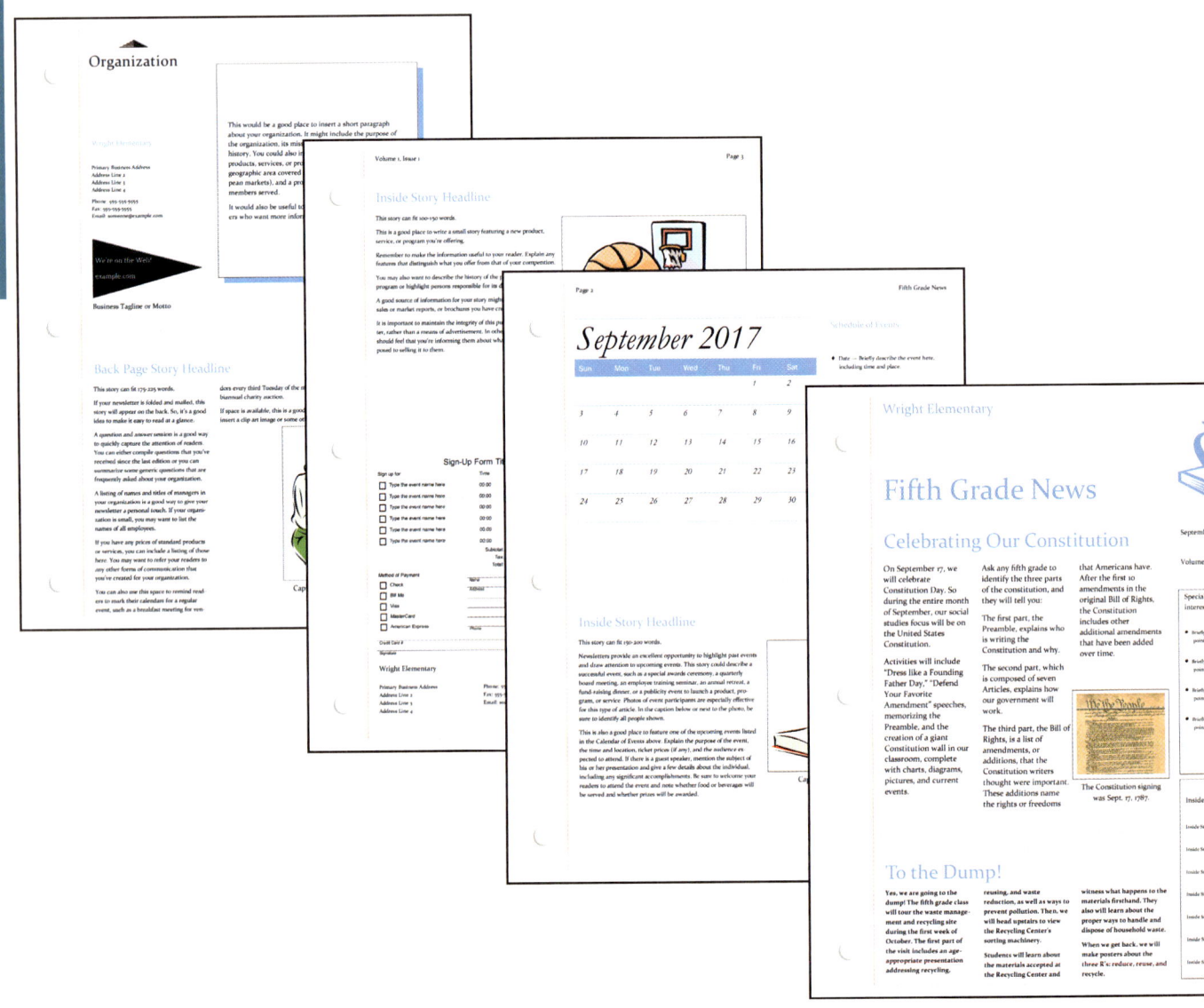

Figure 3–74

Perform the following tasks:

1. Run Publisher. Click BUILT-IN and then click Newsletters.

2. Choose the School newsletter template, the Office color scheme, and the Paper font scheme. Set the Page size to Two-page spread.

3. Create the publication. Navigate to page 2. Use the Options button (Page Design tab | Template group) to include a calendar and a 2-column format on the left inside page. The date of your calendar may differ. Click the Options button (Page Design tab | Template group) again for the right-inside page, and include a sign-up form and a 1-column format.

4. Edit the masthead as shown in Figure 3–74.

5. For the lead story, use the headline, Celebrating Our Constitution. Import the story, Celebrating the Constitution, from the Data Files.

6. Click the Hyphenation button (Text Box Tools format tab | Text group) to display the Hyphenation dialog box. Remove the check mark from the 'Automatically hyphenate this story' check box. Click the Manual button (Hyphenation dialog box) to hyphenate the story manually and to display the first hyphenation choice. Click Yes or No as appropriate, using the rules discussed earlier in this module in the section titled, Hyphenation. Remember that proper names, such as Constitution, should not be hyphenated.

7. If necessary, customize the ribbon to display the 'Edit Story in Microsoft Word' button (Review tab | New Group). Refer to the section in this module titled, To Edit a Story Using Microsoft Word.

8. For the secondary story on page 1, right-click the headline and then click Best Fit on the shortcut menu. Type the headline **To the Dump!** Click the placeholder text of the story. Click the 'Edit Story in Microsoft Word' button (Review tab | New Group). When Word is running, press CTRL+A to select all of the text. Change the font size to 8. Type the following text, pressing the ENTER key at the end of each paragraph except the last:

```
Yes, we are going to the dump! The fifth grade class will tour
the waste management and recycling site during the first week of
October. The first part of the visit includes an age-appropriate
presentation addressing recycling, reusing, and waste reduction, as
well as ways to prevent pollution. Then, we will head upstairs to
view the Recycling Center's sorting machinery.

Students will learn about the materials accepted at the Recycling
Center and witness what happens to the materials firsthand. They
also will learn about the proper ways to handle and dispose of
household waste.

When we get back, we will make posters about the three R's: reduce,
reuse, and recycle.
```

9. Exit Word to return to Publisher. Hyphenate the second story as you did the first (in Step 6).

10. On page 1, click the graphic twice to select it. Use the shortcut menu to change the picture. Use the Bing Image Search to locate photos related to the search term, preamble. (An appropriate image also is included in the Data Files.) Change the caption to read: The Constitution signing was Sept. 17, 1787.

11. If requested by your instructor, change other text and graphics such as the table of contents sidebar, sign-up form, and calendar. Use your name and address at the top of page 4.

12. Save the file with the file name, Apply 3–1 Fifth Grade Newsletter.

13. Remove the ribbon customization as described in the section titled, To Remove All Ribbon Customization and Exit Publisher, earlier in this module.

14. Submit the publication in the format specified by your instructor.

Continued >

Apply Your Knowledge *continued*

15. ✳ Do you think adding a calendar and sign-up form to pages 2 and 3 make them too busy? Why or why not? Would you rather type the story in Step 8 in Publisher or Word? Why?

Extend Your Knowledge

Extend the skills you learned in this module and experiment with new skills. You may need to use Help to complete the assignment.

Creating Page 1 of a Newsletter from Scratch

Instructions: Run Publisher. Your school is planning a first-time callout for a new fellowship club called the Coffee Cup. You have been asked to create a sample page 1, to promote meetings and events. You decide to start from scratch to create the newsletter page shown in Figure 3–75.

Source: Stocksnap.io

Figure 3–75

Perform the following tasks:

1. Click BUILT-IN and then click Newsletters. Scroll to the Blank Sizes area and then click the '1/2 A4 Booklet 5.827 × 8.268' thumbnail to choose a paper size.

2. Choose the Cavern color scheme and the Textbook font scheme. Click the CREATE button to create the publication. When Publisher asks to insert pages automatically, click the Yes button.

3. Use Help to read about Building Blocks. Click the Page Parts button (Insert tab | Building Blocks group) to display the Page Parts gallery and then, in the Headings area, choose the Convention heading to use as a masthead. *Hint:* Point to each heading to see its name. When Publisher inserts the heading, move it to the top of the page. Resize it to fit within the margins.

4. Right-click the Title text, and choose Best Fit on the shortcut menu. Type **THE COFFEE CUP** to change the title. Right-click the subtitle text and then choose Best Fit on the shortcut menu. Change the subtitle to LIBERAL ARTS STUDENT ORGANIZATION.

5. If requested to do so by your instructor, replace the subtitle with the name of your school.

6. Click the Background button (Page Design tab | Page Background group). In the Gradient Background area, click 'Accent 3 Vertical Gradient'.

7. Again using the Page Parts button (Insert tab | Building Blocks group), insert the Convention (Layout 3) sidebar. Resize the sidebar to fit the space below the masthead and at the right margin as shown in Figure 3–75. Your display may differ, depending on how you resize the sidebar.

8. Type **CALL-OUT** to replace the title text. Type **ORGANIZATIONAL MEETING** to replace the sidebar subtitle text. Right-click the text and then click Best Fit on the shortcut menu to autofit the text.

9. Select the text at the bottom of the sidebar. Type **Join us Saturday, Feb. 4, at 10:00 a.m. in the Student Union Coffee Shop for a free cup of coffee with your student ID.** to replace the text.

10. Use the 'Draw Text Box' button (Home tab | Objects group) to add a text box just below the masthead, approximately .5 inches high and 2.5 inches wide. Insert the text, **Volume 1, Issue 1** and then press CTRL+ENTER to create a soft return. Type **Jan. 23, 2017** to insert the date.

11. If instructed to do so, change the date to your birthday.

12. Draw a text box below the masthead, approximately .5 inches tall and 2.5 inches wide. Insert the text, Lead Story Headline, as the new text. Right-click the text and then click Best Fit on the shortcut menu.

13. Draw a text box below the lead story headline to fill the empty space, approximately 4.45 inches tall and 2.5 inches wide.

14. If necessary, customize the ribbon to display the 'Edit Story in Microsoft Word' button (Review tab | New group).

15. Click the first empty text box. Click the 'Edit Story in Microsoft Word' button (Review tab | New group). When Word is displayed, type **=rand(2,3)** and then press the ENTER key to generate random text. Delete any extra hard returns at the end of the text. Exit Word to return to Publisher.

16. Click one of the pictures in the side bar twice, to select only the picture. Replace the picture with a photo you find using the search term, coffee. Repeat the process for the other two pictures.

17. Save the file with the file name, Extend 3–1 Coffee Newsletter.

18. Remove the ribbon customization as described earlier in this module.

19. Submit the file in the format specified by your instructor.

Continued >

Extend Your Knowledge *continued*

20. ✳ When would you use a template instead of creating a newsletter from scratch? What other page parts might you add to subsequent pages? Why?

Expand Your World

Create a solution that uses cloud and web technologies by learning and investigating on your own from general guidance.

Converting Files

Instructions: Run a browser and navigate to zamzar.com (Figure 3–76).You would like to explore converting your newsletter to formats other than the .pub Publisher format. While Publisher has many formats in the Save as type list, a cloud tool may have even more choices.

Figure 3–76

Perform the following tasks:

1. In Step 1 on the Convert Files tab, click the Browse button or the Choose Files button (depending on your browser) and then navigate to one of your completed newsletters.

2. In Step 2, click the 'Convert files(s) to:' box and choose a conversion format, such as html or an e-book format.

3. In Step 3, enter your email address.

4. In Step 4, click the Convert button to send the converted file to your email. If you receive a message indicating the conversion is about to happen, click the OK button.

5. When you receive the email from Zamzar, click the link provided and then click the Download Now button. Your browser should direct you to save the download.

6. If your download is a compressed file, right-click the zipped file to display a shortcut menu. Click Extract or Extract All to extract the file.

7. Open the converted file.

8. Submit the assignment in the format specified by your instructor.

9. ✳ What format might you use to post your newsletter on the web? Would an HTML file be better than a download link? Why or why not? When might you convert to a PDF format?

In the Labs

Design, create, modify, and/or use a publication following the guidelines, concepts, and skills presented in this module. Labs 1 and 2, which increase in difficulty, require you to create solutions based on what you learned in the module; Lab 3 requires you to apply your creative thinking and problem-solving skills to design and implement a solution.

Lab 1: **Creating a Symphony Newsletter**

Note: To complete this assignment, you will be required to use the Data Files. Please contact your instructor for information about accessing the Data Files.

Problem: The symphonic orchestra has asked you to create a newsletter they can distribute to their patrons. Currently, they have given you some content for page 1 and page 4. You are to leave placeholder text and graphics on the inside pages. You create the newsletter shown in Figure 3–77.

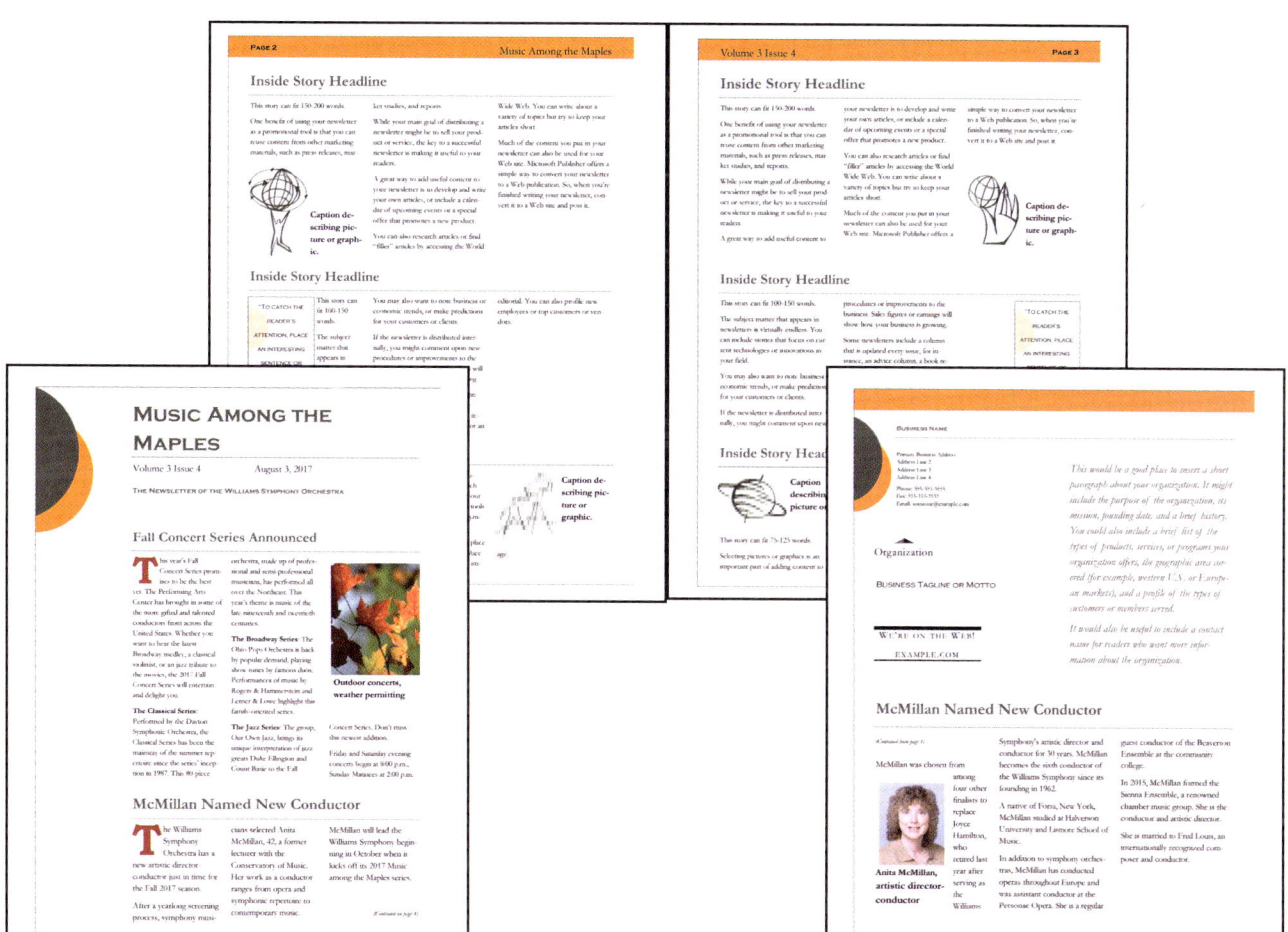

Figure 3–77

Continued >

Perform the following tasks:

1. Run Publisher. In the template gallery, click BUILT-IN and then click Newsletters.

2. In the More Installed Templates area, choose the Eclipse template.

3. Select the Aspect color scheme and the Etched font scheme. Choose to use a two-page spread. Create the publication.

4. As you make changes to the newsletter, scroll and zoom as necessary. Turn on the display of formatting characters if desired.

5. Use the following text to edit the masthead on page 1:

   Newsletter Title: Music Among the Maples

   Volume and Issue: Volume 3 Issue 4

   Newsletter Date: August 3, 2017

   Business Name: The Newsletter of the Williams Symphony Orchestra

6. For the lead story, use the headline, Fall Concert Series Announced. Import the lead story, Fall Concert Series, from the Data Files.

7. Position the insertion point at the beginning of the story. Click the Drop Cap button (Text Box Tools Format tab | Typography group) to display the Drop Cap gallery and then click the 'Drop Cap Style 13' preview.

8. Delete both the Special Points of Interest sidebar and the Inside this Issue sidebar on page 1.

9. Replace the graphic on page 1 using the shortcut menu. Search for the term, maples. Edit the caption to read Outdoor concerts, weather permitting.

10. For the second story on page 1, use McMillan Named New Conductor as the headline. Import the story, McMillan Named New Conductor, from the Data Files. When Publisher prompts you, flow the story to the last story on page 4. Use the same headline on page 4.

11. Navigate to the last text box of the story on page 1. Right-click the story to display the shortcut menu. Click 'Format Text Box' on the shortcut menu to display the Format Text Box dialog box. Click the Text Box tab and then place a check mark in the 'Include "Continued on page…"' check box (Format Text Box dialog box).

12. Navigate to the first text box of the story on page 4. Repeat Step 11 to include a Continued from notice. Use the Previous and Next buttons to follow the story from beginning to end, and double-check your continued notices.

13. Go back to the beginning of the story on page 1 and create a drop cap as you did in Step 7.

14. At the bottom of page 4, click the graphic twice to select it. Replace the graphic using the shortcut menu. Browse to the Data Files and insert the Conductor graphic. Click the Fit button (Picture Tools Format tab | Crop group) to make the graphic fit the area.

15. If requested to do so by your instructor, use your photo instead of the one supplied in the Data Files.

16. Edit the caption to read: Anita McMillan, artistic director-conductor. Check your publication for spelling and design errors, and fix or ignore the flagged items as necessary. Hyphenate the stories according to the hyphenation rules discussed in this module. Delete any graphics in the scratch area.

17. Save the newsletter on your storage device with the file name, Lab 3 – 1 Symphony Newsletter. Save the file again, this time as a Publisher template, named Lab 3 – 1 Symphony Newsletter Template.

18. Submit the file as directed by your instructor.

19. ✹ How do the font scheme and color scheme complement the topic of the newsletter? How do you think page 1 would have looked if you had changed it to a mixed column format? Why might you want to change the format?

Lab 2: **Publisher Newsletter Choices**

Note: To complete this assignment, you will be required to use the Data Files. Please contact your instructor for information about accessing the Data Files.

Problem: Use a copy of a newsletter that you regularly receive, or obtain one from a friend, organization, or school. Using the principles in this module, analyze the newsletter.

Perform the following tasks:

1. Run Publisher.

2. Open the publication, Lab 3 – 2 Newsletter Analysis Table, from the Data Files (Figure 3-78).

3. Use the skills you learned in editing sidebars to fill in each of the empty cells in the table as it applies to your selected newsletter. The topics to look for are listed below:

   • Purpose
   • Audience
   • Paper
   • Distribution
   • Font and color scheme
   • Consistency
   • Alignment
   • Repeated elements
   • Continued notices and ease of navigation
   • Sidebars, pull quotes, patterns, etc.

4. If requested by your instructor, insert your name in the text box at the top of the newsletter, along with the current date.

5. Print the publication and attach a copy of the newsletter. Submit both to your instructor.

Continued >

In the Labs *continued*

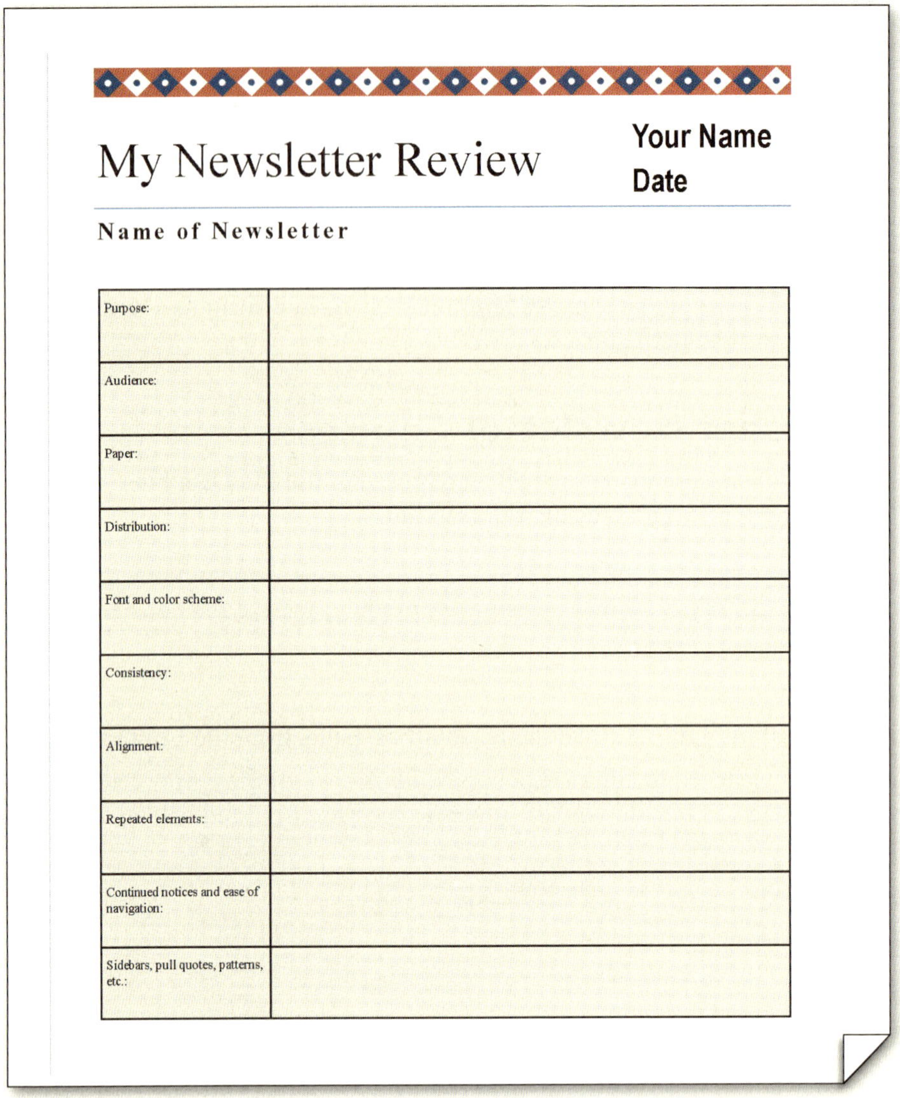

My Newsletter Review

Your Name
Date

Name of Newsletter

Purpose:	
Audience:	
Paper:	
Distribution:	
Font and color scheme:	
Consistency:	
Alignment:	
Repeated elements:	
Continued notices and ease of navigation:	
Sidebars, pull quotes, patterns, etc.:	

Figure 3–78

Lab 3: **Consider This: Your Turn**

Creating a Money Newsletter

Problem: A financial literacy group has asked you to create a newsletter about the wise use of money and spending. You decided to create a newsletter from scratch.

Part 1:   Run Publisher. Use the Cascade newsletter template. Use the Green Color Scheme and the Trek font scheme. Use the title, You and Your Money. On page 1, change the lead story headline to The Road to Financial Freedom (you may use the default text in the story itself). Change the secondary story headline to You Take over the Wheel (you may use the default text in the story itself). Link the story to one of the stories on page 2, and change the headline there as well. Create a pull quote from the story if your template does not have one already. Replace the graphics with suitable pictures and caption. Submit your assignment in the format specified by your instructor.

Part 2:   ✳ What other kinds of stories might you include in a financial newsletter such as this one? Where might those stories come from? Who might be the author/organization for this newsletter? Who might be the audience?

Index

A

active tab, **OFF 17**
add-in, **PA 10**
adding. *See* inserting
additions to publications, PUB 34
address bar, folder windows, **OFF 29**
adjustment handle, PUB 13
align, **PUB 30**
aligning, text, PUB 32
animation emphasis effects, **PA 8**
annotating Webpages, PA 15
applications. *See* apps
apps, **OFF 3**
  exiting Office, with one document
    open, OFF 42
  Microsoft Office Web Apps,
    OFF 8–9
  running from File Explorer,
    OFF 52
  running from start menu,
    OFF 10–12
  running using Search box,
    OFF 46–47
  switching from one to another,
    OFF 31–32
arrange thumbnails, **PUB 82**
AutoCorrect Options button,
    PUB 54–55
autofit, **PUB 25**
autofit headings, PUB 69
AutoFit text, PUB 25–26
autoflow, **PUB 118**
automatic hyphenation, **PUB 145**

B

Backgrounds, using pictures as,
    PUB 63–64
Backstage view
  closing file using, OFF 49–50
  creating new publication from,
    OFF 48
  opening recent file using, OFF 50
black-and-white printing, **PUB 94**
blade-coated paper, **PUB 93**
blank publications, OFF 10–12
bold, **PUB 23**
bold text, PUB 23
borders, changing color and
    weight, PUB 66–67
boundary, **PUB 11**
brochure paper, **PUB 95**

brochures, **PUB 49**
  creating trifold, PUB 52–55
  editing inside panels of, PUB
    73–77
  medium, PUB 51
  options, PUB 52
  page size, PUB 52
  selecting template, PUB 52–53
built-in templates, **PUB 4**
buttons
  AutoCorrect Options, PUB 54–55
  mouse, OFF 4
  Paste Options, PUB 58

C

calendar, editing, PUB 135
Caption gallery, PUB 86–88
captions, **PUB 83**
  editing, PUB 84
  ungrouping, PUB 85
card, **PA 6**
changing
  publication properties, OFF
    23–24
  publications, PUB 33–36
click mouse operations, OFF 4
clip, **PUB 27**
  capturing video, PA 11
  described, **PA 11**
collapsing
  Page Navigation pane, PUB 12
  ribbon, OFF 18–19
color-matching library, **PUB 94**
color printing, PUB 94
colors
  borders, changing, PUB 66–67
  font, changing, PUB 67–68
color scheme, **PUB 6**, PUB 52
commands, **OFF 10**
  and shortcut menus, OFF 19–20
common knowledge, **PUB 115**
continued notices, **PUB 122**
  formatting with, PUB 122–124
copy fit, **PUB 25**
copying, **PUB 56**
  folder to OneDrive, OFF 42–44
  and pasting, PUB 56–57
  text, methods (table), PUB 56
Cortana, **OFF 59, PA 14**
creating
  blank publication from File
    Explorer, OFF 51

drop cap, PUB 140–141
folders, OFF 27–29
folder within a folder, OFF 30
new publication from Backstage
    view, OFF 48
OneNote notebook, PA 2
Sway presentation, PA 6–7
templates, PUB 148–151
trifold brochure, PUB 52–55
Creative Commons license, **PA 7**
CTRL key
  and keyboard shortcuts, OFF 5
customize, **PUB 126**
customizing
  drop cap, PUB 141–142
  Quick Access Toolbar, OFF
    20–21
  ribbon, OFF 14, PUB 126–128
  templates, PUB 6–10
cutting, **PUB 56**

D

default text, **PUB 17**
  replacing, PUB 17–18
deleting. *See also* removing
  files, OFF 55
  objects, PUB 19–20
  pages from newsletters, PUB 113
deleting objects, on pages, PUB
    125–126
deletions from publications,
    PUB 34
deselecting objects, PUB 18
Design Checker, **PUB 88,**
    PUB 144
  running, PUB 90
desktop publishing (DTP),
    PUB 105
desktop publishing (DTP) app. *See*
    Publisher
dialog boxes
  navigating in, OFF 35
Dialog Box Launcher, **OFF 16**
digital printing, **PUB 94**
displaying. *See also* viewing
  formatting marks, PUB 60
  KeyTips, OFF 17
Docs.com, **PA 8**
document properties, OFF 24
double-tap gesture, OFF 3
drag-and-drop editing, PUB
    143–144